HE WAS A GERMAN

A BIOGRAPHY OF ERNST TOLLER

Ernst Toller   Clare Leighton

Wood-engraved portrait of Ernst Toller (1926) by Clare Leighton,
reproduced by kind permission of David Roland Leighton ©

A BIOGRAPHY

OF ERNST TOLLER

He was a German

BY RICHARD DOVE

WITH A PREFACE BY FRANK TROMMLER

LIBRIS

First published 1990
Copyright © Richard Dove, 1990
Preface Copyright © Frank Trommler, 1990

Libris
10 Burghley Road
London NW5 1UE

British Library Cataloguing in Publication Data
Dove, Richard
He was a German: a biography of Ernst Toller.
1. Drama in German. Toller, Ernst, 1893–1939
I. Title
832.912

ISBN 1-870352-85-8

Designed and produced by Cinamon and Kitzinger, London
Typeset by Wyvern Typesetting Ltd, Bristol
Printed in Great Britain by Billings & Sons Ltd, Worcester

CONTENTS

ILLUSTRATIONS

following page 146

PREFACE

by Frank Trommler

Literary historians have expressed a sense of surprise that Ernst Toller was able to understand the threat of Hitler and national socialism as early as 1923 when he wrote his comedy *Wotan Unchained*. Ernst Toller, the famous Expressionist writer, whose involvement in the short-lived Soviet Republic in Munich in 1919 always looked more like an accident than an act of political choice, seemed an unlikely exemplar of political foresight. Typecast as a typical *Gefühlspolitiker* (nowadays bleeding heart) in his quest for a better society, Toller rarely escaped the verdict that, exhilarating as it undoubtedly was as a literary and artistic movement, Expressionism was a poor school of revolutionary tactics. Even as late as 1968, the year of the students' revolt, Toller's revolutionary involvement was characterized as being merely dramatic: in one scene of Tankred Dorst's successful drama-documentary, *Toller*, Toller himself is placed in a symbolic cage from which – in a re-enactment of his own Expressionist play, *Masses and Man* – he advocates his humanitarian activism.

There is no better way to examine the typecasting of Toller as writer and politician than to engage with the historical realities of his unusual career. In his absorbing biography, Richard Dove shows himself to be an enlightened and sympathetic guide through the vicissitudes of Toller's life, from the youthful enthusiasm at the outbreak of the First World War, to the disastrous manifestations of profound despair, culminating in his suicide aged forty-six in 1939, before the outbreak of the Second.

Based on an impressive command of published and unpublished sources, Dove's biography sheds light on Toller's incredible capacity for work, on his moral commitment and public stance, and on his ability to articulate burning issues in theatrical forms which made him one of the most widely-discussed political writers of the nineteen twenties. In particular, Dove provides new insights into that least well-researched period of Toller's life, after his release from prison in 1924. It seems to have been in this period that Toller came to terms with the need constantly to reformulate the concept of 'revolution' as a self-empowering act of the individual.

In his earlier plays, especially *Masses and Man* and *The Machine Wreckers*, he had juxtaposed the harsh needs of political revolution and the humane disposition of the individual so forcefully that contemporaries had taken the juxtaposition for a portrayal of his own indecision. However, the collaboration with Erwin Piscator on *Hoppla, Such is Life!* in 1927 brought home to Toller that the struggle for a better society could not be undertaken with the exclusion of the individual. Reversing Piscator's ending for *Hoppla* – the suicide of the protagonist, Karl Thomas, symbolizing the futility of the revolutionary struggle when undertaken alone – Toller, at the end of the production of the play that followed in Leipzig, decided to let the hero survive. Focusing on the individual's plight and defeat as a metaphor of political commitment remained one of Toller's most central themes.

Toller's dramatic practice, inspired by Expressionist techniques which reduce things and people, art and politics, to a variety of dynamic actions, differs from attempts in the second half of the nineteen twenties to reassemble the individual from the dissolutions of war and mass politics by means of a new essentialism or existentialism *à la* Karl Jaspers or Max Scheler. Toller insisted on the paradigmatic and even redeeming role of the individual in his *failure* vis-à-vis political forces. With the figures of Hinkemann and Karl Thomas he is close to those writers in the nineteen twenties who turn this paradigmatic role of individual failure into a clue for a critique of the prevailing order; for instance, Arnold Zweig in his use of the case of the ordinary Russian soldier, Grischa Paprotkin, for the first comprehensive literary representation of the war machine (in *The Case of Sergeant Grischa*), or Alfred Döblin in his *mise-en-scène* of Franz Biberkopf as the 'outcast/insider' of the big city in *Berlin Alexanderplatz*. 'The artist's voice is the voice of the losers': Leo Lowenthal summed up such a principle in his 1957 essay on Cervantes:

> The marginal figures not only serve the negative function of indicting the social order; they also positively demonstrate the idea of man. They all serve to show the possibilities of Utopia.*

---

*'Cervantes, 1547–1616,' in Leo Lowenthal, *Literature and the Image of Man* (*Communication in Society*, vol. 2), New Brunswick/Oxford, 1986, p. 44.

Toller's utopia differs from the approach of Zweig and Döblin and builds on a curious interplay of outcast and Messiah. Jewish messianism is clearly reflected in the sanctification of the outcast as bearer of the human mission. The same messianism found a tragic but invigorating commitment in the struggle against national socialism. Toller, the failed revolutionary and advocate of human rights, turned into a widely-heard and respected émigré politician. He did not give up the dramatic projection of the individual as the fragile antagonist of the great political and social forces; on the contrary, he transformed it into a viable instrument of his anti-fascist activities. Toller's success resulted from his ability to project himself as the David who challenges the Goliath and thereby commands more attention than a committee with its sweeping resolutions.

In his essay, 'The Head of a Leader', Christopher Isherwood has documented the unusual, almost obsessive zeal with which Toller pursued his goals as an exile politician after 1933 (the capitalization is Isherwood's):

> It was two years before I saw him again, in London, at a time when the newspapers were full of his activities. Single-handed, he was conducting a propaganda campaign on behalf of his compatriots, the starving refugees who were now scattered over half Europe. His success was sensational. He had contrived, somehow, to reach audiences outside the circles of the Left. He had touched the heart of the huge, apathetic Public. He had caught the ears of the right people, the Powers, and the powers behind the Powers. They invited him to their houses, as an honoured guest. Even the conservative press spoke well of him. He was in the process of becoming a respectable institution.

Only one other German literary émigré earned the epithet 'institution' in these years. It was applied, somewhat later in the United States and Britain, to Thomas Mann. In both cases the characterization into hero status was carefully stage-managed, much depending on the capacity for playing to public opinion's perception of the fascist Goliath. However, there the parallel ends. Thomas Mann's characterization was a cultural set-piece. He *became* German culture, demonstrating it in numerous rhetorical statements in which he provided his American audience with metaphors of the Manichaean struggle between Good and Evil. Toller, too, was a great orator; but his was not the rhetoric of the European *Götterdämmerung*, rather of the enlightened outcast who sustains humanity in the night of terror.

Toller carried the torch of humanity for numerous rescue operations on behalf of the victims of the cataclysm of the nineteen thirties. However, using his very existence as the paradigm in this struggle made him particularly vulnerable. Almost all the accounts by his émigré friends after his suicide in a New York hotel in the Spring of 1939 testify to this fact. Toller was able to use the projection of the individual's frailty vis-à-vis political forces for a great humanistic mission, but only at the cost of his own life.

University of Pennsylvania
1990

ACKNOWLEDGEMENTS

A number of people have helped me in writing this book. In the first place I should like to thank the staff of the following libraries and archives: the Archive of the Akademie der Künste, Berlin; the Bayerische Staatsbibliothek, Munich; the British Library, London; the Bundesarchiv, Koblenz; the Deutsche Bibliothek, Deutsches Exilarchiv, Frankfurt; the Deutsches Literaturarchiv, Marbach; the Institut für Zeitgeschichte and the Staatsarchiv für Oberbayern, both in Munich; the Sterling Memorial Library and the Beinecke Library, Yale University and the Leo Baeck Institute, New York.

In the course of my research I interviewed several contemporaries of Toller's, notably Rosa Leviné-Meyer, Fritz Landshoff, Fenner Brockway and Bram Bootman, former secretary of Unity Theatre. I am grateful for their help and inspiration, and for the valuable insight into an historical period which they gave me. I am very grateful to Andrea Valeriu-Grautoff (Mexico City) for permission to quote from her mother's autobiographical manuscript, and to Anne Schönblum (Haifa) for much valuable information about her mother and other members of the Toller family. My thanks also to the late John Lehmann, Sir Stephen Spender, Hugh Hunt and Hermann Kesten for answering my letters.

I am greatly indebted to Professor John Spalek for giving me access to his personal archive and for supplying rare photographic material. I am also grateful to Wolfgang Held for his help in deciphering difficult handwriting. A short section of Chapter X originally appeared in the *Germanic Review*; parts of Chapters XIII and XIV appeared in a slightly different form in *German Life and Letters*. The quotations from Toller's work are reproduced by kind permission of the estate of Sidney Kaufman and Carl Hanser Verlag, Munich. The quotations from Bertolt Brecht's poem 'Concerning the Label Emigrant' (translated by Stephen Spender) and his poem 'Hollywood' (translated by Michael Hamburger) are reproduced from *Poems 1913–1956* by kind permission of Methuen, London; lines from W.H. Auden's 'In Memory of Ernst Toller' are quoted from *Collected Poems* by kind permission of Faber and Faber.

ABBREVIATIONS

The following standard abbreviations for German political parties have been used throughout:

SPD   Sozialdemokratische Partei Deutschlands (German Social Democratic Party)

USPD   Unabhängige sozialdemokratische Partei Deutschlands (Independent German Social Democratic Party)

KPD   Kommunistische Partei Deutschlands (German Communist Party)

NSDAP   Nationalsozialistische deutsche Arbeiterpartei (Nazi Party)

NOTE

Toller's works are referred to by their German titles, with English translation, the first time they are mentioned, thereafter only in English.

INTRODUCTION

Ernst Toller, dramatist, orator and revolutionary socialist, is today almost forgotten. Yet in his lifetime he was a legend. During the nineteen twenties he was probably the best-known living German dramatist, whose fame far surpassed that of Georg Kaiser, Carl Sternheim or Bertolt Brecht, and even threatened to eclipse that of the venerable Gerhart Hauptmann, whose plays had won him the Nobel Prize. By the end of the decade, Toller's work had been translated into twenty-seven languages and his plays had been performed in the major theatre capitals of the world. When he was due to speak at an anti-fascist rally in London in 1933, he was billed as 'the world-famous German author',[1]* which was no exaggeration. His name was familiar to many, particularly on the political left, who had neither seen nor read any of his plays. His fame as a dramatist was inextricably linked with his political reputation, first as a leader of the ill-starred Bavarian Soviet Republic, then as Weimar Germany's most famous political prisoner, and finally as the most celebrated literary exile from the Third Reich.

It seems strange that there is no definitive biography of Toller. He did write a volume of autobiography but, though fascinating, it is fragmentary, ending with his release from prison at the age of thirty. The occasional academic studies of Toller naturally include biographical material, but use it largely to interpret his dramas, turning his life into an aspect of literary history. Yet his biography has greater intrinsic interest than his work: his life contained the drama which his plays sometimes lacked.

Toller was a typical representative of that generation born in the eighteen nineties and brought up in the values of Imperial Germany, which entered the First World War with the highest ideals of patriotism, was radicalized by its experience at the front, and supported the revolution which followed the war. Like many of his literary contemporaries, he enjoyed his most productive years in the nineteen twenties and, like most of them, he was forced into exile after 1933.

*See notes on pp. 269 ff.

He himself was aware of the representative nature of his experience and in his autobiography sought to portray it as both typical of his time and crucial to an understanding of political developments in Germany up to 1933. It is the representative pattern of Toller's life, the extraordinary congruence of public events and private experience, which gives it its interest today.

Toller's career was never far from controversy. As a committed socialist dramatist, he did not aspire to neutrality, and few were neutral about either him or his work. Celebrated on the socialist left as the 'poet of the proletariat', he was vilified by the nationalist right as the incarnation of 'Jewish cultural Bolshevism'. Every new play of his in the nineteen twenties provoked a storm of disagreement, left-wing critics applauding the daring of his political themes, their right-wing counterparts condemning his work as tendentious. (Even today, 'aesthetic' judgement of Toller's work is largely a matter of political *parti pris*.)

The legend which surrounded Toller in his lifetime sprang up around his involvement in the Bavarian Soviet Republic, in which he briefly played the role of the activist writer, transcending the dichotomy between thought and action, art and reality, thereby realizing a dream of German letters which stretched back well into the nineteenth century. It was a legend which helped to launch his career as a dramatist – and which would pursue him for the rest of his life. Literary historians have since written their own version of the Toller legend: a counter-version which portrays him as an essentially lyrical temperament, whose political activity was a youthful indiscretion, whose idealism foundered on the rocks of reality and whose creative talent tragically declined, driving him to despair and eventual suicide. Such a portrait verges on cliché, rehashing the Romantic stereotype of the poet as sensitive idealist, unable to come to terms with the real world and doomed to an early death.

Both legend and counter-legend contain elements of truth. Toller was, and always remained, the youthful activist, the permanent volunteer for great causes, volunteering for the fatherland in August 1914, for the revolution in November 1918 and finally for the struggle against Nazism in 1933. He was also the sensitive poet, whose lyric cycle *Das Schwalbenbuch* (*The Swallow Book*), based on his observation of the swallows which nested in his prison cell, took his name around the world. But he was perhaps above all the observer and chronicler of his times. While his critics dismissed him as a dreamer and a political idealist, his political judgement (certainly after 1920) showed a realism all too rare in the Weimar Republic, and which is perhaps best illustrated by his almost visionary insight into the fatal appeal of Nazism, against which he repeatedly warned: his play *Der entfesselte Wotan* (*Wotan Unchained*), which prophetically depicted the early career of Adolf Hitler, was actually written in prison in 1923.

What kind of man was Ernst Toller? It is always difficult to discern the private person behind the public figure, but the picture of Toller which emerges from the autobiographies and memoirs of the period is both definite and consistent. They reveal a striking and even charismatic figure, who clearly held great fascination for all who met him. This fascination emanated, unlike that of Bertolt Brecht or Georg Kaiser, primarily from his physical presence and personality, which were usually remembered long after his work had been forgotten.

The most famous description of Toller is that contained in the 'Wanted' notice posted throughout Germany in May 1919: 'Slightly built . . . about 1.65 to 1.68 metres tall, thin pale face, clean shaven, large brown eyes, piercing gaze, closes his eyes when thinking, dark, almost black, wavy hair . . . speaks standard German.' Despite his lack of stature, Toller had an upright stance which made him seem much taller than he actually was. His striking physical appearance is well conveyed by the English socialist, Wilfred Wellock, who visited him in prison in May 1920:

> Next moment, the warder entered with his prisoner – a tall, lithe figure, crowned with a rich crop of jet black hair carefully brushed back. The eager face with its clear olive complexion, its bright dark eyes, its penetrating look which appeared to drink me in at the first glance, bespoke great sympathy and intelligence. It was Ernst Toller.[2]

Toller's physical presence imposed itself on all who met him. Christopher Isherwood remembered 'looking into those famous burning dark eyes, which every photograph had failed to reproduce'.[3] Dorothy Thompson, the first American journalist to be expelled from Nazi Germany, paid vivid tribute to his physical attraction in her review of his autobiography:

> I know him only slightly, but I remember his appearance
> vividly . . . his countenance is rather reminiscent of
> some of the wilder of the young John the Baptists by
> Raphael, the true aspect of the poet, sensuous yet
> refined, a combination of strong animalism and
> spirituality.[4]

Toller undoubtedly had a particular attraction for women. The painter George Grosz noted caustically that 'women were devoted to him – and he to them'; Ernst Niekisch, Toller's prison friend and confidant, recalled that 'he always had that winning way that women so love in men – and he was indeed loved by a great many women'.[5]

There were certainly a number of women in his life, often appearing at crucial moments: Margarete Pinner, with whom he founded a pacifist student association in Heidelberg, the well-known actress Tilla Durieux, with whom his name was often linked in Munich, Grete Lichtenstein, who sheltered him after the collapse of the Bavarian Soviet Republic, Netty Katzenstein, the confidante of his prison letters, Betty Frankenstein, with whom he corresponded regularly between 1925 and 1938, Lotte Israel, his close companion of the late nineteen twenties, and Christiane Grautoff, the young actress half his age whom he married in London in 1935. It is often impossible to do more than speculate about such relationships, however, for Toller was always deliberately reticent about them – there is virtually no mention of them in his autobiography. Though many of his letters have survived, there is not one love letter among them; even his published poetry includes nothing approaching a love poem.

Toller's physical presence undoubtedly reinforced his charismatic gifts as an orator, which are confirmed by all who heard him. He had indeed gained a reputation as a political speaker long before he achieved fame as a dramatist. His oratory first brought him to public notice when he addressed mass meetings during the munitions workers' strike of January 1918, and it later took him, despite his lack of political experience, to the forefront of the revolutionary movement in Munich. The messianic figures of his early plays were all projections of his own political activism.

Toller was an emotional speaker, whose power of delivery gained conviction from his evident sincerity and passionate commitment. Otto Zarek, a student contemporary in Munich, remembered:

In his oratorical style, he made no concessions to the
people . . . But in spite of all this, he triumphed. It was
not his matter but his manner which finally won his
hearers. People couldn't make up their minds whether
he was right or not, but they had no doubt he was
sincere.[6]

It was often not so much the power of his argument as the force of
his conviction which carried his audience.

Toller was an ethical socialist who, like many of the generation
who came of age in the First World War, was inspired by the vision
of a new humanity. Ernst Niekisch wrote that 'he believed in the
goodness of human nature', Max Weber testified at Toller's court
martial to his 'absolute moral integrity'.[7] In his autobiography, Toller wrote that the ideal which had sustained him through five years of
imprisonment was 'the belief in a world of justice, freedom and
humanity, a world without fear and without hunger'[8] – ideals which
were synonymous in his own mind with those of socialism. His early
plays were imbued with an ethical idealism which turned the German stage briefly into the 'moral institution' invoked by Schiller. His
critics dismissed the humanitarian rhetoric of his plays as preaching,
but he was genuinely moved by poverty and social suffering, and
convinced that they were politically unnecessary. Ernst Niekisch
wrote: 'Human need, human misery moved him wherever he met it.
His heart was easily touched and he was always willing to help
wherever he could achieve some good.'[9] Toller's character had
indeed a strong vein of selflessness, even altruism. During his first
year in prison, he was offered a pardon, but refused it on the
grounds that it did not include his political comrades. This was no
isolated gesture, for he considered solidarity the supreme socialist
virtue – he donated his earnings from *Die Maschinenstürmer* (*The
Machine Wreckers*) to International Workers' Aid and was always
ready to help fellow-prisoners whose families were living in poverty.
The major relief projects he undertook in exile were financed
entirely out of his own pocket; there are many reports of the material
and moral support he gave to fellow-refugees – an example which
forced even erstwhile enemies, such as the Communist poet J.R.
Becher, to pay tribute to 'the good comrade'.[10]

Toller's striking virtues were matched by equally glaring weaknesses. His critics called him vain, and his altruism certainly coexisted

with a self-esteem bordering on egocentricity. In the years after his release from prison, he grew accustomed to his public role and was finally unable to live without it. The popular biographer Emil Ludwig, himself no stranger to success, felt that Toller was always trying to prove himself, to live up to his own legend.[11] There was a strong theatrical streak in his character: one of his schoolboy ambitions was to be an actor and his penchant for self-dramatization is as evident in his autobiography as in his (often autobiographical) plays. Ernst Niekisch recalled: 'He had theatrical talent, loved the grand pathos, the impressive gesture and was inclined, albeit in a most tasteful way, to put himself in the limelight.'[12] George Grosz, a less friendly observer, felt that Toller always had to be at the centre of the stage:

> With him, telegrams had to arrive and reporters appear. I can still see him in his hotel room after he arrived in New York: half a dozen journalists were there as I came in, two secretaries sat and wrote. Toller was just giving a striking account of the execution of a young anti-Nazi worker called André, a page-boy delivered telegrams, all was activity. Toller was happy.[13]

Grosz's portrait betrays the eye of the caricaturist, but Toller did have a flair for publicity, and in publicizing the causes he espoused often cast himself in the leading role.

Perhaps the most significant, and certainly the most disturbing, flaw in Toller's character was his temperamental instability. He was subject to abrupt changes of mood, in which burning enthusiasm would suddenly give way to deepest melancholy. His manic-depressive tendency, confirmed by all his close friends, was probably exacerbated by the effects of imprisonment and later by the vicissitudes of exile. After 1933, his bouts of depression became more frequent, casting their shadow over his work and his marriage.

All Toller's friends remembered him as an entertaining and engaging companion of considerable personal charm. He had the gift of making people like him – and he liked to be liked. His winning way transcended his native language: Fenner Brockway remembered that, when he visited Britain, 'people were scared of his reputation, but he had the great talent of making friends immediately'.[14] The novelist Hermann Kesten, a close friend of Toller's, remembered the sometimes disconcerting ambivalence of his personality:

> If you saw his depressions and his dreadful end, you
> could hardly believe how gentle and how joyful he could
> be, how gaily he could laugh, his teeth and eyes flashing,
> his young face belying his grey hair.[15]

This youthful quality, noted by many other commentators, so captivated the eminent drama critic Alfred Kerr that some said it
blinded him to the faults in Toller's dramas. In his good moments,
Toller was emphatically alive, emanating energy and vitality. The
successful novelist Lion Feuchtwanger called him 'overflowing with
life': 'if you spent an hour with him, how many plans he would pour
out, outlines of plays, stories, essays. How many relief campaigns he
wanted to undertake – for individuals, for groups, for whole
peoples.'[16] His literary plans, the products of a fertile imagination,
were too often unrealized, a failure which Feuchtwanger attributed
to the energy he spent on other causes.

The Russian writer, Ilya Ehrenburg, who met him frequently
during his restless travels in the thirties, considered him more a
dreamer, who juggled plans and projects like so many castles in the
air. He perceived an almost child-like quality in Toller – who had
indeed the ability to enter the world of children, talking to them on
their terms and winning their confidence. Niekisch recalled how
quickly Toller was able to captivate his ten-year-old son and how he
enjoyed delighting the boy. Feuchtwanger recounted how he
enthralled the pupils at a London girls' school with his stories, until
they were 'hanging on his every word, laughing because he laughed,
crying because he cried'.[17]

Toller was always aware that his fame as a dramatist was due in
part to his political reputation, a conjuncture which both hurt and
frustrated him. He periodically turned his back on public life, feeling inadequate to the role which fate had forced upon him, but then
he would turn back to the public arena, curiously dependent on the
acclaim he tried to shun. He recognized (and often regretted) that his
role as a politically committed writer closed any avenue of withdrawal into the ivory tower of poetic contemplation. Speaking in
1938, just before a visit to Republican Spain, he told fellow-writers:
'We too love the silence of our study and the patient labour devoted
to our work. But a time which betrays the idea of humanity forces us
to denounce this betrayal and to fight wherever freedom is under
threat.'[18]

It was Toller's misfortune to live at just such a time. Unlike his contemporaries Kaiser and Brecht, his principal legacy is not what he wrote but what he did. His was, in many ways, an exemplary life – and it is his example which this book seeks to record.

I

Growing up in Imperial Germany

1893–1914

At first sight, there is little in Ernst Toller's formative years to suggest that he would become a famous dramatist, still less a revolutionary socialist: his upbringing was middle-class, provincial and orthodox Jewish. He did not remember it as a happy childhood: it provided neither the precept nor the inspiration to guide his adult life.[1]

Toller was born on 1 December 1893, one of three children of middle-class Jewish parents living in Samotschin, a small town in the Prussian province of Posen, a part of the German Empire which was ethnically and historically Polish. Samotschin was a small town of some three thousand inhabitants, built on reclaimed marshland in the valley of the river Netze. As a market town, where the produce of the surrounding countryside – mainly wood, grain and livestock – was traded, it had however an economic importance out of all proportion to its size. The town and the surrounding Netzebruch had been annexed to Prussia in the first partition of Poland in 1772 and the succeeding decades had seen German settlers populate the area, colonizing it as a forward outpost of the Reich. In a predominantly Polish province, Samotschin was very much a German town. Toller recalled that ethnic Germans and Jews were equally proud of this German tradition, despising those towns in the province where Poles and Catholics formed a majority which gave the dominant tone.

The Jews in Samotschin were a dwindling minority in Toller's childhood. In 1870, they had numbered over 400, but by 1910 this figure had declined to no more than 130, many having been drawn away to the expanding metropolis of Berlin, now the capital of the new German Reich. Despite this numerical decline, their influence on the town's trade remained considerable. The Toller family had long been established as traders in Samotschin. The official history of the town makes no mention of the family, so that we are thrown back largely on Toller's own sparse comments. His maternal great-grandfather had been the only Jew permitted to settle in Samotschin, a privilege conferred (on payment of an appropriate sum) by a charter from Frederick the Great. His great-grandfather on his father's side was reputed to have come from Spain and to have owned an estate in West Prussia; such was his legendary wealth that he was said to have dined from golden dishes. The wealth of his ancestor had been largely dissipated by succeeding generations, but the family remained modestly affluent.

Toller's autobiography, first published in 1933,[2] says little about his family and even less about his relations with them. He does not mention his elder brother Heinrich, nor his sister Hertha, though he had a close and fond relationship with his sister, which would last all his life. Hertha, four years older than Ernst, was often the guide and confidante of his early youth: she is evoked in the idealized figure of 'the sister' in his autobiographical first play *Die Wandlung* (*The Transformation*). Ernst was a lonely, even solitary child, given to day-dreaming and introspection. He would rarely play with other children, often sitting in front of the house for hours, lost in thought. His mother was worried by his solitary nature: 'Why don't you play?' she would ask. 'What are you doing?' 'I am breathing' was the reply.[3]

The Tollers were one of the solid middle-class families of Samotschin. Ernst's father, Mendel Toller, was in the wholesale grain trade, a business which Heinrich also entered after his father's death in 1911. Though not rich, the family was sufficiently well-off to employ a cook and nursemaid and to educate their children privately; even after his father died, there was enough money for Ernst to continue his education in France.

Mendel Toller was indeed a man of some standing in the local community and in 1906 was elected to the Town Council. He certainly shared the patriotic and conservative values of the Prussian bourgeoisie he obviously aspired to be part of. In the opening scene of *The Transformation* he is apostrophized as 'the good businessman', intent on settling his son into a steady profession and prescribing 'a stable and respectable way of life'. This literary 'evidence' suggests that Mendel Toller did little to encourage his son's ambition to become a writer, but the truth seems to be more complex – it was indeed his father who sent some of Ernst's earliest poems to Kurt Pinthus, then making his way as a young literary critic.[4] He was certainly jealous of the family's good name. When Ernst wrote an article taking up the case of a local vagrant, and the mayor threatened legal proceedings, Mendel Toller was quick to use his influence to get the proceedings dropped, giving his son a lesson in string-pulling which he never forgot.

Toller was seventeen when his father died of cancer, an event which greatly affected him. The account of his death is the only scene in the autobiography in which Mendel Toller plays a central role. Almost with his dying breath, he levels a mysterious accusation at his son – 'It's all your fault'. Many years later, when his mother was seriously ill while he was in prison, Toller had the hallucination of being watched, as he lay in bed, by someone who was both himself and his father. We can certainly infer from these two incidents that the relationship between father and son was a difficult one, in which guilt played a considerable part.

Toller's abiding memories of early childhood were of his mother and the family general store where she held sway. Ida Toller was a capable and hard-working woman, who continued to run the family store long after the death of her husband. She lived her life according to the tenets of the Jewish religion, observing its rites and instructing her children in its precepts. Though Ernst had a close relationship with his mother, it was by no means always a harmonious one. His rejection of his Jewish heritage – he saw his mother's devotion as mere fatalism[5] – undoubtedly hurt her, though she may well have seen it as part of the rebellion of adolescence. 'Even as a boy, he was so defiant,' she told the poet Else Lasker-Schüler. Ernst was nonetheless very much his mother's son. Lasker-Schüler recalled that 'between the lines of her letters, there shone the pride of her generous heart. She had her son's temperament, a purified temperament, blessed by God'.[6]

Though Toller was brought up in the material comfort of a middle-class home, he did not have a happy childhood. He later referred to 'spiritual conflicts' which since early childhood had given his life a peculiar melancholy and which he had been unable to resolve intellectually. The dominant note of his early years, which was to resound through his adult life, was a sense of estrangement. This feeling of not belonging, typical of many of his dramatic protagonists, is largely attributable to his Jewish background.

The situation of the Jews in Posen was typical of that in other parts of Central and Eastern Europe. Although socially and politically emancipated, they had never been wholly assimilated to the society in which they lived. The Jews in Posen were proud of their German heritage, cultivating it assiduously and affirming the aggressive nationalism of the Kaiserreich. Yet, however much they might have wished to regard themselves as Germans, the Germans never fully accepted them as such. Mendel Toller changed his name to the more German-sounding Max, but such gestures of assimilation could not remove the unspoken but insurmountable social barriers: only on the Kaiser's birthday, Toller remembered, were Jews allowed to sit down with reserve officers and old soldiers to drink the Kaiser's health.

Jews and Germans were united only in their contempt for the Polish population. The Poles were treated as a subject people, whose loyalty to Imperial Germany was suspect, and whose language and culture were systematically suppressed. A decree of 1876 made German the sole official language; Polish children were forbidden to speak their mother tongue in school. 'We children called the Poles "Polacks",' Toller remembered, 'and thought they were the descendants of Cain, who killed Abel and therefore had the mark of God on them.'

The political and economic roots of this prejudice are abundantly clear. In 1886 a Settlement Commission was established to buy up Polish estates as farmland for German settlers. German officials were obliged to buy only from German shops, Germans who sold land to the Poles were considered unpatriotic to the point of treason. For their part, the Poles resented the ruling German minority, perceiving the Jews, for reasons of language, to be part of it. The Jews were therefore doubly isolated – to the Poles they were Germans, to the Germans they were Jews. It was an environment bound to produce feelings of isolation and alienation; a similar environment produced Franz Kafka.

Toller's childhood was indeed a paradigm of the social and racial tensions in this remote province of the Reich. There was much to emphasize his difference from other children. His first school was a Jewish school, in contrast to the Evangelical school which other German children attended, or the Catholic school for Polish children, divisions which symbolized the mutual antipathy between Germans and Poles and the anti-semitism latent in both. Some of Toller's earliest memories were of anti-semitism: the enforced separation from Christian children, the taunts of 'Jew-boy', the wild rumours of the ritual killing of a Christian child by Jews. While Toller may have exaggerated the objective importance of such incidents, there is no doubting their importance for his future development. The experience of anti-semitism not only distressed him, but led to feelings of personal rejection: he wanted to stop being a Jew, to be 'like the others', and consequently rejected the Jewish culture and religion which was so much a part of his mother's life. His feelings as a child continued to mark his attitudes as an adult. As a soldier on active service, he wrote requesting that his name be removed from the list of members of the Jewish community of Samotschin; in the anti-semitic atmosphere of his trial for high treason, he protested that he was not 'of Jewish confession', insisting that he was of none. The religious feelings nurtured by an orthodox Jewish upbringing were redirected into socialism, 'the earthly sacrament', as he once described it.[7]

Toller's alienation from his Jewish heritage seems to have been aggravated by feelings of guilt at his own economic privilege. The close friend of his early boyhood was Stanislaus, one of eight children of a Polish nightwatchman. Their friendship had initially transcended the mutual antipathy of Poles and Germans, but by the age of nine they had been separated by the school system which reflected and reinforced the economic differences of class. Toller was sent to the Knabenschule, a private school for boys at which Latin was taught, and was immediately parted from the poorer children who attended the Volksschule. Stanislaus no longer visited him. Puzzled and distressed by such differences, he asked his mother why there were rich and poor. 'Because God wills it so,' she told him, a reply he remembered long after: this was the soil from which his later political conviction would grow. The Knabenschule was run by a Christian pastor, whom Toller later described in derogatory terms. Toller stayed at the school until he was eleven, by which time he was the only pupil.

At the age of ten Toller had fallen seriously ill, having to undergo a major operation. The illness had prolonged after-effects which included heart and nervous disorder. At one point he was apparently able to walk only with the aid of crutches, a disability which seems to have been psychological in origin. Little more is known about this mysterious ailment: Toller was subsequently always reticent about its precise nature, and sensitive to the suggestion that nervous disorder recurred in later childhood. The fact remains that his health was to trouble him periodically throughout his life.

At the age of twelve, Toller continued his education in the regional capital Bromberg (now Bydgoszcz), where he attended the Realgymnasium. Bromberg was some fifty miles from Samotschin and there was no direct rail link, so Toller was boarded out with private families during the term, returning to Samotschin only during the school holidays. The holidays were a welcome release from the 'hard labour' of a Prussian education, but his pleasurable anticipation on the journey home was, he remembered, always tempered by the knowledge that he would have to return in two weeks.[8]

The Realgymnasium purported to offer a more modern and more practical education than the traditional Gymnasium with its classical bias, but in retrospect Toller described it as 'a school of miseducation and militarization'. The Prussian school system was certainly narrow and authoritarian, designed to inculcate obedience to, and respect for, temporal and religious authority. The values it propagated were nationalistic, militaristic and socially conservative, summarizing the prevailing ethos of Wilhelmine Germany. It was a system which only succeeded in nourishing his spirit of rebellion, an experience which prompted his later interest in socialist education. In search of escape from a rigid curriculum and the stultifying conformism of his teachers, he turned to modern literature, particularly drama. The writers whose work fired his imagination were those expressly proscribed by the school: Strindberg and Wedekind, Ibsen and Hauptmann, whose appeal consisted not least in their rejection of bourgeois social values. The death of Toller's father in 1911 emphasized the lack of a guiding figure in the young man's life. He was restless and rebellious, but there was no one to calm his restlessness or harness his rebellion.

Toller's rebellion was perhaps little different from that of many young men of bourgeois origin in Wilhelmine Germany, a rebellion largely identified with the ideals of the Youth Movement. The 'Jugendbewegung' reflected the impatience of the younger generation with the attitudes and institutions of Imperial Germany; in a patriarchal society it represented the revolt of the son against the father. The ideology of the Movement was cloudy and diffuse, but among its aspirations are several which typify Toller's subsequent thinking: the ideal of community (*Gemeinschaft*), the idealization of the natural life of simple people, the faith in social renewal, and in youth as the means of attaining it. Years later, Toller acknowledged its influence on his generation, and by implication on himself, quoting the declaration of the Free German Youth Movement at the centenary celebrations of the Battle of the Nations in Leipzig in 1913:

> The Free German Youth wishes to take responsibility for its own life, to shape it on its own terms with inner truthfulness. We stand united for this inner freedom in all circumstances.[9]

Youth was to remake itself in its own image, the theme of Toller's earliest surviving poem 'Der Ringende' (The Striver), which he wrote in 1912 at the age of eighteen. The poem expresses his alienation from his mother, articulating the feeling that he must die and be reborn through his own efforts:

> I died
> Gave birth
> Died
> Gave birth
> Was mother to myself.

Toller's literary vocation had become apparent at an early age. As a twelve-year-old schoolboy he was already writing articles, mainly accounts of his home town Samotschin, which were published in the Bromberg newspaper, the *Ostdeutsche Rundschau*. While at the Gymnasium, he also tried his hand at other kinds of writing – stories, plays, poems – and while none of this juvenilia has survived, Toller recalled that some of his early verses had 'a rebellious tone'. One of his early ambitions was to be an actor and he played a number of leading roles in school productions. But his main ambitions were literary. In Bromberg, he seems to have frequented a literary circle run by a woman called Clara Rittler. In 1911 he arrived in Berlin with a letter of recommendation from her to her brother-in-law, Sigmar Mehring, the literary editor of the *Berliner Tageblatt*; the poems which Toller submitted do not appear to have been published in the paper (nor indeed elsewhere), but one result of this meeting was Toller's long friendship with Mehring's son Walter, who was to become famous as a poet and lyricist in the twenties.

'Before the war,' Toller later recalled, 'I did not concern myself at all with politics',[11] but in fact he was as receptive as most of his contemporaries to the prevailing atmosphere of strident nationalism.

In July 1911 the German government ordered a gunboat to the port of Agadir, allegedly to protect German interests threatened by French expansion in Morocco. This sudden show of strength provoked a threat of war from Britain. The Agadir crisis caused panic among the population, leading to a run on the savings-banks; the newspapers incited the worst chauvinism with wild stories that France was forming an army of 'Negro' conscripts. War fever spread rapidly. Toller remembered that he and his school-mates greeted the crisis with excitement and enthusiasm. The prospect of war fired their imagination, offering a release from the stifling restrictions of school, an invitation to high adventure. Such reactions were commonplace: the prospect of war had captured the imagination of a younger generation brought up in the ethos of heroic militarism so assiduously cultivated in the Prussian education system. The enthusiasm of that summer was a mere foretaste of the wild hysteria which greeted the declaration of war in August 1914.

In December 1913 Toller passed his Abitur and was finally able to turn his back on the Realgymnasium. As a young man of good family there was no doubt that he should continue his education; the only question was – where? In February 1914 he travelled to France to study at the University of Grenoble, enrolling in the faculties of Philosophy and Law. Grenoble attracted a large number of foreign students, enjoying a reputation as a showplace for the achievements of French culture and learning. Toller was not a good student and on his own admission attended few lectures, finding neither their style nor their content much to his taste.

Translated over a thousand miles from the provincial seclusion of Posen, the twenty-year-old Toller had initially seen France as a land of romance and adventure, but before long he began to keep the company of his compatriots, adopting their aggressive chauvinism. The German students kept very much to themselves, behaving as the representatives of a higher culture. They treated the French with contempt and even suspicion: France was the traditional enemy, who had been defeated in the war of 1870 and still sought revenge and retribution. The German students' association would close its meetings by throwing open all the windows and giving a thunderous rendering of the German national anthem. Toller later summed up his life in Grenoble with typical brevity: 'I am living in France and have never left Germany.'[12]

In the summer of 1914 Toller spent a walking holiday in the South of France and Northern Italy, where he dreamed conventionally romantic dreams of adventure in foreign parts – in Marseilles, he even toyed briefly with the idea of joining the French Foreign Legion. His experience in France seems to have made little lasting impression on him. Though he devoted a few pages of his autobiography to this period of his life, it left virtually no trace in his poems or plays. His later aspirations were internationalist, but his inspiration always remained Germany. His years in exile in England and the USA merely confirm this: the only two plays he wrote in exile were both about Germany. After 1933 he was cut off, not merely from his reading public, but from the very roots of his inspiration.

His carefree life in France did at least make him reflect briefly on the injustice of a social order which allowed him to enjoy the customary privileges of a middle-class education, while his childhood friend, Stanislaus, had had to leave school at the age of fourteen to help support his family. He recognized that it was money which gave him freedom, and although he enjoyed money, it was not without a sense of guilt: 'I loved money, but with a bad conscience.' Toller never lost his taste for good living: even during the last few weeks of his life, he continued to live in an expensive hotel far beyond his means.

In July 1914 he decided to apply himself to learning French, intending to enrol on a French-language course at the Sorbonne. The international situation was tense, having deteriorated rapidly following the assassination off the Austrian Archduke Franz Ferdinand in Sarajevo. On 28 July Austria-Hungary declared war on Serbia, and when Toller set out for Paris on 31 July, a European war seemed inevitable. Alarmed at the prospect, Toller broke his journey in Lyons to consult the German consul as to the best course of action. The consul was reassuring: there was no real cause for alarm, the only thing students should be thinking about was studying. The following day, 1 August, brought news of German mobilization. On the streets of Lyons, Toller heard the newspaper boys shouting that a German declaration of war on Russia was imminent.

As war fever began to spread about him, Toller felt all the alarm of being an alien in an enemy country. Popular feeling was running high. German troops were reported to have crossed the French border, Germany had issued an ultimatum to France. As the final preparations for war were made on either side, Toller's only thought was to get back to Germany. He found that a train was due to leave for Switzerland at 2 a.m. and settled down to wait in a small café. As he waited, a French army sergeant, who had been telephoning, suddenly turned and shouted out that Germany had declared war on France. People at the surrounding tables rose and sang the 'Marseillaise'.

The train from Lyons was full of Germans trying to flee the country. As it made its way slowly towards Geneva, it was repeatedly stopped. Finally, fifteen miles from the border, all the passengers were ordered out and those with German passports detained. It was not until the evening that they were finally allowed to travel on, reaching Geneva at midnight. Shortly after, the French closed the border. As the Germans finally got out of the train, the relief was too much for them: they fell into each others' arms and sang 'Deutschland über Alles'.

II

From Patriotism to Pacifism
1914–1917

Once back on German soil, Toller was swept up in the patriotic enthusiasm which had taken hold of virtually the entire population. Germany was in the grip of war fever. The chauvinism of the Kaiser-reich had erupted even before war had been declared, feeding on the reports of mobilization, frontier violations and ultimatums which had followed each other with bewildering rapidity. The situation had indeed succeeded in uniting the nation as never before. Even the SPD, forgetting the internationalist principles it had always pro-claimed, had supported the government, the SPD group in the Reich-stag voting unanimously to approve the government's war credits. Press censorship and tendentious government statements made it impossible to gain an objective picture of the international situation. It was widely believed that Germany was the victim of aggression, that French airmen had dropped bombs on Nuremberg, and that the Cossacks had crossed the border into East Prussia, a belief carefully fostered by government propaganda. Toller shared the universal conviction that Germany had been attacked and that it was the duty of every German to come to the defence of the Fatherland. No sooner had he arrived in Munich than he decided to volunteer for the army.

In the prevailing war fever, there was no shortage of recruits: both the infantry and the cavalry were turning away volunteers. Toller was apprehensive that he might be rejected altogether because of his slight physique and his history of childhood illness, but he need not have worried. A complaisant doctor passed him medically fit and on 9 August he enlisted in the First Bavarian Foot Artillery Regiment. Toller later recalled the atmosphere of total euphoria amongst the volunteers: 'Yes, we live in an intoxication of feeling. The words Germany, Fatherland, War have magical power; when we pro-nounce them, they do not vanish, but remain floating in the air, circling round, inflaming themselves and us.'[1]

During these early weeks of the war, writers and intellectuals were

as prone to patriotic euphoria as any other section of the population.
For most of them, the outbreak of war was a momentous event
which they felt privileged to live through. The verse which it
inspired shows that for many it was a semi-mystical experience,
transcending rational explanation. Thomas Mann recorded the feelings of relief, even of catharsis, which it evoked: 'What we felt was
purification, liberation, an immense hope. This is what the poets
spoke of.'[2] The poet Rilke was overcome by feelings of solemn awe:
in the first of his 'Fünf Gesänge' ('Five Songs'), written in August
1914, he invoked the 'hörengesagter, fernster, unglaublicher
Kriegsgott' ('the rumoured, most distant, unbelievable God of
War'). Others succumbed to the sentiments of crude chauvinism
which swept through the population – Ernst Lissauer composed his
notorious 'Haßgesang gegen England' ('Hymn of Hate against England'), even the sober Thomas Mann abandoned his normal ironic
detachment to write essays of unalloyed patriotism. Many of the
younger writers who would later oppose the war – Fritz von Unruh,
René Schickele, Klabund – joined in this chorus of patriotic
celebration.[3]

Such jingoism was by no means limited to Germany, of course,
but in Germany it had particular connotations. In one sense, the
blind nationalism of August 1914 was itself a manifestation of a deep
longing for national unity. The poet Richard Dehmel, who volunteered for the army at the age of fifty-one, was typical of many who
welcomed the war in the belief that it would create a community of
spirit and purpose. Dehmel recorded in his war diary:

> All the hampering, paralysing mistrust between
> individual classes and groups in society . . . all the
> demoralizing display of class snobbery which was adop-
> ted in Germany from the English wage-slave system . . .
> suddenly all this was magically gone.[4]

The Kaiser himself had invoked national unity and community in
his famous speech from the throne proclaiming the 'Burgfrieden'
(civil truce) – 'I no longer know any parties, I know only Germans.'
Toller recounted that, on his journey back to Munich, people at the
stations they passed through had handed them postcards bearing the
picture of the Kaiser and the words of his famous declaration.

Toller's impulsive decision to enlist was of course in keeping with
the tremendous popular enthusiasm for the war, but in his case it

also had a deeper personal significance. It seemed suddenly to resolve the spiritual conflicts of his youth, to enable him to transcend his isolation through acceptance into the national community from which his race had always so subtly, but so successfully, excluded him. He wished to prove that he was a German, and only a German. At his later trial for high treason, he recalled that when he had volunteered, no one had asked him if he was a Jew.

Toller's patriotic commitment was typical of the Jewish community in general. The Kaiser had explicitly embraced his Jewish subjects in a famous address 'To my dear Jews' and most Jews had responded with gratefulness and relief that their separate identity had been rescinded. Prominent liberal Jewish intellectuals, such as Alfred Kerr, Maximilian Harden, Siegfried Jacobsohn and Kurt Tucholsky were converted overnight to a militant patriotism. The number of Jews who died fighting for Kaiser and country was proportionally greater than any other racial group in the Reich, including the 'pure' Germans: it was their last desperate attempt at assimilation.

Toller joined his regiment at Milkertshofen in the north of Munich, and it was here, on the church square, that he took the soldier's oath of allegiance. The father of a fellow recruit who met Toller at this time remembered him as 'a pale, almost boyish young man . . . a modest, rather shy person'.[5]

The regiment left Munich in mid-August. As the long field-grey columns marched off to war in the blazing summer sunshine, flowers in the muzzles of their rifles, they were cheered on their way by admiring and enthusiastic crowds. Toller was anxious to see active service, but the regiment was not immediately bound for the front. It spent some months stationed behind the lines, firstly at Bellheim in the Palatinate, then from January 1915 in the vicinity of Strasbourg. These long and often tedious months in different training-camps, a time of parade-ground drill and pointless spit-and-polish, failed to dispel Toller's spirit of commitment.

Among those serving in Toller's regiment was the young bookseller and publisher Heinrich F.S. Bachmair, who had already published the early poems of the Expressionist poet J.R. Becher. The two men met at the end of 1914: four years later Toller would appoint Bachmair as commander of the local Red Army's artillery in Dachau.

Toller's letters to family and friends in 1915 were still full of patriotic enthusiasm; fellow-soldiers remembered his fervent desire to get to the Front. Finally, in March, he volunteered for front-line service and was assigned to an artillery unit near Pont-à-Mousson. His diary contained the entry: 'How happy I am to go to the front at last. To do my bit. To prove with my life what I think and feel.'[6] The spirit of self-sacrifice, of eager commitment to what he regarded as a just cause, were to remain typical of Toller – only the political perspective would change.

Toller's service in the front line lasted fourteen months, from March 1915 to May 1916. It was the most formative period of his life, turning his system of beliefs upside down. The experience marked him not only morally but physically. A photograph taken in uniform in August 1914 shows a dapper, fresh-faced young man with dreamy eyes. Another picture taken a year later shows him pensive and questioning: a face that has already seen too much. Toller's transformation was far from immediate, for his idealistic patriotism was not easily dispelled. He initially served as an observer with an artillery unit, rejoicing, as he afterwards admitted, at each direct hit. In August 1915 he was transferred, at his own request, from the artillery to the infantry. The reason for his request was not only that he had been consistently victimized by his platoon commander, but also that the artillery war seemed strangely impersonal: he wanted to see who he was shooting at. He requested a posting to a machine-gun unit in Bois-le-Prêtre, one of the bloodiest sections of the front, and it was here that he gained first-hand experience of trench warfare.

If service in the artillery had made the enemy seem remote, the trenches brought him all too close. The French and German lines ran through the middle of the wood, close enough for the opposing soldiers to shout across to each other – if any of them had dared to raise their heads to do so. It was Toller's experience in Bois-le-Prêtre which first made him question what he was doing. A few hundred yards from the German positions was a blockhouse which had changed hands frequently in the fighting. Stumbling on it one day, Toller found himself confronted by a pile of corpses – French and German soldiers lying together in a last embrace, covered with a light coating of lime. This terrible scene, summarizing the violation of humanity in war, was to haunt him long after, inspiring one of his most deeply-felt poems.

Toller had continued to write poetry during his military service.

Much later, he published a selection of his poems in *Vormorgen*, studiously arranged to demonstrate his own transition to pacifism and activism. Though he certainly wrote poems in 1914, none has survived and it seems likely that he chose to suppress them, disowning the patriotic note which they undoubtedly struck. Only one poem, entitled 'Frühling 1915' ('Spring 1915'), has survived amongst his unpublished papers, documenting the feelings of patriotic euphoria he took to the front:

> In spring I go to war
> To sing or to die.
> What do I care for my own troubles?
> Today I shatter them, laughing, in pieces.
>
> Oh, Brothers, know that young spring came
> In a whirlwind.
> Quickly throw off tired grief
> And follow her in a host.
>
> I have never felt so strongly
> How much I love you, Oh, Germany,
> As the magic of spring surrounds you
> Amidst the bustle of war.[7]

This mood did not last long. The poems he began to write at the front in 1915 were more sober and factual in tone, unembellished, almost laconic in style:

> We muster at the forest graveyard.
> By the mass grave, one man dreams
> 'As a child, I always wanted
> Piles of Christmas cakes
> Like these . . .'
> A mine blew up fourteen comrades.
> Whenever was it?
> Yesterday.[8]

By 1916, the tone has changed. The subject had become more urgent and the style more declamatory. Perhaps the best example of this is 'Leichen im Priesterwald' ('Corpses in Priest's Wood'), a poem inspired by the dreadful scene he had witnessed in Bois-le-

Prêtre. In retrospect, the scene seemed to symbolize the essential brotherhood of mankind, made more poignant by death.

> A dung heap of rotting corpses:
> Glazed eyes, bloodshot,
> Brains spilt, guts spewed out
> The air poisoned by the stink of corpses
> A single awful cry of madness.
>
> Oh, women of France,
> Women of Germany
> Regard your menfolk!
> They fumble with torn hands
> For the swollen bodies of their enemies,
> Gestures, stiff in death, become the touch of
>   brotherhood,
> Yes, they embrace each other,
> Oh, horrible embrace!
>
> I see and see and am struck dumb.
> Am I a beast, a murderous dog?
> Men violated . . .
> Murdered . . .[9]

Following his service in Bois-le-Prêtre, Toller was promoted to corporal, and posted to a battery east of Verdun, where he was on regular night-duty in the trenches with the task of determining the precise position of the enemy guns. His enthusiasm for the war gone, only his sense of duty sustained him. Appalled by the physical slaughter, he still sought to justify it as necessary in the cause of national defence. The chauvinism of his student days had vanished: he indignantly rejected the government propaganda within Germany which depicted the enemy as brutal and degenerate. He protested against such distortion in an article he sent to the journal *Der Kunstwart*, but the article was returned as unsuitable 'in view of the current state of public opinion'. Toller was already beginning to realize what he later made explicit:

> Most people have no imagination. If they could imagine
> the sufferings of others, they would not make them suf-
> fer so. What separated a German mother from a French

mother? Slogans which deafened us so that we could not hear the truth.[10]

Whatever his private doubts, he continued to carry out his military duties to the best of his abilities; indeed his military record remained unblemished to the end. Even at his trial, his former officers testified that he had been a good and conscientious soldier; fellow-soldiers praised his courage and comradeship.

In his autobiographical account of life at the front, Toller made little reference to the 'camaraderie' of the front-line soldier, no doubt because this virtue had by then been appropriated by the nationalist right, but in fact he always had a strong sense of solidarity with his comrades-in-arms. In a letter defending his anti-war activities in December 1917, he wrote that 'precisely those of us who have been at the front feel doubly obliged to speak on behalf of those still there'. Over a decade later, reviewing Remarque's best-seller *All Quiet on the Western Front*, he praised the author for having spoken

> on behalf of all of us, all those who lay in the trenches, filthy and infested with lice, who shot and were shot at, who saw the war, not from the perspective of the General Staff or from behind a desk, but for whom it was everyday life, terrible and monotonous.[11]

Toller's experience at the front led to a gradual deadening of feeling and perception: 'I see the dead, and I don't see them,' he wrote later, 'they have the unreality of waxworks, inspiring only horror, not pity.' He described his final conversion to pacifism as a process of sudden revelation, coming when he accidentally dug up the intestines of a dead body:

> A dead human being is buried here. A dead human being! And suddenly, as though the darkness were parted from the light, the word from its meaning, I grasp the simple truth about humanity, a truth which I had forgotten, which lay buried, overlaid: the common interest, the single unifying quality. A dead human being. Not: a dead Frenchman. Not: a dead German. A dead human being.[12]

This revelation of the common humanity of friend and foe, consciously borrowing the language of the biblical creation, has all the marks of literary stylization, but while Toller's actual realization was probably more gradual, its effect was no less dramatic.

In May 1916 Toller suffered a physical and nervous breakdown. He was taken to hospital near Strasbourg – it was in fact a Franciscan monastery which the monks had converted into a field hospital – where he remained for about two months before being transferred to a sanatorium at Ebenhausen near Munich for further treatment. Toller was always reticent about the precise nature of this illness, referring only to 'heart and nervous disorder', but whatever the physical manifestations of the illness, it is clear that it was psychological in origin. Dr Julian Marcuse, who treated him at the Ebenhausen sanatorium, diagnosed 'physical exhaustion and a complete nervous breakdown'.[13] It was two months before Toller recovered sufficiently to be released from hospital; he was posted to a convalescent company near Mainz, where he spent a further two months. On 4 January 1917 he was finally discharged from the army as 'unfit for active service'.

Toller's experience of war was to remain the most formative of his life, and henceforth pacifism was to be his dominant conviction, a thread running through all his work. His first play was the anti-war drama *The Transformation*, almost his last was the satirical comedy *Nie wieder Friede!* (*No More Peace!*). His earliest political manifesto in 1919 was an appeal for peace; his first major speech after his release from prison five years later was to an anti-war meeting in Leipzig on the tenth anniversary of the outbreak of war. While he was to give a symbolic version of his experience in *The Transformation*, it was a decade and a half before he felt sufficient distance from it to be able to narrate it directly in his autobiography.

Even before his official discharge, Toller had returned to Munich to resume his studies: in November 1916 he registered as a student in the faculties of Law and Economics. He found lodgings in the fashionable Kurfürstenstrasse, but soon moved to Schwabing, the student and artistic quarter, which even in war-time had retained some of its Bohemian character. In retrospect, he described this period as one in which he 'gradually found himself', both politically and artistically, but the process was neither rapid nor easy.

The winter of 1916–17 was a drab and straitened time in Germany. Food shortages increased, as the Allied blockade began to bite. The stalemate on the Western Front continued and casualties climbed inexorably. Munich itself was no longer the 'Athens on the

Isar' of pre-war years. Conscription and the rapid growth of war industries had changed the face of the city, but after the half-life of the trenches or the ordered sterility of the sanatorium, Munich seemed full of life and colour. In his autobiography, Toller writes that his enthusiasm and thirst for knowledge were boundless – and yet the specific knowledge of individual academic disciplines seemed divorced from real life.

As at other German universities, students were able to draw up their own syllabuses and it was considered a virtue to attend lectures on a wide variety of subjects. Toller's interests were predominantly literary, interests which he seems to have pursued to the neglect of his legal and economic studies. He joined a seminar in German literature given by the well-known Professor Artur Kutscher, who enjoyed a reputation as a champion of modern writing. He would later write a definitive biography of the playwright Frank Wedekind, who was among his many literary friends in Munich. Once a week, Kutscher would invite his students to a Gasthaus, where Wedekind would sing his ballads, or such literary notables as the poet Karl Henckell, the Naturalist dramatist Max Halbe, or Thomas Mann would read from their work.

Mann was the doyen of literary circles in Munich. He lived in a house in the Herzogspark, a residential district as far removed as he was from the Bohemian excesses of Schwabing. His house was nonetheless a Mecca for young writers, whom he was always willing to help with advice and criticism. Toller was among those whom Mann invited to visit him. He arrived with his pockets stuffed full of poems, some of which earned measured praise from the great writer. Toller must have made more than a passing personal impression, for two years later Mann came forward to testify on his behalf. Mann's son Klaus was later to become a close friend of Toller's in exile.

It was not only literature which absorbed Toller. In the company of his girl-friend Grete Lichtenstein, he visited concerts and art galleries and made excursions to the lakes and countryside around Munich. There was an element of escapism in this feverish activity, which Toller later summarized in the chapter title 'I Want to Forget the War'. He certainly made a conscious effort to escape from it mentally, as he had escaped from it physically, but the war pursued him wherever he turned: crippled figures in field-grey uniform confronted him on every street corner. Memories of war mingled in his mind with images of war. He recalled how the Crucifixion by

Matthias Grünewald, the so-called Isenheimer Altar in Colmar, evoked the scenes he had witnessed in Bois-le-Prêtre. The comparison is forced, but is nonetheless eloquent of Toller's state of mind.

By early 1917 his literary ideals had become those of Expressionism. What we now call Expressionism was not a product of the war years. Its origins lay in the rebellion against the rigid conventions of the Kaiserreich common in intellectual circles before 1914. The younger generation of writers rejected what Carl Sternheim derisively termed 'the heroic life of the bourgeoisie' – and the culture which it officially endorsed. There was a widespread desire for 'Aufbruch', a new beginning, a break with the old, which Expressionist poets evoked in fevered and often visionary language. In August 1914 the rebellion of Expressionism had been subsumed in the general enthusiasm for the war. Many of the younger poets believed that this event heralded a new beginning, perceiving the death and destruction of war semi-mystically in terms of cultural and spiritual renewal. Once confronted by the realities of modern warfare, they had rapidly recanted their enthusiasm. By 1916 virtually all the writers associated with Expressionism were opposed to the war. Expressionist periodicals, like *Die Aktion* and *Die weißen Blätter*, became foci for anti-war feeling. The former assumed in 1917 the forthright subtitle: 'Organ of the most radical friends of peace for anti-national politics and culture.' The latter, having been transferred to Zurich by its editor, René Schickele, was able to evade German censorship, publishing an impressive variety of pacifist contributions.

In 1916 the pacifist writer Kurt Hiller published the first of his yearbooks *Das Ziel*, in which he expounded the idea that all true thought was political, demanding the enrolment of art in the service of politics. Hiller, the originator of the concept of Activism, found an enthusiastic audience among the younger Expressionist writers, who, reworking their earlier convictions, had now come to believe that the suffering of war would produce a new humanity. Increasingly visionary and apocalyptic, their work proclaimed that a new era of peace and brotherhood was at hand – if only people could be incited to act. Here lay the responsibility of the Activist writer, the 'political poet' espoused by J.R. Becher and (above all) Walter Hasenclever.

In 1917 Hasenclever published a volume of poems with the quintessentially Expressionist title *Tod und Auferstehung* (*Death and*

Resurrection) which ended with a poem entitled 'Der politische Dichter' ('The Political Poet'):

> The poet no longer dreams of blue bays.
> From back yards he sees bright crowds ride forth,
> His foot rests on the corpses of the loathsome
> His head is raised to accompany the people.
>
> He will be their leader. He will proclaim.
> The flame of his words will be music.
> He will establish the great community of states,
> The rights of man. The Republic.[14]

The role of the poet was therefore not only to decry the war, but to lead humanity towards his vision of a peaceful, just and communal society, a theme repeated in many variants in the literature of the later war years.

Ernst Toller's poetry in 1917–18, including his anti-war drama *The Transformation*, must be seen in this perspective. He felt that his generation, which had born the brunt of action in the front line, had been betrayed by its elders. He believed the time was right for social transformation, though like many of his contemporaries he still conceived of social change in terms of the spiritual regeneration of the individual. In July 1916, less than three months after the end of his active service, he had written to the novelist Cäsar Flaischlen, praising his book *Jost Seyfried*.[15] The theme of the novel is the struggle of the artist at an historical turning-point. 'We must become new people,' declares its protagonist, 'we must create new souls, new values to live by!' The appeal of this novel for the twenty-three year old Toller needs little elaboration. A fellow-student in Munich, invited to read some of Toller's poems, remembered that he was scornful of 'art for art's sake': the purpose of art was no longer simply aesthetic, for the time was long past when anyone could take refuge in pure aestheticism. There was no time left to discuss 'what poetry is or should be'. Poetry had to confront the issues of the day, and in a time of mass slaughter, the only issue was the war.[16]

Toller's poems from this period sound the authentic note of war Expressionism: declamatory in manner and Activist in intent. Typical in both content and style is the poem 'Den Müttern' ('To the Mothers'):

Mothers,
Your hope, your joyful burden
Lies in churned-up earth
Groans between barbed wire . . .
Mothers!
Your sons did this to each other.

In its original version, the poem ended with a direct incitement to action:

Dig deeper into your pain,
Let it strain, etch, gnaw
Stretch out arms raised in grief
Be volcanoes, glowing sea:
Let pain bring forth deeds![17]

He shared the general feeling of the poet's special responsibility:

I accuse you, you poets
Wanton with words, words, words . . .
Cowardly hiding in your paper-basket.
On to the rostrum, accused![18]

The poet had to be more than a mere confectioner of words, for words must prompt action. Indeed poetry itself was conceived as action: action as exhortation, as revelation, as inspiration.

When Toller left Munich in the summer of 1917, his revulsion against the war had hardened into opposition to the forces which prosecuted it. He had still not fully recovered his health and he spent some weeks during August and September in a sanatorium in Bad Schachen on Lake Constance. It was the lull before the storm of his first active involvement in politics.

III

Call to Socialism
1917–1918

The Anti-War Movement

By the autumn of 1917 the tide of public opinion was running strongly against the war and the peace movement was gathering momentum. In April the Social Democratic Party (SPD) had finally split, and the Independent Social Democrats (USPD) had been formed as a specifically anti-war party. Also in April, a wave of anti-war strikes had broken out in Berlin and other big industrial cities, followed during the summer by unrest in the Imperial Navy. On 19 July, the Reichstag passed its famous Peace Resolution, appealing for a negotiated peace and renouncing the government's policy of annexations. The resolution was strongly attacked by nationalists and led within a month to the founding of the Deutsche Vaterlandspartei, which made resounding propaganda for the cause of 'peace through victory'.

It was against this background that, in September 1917, Toller was invited to attend the 'Kulturtagung', a conference of artists and intellectuals organized by the publisher Eugen Diederichs at Lauenstein Castle in Thuringia. Toller himself later referred to the occasion as his 'first active involvement in politics'.[1] Among the participants were many of the leading figures in German intellectual life. There were notable academics, like the sociologists Max Weber and Ferdinand Tönnies, the economist Werner Sombart and the historian Friedrich Meinecke. There was also Max Maurenbrecher, Lutheran pastor turned pan-German publicist. And there were such leading literary figures as Walter von Molo, Richard Dehmel, Paul Ernst and the worker-poet Karl Bröger. Diederichs had also invited a number of younger men, among whom were Theodor Heuss (later President of the Federal Republic) and Ernst Toller. Toller was not yet twenty-four, unknown and unpublished, but his invitation to such a gathering suggests that he had already made some impression on established literary circles in Munich.

The basic theme of the conference was 'The Problem of Leader-

ship in State and Culture'. Diederichs himself had a more grandiose
vision, which may also help to explain how Toller and other younger
writers came to be invited:

> The (first) Lauenstein conference was unsatisfactory, in
> that the creative political man was lacking . . . What is
> needed is the New Man, whose inspiration is grounded
> in the spirit, and who is therefore not impressed by the
> economic laws of life, but rather taking the Platonic
> view, feels that it is the spirit which also shapes econ-
> omic and political life. This has nothing to do with moral
> precepts, but rather with a chivalrous humanity, which
> affirms life though it believes it to be tragic. The prob-
> lem is, therefore – how is this type to develop in the
> state, how does he achieve leadership?[2]

Diederichs's comments typify the cloudy idealism of many German
intellectuals in 1917, suggesting both the messianic pretensions of
Expressionism and the mystical undercurrent which would lead to
Nazism.

Toller went to the Lauenstein conference in search of kindred
spirits, of others who found the continuation of the war intolerable.
He seems to have expected the occasion to produce some positive
initiative for peace, but in this he was disappointed. The proceedings
turned into a personal contest between Maurenbrecher, summoning
up a future Germany perceived mystically in terms of the past, and
Max Weber, who asserted that the Prussian 'Obrigkeitsstaat'
(authoritarian state) must be democratized and who regarded the
Kaiser as the person principally responsible for Germany's misfortunes. Toller considered these exchanges to be proof of the
futility of intellectual discussion at a time which cried out for action.
Initially hesitating to speak in such distinguished company, he
finally rose to make a passionate appeal for some initiative against the
war. There was no response. Toller left Lauenstein bitterly critical
of 'the confusion, the cowardice, the lack of courage of the older
generation'[3] – a generation he and his contemporaries held responsible for the war. His memoirs suggest that one of his few positive
experiences in Lauenstein was his meeting with Richard Dehmel,
who offered praise and encouragement of Toller's poems. Even this
memory is misleading, for he wrote to the older man later that year,
reproaching him with the patriotic tone of his war poetry: 'I read

some of your war poems today. Glorifications of war. Do you still stand by them?"[4] There is no record of Dehmel's reply.

Immediately after the Lauenstein conference, Toller went to Heidelberg, registering as a student of law and economics for the winter semester. Heidelberg, surrounded by wooded hills and crowned by its romantic ruined castle, is the best-known of all German university towns, celebrated by Hölderlin and the German Romantics and popularized in Sigmund Romberg's *The Student Prince*. In 1917 it had lost much of the chocolate-box splendour of pre-war years. The traditional student corporations still held sway, but the majority of the students were now either young women or ex-soldiers who had been invalided out of the army.

Toller found lodgings in Friedrichstrasse, one of the narrow streets in the heart of the Old Town. Heidelberg enjoyed the dubious reputation of being a 'doctoral factory'. When Toller visited the venerable Professor Gothein to discuss a topic for dissertation, he was recommended to write on 'Pig Breeding in East Prussia'. He had more pressing concerns.

Toller never stated why he chose to transfer his studies to Heidelberg, but it was most probably to further his acquaintance with Max Weber, who had made a deep impression on him at Lauenstein. Though Weber had not actually lectured in Heidelberg for several years, he remained one of the University's outstanding academic figures. Toller wrote later: 'Max Weber was the only German professor who was a real politician and – what was even more of a rarity at German universities – a character.'[5] Their meeting had also impressed Weber, who had found Toller likeable and, while recognizing his political immaturity, respected his obvious sincerity and moral integrity. He was soon amongst those who regularly attended Weber's famous Sunday 'open house'. It was not long before he felt sufficiently confident to read aloud some of his war poems which, according to Marianne Weber, greatly affected his audience. His friend Margarete Pinner remembered that on several winter evenings he recited his poems to a small circle of fellow-students – 'and we were deeply moved'.[6] Among the works he read were scenes from his anti-war play *The Transformation* which he had begun the previous summer and which, within two years, would establish his reputation as a dramatist. Toller did not read his work in search of literary comment or criticism, but consciously 'to agitate against the war'. He wished 'to rouse the dulled, mobilize the hesitant and show the way to those still groping'.[7] Toller's comment, written in 1920, is eloquent of his whole conception of political theatre – and indeed of political activity in general.

Toller's pursuit of Max Weber to Heidelberg suggests his need of a father figure, his search for an intellectual mentor who could point the way forward. Weber, with some justification, later called him 'a disciple by nature',[8] but it was not Weber whose disciple he was to be. He admired the older man's courage and honesty, but he did not share his ideology. Weber believed that Germany must continue to prosecute the war, for only national defence would ensure the survival of the nation; he also argued for a process of parliamentary and electoral reform. Even his assertion that, when the war was over, he would provoke the Kaiser into prosecuting him for lèse-majesté in order to force the politicians responsible for the war to testify under oath, revealed a basic attachment to institutions which Toller increasingly dismissed. If Weber's approach was cautious and legalistic, Toller was moving towards a revolutionary perspective. Above all, he had now committed himself actively to the growing peace movement.

Toller had come to Heidelberg more determined than ever to find others who shared his opposition to the war. Among those he found was Margarete Pinner, who had lodgings at the boarding-house where he took lunch. Their relationship began as a romantic friendship – 'we rowed on the river and thought we were happy,' she remembered.[9] They shared a liking for the countryside around Heidelberg, but above all they shared opposition to the war. Margrete introduced him to a group of students who met informally for political discussion. The meetings had been initiated by a Viennese student called Käthe Pick (later prominent in the Austrian Social Democratic Party) in order 'to clarify our thoughts by reading and discussing socialist books'. Margarete Pinner recalled that the group was 'closely knit and strong in its socialist zeal' and it therefore seems unlikely that Toller would have been invited to join them if he too had not already been a socialist. It was only with great difficulty that she was able to convince Toller to join the group; the Lauenstein conference had suggested that all discussion was pointless. He was, however, finally persuaded to come and was soon urging the group to embark on action: it was this group which formed the nucleus of a pacifist association for which Toller coined the grandiloquent name 'Cultural and Political League of German

Youth'. It is clear that Toller was both the instigator and main spokesman of the League – and equally clear that its influence failed to match its pretensions, since it never numbered more than a dozen members. Toller was later at pains to distance himself from it, dismissing it as 'a Don Quixote of 1917', but its activities were both more practical and more socialist than his description suggests. At his trial for high treason, Toller spoke of the League's 'cultural, political and socialist aims'.[10]

The League began its work by seizing on a current 'cause célèbre'. In October 1917, nationalist students in Munich disrupted a lecture by the eminent Professor F.W. Foerster, a man well known for his pacifist views. Foerster himself was threatened with physical attack and rescued only by student sympathizers. Toller and his friends used this incident to demand the removal of restrictions on students' rights of association and assembly, which the University authorities enforced largely to prevent socialist or pacifist activity. This demand was made in a leaflet signed by Toller 'on behalf of 135 Heidelberg students', which was widely distributed and also published in the *Münchener Zeitung* on 10 November 1917. It was Toller's first political publication.[11]

In a wider context, the League aimed to counter the annexationist demands of the Deutsche Vaterlandspartei and to canvass support for socialist initiatives for a 'peace without annexations and reparations'. To this end, Toller drafted an appeal to be circulated to students at other universities. He was eager to enlist the support of Max Weber, but the latter was not to be drawn. He considered the appeal confused and was, moreover, reluctant to endorse any action which might undermine the morale of the German army in the field. Toller was not so easily diverted. He sent copies of the appeal to leading literary and academic figures, receiving messages of support from F.W. Foerster and such writers as Heinrich Mann, Carl Hauptmann (elder brother of Gerhart), Walter Hasenclever and Walter von Molo, whom Toller had met in Lauenstein.

By November 1917 Toller was in touch with leading pacifist figures in Germany and abroad, including the Alsatian poet and novelist, René Schickele, in Zurich.[12] As the war continued, Switzerland had become a haven for several German or Austrian writers of pacifist or socialist conviction, who included the Dadaists Arp and Ball, and others such as Albert Ehrenstein, Leonhard Frank, Ivan Goll, Ludwig Rubiner and Schickele. Schickele, editor of the journal *Die weißen Blätter*, had left Germany for Switzerland in the autumn of 1915 and had thereafter edited the journal from Zurich, a move enabling him to avoid the strict censorship which stifled much of the criticism of the war in Germany. After 1916, *Die weißen Blätter* published many of the crucial anti-war texts and it was almost certainly here that Toller first read Hasenclever's anti-war drama *Antigone*, here that he read the stories by Leonhard Frank, later collected under the title *Der Mensch ist gut* (*Man is Good*), and here too that he must have read the translation of Henri Barbusse's novel *Under Fire*, a work which quickly became the guiding light of a generation of European intellectuals. Toller was certainly familiar with all these works, for he intended to distribute pamphlets containing extracts from them as part of his anti-war agitation in Heidelberg.[13]

Toller's state of mind at this time was curiously ambivalent: he sought both political involvement and solitude. He began to take long walks in the hills surrounding Heidelberg, sometimes disappearing for days on end without telling any of his friends. Politically, matters were now coming to a head. The appeal Toller had drafted had been sent to socialist groups at other universities in order to rally support before publishing it, but the appeal was prematurely leaked to the (nationalist) *Deutsche Zeitung*, which printed it in full on 11 December. The official Heidelberg Students Committee instantly disowned 'the very narrow circle of Heidelberg students under the leadership of one Ernst Toller', the Vaterlandspartei began a virulent campaign against them. One Heidelberg professor used his final lecture before Christmas to denounce the association's 'treason against the Fatherland'. Toller replied to these attacks in a letter to the *Heidelberger Tageblatt*: 'For us, politics means that we feel morally responsible for the fate of our country and act accordingly.'[14]

This public controversy succeeded in alerting the military authorities, which rapidly intervened to disband the League and disperse its members. Käthe Pick and another Austrian student were refused re-entry into Germany, German students were expelled from Heidelberg and forced to return to their native states – in Toller's case Prussia, of which Posen was then still a province. He was indeed threatened with being recalled for military service. The police called at his lodgings with a warrant for his arrest, but failed to find him as he was ill in hospital. Toller hurriedly left Heidelberg, having been there less than three months. Arriving in Berlin on 22

December, he hastened to alert sympathetic Reichstag deputies to the action of the military authorities. The socialist deputy Wolfgang Heine did indeed raise the question of exclusion orders against Austrian students in the Central Committee of the Reichstag – but to no avail.

While Toller's pacifist association was intrinsically of little political significance, it nonetheless represented an important step in his political development. He clearly considered it a focus for opposition to the war ('we want to rouse the uncommitted, rally the like-minded')[15] and as a means of converting that opposition into practical activity. The League's outline programme, drafted by Toller, articulates his ideology at this time: pacifist in tendency, Activist in intent, appealing to youth as the means of effecting international reconciliation. It reveals the formative influence of the anarchist philosopher, Gustav Landauer, 'whose *Call to Socialism* decisively moved and influenced me'.[16]

The Influence of Gustav Landauer

Landauer was a self-styled anarcho-socialist, whose ideas derived from Proudhon and Kropotkin; his philosophy is essentially a poetic interpretation of the tradition of European Anarchism. In his *Aufruf zum Sozialismus (Call to Socialism)*[17] Landauer defined socialism as 'a tendency of the human will . . . a striving to create a new reality with the help of an ideal' (p. 1). Men invoked this ideal precisely because the modern state, and the capitalist system on which it rested, failed to provide the basis for a satisfying life. Landauer did not share Kropotkin's belief that the state could be destroyed by political revolution, believing that the social order could only be changed in so far as the existing relationship between human beings was changed, and they came together again as 'Volk' (people).

> It is essential that we understand socialism, the struggle for new relations between men, as a spiritual movement . . . that there can only be new relations between men in so far as men who are moved by the spirit create them for themselves (p. 98).

New social forms would not be created by political revolution alone, but by 'a peaceful work of construction, an organizing from new spirit and for new spirit – and nothing else'. The driving force of social change was therefore 'Geist' (creative spirit).

'Geist' is a central concept in Landauer's philosophy though, for all his attempts to define it, it remains an ambivalent, almost mystical, one. It was both a motive force within the individual and a bond between individuals. It determined the manner of social relations, and the social and economic institutions in which they found expression. It was the spirit of community, but also produced the will to achieve that community. It was 'Geist' which would inspire people and unite them in pursuit of a common ideal: people united in this way were, in Landauer's terminology, 'Volk' (a people). Whereas 'Volk' was an organic entity, created by an identity of consciousness and aspiration, the state was an artificial structure, resulting from historical chance. If the unity of a people was created by 'Geist', the unity of the state was imposed ultimately by force: in Landauer's system of thought, 'Geist' and 'Staat' are roughly antithetical.

The most obvious sign of the absence of 'Geist' in modern society was the plight of the proletariat. Separated from the earth and its products, and forced by the factory organization of capitalism to produce goods unconnected with their own needs, they became alienated, often succumbing to poverty, sickness and alcoholism. The analogy with the Marxist concept of alienation is only superficial. Landauer maintained that the proletariat was not 'the class chosen by God on the basis of historical inevitability, but rather the section of the population which suffers most' (p. 112). That is, as the class most exploited by capitalism, it represented human suffering at its most acute. Toller's efforts to come to terms with this conception of the proletariat, and to reconcile it with materialist ideas of historical development, are apparent in all his early plays.

Landauer was a severe critic of Marxism, which he described as 'the bane of our time and the curse of the socialist movement' (p. 42). He rejected, above all, its scientific pretensions. Under the influence of Fritz Mauthner's 'critique of language', he believed that scientific language was inadequate to convey the essence of reality, which he believed could only be evoked indirectly through poetic language and image. Socialism, he maintained, was not the result of a particular stage of material development, but the product of human will:

> The possibility of socialism does not depend on any form of technology or the satisfaction of material needs.

> Socialism is possible at any time, if enough people want
> it . . . (p. 61).

Accordingly, he believed that the dominant historical force was the working of 'Geist' in society.

While Landauer acknowledged that the force of 'Geist' had been suppressed by the state and by industrial capitalism, it had not died out entirely. It had remained active in individuals of heightened awareness – the poets and thinkers – and it was their duty to reawaken it in others, to summon up the new reality through the propaganda of word and deed: 'Our spirit must arouse others, must light the way, must entice and attract. That was never done by words alone . . . but solely by example – example and self-sacrifice' (p. 152).

Landauer's *Call to Socialism* was first published in 1911, exerting some influence within a limited circle. The book's real popularity had emerged during the war: from 1916 Landauer had received a steady stream of requests for copies. At a distance of over seventy years, it is difficult to apprehend the evident appeal of the book to intellectuals. Landauer's socialism now seems remote: excessively romantic in its evocation of community and its hostility to modern industrial society. The fact that Landauer's ideas are consonant with those of Expressionism may explain much of its appeal to a younger literary generation. There are obvious parallels in the messianic tendency of Expressionism, in its emotional and often apocalpytic language and in its belief in the primacy of 'Geist'.

It is uncertain when Toller first read Landauer's *Call to Socialism*, though it was probably during the summer of 1917 and certainly before his move to Heidelberg in October. Margarete Pinner confirmed that the book had made a profound impression on him – as it had on her. Shortly before his expulsion from Heidelberg in December 1917, Toller wrote to Landauer in terms which show that he was not only familiar with Landauer's philosophy, but had adopted it very much as his own. His letter specifically requested Landauer's support for the work of his student League – and Landauer's influence is paramount in the League's 'Leitsätze' (outline programme) which bears Toller's name.[18]

The outline programme of Toller's student League is a programmatic restatement of some of Landauer's most typical ideas. Anarchist in its inspiration, Expressionist in its diction, it documents the literary quality of Toller's early political commitment. Toller called the League 'a community of those of like mind and like will', who were guided by 'the unifying idea of true spirit' and defined the League's task as 'awakening a sense of responsibility in young people and introducing them to politicaly activity'. It would achieve this aim – and here too the anarchist inspiration is clear – through the force of moral example: 'we wish to lead by taking action, to fire others with our own flame'. Furthermore, it is evident that 'Geist' is seen as the motive force of social change:

> The League will work for developments in which forms and institutions which have become inflexible are replaced by creative forces, arbitrary organization by the growth of organism imbued with creative spirit.

The outline programme goes on to propose 'practical work . . . to overcome the ever-widening gulf between the common people and the intellectuals'. It is the task of the few ('artists and those who create from a sense of love') to take the message to the many 'whose creative impulses are buried by the dirt and refuse of the factories and big cities'.

The outline programme in fact lists a number of concrete political demands – for the separation of Church and State, the humane administration of the law, the abolition of the death penalty, the reduction of the voting age, the reform of education – but its ultimate aspirations were purely utopian: 'Only through human transformation from within can there grow the community which we are striving for.' The transformation of the individual, as a model for the transformation of society, was a prescriptive aim which Landauer shared with the younger generation of Expressionist writers, a watchword which Toller would encapsulate in the title of his first drama *The Transformation*.

The January Strike

In December 1917 the news of the war seemed briefly to give grounds for optimism. Peace negotiations between Russia and Germany were opening at Brest-Litovsk and there was hope that they might preface a general armistice. Toller was in contact with pacifist circles in Berlin, speaking at a meeting held under the slogan 'Workers by brain and by hand – unite!': it was his maiden speech to a political meeting. He also gave further readings of his war poems at the house of a friend, when Grete Pinner was again among those present.

It was also at this time that Toller received some of the underground pamphlets which circulated clandestinely in war-time Germany, among them a letter by the ex-Krupp director Mühlon, and the Lichnowsky memorandum, written by the former German ambassador in London. Both these documents, illegally printed and distributed by the Spartacus League, revealed the diplomatic manoeuvres on the eve of war, contradicting the official government version of events. For Toller, they were a revelation, exposing Germany's responsibility for the outbreak of hostilities. Toller had volunteered in 1914 in the belief that Germany was fighting a defensive war, a belief he continued to cling to long after he had been discharged; his sense of betrayal at this exposure of Germany's war guilt was therefore all the more acute. Even more disturbing was his discovery of the expansionist aims of German capital, which immediately put the annexationist demands of the German government in a new light. 'The question of war guilt paled before the guilt of capitalism' he wrote fifteen years later, but it is unlikely he would have perceived it with such clarity in 1917.

The events which finally precipitated Toller into the growing revolutionary movement were his meeting with Kurt Eisner and his consequent participation in the munitions workers' strike in Munich. Toller's pacifist activities had made it almost inevitable that he would come into contact with socialist circles. The burgeoning anti-war movement had focused around the USPD, which had been formed as a party of protest against the war. Opposition to the war was the common denominator of the party's otherwise disparate membership, which embraced the Spartacists on the left and reformist socialists like Eduard Bernstein on the right.

Toller was introduced to Eisner in January 1918, when the latter came to Berlin for a meeting of USPD leaders to coordinate strike action against the war. Eisner, the leader of the USPD in Munich, had been a life-long opponent of Prussian militarism. He had opposed the war since September 1914 and had become obsessed with the question of German war guilt. He had written a careful analysis of the role of German mobilization in the outbreak of war, which the military censorship had prevented him from publishing. Eisner was a somewhat unlikely political leader. He was very much a literary man, who had made his living as a political journalist and drama critic; he had written verse and was the author of an Expressionist play which he would complete in prison following the January strike.[19]

Eisner's conception of socialism resulted from the intensive study of Kant, which he had pursued in Marburg under the tutelage of Hermann Cohen, the leading neo-Kantian scholar. Cohen believed that Kant's philosophy was essentially political. Philosophy, Cohen maintained, had come to see the state, not as a power structure, but as the embodiment of ethical consciousness. The empirical state, the 'Kaiserreich' of the Hohenzollerns, failed to conform to this ideal, being all too evidently 'the state of the ruling classes'. This power state (*Machtstaat*) would become a just state (*Rechtsstaat*) only when it ceased to serve particular class interests. What Cohen specifically suggested, therefore, was the compatibility of Kant's system of ethics with the objectives of democratic socialism.

Eisner tried to take these ideas further, asking if it were possible to reconcile the idea that socialism was ethically desirable with the view that it was scientifically determined. Could socialists adhere to both Kant and Marx? In 1904 he had published an essay seeking to 'dissolve the synthesis Marx–Hegel in the connection Marx–Kant – for objectively Marx belongs with Kant in the ranks of the eighteenth-century Enlightenment'. Eisner tried to place Kant in the perspective of historical development. While conceding that his ethical principles were the product of bourgeois liberalism, he maintained that they could no longer be identified with a bourgeois society bereft of all ideals. At the present stage of economic and political development they could be realized only through democratic socialism.[20]

Most historians have chosen to dismiss Eisner as an impractical dreamer, but his charismatic appeal for Toller and other young intellectuals lay precisely in his apparent success in translating ideals into reality. He would often invoke 'the greatest idea known to humanity, that between thought and action there should be no contradiction and no delay'.[21] In December 1916, he had organized a discussion group which began to meet on Monday evenings at the 'Golden Anchor' in the Schillerstrasse. The original group comprised no more than twenty-five people, but in the course of 1917 it grew to over a hundred, providing the nucleus of the later revolutionary movement in the city.

In January 1918 the political situation had suddenly acquired a new urgency. German demands in the peace negotiations at Brest-Litovsk had dispelled any hopes that the government would settle for a peace without annexations. It had become clear that peace in the East was not the prelude to a general armistice: the High Command was already planning a new spring offensive on the Western Front. Against this background, the shop stewards (*Obleute*) in the Berlin factories had met USPD leaders to agree plans for a mass strike in support of the demand for immediate peace without annexations. Returning to Munich on 19 January, Eisner immediately set about gaining support for the strike. At the weekly meeting at the 'Golden Anchor' on 21 January, in the presence of the usual police informers, he read out the strike resolution, roundly declaring that the aim of the strike was not simply to bring the war to an end but to end militarism and bring down the monarchy.

Toller's meeting with Eisner made such a deep impression on him that only days later he followed him to Munich. In a later statement to the police, he claimed that when he came to Munich, he had known nothing of the plans for a strike. However disingenuous this statement, it was certainly some days before he actually contacted Eisner. Indeed he took up in Munich where he had left off in Heidelberg. He addressed a student meeting, where (under the heading of 'any other business') he appealed for support in a campaign against the banning of his student association. He later held a literary evening, consisting of readings from his poems and the performance of scenes from *The Transformation*: it was the first of many public readings by Toller. Not every member of the audience had cultural motives for attending: one of those present was a police spy who reported that Toller's poems were 'crass and ultra-revolutionary'.[22]

It was 26 January when Toller finally went to see Eisner, who invited him to the public meeting organized by the USPD at the Kolosseum the following evening. The hall was filled with over 250 people, mainly factory delegates, when Eisner rose to speak. He spoke forcefully, announcing the decision by Berlin workers to hold an anti-war strike and ending with an appeal for delegates to canvass support for the strike at factory level. The other main speaker was Sonja Lerch, also of the USPD, on whom Toller would loosely base the protagonist of his revolutionary drama *Masse-Mensch* (*Masses and Man*).

Toller was instantly involved in a movement which seemed to have aims identical to his own. He was invited to attend the weekly meeting at the 'Golden Anchor' the following evening. When he arrived, the back room of the Gasthaus was already packed, the atmosphere tense and expectant. Toller was not slow to speak. Eyewitness accounts of the meeting bear vivid testimony to his state of mind and to his extraordinary power as an orator. He delivered an impassioned exhortation against the war, graphically depicting its horror and suffering. At times, he seemed scarcely in control of himself, salivating and trembling with emotion. He addressed himself particularly to the women there, mainly workers from the munitions factories: 'You mothers!' he would begin each new tirade, 'you brothers and sisters!' The speech was a rhetorical *tour de force*, full of Expressionist pathos, and it produced an astonishing effect. Some women were in tears, others were on their feet, but the entire meeting was with him: 'Hang Ludendorff!' they shouted and 'Down with the war!'[23] Toller's involvement in the strike movement was now irrevocable.

The strike quickly gathered momentum. In the next two days, Eisner appealed for support at a number of factory meetings. Toller accompanied him to some of these meetings and, eager to play an active role, handed out leaflets containing scenes from his play *The Transformation*. His intention was the same as in Heidelberg – to arouse feelings against the war. Workers in the main factories finally decided to strike from Thursday 31 January – 'the great and splendid Thursday', as Eisner would call it. A series of strike meetings adopted a declaration written by Eisner which the Bavarian government was called on to send to workers in 'enemy' countries:

> Unite with us to enforce a peace which will ensure freedom and happiness for all mankind in the building of a new world ... The struggle for peace has begun. Workers of the world unite![24]

The mixture of moral idealism and revolutionary rhetoric, so typical of Eisner, made a powerful impact on the impressionable Toller: he professed himself overjoyed that workers should strike, not for their own material interests, but on behalf of their comrades in the field.[25]

Eisner and other strike leaders were arrested late that evening. Early the following morning, Toller carried out his first direct assignment in the strike, speaking to women workers at a cigarette factory and then accompanying them to the strike meeting at the Schwabingerbräu beer-hall. The news of the arrest of the strike leaders threw the meeting momentarily into confusion. After some discussion, it was decided to send a deputation to the Chief of Police to demand their release. Toller volunteered to join the deputation and was promptly asked to address the meeting. It was the first time he had spoken to a mass meeting and his customary eloquence momentarily deserted him, but he soon began to speak freely and forcefully. His later accounts make only a laconic reference to the occasion, but it is clear from the poem which it inspired that he found it an exhilarating experience.[26] The strike, he declared, should be continued until all the arrested leaders had been released; it would demonstrate that the majority of the German people wanted 'a peace of understanding'. The tone of Toller's speech was pacifist; the inevitable police informers in the audience called it 'provocative in the extreme'.

The deputation to the Chief of Police got little satisfaction, being fobbed off with vague promises to look into the matter. Toller was elected to a new strike committee, formed to win support for a continuation of the strike. On Friday, 1 February, 8,000 workers were on strike, including those at Krupp, Maffei and other major factories producing war materials. There were more mass meetings on the Theresienwiese on 2 and 3 February. At the first of these, attended by over 6,000 strikers, Toller was one of the three main speakers: almost overnight, he had become a leading figure in the strike movement.

Toller's rapid and total involvement in the strike was typical of his emotional and often impulsive commitment: as in 1914, he was once more eager for active service. His experience of the strike – his first contact with the labour movement – served to give his convictions a class perspective. He had joined the strike, as he stressed in all his later accounts, for pacifist, not socialist, reasons: 'what attracted me was their struggle against the war.' But his actual experience was a revelation: 'I saw in the strike a movement pursuing completely ideal objectives.'[27] The strike was indeed to remain his most positive experience of revolutionary action, seeming to demonstrate the capacity of the working class for a fundamental change of attitude. Despite its ultimate failure, it suggested the latent power of mass action to bring about non-violent social change. From it emerged two of Toller's most typical political ideas – the mass strike as the ultimate revolutionary weapon and the idea of the 'Einheitsfront', the united front transcending party allegiance. But the strike also illustrated the opportunism and cynicism of the SPD, whose leaders had opposed it from the beginning and now set about bringing it to an end. Declaring themselves in complete agreement with the strikers' demands, and appealing to traditional party loyalty, they were able to assume leadership of the strike – and forced through a resolution that work should be resumed on Monday 4 February. In an attempt to combat their influence, Toller and other students printed a leaflet (which Toller wrote) calling for the strike to be continued, but by 4 February it had virtually collapsed.

That evening, detectives called at Toller's lodgings in the Akademiestrasse in the city's student quarter, and arrested him at gunpoint: pacifists were obviously dangerous people. He was taken to the military prison in the Leonrodstrasse, where he was held on a charge of 'attempted treason'. His exemption from military service had technically expired, and although he was still classified as 'unfit for active service', he was immediately reconscripted and forced to wear uniform again.

Toller was subjected to lengthy interrogations which were evidently intended to implicate him in the proceedings against Eisner. The authorities clearly believed that Eisner had been suborned by foreign, probably Bolshevik, money, as part of a conspiracy to undermine the morale of the army. Toller, technically still a soldier, provided the military link necessary to substantiate this crackpot theory. The examining magistrate refused to accept Toller's more straightforward account of events, resorting to threats to make him sign an untrue statement. Toller refused. During this time, he was held in complete isolation, being denied any visits, even from a lawyer, a measure against which he finally protested by going on hunger strike. Not everyone arrested was so tenacious. Sonja Lerch, who had been arrested at the same time as Eisner, was so downcast by her experience that she hanged herself in Stadelheim prison at the end of March.

Prisoners were allowed half an hour's exercise a day and it was in the grey quadrangle of the exercise yard that Toller composed the first of his prison poems and that he visualized the final scenes of *The Transformation*.[28] In his autobiography, Toller portrays the prison as a social microcosm, prefiguring the political disintegration of Imperial Germany. The prison is filled with deserters, demoralization and disaffection have reached epic proportions, the warders fraternize with the prisoners and ask Toller when the 'fraud' will finally be over, an officer has words of encouragement for him, and a sympathetic doctor connives in his discharge.

Toller was finally released from prison in May 1918 and posted to a reserve battalion of his regiment at Neu-Ulm. The charge of 'attempted treason' was still hanging over him. This second (involuntary) spell of military service was relatively uneventful. Toller took no public part in politics, but devoted himself to the study of the socialist classics. He read works by Marx, Engels, Bakunin, Lassalle and Luxemburg – reading which provided a conceptual basis for what had previously been an emotional commitment. It was only now, he later recorded, that he became 'a socialist of intellectual conviction'.[29] Toller was also secretly in touch with Gustav Landauer, whom he contrived to visit in the Swabian village of Krumbach, where Landauer had spent the war in self-imposed exile. Why, Toller demanded, had Landauer remained silent during the holocaust of the last four years? The latter replied that he had predicted the outbreak of war and now predicted the revolution which would inevitably follow it: when the time came, he would be ready to play his part.

There was one significant interruption to these months of reading and reflection. In August, Toller was committed to the Psychiatric Clinic in Munich for examination. While in the military prison he had been examined by a series of doctors, who had variously diagnosed him as 'a neurasthenic with a pronounced sense of ego' or 'severe hysteric with an abnormal urge to make himself interesting', one or two noting for good measure signs of 'hereditary degeneration'.[30] Their diagnosis must, of course, be treated with considerable caution: they were employed by the military authorities, and it is not difficult to detect the intention of marginalizing political dissent by simply categorizing it as abnormality.

Toller remained extremely sensitive to all such attempts to undermine his political position. At his subsequent trial for high treason, he insisted that he had been committed to the Clinic only as the result of steps taken by his mother, who had written to the military authorities with medical certificates which testified to Ernst's childhood history of nervous illness. 'My family felt that its bourgeois honour was threatened and did all it could to suggest that I was not responsible for my actions.'[31] In the Psychiatric Clinic he was examined by Professor Emil Kräpelin, a fanatical nationalist whose expertise had always been at the service of the state – in 1913, he had written a detailed memorandum for the State Prosecutor in the latter's move to ban Frank Wedekind's sexual drama *Lulu* on grounds of obscenity. He pointedly told Toller that it was only scoundrels like him who had prevented Germany from winning the war already. The experience made a profound impression on Toller, surfacing almost a decade later in his play *Hoppla, wir leben!* (*Hoppla, Such is Life!*) in which the motif of the mental hospital symbolizes the play's theme of the madness of the social order. In his autobiography Toller recounts the episode in a chapter pointedly entitled 'Madhouse', in which it is the staff rather than the patients who need locking up. Kräpelin is portrayed as the manic voice of German nationalism, still demanding total victory at a time when defeat was already inevitable.

Toller was released from the Psychiatric Clinic after only four days. The medical experts concluded that he was 'clearly one of the politically immature, aestheticizing and hyper-sensitive young people, who live entirely in their ideas'. He was discharged from the army in September 1918, when it was formally decided not to proceed with the charges against him. None of the strike leaders was ever charged, but the proceedings against them were not finally dropped until the autumn. Eisner himself was not released until 14 October – by then, the war was lost and the political climate transformed.

After being discharged, Toller returned to his mother's home. She was now living with his sister Hertha in Landsberg-an-der-Warthe, where they had moved earlier in the year. Germany's situation was increasingly hopeless. Admiral Scheer, Commander of the German Navy, advocated a mass levy as a last desperate measure of national defence, a call echoed by leading politicians such as Walter Rathenau. Protest meetings were hurriedly called to rally opinion against such proposals, and Toller was briefly in Berlin to speak at one such meeting called by the Reichstag deputy Wolfgang Heine. It was Toller's last political action before the outbreak of revolution. By early November, he was once more in Landsberg.

IV   The Transformation: *Drama as Political Action*

The Transformation, like many first plays and novels, contains strong elements of autobiography. Toller wrote the first draft in the summer and autumn of 1917, and completed the final version while he was in prison following the January Strike.[1] The composition of the play therefore runs roughly parallel to his early involvement in the anti-war movement, an experience which it reworks, translating it into the symbolic conventions of theatrical Expressionism.

The breakthrough of Expressionism into the theatre did not occur until the last two years of the war, for though the earliest examples of Expressionist plays – Reinhard Sorge's *Der Bettler* and Walter Hasenclever's *Der Sohn* – were actually written before 1914, they were not staged until 1916–17.[2] The emergence of Expressionism in the theatre closely follows the growth of the anti-war movement. During 1916–18, as opposition to the war grew and the pace of public protest quickened, a number of plays in the Expressionist style, all strongly pacifist in theme, were written, published, and in isolated cases even performed, despite the strict censorship then in force. They included some of the works which would make Expressionism internationally famous: Georg Kaiser's *Gas* (written 1917–18, published and performed 1918), Fritz von Unruh's *Ein Geschlecht* ('One Race') (written 1916, published March 1917, performed June 1918), Walter Hasenclever's *Antigone* (written, published and produced in 1917) – and *The Transformation*, which though written in 1917–18, was not published or produced until almost a year after the armistice.

The Transformation is, in both theme and structure, a typical (if not *the* typical) example of Expressionist theatre. The theme of the play, summarized in its title, is the representative Expressionist theme of spiritual regeneration, leading to social renewal. The play is written in the typically Expressionist form of the 'Stationendrama', in which the spiritual progress of its central character is portrayed through a series of loosely-connected tableaux, linked only through the protagonist's experience. This particular dramatic form had been pioneered by Strindberg in such plays as *To Damascus*, *A Dream Play* and *The Ghost Sonata*, which were all performed in Germany in the pre-war period and which were a decisive inspiration to the younger playwrights. Toller frankly acknowledged the influence of Strindberg, whose name is actually pronounced in the opening scene of *The Transformation*.[3]

The 'Stationendrama' abandoned both the logically-structured plot, dependent on cause and effect, and the realistic setting which were intrinsic to Naturalism. The stage directions in *The Transformation* indicate time and place only in the most general terms: the action of the play is set 'in Europe before the beginning of rebirth'. The dramatis personae are not individual characters but types who embody particular social roles: 'doctor', 'war cripple', 'student', 'soldier'. There is also the emblematic figure of 'death as the enemy of the spirit', in the guise of a soldier, a professor, a judge and so on. Even Toller's protagonist, Friedrich, is less an individual than a paragon, whose spiritual rebirth is a model for the hoped-for regeneration of mankind.

Strindberg called his experimental dramas 'dream plays' – and they were indeed written in the years following the appearance of Freud's *Interpretation of Dreams*. Perhaps the keynote of Expressionist theatre was the attempt to convey inner experience in visual and dramatic terms, representing dream effects through the use of lighting and division of the stage. Toller draws on these experimental techniques in *The Transformation*, dividing the action of the play between 'realistic' scenes, which are played front stage and which give a roughly consecutive narrative of Friedrich's conscious experience, and 'dream' scenes, played rear stage 'in inner dream-like distance', which represent the subconscious reality of the struggle through which Friedrich achieves his transformation. While the 'realistic' scenes use prosaic dialogue and situations, the 'dream' scenes are written in the heightened poetic language which is the hallmark of Expressionism.

The Transformation is a carefully constructed play, consisting of six stations, which are further divided into thirteen scenes. The play centres on the crucial seventh scene, which marks a dramatic climax and turning-point, so that the six scenes which precede it are balanced against the six which follow it, giving the play a conscious dramatic symmetry. The plot and meaning of the play are probably best understood by following the successive stations which mark the spiritual development of the protagonist. The first three stations all follow the same structural pattern, the narrative exposition of a 'realistic' scene alternating with a 'dream' scene which provides oblique commentary on it.

In the opening scene Friedrich, a young sculptor, feels that he is a social outcast, 'eternally homeless', akin to Ahasuerus, the wandering Jew. He is cut off from society by the supposed stigma of his (Jewish) race, yet alienated from the attitudes of his family: 'a stranger to those over there, distant from the others' (p. 17). To break out of this isolation, he volunteers for a colonial war, in which he sees an opportunity to prove himself: 'Oh, the struggle will unite us all. The greatness of the times will make us all great . . . Now I can do my duty. Now I can prove that I am one of them' (pp. 20–21). The ensuing dream-scene ('Troop-train') contrasts Friedrich's naive enthusiasm with the cynicism and resignation of his fellow- soldiers, who speak of the horrors of war in a choral lament. The symbolic figure of Death, in the form of a soldier with a skull instead of a head, accompanies them.

In the second station, Friedrich volunteers for a dangerous mission in order to prove his devotion to the Fatherland. It is only after the successful conclusion of this mission that he begins to perceive the brutal reality behind the fine words of patriotism. His realization is prefigured in the dream scene 'Between the barbed wire', in which four skeletons, representing humanity used and abused by war, are united in death, as they hang in the barbed wire in No Man's Land: 'Now we are no longer friend and foe/Now we are no longer black and white./Now we are all alike (p. 26). At the end of the scene, they perform a 'danse macabre' to the music of the rattling bones of other corpses.

The third station again begins with a realistic scene, in which Friedrich, now in hospital, is decorated with the Iron Cross, the ultimate symbol of the acceptance he sought. Simultaneously, the victory of the Fatherland is announced, a victory bought at the cost of ten thousand enemy dead. For the first time, he questions the ideal of patriotism at a conscious level: 'Ten thousand dead! Ten thousand have died that I may find a country . . . Is that liberation? Is this the Great Epoch? Are these the people of greatness? . . . *Now I am one of you*' (p. 29). In the corresponding dream scene, Friedrich appears in the guise of an observer in a military hospital – as a

professor parades the crippled and mutilated soldiers whom he has
fitted with artificial limbs. He wishes to show off the advance of
medical technology: they wish only for the ultimate release of death.

These first six scenes, probably completed in the summer of 1917,
are theatrically among the most effective of the play, translating
Toller's experience of war into dramatic images of great force. The
remainder of the play traces Friedrich's emergence as a popular
leader, reflecting Toller's own politicization and the mood of radical
activism emerging in Germany in 1917–18. The dramatic narrative is
resumed in the fourth station, consisting of a single scene which
alternates the realistic and symbolic modes. We find Friedrich working on a statue of a huge human figure, representing the Victory of
the Fatherland, but he is troubled by growing doubts which impair
his ability to complete the work: the statue 'has a brutal effect'. His
doubts are finally confirmed by the appearance of a former fellow-
soldier, now ravaged by syphilis, a meeting which confronts
Friedrich with the true price of victory. His ideal of patriotism
finally destroyed, he destroys the statue which portrays it. As he
contemplates suicide, his sister enters to show him the new direction
he must take:

> To God who is spirit, love and strength,
> To God who dwells in humankind,
> Your way leads you to humanity (p. 40).

At the end of the scene, Friedrich 'walks out ecstatically' to pursue
his new mission. While this scene lacks dramatic conviction, it is
structurally crucial to the play, representing a dramatic and psychological turning-point.

Before he can begin his mission to embrace humankind, he must
attain full realization of his own humanity:

> He who seeks to find humanity
> Must find it first within himself (p. 40).

Scene 8 portrays symbolically Friedrich's experience of the lot of the
proletariat, firstly as a lodger in a slum dwelling, then in the Great
Factory. The ninth scene, representing the final stage of Friedrich's
spiritual development, has the typically Expressionist title 'Tod und
Auferstehung' ('Death and Resurrection') indicating that Friedrich
will progress through suffering and death to redemption and rebirth.
The setting is a prison, in which Friedrich appears in the guise of a

prisoner who has thrown himself downstairs to his death. He lies in an attitude of crucifixion:

> Perhaps through crucifixion he can liberate himself
> . . .
> Perhaps through crucifixion he can find salvation
> (p. 45).

Even in death, he is to be reborn: as he dies, his wife, who has come to visit him, symbolically bears his child.

Redeemed and reborn, Friedrich is now ready to take his message to the people. The final scenes transpose his spiritual regeneration on to a social plane, offering his own rebirth as a model for the rebirth of society. The setting of the eleventh scene is a mass meeting, which is addressed successively by representatives of the Old Order – the old soldier evoking the glorious military successes of 1870, the priest who preaches the doctrine of the just war, the professor who extols a learning which is irrelevant to his starving audience. These spokesmen for the Old Order are condemned by the final speaker, a demagogue who incites the people to bloody revolution. At this point, Friedrich demands to be heard, denouncing the solutions of the demagogue as half-truths, imploring the people to wait until the following day, when he will address them again.

The sixth and final station again begins with a dream scene, in which Friedrich, this time in the guise of a mountaineer, scales a steep summit, leaving behind his companion in order to be true to himself: 'Because I will not leave myself/I must leave you' (p. 54). In reaching the summit, Friedrich has symbolically reached the height of his mission as a leader of the people. In the final scene, he addresses the people who have gathered on the church square. In the heightened language of stage Expressionism, he tells them that he knows of the suffering and deprivation of their daily lives. The existing social order, he tells them, has twisted their lives: they are no longer men and women, merely the distorted likenesses of their true selves. To become men and women again, they must believe in themselves and their own humanity. Under the impact of his words, many in the crowd undergo a symbolic transformation: 'That we forgot! We are human beings!' The play ends with Friedrich's call for revolution:

> Brothers, stretch out your tortured hands
> In blazing, joyful tones.
> Let there stride through our liberated land
> Revolution, revolution! (p. 61).

The Expressionist style of *The Transformation* makes excessive demands on a modern theatre audience, but the play remains a biographical and historical document of great interest. It illuminates in particular two crucial aspects of Toller's thinking: his attitude to Judaism and Jewishness, and his conception of revolution. Toller's childhood had alienated him from his own Jewish identity. While Jewishness is the theme of the opening scenes, it is eloquent of Toller's attitude at this time that the word 'Jew' is never pronounced in the play. In the opening scene, Friedrich gazes out at the Christmas lights in the houses opposite, symbolizing his attraction to, and exclusion from Christianity. He calls himself 'a disgusting hybrid', feeling that he can only resolve the ambiguities of his own identity by assimilation to the dominant culture.

Toller's attitude to his Jewish heritage is formulated in Friedrich's conversation with his mother. Friedrich feels alienated from the Jewish community by its materialism and lack of spiritual values: 'You looked after my material needs, but what did you do for my soul?' (p. 18). Religious observance has been perverted to a largely secular purpose. When his mother urges him to attend divine service, Friedrich replies:

> Don't call it divine service, call it the service of people. You have turned God into an antiquated, narrow-minded judge, who judges all men by the letter of some dead Law (p. 19).

He feels stifled by Jewish family life: 'those tastefully arranged portraits of well-bred family houses'. *The Transformation* follows his attempts at assimilation, offering no hint of reconciliation with Jewishness; it was only fifteen years later, in his autobiography, that Toller could finally speak with a different voice.

The Transformation also bears testimony to Toller's conception of revolution less than a year before his involvement in the revolutionary events in Bavaria. The revolution of *The Transformation*, framed, as it is, by the symbolic conventions of theatrical Expressionism, cannot be taken literally: it must be understood within a specific frame of reference, that of Landauer's *Call to Socialism*. Friedrich's decision to go to the people and his subsequent experience of working-class deprivation imply a conception of the proletariat and of the political role of the intellectual which derive directly from Landauer. If Friedrich is to embrace humanity, he must first embrace human suffering, epitomized by the proletariat which, as the class most exploited by capitalism, is also that which suffers most acutely. Friedrich is therefore led to the Great Factory, which proves to be a prison roofed with gold: a striking metaphor for the condition of the working class. Toller presents the proletariat as a class which merely suffers: in the final scenes, the people play a purely passive role, redeemed, not by their own efforts but by Friedrich's rhetoric.

Friedrich's attempt to take his mission to the people evokes Landauer's belief that society could be revolutionized only if artists and intellectuals, those in whom 'Geist' was still active, could invoke it in others through precept and example. One of the main precepts of Toller's Heidelberg association was the need to bridge the gulf between intellectuals and the common people; in December 1917, he had spoken at a meeting in Berlin held under the slogan: 'Workers by hand and by brain – unite!'

In Landauer's philosophy, the process of revolution is the reawakening of the creative spirit which is latent in every human being, and its realization in new forms of social cooperation. It is this process which Toller evokes in the final scene of his play. Having shared the prison of working-class experience, Friedrich can justly claim: 'I know none of you and yet I know you all.' He compares the wretchedness of their lives with the artist's sublime vision of humanity:

> I know of your astonishment when you see a striding youth created by the hand of an artist. How could he create him? Because he is there, really there (p. 59).

That is, artists can visualize only what is already innate in them, but their humanity has been overlaid – creative spirit buried beneath the accretions of industrial society:

> And so you are all distorted images of true humanity: buried alive, bound together, gasping for breath, joyless and embittered, for you have buried the spirit . . .

They are no longer men and women, but they could be reborn, if they could rediscover their essential humanity:

> You are all of you no longer men and women, you are only distorted images of your true selves. And yet you could be men and women once again, if you had faith in yourself and in humanity, if you were fulfilled in the spirit (p. 60).

The process of regeneration which Friedrich initiates is therefore the rediscovery of something innate in every human being, the unearthing of the creative spirit which will enable men and women to transform social relationships – and hence society itself.

As Friedrich speaks, some in the crowd undergo a symbolic transformation. Now – and only now – can he call on them to rise against the social order which has subjected them:

> Now go to your rulers and proclaim to them with roaring organ voices that their power is only an illusion. Go to the soldiers and tell them to beat their swords into ploughshares. Go to the rich and show them their hearts, buried beneath rubbish. But be kind to them, for they too are poor and gone astray (pp. 60–1).

The revolution Friedrich proclaims is clearly anarchist in inspiration, calling not for the dictatorship of one class, but the sublimation of all classes in the unifying spirit of community. The final scenes of *The Transformation* are therefore a dramatic reading of Landauer's philosophy of social revolution, in which the role of the socialist is to invoke socialism through the propaganda of word and deed.

The biographical significance of *The Transformation* is not simply as a dramatic confession, recording the author's personal and political development. His rapid politicization had led him to espouse an extreme Activist conception of art, in which the artist himself was both advocate and exemplar. As part of his anti-war agitation in Heidelberg, Toller had planned to distribute pamphlets containing extracts from such works as Tolstoy's *Resurrection*, Barbusse's anti-war novel *Under Fire* and the pacifist stories of Leonhard Frank.[4] Similarly, *The Transformation* became part of the peace campaign:

> In 1917 the play served as a leaflet. I read scenes from it to the circle of young people in Heidelberg and wanted

to *stir* them (incite them against the war). After being expelled from Heidelberg, I went to Berlin – and again gave readings from the play. Always with the intention of stirring the dulled, mobilizing the hesitant and showing the way to those groping for it – and of winning them all for the concrete day-to-day tasks of revolution.[5]

In January 1918 he distributed scenes from the play at Eisner's strike meetings and even included snatches from them in his speeches. Nor did his Activism end with the January Strike. The historian Gustav Mayer was among those at a private gathering in the summer of 1918 at which Toller gave a reading of *The Transformation*. It was there that Mayer first heard the coming revolution talked of as an event which was inevitable and for which preparations had to be made.[6] Toller's hosts on that occasion were Erich and Netty Katzenstein, friends of his since his time in Munich in 1917. Netty Katzenstein, under the pseudonym Tessa, would become the main confidante of Toller's prison letters.

Mayer recognized the derivative nature of Toller's play, but was nonetheless impressed by the 'genuine emotion with which he gave vent to his pacifist conviction'. The play made a profound impression on many of those who read it later. At Toller's trial for high treason, several eminent literary men testified to its outstanding moral and poetic qualities. The journalist Stefan Großmann described reading the play at this time in a Munich hotel room to a group of friends who listened in solemn, even reverent, silence.[7] The publisher Kurt Wolff suggested, perhaps better than anyone else, the reasons for the play's evident contemporary appeal:

> ... reading the play, I cannot help feeling that the author has not quite succeeded in realizing the conception which he carried, burningly alive, within him, but the whole work is of such compelling authenticity and honesty and contains so much blood, breath and pain of these times, that you will certainly have no need to be ashamed of the work – now or later. *The Transformation* will, in a very special sense, belong to the history of contemporary literature and the German revolution.[8]

Wolff's letter suggests not only the play's emotional resonance, but its representative nature, which documents several aspects of the intellectual atmosphere of the November Revolution.

Toller's transition from idealistic patriotism to radical pacifism was one experienced by many of his contemporaries and is frequently recorded in the creative literature of 1916–18. Pacifism nourished the hope that revolutionary social change could be achieved by non-violent means. This belief was particularly prevalent in the USPD, the party in which left-wing artists and intellectuals began to gather and which Toller joined in 1918. Opposition to the war was often accompanied by utopian expectations of the ensuing peace. As the ruling powers faded away in November 1918, there were many who believed that the ideal of non-violent revolution had been vindicated and even that the fantastic vision of a new mankind might become reality. The young dramatist Friedrich Wolf was among many who were carried away by the euphoria of those early days:

> The revolution took possession of minds and hearts. There were brothers, only brothers ... A wave thundered over the bridge, soldiers arm in arm, all in step, one heart, one idea, one goal – brothers ... Down with the individual! We are brothers. Everything must become fairer, freer, more fraternal.[9]

René Schickele, from the calm of Swiss exile, was no less effusive: 'The New World has begun! The day of unromantic realization has come ... now the new age is here, the Socialist age.'[10]

The Transformation is a work of political and artistic immaturity, derivative in style and ideology, but its overnight success in the theatre in 1919 established Toller alongside Kaiser and Hasenclever as a leading dramatist of the younger generation. The play was first produced at the Tribüne, Berlin on 30 September 1919, running for well over a hundred performances and attracting the enthusiasm of audiences and critics alike. It owed its success partly to a conjuncture of political and theatrical circumstances which would remain typical of Toller's career as a dramatist. Interest in the play was stimulated by the fate of its author, then beginning a five-year prison sentence, but its success also owed much to the skill and originality of the production, which many critics greeted as the first truly Expressionist production in the theatre. Alfred Kerr, doyen of Berlin theatre critics, hailed it as the victory of the 'theatre of suggestion' over the 'theatre of illusion' – that is, the Expressionism over Naturalism. The success of the production established not only Toller's fame as a dramatist, but the reputation of the director Karlheinz Martin, who was promptly put under contract to Max Reinhardt, and of the leading actor Fritz Kortner, who recalled that after the first night 'I was able to stop worrying about my career: the theatres were making eager overtures to me'.[11] Politically, the play was already an anachronism: the revolution it proclaimed had been defeated, its faith in the New Mankind disproved by events. It was part of an artistic revolution which had far outstripped social reality – but that is to anticipate the political events to which we must now return.

V

Revolution in Bavaria: The Writers' Republic
November 1918–May 1919

Ernst Toller's involvement in the revolution in Bavaria, a period lasting less than six months, was only an episode in his life, but it was to be his most formative experience, shaping his political development and helping to create the literary legend which surrounded him for the rest of his life. The revolution – and its failure – were to be the theme of all his major work up to 1933. His own account of these events occupies about a quarter of his autobiography, documenting the crucial importance it had for him some fifteen years later.[1]

The German Revolution began early in November 1918 with a mutiny by the sailors of the High Seas Fleet, who refused to obey the order to put to sea for a final death-or-glory engagement with the English. Instead, they took control of their ships, elected Sailors' Councils, and occupied the ports of Kiel and Wilhelmshaven, starting a movement which quickly spread to other parts of Germany.

In Munich, on 7 November, a peace demonstration called by the SPD turned into a spontaneous revolt when a section of demonstrators, led by Kurt Eisner, raised a red flag, marched on the city's barracks and persuaded the soldiers to join them. Late that evening, the revolutionaries met in the enormous Mathäserbräu beer-hall to elect a Workers' and Soldiers' Council which proclaimed the Revolutionary Republic of Bavaria and elected Kurt Eisner as its first Prime Minister. The same night, Ludwig III of Bavaria, last of the Wittelsbach kings, fled from Munich, the first of many German princelings forced to abdicate in the face of pressure from the streets. All over Germany, revolutionary Workers' and Soldiers' Councils began to spring up. On 9 November, the Kaiser fled from Berlin and the SPD deputy Philip Scheidemann proclaimed the German Republic from the balcony of the Reichstag.

Toller, who had fervently wished for this revolution, took no part in the actual events. News of the revolution reached him at his mother's home in Landsberg, where he lay ill, a victim of the virulent flu epidemic which had swept Germany that autumn. Almost immediately, he set out for Berlin; a few days later he was in Munich. In his autobiography, Toller suggests he was invited to Munich by Eisner, but this is certainly an example of his tendency to self-dramatization; he told his court martial that he had sent Eisner a telegram of congratulation and while the latter's reply 'did not contain an actual invitiation', he felt that 'his presence would be welcome'.[2] He was in fact once more volunteering for active service. Arriving in Munich in mid-November, he plunged headlong into the revolutionary activity which was to convulse Germany for the next six months.

In Munich, as elsewhere in Germany, the symbol of political change was the revolutionary councils. While the councils were certainly inspired by the Russian example of Soviets, they were also very different from them. Emerging spontaneously at local level, they rapidly assumed some of the duties of municipal administration, replacing or coexisting with the established bureaucracy. It was in the day-to-day work of the councils that Toller served his political apprenticeship. Hardly had he arrived in Munich than he was coopted onto the Zentralarbeiterrat (Central Workers' Council), an ad hoc body formed in the immediate aftermath of the revolution. Toller's political experience was negligible, but many of the leading revolutionary activists remembered his role in the January strike, a fact which goes far to explain his rapid rise within the revolutionary movement. He became in quick succession a delegate to the Bavarian Workers' Council, the Bavarian Congress of Councils (of which he was elected vice-chairman) and the Provisional National Assembly, which Eisner had created from the ranks of the councils and the political parties. Toller also achieved prominence in the USPD, becoming vice-chairman of the party's Munich branch. He was therefore closely associated with both the councils and the USPD; inevitably, he was also identified with his chosen political mentor Kurt Eisner.

It was Eisner who from the first had imposed his personal stamp on the revolution in Bavaria: he intended it to be 'a revolution, perhaps the first in the history of the world, to combine the idea, the ideal and the reality'.[3] Eisner believed that it was possible to transcend Kant's distinction between politics and ethics. The proclamation of the new Bavarian Republic is typical of the high moral tone which he attempted to instil into public life:

> A new age is dawning. Bavaria will prepare Germany for the League of Nations. The Democratic Social Republic of Bavaria has the moral strength to gain a peace which will preserve Germany from the worst . . . We count on the creative assistance of the whole population . . . In this time of wild and senseless killing we shun bloodshed. Every human life is sacred. Keep calm and help to build the New World . . .[4]

Eisner's vision of a new society called for the cooperation of all its members, releasing their creative energy in the task of social reconstruction. His public speeches struck a note which was utopian, internationalist and, above all, pacifist – the greatest achievement of the Bavarian revolution was, in Eisner's eyes, that it had succeeded entirely without bloodshed, a success which encouraged him and his supporters, including Toller, in the fatal delusion that they could carry through a socialist transformation without force.

In the early weeks of the revolution, the crucial question in Bavaria, as elsewhere in the Reich, concerned the respective roles of the revolutionary councils and parliament, a question which soon divided Eisner from the SPD colleagues he had called into his cabinet. Eisner rejected the formal democracy of parliament, postulating a new participative democracy in which 'the masses themselves assist directly and continuously in the affairs of the community'.[5] The vehicle for this direct democracy would be the councils which he called 'the great school of democracy and socialism' – that is, a means of politicizing the masses and educating them to political power. He believed that immediate elections to a parliamentary assembly would simply reinstate the ruling class which had plunged Germany into a disastrous war and that they must therefore be deferred until the council system had had time to put down roots.

While Eisner and the USPD placed their faith in the councils, the SPD treated them with suspicion, advocating a parliament which they calculated would maximize their own representation and influence. In the ensuing power struggle, Eisner was finally outvoted by the SPD members of his cabinet and forced to call elections to the

Bavarian Landtag (Provincial Assembly) for 11 January 1919. Eisner himself was a candidate for the USPD; among the other candidates was Ernst Toller.

Toller had been from the first an enthusiastic advocate of the revolutionary councils. At the inaugural meeting of the Bavarian Workers' Councils, he addressed the delegates as 'the bearers of the revolutionary idea which has the power, not only to transform the economic order, but to revolutionize the human spirit'.[6] He shared Eisner's scepticism about the formal democracy of parliament, but when elections to the Provincial Assembly were declared, he nonetheless became a candidate for the USPD, and even took out Bavarian citizenship to enable him to do so. He believed that Parliament would coexist with the councils, which 'would gradually supersede it by a process of evolution'.[7] He was rapidly disabused. Shortly before Christmas, he attended the Deutscher Rätekongreß (German Congress of Councils) in Berlin. The Congress denied the Spartacist speakers Rosa Luxemburg and Karl Liebknecht a hearing and voted in favour of elections to a National Assembly, thereby renouncing its own claim to political power and influence. This experience strengthened Toller's conviction that the same should not be allowed to happen in Bavaria. Like many others, including Eisner, he cherished the separatist illusion that events in Bavaria could take a different course from those in the rest of the Reich.

Toller's most prominent political intervention during the early months of revolution in Bavaria was in the so-called 'Bürgerwehr' crisis. On 27 December, posters announcing the formation of a Bürgerwehr (Citizens' Defence Force) had appeared over the signature of the Interior Minister and SPD leader, Erhard Auer. In an impassioned speech to the Provisional National Assembly, Toller exposed the reactionary forces behind the undertaking and attacked Auer as either naive or an enemy of the revolution. 'The revolution is in danger,' he cried. 'There can be no cooperation between reactionary bourgeoisie and proletariat' – and he called for the establishment of a Workers' Defence Force.[8] Auer was forced to withdraw support for the undertaking, leaving Toller to close this session of the Assembly by proposing a resolution calling for 'a united front and thoroughgoing socialization'.[9] The idea of the united socialist front, in which workers would unite across formal party divisions, was one closely associated with Eisner. It was the keynote of Toller's political activity in the coming months, would colour his political thinking throughout the Weimar Republic, and influence his support for the Popular Front during the thirties.

The elections to the Landtag on 11 January 1919 showed little sign of Eisner's 'new democracy': the USPD suffered a crushing defeat, gaining only 2.5% of the vote and three seats in the Assembly. Toller was not one of those elected. The result confirmed him and other council supporters in their conviction that parliamentary government would serve only to reinstate the old ruling class. There was fevered debate within the councils themselves as to their future role. Toller himself was in no doubt, reproving some of his comrades for being too attached to the parliamentary principle: 'Basically, the Assembly and the Councils are incompatible.'[10]

Toller's headlong plunge into politics left him little time for writing, but he did not abandon his literary ambitions. His early poems had already begun to appear in avant-garde literary publications like *Die Aktion* and *Die weißen Blätter*. He knew Kurt Wolff, the friend and publisher of so many Expressionist poets, and the Berlin publisher and art dealer, Paul Cassirer, to whom he submitted *The Transformation* (his name was also linked with Cassirer's wife, the actress Tilla Durieux, then playing a season at the Münchener Nationaltheater). Toller's acquaintance with the dramatist Georg Kaiser also dates from this period. Kaiser, finally established in the forefront of German dramatists with the success of *Gas* in November 1918, strongly advocated the publication of *The Transformation*. His friendship with the 'Communist' Toller would be used in evidence against him when he was tried for 'embezzlement' two years later. Toller was also acquainted with the poet Rainer Maria Rilke, whose work he greatly admired. Rilke's *Stundenbuch* remained one of the works which moved him most deeply in prison: he sent the author a copy of his own *Gedichte der Gefangenen* (*Prisoners' Poems*) as 'a token of deep gratitude' for 'many rich hours of silent fulfilment'.[11] Rilke's association with Toller proved fateful in the aftermath of the Soviet Republic, when he was subjected to police harassment which finally drove him out of Munich. Among other contacts of Toller's at this time were old friends like Alfred Wolfenstein and new acquaintances like the novelist Lion Feuchtwanger, whose 'dramatic novel' *Thomas Wendt* contains a portrait of Toller the revolutionary.

The whole revolution in Bavaria had a pronounced literary flavour. In the revolutionary councils, it was often 'literati' like Toller, Landauer and the anarchist poet Erich Mühsam who set the tone. Other writers, such as Kaiser, or Ret Marut (later famous as the novelist B. Traven) also played minor political roles. Above all, Eisner himself was a literary man, who used the Provisional National Assembly as a forum to extol the political function of the artist:

> A politician who is not an artist is also no politician. It is a delusion of our unpolitical German people to believe you can achieve something in the world without such poetic power. The poet is no unpractical dreamer: he is the prophet of the future.[12]

Eisner not only believed in the creative role of the politician but regarded politics itself as a creative process. The classical age, he maintained, had turned away from reality, seeking refuge in the pursuit of formal beauty. Now, he declared, 'art should no longer be a refuge for those who despair of life, for life itself should be a work of art, and the state the greatest work of art'.

History would soon pass its own verdict on Eisner's utopian propositions, but it is important to note their contemporary resonance: his speech was greeted with 'prolonged applause'. Among the audience in the Assembly was Ernst Toller, whose own speeches document the literary nature of his conception of revolution. He told the Bavarian Congress of Councils that the German people 'will go from misery to misery, from station to station, until it finally discovers within itself the humanity which binds it in love and freedom to its fellow human beings'.[13] The stations of his drama *The Transformation* were to prefigure political reality: the poet was indeed to be the prophet of the future.

At the end of January Toller went to Switzerland to attend the conference of the Second International in Bern, where delegates from the socialist parties of the main combatant nations met for the first time since the outbreak of war. There was an atmosphere of mutual suspicion and recrimination. In the eyes of the French and the British, the SPD was still hopelessly compromised by its support for the German government during the war, whereas the USPD, represented by Karl Kautsky and Kurt Eisner, enjoyed great sympathy. Eisner's moral stature as a leader of the anti-war movement ensured him a sympathetic audience when he rose to address the delegates. He acknowledged Germany's war guilt and appealed for volunteers to rebuild the devastated areas of Belgium and Northern France as a gesture of reconciliation. Most observers felt that his speech was the climax of the conference. Certainly, it was received with tumultuous applause. Heinrich Mann later declared that as long as Eisner was speaking, Germany no longer had any enemies.

It was Toller's first appearance on the stage of international politics, but he was not overawed, taking the rostrum to make a grandiloquent appeal 'To the Youth of all Nations'. He conceded that 'the revolution has not yet taken hold of the entire German people', but declared that socialist youth in Germany would continue the revolution until its ultimate triumph. Echoing Eisner's appeal, he called on socialists in the Entente countries 'to resist the strangling conditions of the armistice' and prevent a peace treaty which would put German workers at the mercy of foreign capitalists: the struggle against militarism and capitalism was an international one. He ended on a note of pure rhetoric:

> And if our elders leave us in the lurch, the youth of all nations will establish the social commonwealth . . . We shall live for a new society, a new pure relationship between man and man, people and people . . .[14]

There is no record of how Toller's words were received, but their utopian internationalism moved at least one member of the audience. C.R. Buxton, later treasurer of the British ILP, was so impressed that he sent the text of Toller's speech to the pacifist journal *The Crusader*, which published it in translation.

Following the conference, Toller remained in Switzerland for some days to stay with friends in the Engadine. During this brief interlude in St Moritz, he saw the gilded youth of European society enacting international reconciliation. He was soon returned to political reality. On the journey back to Munich, as his train was standing in a Swiss station, he heard excited voices on the platform shouting that Kurt Eisner had been assassinated.

Eisner's speech in Bern, though acclaimed by the International, had earned him the implacable hatred of German nationalists. A scurrilously anti-semitic campaign was conducted against him in the German press, which disputed his right to speak for Bavaria, let alone Germany. A leaflet circulated by students in Munich openly called for his murder, quoting the allusive but unmistakeable line from Schiller's *Wilhelm Tell*: 'Mach hurtig, Landvogt, deine Uhr ist abgelaufen' ('Make haste, Governor, your time is up'). On the morning of 21 February, Eisner left his office in the Foreign Ministry for the nearby Provincial Assembly to tender the resignation of his government. As he walked up the Promenadestrasse, a twenty-one-year-old Nationalist, Count Anton von Arco-Valley, stepped out of a doorway and shot him. The assassin's bullet robbed Bavaria of its dominant political figure – and Ernst Toller of his political mentor and guide.

Eisner's assassination threw Bavaria into political turmoil. Barely an hour after the event, a butcher called Alois Lindner burst into the packed Chamber of the Provincial Assembly, shot and wounded the SPD leader Erhard Auer, and killed two other deputies who tried to detain him. The members of the Assembly fled in panic, leaving behind them a political vacuum. In the prevailing chaos, the only authority left intact was that of the Councils. A new Central Council took control, chaired by Ernst Niekisch, a twenty-eight-year-old school teacher, who would later become a close friend of Toller's and later still achieve fame as a prisoner of the Third Reich.

Eisner's death once more put the question of a Soviet Republic on the political agenda. When the Bavarian Congress of Councils was reconvened, Erich Mühsam proposed that 'Bavaria be declared a Socialist Soviet Republic', but the Congress rejected the resolution. After three weeks of confused negotiation, a socialist government under Johannes Hoffmann (SPD) emerged, which was to be approved by the Provincial Assembly. The so-called Nuremberg Accord therefore seemed to reestablish the legislative and executive authority of Parliament, reducing the councils to a purely consultative function.

Toller's role in these confused events was marginal, though he left no doubt about his own political position:

> The great question here is: Soviet Republic or Parliamentary Republic? I have no illusions and advocate as a matter of principle a Soviet Republic . . . But we cannot establish the Council system unless the whole working class is united.[15]

He bitterly denounced the Nuremberg Accord as a device to reintroduce parliamentarianism: so bitterly that the pacifist Professor Foerster wrote admonishing him that such intransigent opposition to parliament gave 'the fateful impression of a striving for dictatorship'.[16] In early March Toller became Chairman of the Munich USPD. Under his leadership, the party pursued a policy of creating mass support for a government of the revolutionary councils, though Toller was still adamant that a Soviet Republic would be established 'through a peaceful process, not by force'.[17] It is evident that he increasingly considered this to be the legacy of Kurt Eisner – and himself to be the heir to that legacy.

On 17 March the Landtag met briefly, for the first time since Eisner's death, to approve the new government of Johannes Hoffmann; but within days the political mood had once more been transformed, this time under the impact of events outside Bavaria. On 22 March, a coalition of Socialists and Communists, under Bela Kun, declared a Hungarian Soviet Republic in Budapest. News from Vienna seemed to suggest that a similar development was imminent in Austria, offering the prospect of a revolutionary corridor in Central Europe. When the Hoffmann government announced that the Landtag would reconvene on 8 April, the mere announcement was enough to provoke a new wave of revolutionary feeling. The Central Council announced that the Landtag would not be permitted to meet; the Munich garrison declared that, if it did, it would receive no military protection. Mass meetings were held to rally support for a Soviet Republic. In the prevailing atmosphere, what had seemed impossible only a few weeks ago now began to seem inevitable.

The Bavarian Soviet Republic can only be described as a tragic blunder; fifteen years later, Toller himself conceded that it was a mistake which was doomed to failure from the outset. His own role in these events pursued him for the rest of his life. It was the object of intense judicial scrutiny during his trial for high treason. It was the pretext for virulent attacks throughout the 1920s by both the extreme right and the extreme left, the former accusing him of complicity in the so-called 'hostage murders', the latter of having 'betrayed the revolution'. Charge and counter-charge determined his reception in Soviet Russia in 1926 and in the USA in 1929; they were used as late as 1938 by the Nazis in order to cast doubt on the good faith of his Spanish Relief Project.

Strangely, the final impetus for the proclamation of a Soviet Republic came from the Social Democrat Ernst Schneppenhorst, Minister for Military Affairs in the Hoffmann government. His motives have often been debated, but essentially he seems to have wanted to abort the idea of a Soviet Republic by instigating a premature action. In the early hours of 5 April, he convened a meeting in the War Ministry, attended by delegates from every section of the revolutionary movement in Munich. There was general amazement when Schneppenhorst declared himself warmly in favour of a Soviet Republic, a step known to be opposed by the government he belonged to. His statement was echoed by the Chief of Police and the Military Commander of Munich and before long the proclamation of a Soviet Republic had been agreed in principle. The only dissent came from Eugen Leviné, the Communist spokesman, who declared the outright opposition of his party to any such move. Leviné, born in Petersburg of German-Jewish parents, was a cool-headed, if domineering revolutionary who had taken part in the 1905 uprising in Russia. He voiced his suspicion of Schneppenhorst's motives: the KPD was not prepared to cooperate with a party like the SPD, which had twice used 'Freikorps' irregulars to put down a revolt of Berlin workers. Leviné's statement threw the meeting into some confusion, before it was finally decided to postpone the official proclamation for a further forty- eight hours, while delegates, who included Schneppenhorst, were sent to prepare the ground in the Northern Bavarian towns.

One notable absentee from this meeting was Toller, who was in Nuremberg, on his way to Berlin for a meeting of the German Congress of Councils (*Rätekongreß*), when the news of the imminent proclamation of a Soviet Republic reached him, forcing him to return to Munich in great haste. Opinion in the USPD seemed strongly in favour of an immediate proclamation; Toller's own attitude was more ambivalent. He had invested his Expressionist vision of the renewal of man in the idea of a Soviet Republic. For months he had enthusiastically advocated it: was it credible to turn away from it now? However, such hopes had to be weighed against practical realities. He felt that the proclamation was premature. A minimum condition for its success was the unity of the three socialist parties, the lack of which made him hesitate. On the other hand, events seemed to be gathering a momentum of their own. Reports were arriving in Munich that in towns all over Bavaria there had been spontaneous declarations of support for a Soviet Republic. This seems to have been the decisive factor for Toller. The masses, he later wrote, had declared the Soviet Republic over the heads of their party leaders: the leaders had no right to leave them in the lurch.[18]

The final decision to proclaim a Soviet Republic was taken at a meeting on the night of 6–7 April in the Residenz, the former palace of the Wittelsbachs, where some sixty delegates gathered in the bedroom of the former queen.[19] The Communists had been invited, but had failed to appear; the delegates to Northern Bavaria had not returned to report. Unknown to any of those present, the SPD leaders had met in Nuremberg and rejected the idea of a Soviet Republic, whereupon Schneppenhorst had changed his mind and rejoined the Hoffmann government.

Ernst Niekisch, who conducted the meeting in his role as Chairman of the Central Council, had scarcely opened the proceedings when Gustav Landauer proposed that the meeting should declare itself a constituent assembly: revolution was always a creative act, he explained, which must begin with an unexpected step. There seemed broad agreement amongst the various organizations present that a Soviet republic should be proclaimed: the Peasants' League was in favour, even the SPD and trade union delegates raised no objections. When the meeting went on to discuss the distribution of various ministerial posts, the proceedings often strayed into the absurd. Erich Mühsam proposed himself as Commissar for Foreign Affairs, but was persuaded to withdraw in favour of Dr Franz Lipp, whose credentials were claimed to be impeccable – and about whom so little was known that no one could dispute his claim. He turned out to have a history of mental illness and soon had to be removed from his post to a mental hospital. Silvio Gesell, known as a theorist of a 'free currency' economy became Commissar for Finance, Gustav Landauer for Education.

Discussions were still in progress when Eugen Leviné finally arrived, reading a prepared statement condemning the venture and refusing the support of his party: a 'Räterepublik', he declared, could only emerge from a successful workers' struggle, it could not be 'proclaimed from a green conference table'. His statement was greeted with dismay, particularly by Toller and Landauer, who implored him to change his mind, but Leviné was adamant. Niekisch then suggested that the meeting should reconsider its original decision and the various party delegations withdrew to confer privately. The USPD delegation was divided. Toller suggested that the opposition of the Communists now absolved his party from its commitment, but his colleagues wanted to stand by their original decision. In all his later accounts, Toller insisted that he privately opposed the venture, but supported it publicly 'as a decision of the party'.[20] When he returned to the plenary session, he was clearly agitated, tie loose, hair tousled, as he announced that the USPD would support the proclamation 'in the interests of working-class unity'.[21] Landauer had thoughtfully drawn up the proclamation before the start of the meeting: he now proposed that the occasion should be marked by the ringing of church bells throughout Bavaria.

As the members of the new government left the Wittelsbach Palace in the cold light of early morning, many of them must have shared Toller's misgivings. Ernst Niekisch alone had abstained from voting on the question of the proclamation. He feared that the undertaking was bound to fail and he now tendered his resignation as Chairman of the Central Council. Toller was elected to succeed him, thus becoming the head of the new Soviet Republic. He was almost certainly the youngest head of government in German history, bringing to his office a mixture of idealism and political inexperience which was certainly unequal to the tasks which lay ahead. He assumed his new office reluctantly: paradoxically, it was Niekisch who, as he later testified, persuaded Toller to accept it.

From the beginning the position of the Soviet Republic was tightly circumscribed, its fate depending largely on events outside Bavaria. It had been conceived partly as an exemplary action, intended to inspire emulation in other parts of the Reich. The original proclamation, with its connotations of 'propaganda by deed', suggests the Anarchist inspiration of the whole venture:

> The Bavarian Soviet Republic is following the example set by the Russian and Hungarian peoples . . It appeals in brotherhood to all other German peoples to follow the self-same path . . .[22]

More specifically, it was hoped that it would inspire the German Congress of Councils, on the eve of its meeting in Berlin, to declare a German Soviet Republic, but the Congress made no such move. Hopes that the revolutionary example of Bavaria would encourage similar action in Central Germany and the Ruhr also proved vain.

The news from Northern Bavaria was even worse. In Nuremberg and Bamberg the Soviet Republic had been still-born, in Würzburg and other smaller towns it had been suppressed after street fighting. The Hoffmann government, which now established itself in Bamberg and declared itself the sole legitimate authority, controlled the whole of Northern Bavaria. The jurisdiction of the Soviet Republic was confined below the Danube, extending no further than the area bounded by Augsburg, Rosenheim and Garmisch. The threat to its existence was soon explicit. The Hoffmann government dropped leaflets on Munich, announcing a blockade of the city, and issued an appeal throughout Northern Bavaria for armed volunteers. In Ohrdruf, just across the state border in Thuringia, the reactionary Colonel Ritter von Epp was recruiting members of a Freikorps (volunteer force). The Freikorps Epp, numbering among its officers Captain Ernst Röhm, the future leader of the Nazi stormtroopers, was to play a leading role in the 'liberation' of Munich less than a month later.

Even in Munich itself, the Soviet régime had encountered opposition. The KPD, under the leadership of Leviné, had moved from non-participation to outright condemnation. At hastily-convened public meetings, and in the columns of the *Rote Fahne*, the party denounced the 'Scheinräterepublik' (pseudo Soviet Republic) and exhorted workers to 'follow only the instructions of the Communist Party'.[23]

It was against this background of confusion and instability that the new government began its work. During the six days it held power, it issued a steady stream of proclamations. It declared the 'Landtag' dissolved and the Hoffmann government deposed, announced the socialization of industry, the requisition of housing, the censorship of the press, the disarming of the bourgeoisie and the formation of a Red Army. Fraternal relations were to be established with Soviet Russia and the new Soviet régime in Hungary. It was Toller, as Chairman of the Central Council, who signed the proclamations of the new government, an action later considered sufficient to prove the charge of high treason brought against him.

In the Wittelsbach Palace, the seat of the new government, Toller was besieged by those seeking the favour of the new regime. The wrong demanded redress, the ambitious preferment; cranks and inventors came to offer their universal remedies. Even the activity of the government had an air of unreality. Many of the decrees existed only on paper, for the Central Council was simply not in a position to enforce them. The decree ordering the bourgeoisie to surrender its weapons had little effect. A Red Army recruiting office did open on 10 April, but there were few volunteers. Less than eight hundred rifles were distributed to workers and Toller later admitted that the Central Council did not even know how many weapons it had at its disposal. Radio messages were sent to Moscow and Budapest and a reply was even received from Lenin:

> Please give us details of the revolution carried out in
> Bavaria . . . Please report to us how things are progress-
> ing there and whether the new order is fully and com-
> pletely in control . . .[24]

Nothing could have been further from the case. The new government seemed in fact to have a sense of its own transience. The
Central Council decided that all its decrees should bear the desig-
nation 'Provisional Central Council', the list of Commissars was also
'provisional'. Gustav Landauer, who had ambitious plans for revolu-
tionizing the university, wrote a postcard to his friend Fritz Mauthner: 'If I am given a couple of weeks, I hope to achieve something,
but quite possibly, it will be only a couple of days and then it will all
have been a dream.'[25]

Opposed by the SPD on the right and the KPD on the left, the
Central Council had little room for manoeuvre. Toller was all too
aware of its weakness and made determined efforts to win the support of the Communists. On 7 April he responded to Communist
attacks on the 'pseudo Soviet Republic' with an appeal for working-
class unity. The Central Council convened a series of mass meetings
in the Munich beer-cellars to explain its position. Toller issued a
declaration that 'the unity of the revolutionary proletariat is
absolutely essential' and even asserted that 'the differences between
the Central Council and the Communists are in no way fundamental'.[26] His optimism was sadly misplaced, for Leviné remained adamant in his opposition: the KPD would join only a government which
it effectively controlled.

The economic situation was deteriorating rapidly, as the blockade
of Munich began to bite. Supplies of coal and food from Northern
Bavaria had been cut off: the normally bustling markets in Munich
were ominously quiet. Toller himself felt that the position of the
Soviet Republic was fast becoming untenable and he attempted to
contact the Hoffmann government through an intermediary in order
to open negotiations and forestall military intervention. These
attempts were pre-empted by the so-called Palm Sunday Putsch.

In the early hours of Sunday 13 April, a detachment of the
Republican Guard, suborned by payments from the Hoffmann
government, occupied the station and other strategic buildings,
including the Wittelsbach Palace, and arrested several members of
the Central Council. Posters appeared in the city announcing that

the Central Council was deposed and the Hoffmann government re-instated. Toller avoided arrest in this action. Rumours of a putsch had been circulating the night before and he had taken the pre-caution of leaving his lodgings and sleeping at a friend's house. Waking next morning to news of the coup, he decided to lie low and await developments.

That afternoon, Soviet sympathizers began to gather on the Theresienwiese; armed workers and soldiers moved on the centre of the city, driving the putschists back into the railway station, which was recaptured after several hours of fighting. It was this spon-taneous action by Munich workers which convinced Eugen Leviné that the time had come to declare a 'real' Soviet Republic. His motives for taking control of what he had deemed, only a week earlier, a hopeless situation, have long been debated. The historian Arthur Rosenberg suggested that he thought it the duty of the KPD to step into the breach 'to save the honour of the revolution'.[27] Certainly, Leviné had not changed his assessment of the situation: he knew that a Soviet Republic in Bavaria could not sustain itself independently for long, but in the short time available he hoped to establish a Soviet Republic which would serve as a model and inspiration for the Munich workers. He saw struggle – and defeat – as inevitable, but if it *was* inevitable, it was the duty of the KPD to ensure that the workers emerged from that defeat with a clear idea of what they had been fighting for.

To some extent, he was also the prisoner of his own arguments. Had he not said that a Soviet Republic could only be founded after a victorious workers' struggle? Had he not also said it could only be declared by the Factory Councils? – and this they now proceeded to do. Before the last shots of battle had died away, the Factory Councils were meeting in the main hall of the Hofbräuhaus, which became for the first time a landmark in Bavarian politics. The dele-gates seated at the long wooden tables, informed that the members of the old Central Council had been arrested, voted to transfer power to a fifteen-member Action Committee. However, real power lay with the Executive Committee, consisting of Leviné as Chairman and three other Communists – Max Levien, Carl Dietrich and Paul Werner.

Toller had spent much of the day waiting for news, but on hearing that fighting had broken out, he had emerged from hiding. It was already evening and, shortly after, the workers had finally captured the main station. A unit of the Republican Guard was still holding out in the Luitpoldgymnasium, and Toller joined a group of armed workers in attacking the building and forcing the defenders to surrender. It was only later, in the early hours of the morning, that he finally made his way to the city Kommandatur where he found a meeting of the four-man executive of the new government in session. Astonished by the turn of events, he challenged their legitimacy, whereupon he was placed under arrest – and released only after lengthy altercation.

Toller was sceptical about the new régime, from which he expected 'nothing of much value', but having satisfied himself that its authority derived from the Factory Councils, he issued a statement calling on workers to unite behind it. Whatever his reservations, he felt more strongly than ever that he could not leave the workers in the lurch. The imperative of revolutionary solidarity overcame all private scruple.

Leviné issued a proclamation that the dictatorship of the proletariat had been established: there were certainly immediate signs that the new government meant business. The Factory Councils met in almost permanent session in the Hofbräuhaus. The new Executive Committee called a general strike, banned all the Munich newspapers and ordered the distribution of arms to the workers. A young sailor called Rudolf Egelhofer was appointed military commander of Munich and immediately ordered armed workers onto military alert. The city itself was transformed into a virtual state of siege – access roads into Munich were closed, telephone and telegraph communications were broken off.

The anticipated military threat to the Soviet Republic soon materialized: 700 troops waiting at Ingolstadt began to advance on Munich in the afternoon of 15 April. As the news reached the city, church bells were rung; mounted soldiers appeared on the streets, ordering the population into their homes. In an atmosphere of some confusion, groups of armed workers and soldiers began to form spontaneously, streaming out of the city to the north to meet the White advance.

News of the attack reached Toller in the Hofbräuhaus, where a meeting of the Factory Councils was in session. He immediately left the meeting and, together with armed workers who were on guard outside the building, hurried through the side-streets to the onion-domed Frauenkirche. He demanded to know who had given the order for the bells to be rung, but the sacristan could tell him nothing. In the prevailing confusion, rumours abounded: a new putsch had been started, the Whites had occupied the station. Finally, in the Communist Party office in Sendling, he learned that the Whites were advancing on Allach, to the north. Commandeering a lorry, Toller drove out along the Nymphenburgerstrasse, the main route out of the city to the north, finally stopping at a Gasthaus in search of more news. He could find none, but he did find three cavalry soldiers drinking beer. One of them gave Toller his horse, the others agreed to accompany him and in bright moonlight they rode out across the silent countryside towards Allach. When they reached Karlsfeld, they came upon the main body of the improvised Red Army, which had managed to halt the advancing White troops and force them to retreat towards the small town of Dachau. In the aftermath of victory, the workers were waiting, flushed with success but uncertain what to do now. Toller and his two companions undertook a reconnaissance patrol along the road to Dachau. Halfway there, they suddenly came under fire and they were forced to withdraw, leaving one of the cavalrymen behind, dead.

Returning to Karlsfeld in the early hours of the morning, Toller found a hastily-convened meeting of shop-stewards in progress in a local tavern where, after brief discussion, he found himself elected Commander of Red troops. He protested in vain that he lacked the necessary military knowledge and experience, but when they insisted, felt that he had no choice but to accept. Toller thus found himself Commander of the first Red Army to be formed on German soil.

Toller's career as Red Army Commander lasted only ten days, but it helped to create the legend which surrounded him throughout the nineteen twenties. The paradox of a pacifist poet as military commander is one which has continued to fascinate the imagination up to the present day. The actress Tilla Durieux, who encountered him during one of his visits to Munich from the front, was amazed to see him in uniform: Toller himself conceded the paradox.[28] In fact, all his actions as military commander reveal the inherent ambivalence of his position, torn between the principle of non-violence and the imperative of revolutionary solidarity. He had joined the spontaneous defence of Munich without hesitation but not without misgiving. He saw the prospect of armed conflict as 'a tragic necessity', a phrase which runs through all his subsequent accounts. He felt 'obliged' to join the workers; the same sense of moral obligation made him accept command of the Red Army. He repeatedly stressed that he had gone to the front not as Commander, but as an ordinary soldier, that he had accepted and retained command 'only at the insistence of the Factory Councils'. It was little more than three months since he had declared that the revolutionary leader was merely the instrument of the will of the working class: now revolutionary rhetoric had been overtaken by reality.

In Munich, Rudolf Egelhofer had become Commander-in-Chief of the Red Army. In the prevailing confusion, he had little choice but to acknowledge the 'de facto' situation and confirm Toller as Field Commander, with his USPD colleague Gustav Klingelhöfer as his deputy. Toller's problems were enormous – he did not know what weapons his men possessed, nor even how many men he had under his command. His first task was to organize the army along more or less military lines; he formed a general staff comprising a few officers who had wartime experience. The troops took up positions before Dachau, some twelve miles north-west of Munich. The name of Dachau was to become notorious as the site of the infamous concentration camp, but in 1919 it was a small town which was the centre of a prosperous farming community. It was also the site of a munitions factory and, commanding a strategic position on the northern approaches to Munich, represented a military target of some importance.

Egelhofer's first order to his new commander was to bombard Dachau. Toller ignored the order, considering it militarily unnecessary and politically unwise, since it would only have antagonized the peasants who farmed the surrounding countryside and whose support was indispensable. Instead, Toller opened negotiations with the enemy, sending delegates with an ultimatum that the White should evacuate Dachau and withdraw behind the line of the Danube. A cease-fire was agreed for some hours while the demand was considered. There followed one of the bizarre incidents which punctuated the Bavarian Soviet.

Shortly before the cease-fire was due to expire, the Red artillery opened fire on Dachau and the waiting troops began to advance on the town. Toller later found out that the advance had been ordered by an *agent provocateur* who would march into Munich two weeks later with the victorious enemy. At the time, he was alarmed that the breach of the cease-fire would endanger the lives of the delegates who were being held as hostages in Dachau. He gave orders for the bombardment to cease and, jumping into an available staff-car, drove towards Dachau to find out in person what was happening. He quickly realized it was impossible to stop the advance of his troops and therefore ordered up reinforcements and himself pressed forward to join the attack. In Dachau itself, workers from the munitions factory, many of them women, began to harry the defenders from the rear, calling on them not to fire, disarming some of them and forcing the rest to flee the town. Toller and his makeshift Red Army were able to occupy the town, capturing five officers and thirty-six men, as well as large quantities of guns and ammunition. Toller had become, almost despite himself, the 'victor of Dachau'.

The government in Munich celebrated this minor skirmish as a major military success, issuing a communiqué in Toller's name which was posted all over the city, hailing a 'great victory' and even announcing that there was no military danger to Munich. Toller knew better: he tried to dissociate himself from the communiqué, claiming he had neither written nor authorized it. He felt that the real significance of the victory was ideological. Workers of all parties, and none, had come spontaneously to the defence of the revolution: the united workers' front, for so long a political watchword, had become a reality.

Unknown to Toller or the Communists in Munich, the victory at Dachau was to prove the moment when the tide finally turned irreversibly against the Soviet Republic. The same day, 16 April, the Reich government in Berlin acceded to the requests of the Hoffmann administration for military assistance, agreeing to send up to 20,000 troops into Bavaria. It began to assemble a force under the command of the Prussian General von Oven, comprising a mixture of regular troops and large contingents of Free Corps mercenaries.

The victory at Dachau also marked the first of the bitter disagreements which were soon to divide Toller from the Communist régime in Munich. He received an order from Egelhofer that the officers taken prisoner should be shot, an order he refused to carry out, finding it incompatible with the humanitarian principles he was fighting for. He ordered the soldiers who had been captured to be released; some of them returned to fight once more against the Red Army. This was not the only bone of contention. Toller had wanted to consolidate the victory at Dachau by advancing as far as the Danube, thus occupying a fertile agricultural area and increasing the supply of food available to Munich. This plan was turned down by Egelhofer, for reasons which Toller suspected were not military but political – he mistrusted his USPD commanders.

Once the Red Army had secured its positions around Dachau, there was relatively little to keep the troops occupied. They were mustered twice a day in the market square in Dachau where, under the eyes of the local population, Toller would deliver a political address. On one occasion, he justified his policy of releasing prisoners ('We are not making a Russian or Berlin revolution of bloodshed, but a Bavarian revolution of love'); on another, he instructed officers and men to address each other with the familiar 'du'. Toller's military command was indeed ultra-liberal. He reasoned that if militarism was intrinsic to the social order they were fighting to overthrow, blind military discipline had no place in a revolutionary army. Regular drill was discontinued as a relic of the Ludendorff era. Officers no longer gave commands, but directives; if other ranks disputed them, the matter was referred to a 'Soldatenrat' for arbitration. Within three days, many of the troops had returned to Munich or were drinking in the beer-houses and the old military discipline had to be partly reintroduced.

Both Leviné and Egelhofer would have liked to remove Toller from his military command, but as the 'victor of Dachau' he enjoyed considerable popularity, the closest thing to a military hero which the Soviet Republic had. At the meeting of the Factory Councils on 17 April, Leviné attacked the absent Toller for having concluded a truce 'behind the backs and against the wishes of the Executive Council'.[29] Two days later, Toller himself appeared unexpectedly in the Hofbräuhaus parliament to make a spirited defence of his actions. He criticized the military strategy of the overall General Staff and complained bitterly of the disorganization in Munich which left his troops without essential supplies.

The disagreements between Leviné and Toller over military strategy were in fact political differences which reflected the mutual distrust between Communists and Independents. At a special meeting of the Factory Councils held on Easter Monday, 21 April, they flared into open conflict. Toller and Klingelhöfer reported on the military situation, particularly their attempts to secure a further truce with the White troops facing Dachau. In the ensuing discussion, Leviné bitterly criticized them for having exceeded their authority: Toller retorted that Leviné did not represent the working class but only a small clique. Max Levien then sprang to his feet, accusing Toller of behaving 'like the King of Southern Bavaria', a remark which produced noisy disagreement from many of the delegates. Levien insisted that Toller had exceeded his authority: he had behaved as though he were the Commander-in-Chief instead of merely a Field Commander. When Toller left the meeting at one o'clock in the morning to return to his troops at Dachau, the conflict was still unresolved.[30]

The military situation was rapidly deteriorating. White troops had captured Augsburg; the airfield at Schleissheim had been lost without a fight, exposing the flank of the Red Army at Dachau. Toller was increasingly convinced that they should negotiate, Leviné was adamant they should not. The split between Independents and Communists became public: writing in the *Rote Fahne*, Leviné called for 'iron logic in establishing the dictatorship of the proletariat' and rejected any attempt to negotiate: 'We must hold our position to the last.'[31]

In the early hours of 26 April, Toller finally resigned his military command, declaring that he could no longer work with the Executive Committee or the military General Staff. He issued a brief statement in which he called the Communist government 'a disaster for the working class' and its leaders 'a menace to the Soviet idea': 'incapable of anything constructive, they are bent on senseless destruction'.[32] Toller's resignation was, of course, intended to bring matters to a head in Munich in the hope of deposing the Executive and getting peace talks started.

Time was running out. At the meeting of the Factory Councils on 27 April, Toller and his party colleagues, Klingelhöfer and Emil Maenner, conducted a joint attack. Toller accused Leviné of having concealed a disastrous economic and military situation. He stressed that the Red Army was confronted by vastly superior forces: 'I made clear that we must open negotiations because there was no alternative.'[33] Leviné responded by accusing Toller and the Independents of treachery and cowardice; he demanded that the delegates should decide whether they wanted to continue to pursue Communist policies or whether they wanted the present Action Committee to resign. The meeting then passed a vote of 'no confidence' in the Action Committee, thus apparently bringing Leviné's rule to an end. A new Committee was to be elected, charged with opening peace negotiations.

But by now mutual hostility had degenerated into open strife. As the Factory Councils met the following afternoon (28 April) to elect a new committee, the Hofbräuhaus was surrounded by armed Red Guards, who demanded that all power should be vested in the Red Army High Command. A group of Red Guards entered the building to arrest Toller and it was only with the help of the landlord that he managed to escape through a side door. Fearing that he might still be arrested, he did not return home, turning instead to Tilla Durieux, who agreed to shelter him for the night at the Hotel Marienbad. He was emotionally overwrought, seeming to be on the verge of despair. He felt so threatened that he spoke of going into hiding or even disguising himself with a false moustache (Toller's theatrical bent was never far from the surface). He left early next morning and spent each of the following two nights at different addresses; he was now permanently escorted by the young sailor who had been his adjutant in Dachau, who was reported to be heavily armed.

Munich was now completely surrounded by advancing Free Corps units. The split in the ranks of the revolutionaries was total. As the Independents tried to open peace negotiations, the Communists set about organizing armed resistance. In the *Rote Fahne*, Leviné denounced any attempt to negotiate as 'between weakness and treachery'.[34] The differences between Toller and Leviné of course transcended military strategy, being symptomatic of the ideological division between Independents and Communists. Toller was convinced that the Red Army faced overwhelming odds and argued for negotiations as a form of tactical retreat. While he shared the Communists' ends, he rejected their means, accusing them of being prepared to sacrifice workers' lives in the dogmatic (and illusory) belief that only present defeat could ensure ultimate victory. Leviné's political analysis cast Toller and the Independents in the role of involuntary traitors to the revolution. The very humanitarian ideas they held forced them into positions of compromise and negotiation; they would always draw back from the struggle which was the inevitable result of the revolution they themselves proclaimed. They willed the end but not the means. By proposing negotiations, and awakening the illusion that they were possible, they weakened the workers' will to fight – and so betrayed the revolution into the hands of its enemies. Leviné believed that armed struggle was inevitable – but also that it would serve to heighten revolutionary consciousness in the working class. It was these irreconcilable positions

which Toller later transposed into the dramatic conflict of his play
Masses and Man.

While history did not corroborate Leviné's thesis, in one respect
he was proved right: the time to negotiate was past. The delegates
sent to parley with the advancing enemy were sent back with a
demand for unconditional surrender, a demand which the Factory
Councils could not have complied with, even if they had wanted to.
Power now lay with the Red Army, and how that power would be
used was abundantly clear. Egelhofer issued a statement that the
Red Army would 'defend the revolutionary proletariat, whatever the
cost'; in the *Rote Fahne*, Leviné called for 'struggle and death for the
cause of Communism'.[35]

As the ring closed around Munich, morale and discipline began to
crumble. In an atmosphere of mounting panic and desperation, the
Red Guards began to take hostages. There were open threats to the
lives of Erhard Auer and Eisner's assassin Count Arco. During the
final twenty-four hours of the Soviet Republic, Toller spent his
failing energies in trying to prevent such actions. On hearing that
two hostages had already been executed, he hurried to the War
Ministry, demanding – and securing – an assurance from Egelhofer
that no more hostages would be taken. He then went to the Surgical
Clinic, imploring the Director, Professor Sauerbruch, to move Auer
and Arco to a place of greater safety. He was in a state of great
agitation. Sauerbruch caustically described him as barely in control
of himself, let alone the political situation.

Toller returned to the War Ministry to find the building now
almost deserted. Only Egelhofer and a couple of his aides were still
at their posts. Toller again implored Egelhofer to order the workers
to lay down their arms to avoid unnecessary bloodshed, but he again
refused. From there, Toller made his way to the Wittelsbach Palace.
The streets were almost deserted, the silence broken only by the
marching feet of the occasional detachments of Red Guards. The
Red Flag was still flying over the Wittelsbach Palace, but the building itself was virtually empty: Toller found only the Chairman of the
new Action Committee, writing directives that no one would now
follow. That evening Toller returned to the Hofbräuhaus, where the
Factory Councils were meeting to hear the report of the peace delegation. While the meeting was in progress, a messenger arrived with
the news that eight hostages had been shot in the Luitpoldgymnasium. The meeting was stunned. Toller himself was close

to tears. This was not an act of communism, he declared, but an act of nihilism. At his instigation, the Councils issued a statement dissociating themselves from the shootings, which was posted throughout the city. They then called on the workers to lay down their arms, appealing for a final protest demonstration on the following day. Such appeals were, of course, hopeless, even if they could have been heard: brute force was now the order of the day.

Toller left the meeting to go straight to the Luitpoldgymnasium. He later testified that the news of the hostage murders had been a 'shattering blow': it was the final contradiction of his own ideals of revolution. When he reached the Luitpoldgymnasium, he found that the troops had already fled. He found six prisoners still alive, cowering in a cellar. The door was barred and he could not break it down, having to release the prisoners through the only window. In a nearby shed, he also found the bodies of the eight who had been shot. He afterward learned that they were all members of the proto-Nazi Thule Society, whose symbol was the swastika. At the time he was more concerned with disposing of the bodies, realizing – as he candidly acknowledged – that their discovery would provide a pretext for even more brutal reprisals. He went back to the Surgical Clinic, pleading with Sauerbruch to have the bodies removed to the hospital mortuary, but they were left where they lay, to be discovered by the victorious Free Corps.

It was now three o'clock in the morning and, in a state of almost complete exhaustion, Toller turned his mind to finding a refuge for the night. He already knew what was in store for him if he fell into the hands of the enemy: stories were circulating that a Red ambulance team had been murdered in Starnberg by the advancing Free Corps. The homes of his political friends were no longer safe: he turned instead to Grete Lichtenstein, his girl-friend during his student days in Munich. It was from the window of her room in Schwabing's Franz-Josef-Strasse that he watched the advance of White troops into Munich the following morning. It was 1 May.

The military struggle for Munich was brief and brutal. The Red Army, hopelessly outnumbered, defended the city courageously, but by 3 May, the whole city was in the hands of government troops. In the aftermath of victory, the Free Corps exacted a revenge more terrible than even their opponents had thought possible. Under the cover of martial law, hundreds of workers were arrested and shot, often on evidence no stronger than a denunciation. The estimates of the numbers killed vary between 600 and 1,200, but all the reports are virtually unanimous about the ruthless and often arbitrary nature of the killings. Toller had already gone into hiding, a fact which undoubtedly saved his life, for those leaders who were caught in the immediate aftermath received short shrift. Egelhofer was dragged from a car and shot during interrogation; Landauer was beaten to death in the yard of Stadelheim Prison. Leviné was not arrested until a fortnight later. He was brought before a Court Martial, but the verdict had been reached before the trial: he was found guilty of high treason and shot.

The bloodthirsty rampage of the Free Corps was lent a spurious legality by the approval of a Social Democratic government. Defence Minister Gustav Noske sent a telegram congratulating General von Oven on 'the successful conduct of the operation' and offering his 'warmest thanks to the troops'. The killings were finally halted only after the massacre of twenty-one members of a Catholic working-men's association, who were mistaken for a Communist cell. The Free Corps have been called 'the vanguard of Nazism'.[36] Certainly, they provided some of the most ruthless and loyal supporters of the Nazi Movement: Major von Epp himself became Governor of Bavaria after 1933. The political lines in Germany had been drawn for the next fourteen years.

In the week after the massacres, the Munich cemeteries were filled with unburied corpses. One of the bodies in the Ostfriedhof was at first identified as Toller's and his death was officially announced. it was only on 7 May, when the body was seen by Dr Marcuse, who had treated Toller at his Ebenhausen sanatorium, that it was established that the body was not his. The man-hunt for Toller then began. A warrant for his arrest was issued, a reward of 10,000 marks was placed on his head. His photograph appeared on wanted notices outside every town-hall and police-station in Bavaria, and in every major town in Germany. Border police were put on special alert, particularly along the frontier with Austria. Soldiers and Free Corps irregulars searched every working-class house in the city.

The police file covering the man-hunt for Toller, still scrupulously preserved in the State Archive, has all the elements of a classic detective story, containing clues, false leads, suspects and inform-ants. Munich was full of professional and amateur spies, many of whom were attracted by the high reward, and reports that he had been seen came in thick and fast. He had been seen in the Ethos, a vegetarian restaurant he had been known to frequent, and had been overheard discussing the garden flat at 8 Schubertstrasse – a police raid failed to find a garden flat. A cook called Maria Webersdorfer reported that she had overheard her master and mistress discussing a hiding-place for Toller. An engineer reported that a man working at his factory *was* Toller.

The police were authorized to intercept Toller's mail, his known friends and acquaintances were kept under observation. A search of his flat yielded only a few items of clothing which his landlady had put in the cellar because he had not paid the rent since mid April. Toller's movements since 24 April were painstakingly reconstructed by Gradl, the detective in charge of the case, whose reports end abruptly in tragi-comedy. Searching a house in which Toller was reported to be hiding, he suddenly heard the door-bell ring; he opened the door to a detachment of soldiers carrying out a house search who, mistaking him for Toller, shot him dead on the spot.

Toller had in fact kept on the move since 1 May. He had left Grete Lichtenstein's room the same day for the home of Eduard Trautner, a friend and political comrade. Trautner had only a studio flat and had understandable reservations about sheltering Toller there. Waiting only for the cover of darkness, he accompanied Toller to a new hiding-place in the house of Prince Karl zu Löwenstein.[37] The young aristocrat was an unlikely accomplice who neither knew Toller nor shared his political views but agreed to shelter him for humanitarian reasons. His name and rank afforded considerable protection, for he was spared the house-searches which were now commonplace. On one occasion, Toller woke to the sound of marching feet, as a detachment of soldiers halted before the house. He and his host sat listening, as the soldiers began to search every other flat in the building. At last they heard footsteps stop directly outside the door – only to go away again. The officer had seen the aristocratic name on the door and had waved his troops away.

Trautner visited Toller every day in his new hiding-place. He found him ill and moody: one day ready to give himself up, the next determined to escape.[38] The Prince recalled that Toller was nervous and volatile, making wild and often contradictory plans: to escape, to hide, to give himself up. One day Trautner failed to appear. He had been arrested. A police officer held a pistol to his head and threatened to shoot him if he did not reveal Toller's whereabouts, but Trautner refused to be intimidated. He was later sentenced to five months' imprisonment for harbouring Toller.

Toller had been in this hiding-place about ten days, when the Prince became aware that the house was being watched. A man was standing across the road, observing everyone who went in or out. If Toller was to escape, there was no time to lose, but the only way out of the house was the front entrance, so that it was impossible to leave without being seen by the spy across the road. The Prince finally had the idea that they should impersonate a funeral party. They dressed in morning-clothes, including the customary top-hats and, accompanied by a young woman in a black hat and veil, left the house and walked up the road at a suitably dignified pace. The Prince recalled that they made their escape 'without attracting undue attention'.

Toller's last refuge was in the house of an artist called Johannes Reichel, who was known in Schwabing as an early disciple of Paul Klee. Reichel and his wife lived in a large house set in its own garden, which still stands on the corner of Schwabing's Werneckstrasse. Toller spent the days in Reichel's studio, taking care to keep well away from the windows. At night, he slept on a couch in the living-room. In an emergency, he was to hide in a cubby-hole, closed by a secret door, which Reichel hung with paintings in order to hide it from view. Toller's arrival in his new hiding-place coincided with the announcement that Leviné had been arrested, news which threw Toller into some agitation: he spoke of giving himself up as a demonstrative gesture 'that we revolutionaries do not fear the court martial'. At the same time, he further disguised his appearance. He had already grown a moustache, now he dyed his hair with peroxide, giving it a reddish colour. 'When I looked in the mirror,' he wrote later, 'I hardly recognized myself.'[39]

During the next three weeks, while Toller vacillated between surrender and escape, the search for him intensified. After Trautner's arrest, Grete Lichtenstein was questioned, Prince Löwenstein's house searched. The police were now certain that Toller was in Schwabing. On 4 June, at four o'clock in the morning, a detachment of armed police and soldiers, acting on a tip-off, surrounded the house in Werneckstrasse and searched it. Their knocking had already awakened Toller, who had withdrawn to his bolt-hole; crouched inside, he listened to the heavy feet of soldiers searching the house. Later, they began to tap the woodwork: they already knew about the bolt-hole. It did not take them long to find him, still wearing only his night-shirt. He was taken to Stadelheim Prison, where he was interrogated, finger-printed and clapped in chains. The following day, 5 June, Eugen Leviné was executed by firing-squad. The campaign to save Toller from a similar fate began almost immediately.

VI

High Treason

Toller's trial for high treason summarized in many respects the prevailing political atmosphere following the overthrow of the Soviet Republic: a singularly Bavarian mixture of conservatism, separatism and anti-semitism. While the Hoffmann government had nominally been reinstated, it was in fact a hostage of the very forces it had conjured up. In the name of a return to constitutional legality, it was obliged to endorse martial law and the excesses which it permitted. The clearest indication of the impotence of the Hoffmann cabinet is that it could find 'no reason for remitting the sentence of death' on Eugen Leviné,[1] even though his trial and sentence were a clear perversion of justice.

Real power lay with the army. The political section of the High Command established a press and news bureau with the dual task of conducting political propaganda within the army and monitoring political activities outside. (One of its earliest recruits was Adolf Hitler.) In the following weeks, those with extreme Nationalist sympathies were appointed to crucial positions of power. Among the officers of the VII District Command were Major von Epp, Free Corps leader and later Nazi Governor of Bavaria, and his right-hand man Ernst Röhm. The new Chief of Police in Munich was a magistrate called Pöhner, who when subsequently asked if there were right-wing murder squads in Bavaria answered, 'Yes, but not enough of them.' His assistant, Wilhelm Frick, was to become Nazi Minister of the Interior.

It was some weeks before Toller was brought to trial. After initial cross-examination at police headquarters, he was transferred to Stadelheim Prison, which had witnessed some of the worst excesses of the Free Corps. Graffiti above the main gate announced: 'Here we dispatch Spartacists free of charge' and 'Spartacist blood made into black pudding and liver sausage'. It was here that Landauer had been beaten to death, that revolutionary prisoners had been summarily shot and that Leviné had been executed by firing-squad. Toller was held in solitary confinement. He began to feel at this time that he had not much longer to live, a feeling heightened by the fact that the prison authorities, with sadistic refinement, had put him in the cell lately occupied by Leviné. It was situated in the block housing criminal convicts – the cell on one side was occupied by a prisoner serving a life sentence, that on the other by a murderer awaiting execution. There was an almost total absence of sound, a silence broken only at night, when the soldiers would fire volleys of shots to relieve their own boredom.

Toller's case was the subject of lively controversy long before it came to court. There were concerted attempts by socialists to mobilize public opinion against a possible death sentence. The left-wing press was unanimous in demanding that 'he be spared the same fate as Leviné'.[2] Well-known liberal papers, such as the *Berliner Tageblatt* and the *Frankfurter Zeitung* lent their weight to the campaign. Leading intellectuals and politicians interceded on his behalf, the most influential being Wolfgang Heine, SPD deputy and now Prussian Minister of the Interior, who wrote to the Court that he could 'say nothing but good about Toller's character', calling him 'an incorrigible optimist . . . who rejects all violence' and concluding that 'his execution could have only the most unfortunate consequences'.[3] The wave of solidarity with Toller was international: socialist students in France elected him their honorary president, Romain Rolland, the noted French pacifist, wrote to express his support. The right-wing press reacted by demanding that Toller should pay for his supposed crimes; in the Provincial Assembly, Prime Minister Hoffmann invoked the 'full force of the law for those who had led the people astray'. But there were those who were determined that Toller should not even stand trial.

The most traumatic event of Toller's imprisonment in Stadelheim was an attempt to murder him.[4] As he was escorted from his cell for interrogation one day, he found himself forced to push past a group of six men standing in the corridor. They were wearing the uniforms of ordinary soldiers, though from their manner and bearing he judged them to be officers or students. Two hours later, when he was finally returned to his cell, the men were still waiting, pursuing him down the corridor, calling threats and abuse. Shortly after, a young warder came into his cell to warn him that he should on no account allow himself to be taken down to the yard for exercise. He had overheard the six men planning to murder Toller, intending to push him from behind, so that when he stumbled, he could be shot 'while trying to escape', a pretext already used to justify the murder of

several revolutionary prisoners. When Toller was escorted from his
cell for exercise shortly after, the six men were indeed lying in wait,
following close on his heels along the corridor and down the stairs to
the iron gate which led into the exercise yard. Toller was saved only
by the presence of mind of the warder escorting him, who unlocked
the gate and suddenly gave Toller a violent push into the yard,
quickly following and slamming the gate shut again, leaving the
would-be assassins to shout imprecations from the other side. Toller
later submitted a complaint to the prisoner governor about the
incident, his story being substantiated by both the warders concerned. The governor actually opened an official inquiry, but
quickly closed it again on the grounds that it was impossible to
establish which unit had been on duty on the day concerned.

Toller's trial finally opened on 14 July 1919;[5] the proceedings were
held in a small court-room which had space for little more than thirty
members of the public. Intensive security measures were in force.
Toller was brought to court under armed military escort; inside the
building, witnesses were searched before being allowed into the
court-room. Armed police were present throughout the trial. On
either side of the judges' table sat an officer representing the military
authorities. There was a large number of reporters, who overflowed
the press table into the public gallery. Among other observers was
agent A 47 of the army's Press and News Bureau, whose confidential
report stressed that two of Toller's three defence lawyers were Jews,
as were several of the journalists reporting the trial, and even some
members of the public: 'the whole trial was held under the sign of
Israel'.[6] The proceedings themselves had an anti-semitic tone which
was established at the very outset, when the presiding judge
Stadelmayer, who had pronounced sentence of death on Leviné,
questioned Toller's statement that he was 'of no religious confession', interpolating: 'You didn't come into the world with no
religious confession – what confession were your parents?' The
stenographic record duly described Toller as 'Israelite, now of no
religious confession'. Throughout the trial, the prosecution sought
to portray Toller and other leaders of the Soviet Republic as 'alien
elements' who had subverted the natural order of Bavarian society.

Toller seemed ill at ease during the early part of the trial. He was
quickly forced to realize that it was not only his political actions
which were on trial, for the court consistently tried to undermine his
mental and moral standing. Though his bank account was found to

contain only a few marks, it was none the less suggested that he had embezzled funds. He was obliged to refute the implication that he had venereal disease, while his relations with Tilla Durieux were the subject of prurient speculation. The presiding judge dwelt at length on Toller's history of childhood illness, confronting him with the psychiatric reports written at the time of the January Strike. Dr Rüdin, who had examined Toller at that time and had categorized him as 'a severe hysteric', was called as a witness for the prosecution. The intention was clear – it was not enough to have defeated the Soviet Republic militarily, the credibility of its leaders had to be destroyed. In the face of these attacks, Toller defended himself with courage and dignity. The journalist Stefan Großmann noted that – quite contrary to the intention of the Court – this minute examination of Toller's life 'revealed ever more clearly the outline of a moral personality'.[7]

Toller's defence was conducted by three lawyers, the most eminent of whom was Hugo Haase. A noted Berlin advocate, Haase was also the Parliamentary leader of the USPD and had belonged to the Council of People's Commissars in the early days of the revolution. Haase's defence of Toller was his last major legal assignment: a few months later he was murdered by a right-wing assassin. Haase rested his defence of Toller on two main arguments. Firstly, he contended that there was really no charge to answer: Toller was accused of high treason under a law promulgated in Imperial Germany which had effectively lapsed with the overthrow of the monarchy it had been framed to protect. The Reich government itself had come to power through revolution and it was nonsensical, Haase argued, 'that the revolutionaries of yesterday should imprison the revolutionaries of today for the very crime which they themselves had committed'. Haase anticipated, however, that this argument would be rejected. The sentence of death passed on Leviné had been justified by the attribution of 'dishonourable motives'. Toller's defence therefore sought to prove that his political actions had been guided by honourable motives, establishing that he had gone to great lengths to avoid bloodshed.

Various witnesses were called to testify to his idealism and moral integrity. His former officers confirmed that his military record had been unblemished; fellow-soldiers paid tribute to his comradeship and courage. Among the famous figures who gave evidence on Toller's behalf was Max Weber, who testified to his 'absolute moral integrity, combined with extraordinary unworldliness and innocence of political and economic realities', concluding with the much-quoted phrase that 'only God in his wrath had made Toller a politician'. He was followed into the witness-box by distinguished literary figures such as Thomas Mann, the novelist Max Halbe, and the Norwegian writer and actor Björn Björnsen, each of whom affirmed Toller's literary talent and the ethical idealism evinced in his (as yet unpublished) drama *The Transformation*. It was indeed here that the public first heard of the play which would establish Toller's fame as a dramatist when it was produced in Berlin three months later. Max Martersteig, a respected elder of the Munich theatre, called the play 'the personal confession of a man imbued with the highest sense of morality'. Toller was embarrassed by such fulsome praise; he later wrote that he was ashamed that it was intended to secure a lighter sentence, but the strategy of the defence was certainly effective. Even the State Prosecutor, though maintaining that the proceedings had proved the case against Toller, conceded that they had also served to reveal his character in a much more favourable light. He asked for a sentence of seven years, the defence called for Toller's acquittal.

Before judgement was passed, Toller made use of the prisoner's traditional right of final address to the Court. One observer noted that he had recovered the confidence and composure which had deserted him at the start of the trial. He spoke briefly, but 'not without the warmth of inner conviction'.[8] He made virtually no reference to the actual proceedings. Addressing an audience outside the Court, he reaffirmed his belief in the inevitability of revolution and its final triumph. Significantly, he began by addressing the question of revolutionary force, a moral problem which was to form the dramatic conflict of *Masses and Man* and which would remain the central conflict of his ideology for many years:

> I would not call myself a revolutionary, if I were to say that I would never countenance the use of force to change existing conditions. We revolutionaries acknowledge the right to revolution when we see that the situation is no longer tolerable, that it has become frozen. Then we have the right to overthrow it.[9]

His words were often rhetorical, his sentiments sometimes utopian:

The working class will not halt until socialism has been realized . . . The revolution is like a vessel filled with the pulsating heartbeat of millions of working people. And the spirit of revolution will not die while the hearts of these workers continue to beat. We who know the situation do not promise the working class a paradise. We know full well that the coming decades will bring terrible economic conditions and that the utmost effort of every individual will be necessary to remove them. But we also know that when we have overcome these difficulties, future generations will reap the reward . . .

You say that the revolution is merely a wage struggle by the workers and thus seek to denigrate it. If you go among the workers and see their wretched conditions you will understand why they must first satisfy their material needs. But you will also find a great longing for art and culture, a struggle for spiritual liberation. This process has now begun and will not be suppressed by the bayonets and court martials of the capitalist governments of the entire world.

The hostility to the state, the prescriptive idea of community and the belief in the liberating function of art all suggest the continuing strain of utopian anarchism in his thinking. He ended with a defiant anticipation of the Court's verdict:

Gentlemen! I am convinced that, by your own lights, you will pronounce judgement to the best of your knowledge and belief. But knowing my views you must also accept that I shall regard your verdict as the expression, not of justice, but of power.

The judges found Toller guilty of high treason but, acknowledging his 'honourable motives', sentenced him to the minimum term of five years' fortress imprisonment. Toller listened to the verdict 'without any visible sign of emotion'.[10]

VII

Five Years'
'Honourable Imprisonment'
1919–1924

Toller spent the early months of his sentence in the prisons of Stadelheim, Neuburg and Eichstätt, until in February 1920 the Bavarian government finally decided to concentrate all revolutionary prisoners in the fortress prison of Niederschönenfeld. Situated near the village of Rain am Lech, Niederschönenfeld still stands isolated in a low-lying plain near the confluence of the Lech and the Danube. Stranded in this remote corner of Bavaria, it must have seemed an ideal place to consign unwelcome political opponents.

Toller entered Niederschönenfeld on 3 February 1920. He arrived by train and was brought under escort across the fields to the prison. He remembered the strong smell of earth and damp grass. Across the flat landscape, he could see a lonely birch-tree, its branches outlined across the sky: they were the only impressions he could salvage to tide him over the next four and a half years.[1]

Niederschönenfeld had originally been built as a cloister before being converted into a reformatory for young offenders – a purpose it again serves today. With the arrival of revolutionary prisoners, the building was surrounded by a cordon of barbed wire and patrolled by armed guards. The building itself was divided into two blocks of cells, the first block housing ordinary criminals and the second the political prisoners. There were initially about a hundred revolutionary prisoners in Niederschönenfeld. During the early months, they talked of little but the recent past, reliving the revolution in animated discussion and polemic. Many of them hoped they would soon be liberated by a new wave of revolution, but such hopes rapidly receded. In July 1920 Toller wrote to his publisher Kurt Wolff that 'the historians of the day may doubt it, but it is nonetheless an historical fact that in pre-historic, so to speak legendary times, Kurt Eisner was Bavarian Prime Minister'.[2] The tone of the letter, in which a sense of unreality vies with a feeling of historical distance, is symptomatic of a development in which political reaction had triumphed so completely that the very events of the revolution had come to seem remote and unreal.

Oskar Maria Graf recalled that Toller once referred to his years in prison as a time when he was really happy: Toller's prison letters tell a very different tale.[3] When he began his sentence, he was still only twenty-five, a man who had already tasted – and enjoyed – popular acclaim, whose literary ambitions were in the public domain of the theatre, whose lyrical sensibility craved the stimulus of sights and sounds. His letters constantly repeat his feeling of being cut off from public events, his impatience with a drab and colourless prison routine, and his frustration at being unable to see his own work on stage – it was 1924 before he attended a performance of one of his own plays.

These five years were certainly the most artistically productive of his life, during which he wrote the plays which made him internationally famous: *Masses and Man*, *The Machine Wreckers*, *Hinkemann* and *Der entfesselte Wotan (Wotan Unchained)*, as well as various other works. They were also the years in which he became a 'cause célèbre'. Following the success of the production of *The Transformation* in Berlin in the autumn of 1919, Toller's lawyer, Adolf Kaufmann, wrote to him that 'many prominent people have inquired of me about your fate'.[4] The success of the play and the growing fame of its author threatened to make him a political embarrassment and early in 1920, on the occasion of the hundredth performance of the play, the Bavarian government offered Toller a pardon. Toller, however, refused the pardon on the grounds that he did not want individual clemency but a universal amnesty. It was in fact a matter of deep principle: in 1921–22 he dissociated himself from the public campaign for his release 'as long as it is intended for me alone'.

If the success of *The Transformation* and later *Masses and Man* made Toller the most famous political prisoner in Germany, his renown as a political prisoner in turn reinforced his success as a dramatist. He became a focal point for political differences, inspiring fervent admiration and fanatical hatred, so that almost every Toller play became the occasion of controversy or scandal. The performance of *Masses and Man* in Nuremberg in 1920 was interrupted by anti-semitic heckling and fighting in the audience which the authorities used as a pretext to ban all further performances. The Berlin première of *The Machine Wreckers* was turned into a tumultuous demonstration for Toller's release, endorsed in an appeal from the stage by the play's director Karlheinz Martin. The production of *Hinkemann* in Dresden in 1924 was violently disrupted by nationalist extremists and the play had to be taken off.

For all his success as a dramatist, Toller suffered both physically and psychologically in prison. He was troubled by persistent ill-health, which was sometimes aggravated by the lack of prompt medical treatment (the prison doctor told him that he considered himself 'first and foremost an official of the state').[5] He suffered from violent headaches which for long periods made it impossible for him to work; while in prison, he went prematurely grey. The effects of imprisonment certainly contributed to the illnesses which troubled him in later years, seeming above all to have exacerbated his manic-depressive tendencies.

Toller's letters graphically record his loathing of the impersonal but inescapable routine of prison life:

> It is dreadful to be exposed day after day to the monoton-ous, repetitive noises of this place, where the walls are so thin you can hear every noise from the cells above, below and on either side of you. Noise in the corridors, the rattling of keys, slamming of the iron doors, warders calling the roll, hob-nailed boots stamping on the stone floors, or worse still, the shuffling of rubber soles.[6]

He undoubtedly suffered most acutely from the loss of personal freedom. The epigraph to his *Prisoner's Poems* is a quotation from Kant: 'There is surely nothing more terrible than that the actions of one person should be subject to the will of another.'[7] This feeling was fed by an abiding sense of injustice.

Fortress detention (*Festungshaft*) had originally been devised as a form of 'honourable imprisonment', involving the least possible infringement of personal liberty: fortress prisoners were entitled to receive regular visits without surveillance, to write and receive let-ters uncensored and even to periods of leave. However, the new Bavarian Minister of Justice, Müller-Meiningen, soon introduced a much stricter régime which entailed the withdrawal of many of the customary privileges: letters and newspapers were strictly censored, food parcels opened, visits restricted and subject to surveillance. Cell doors were left open in daytime, however, and prisoners could visit each other and walk freely in the prison yard for several hours a day.

The severity of the regime inside Niederschönenfeld closely followed political developments outside. In the wake of the right-wing Kapp Putsch in March 1920, the Hoffmann administration had finally been deposed and replaced by an authoritarian right-wing regime. A new prison governor was appointed to Niederschönenfeld – a lawyer named Kraus whose reactionary credentials were impeccable. He informed prisoners that complaints to the judicial authorities were pointless: 'I can do what I like with prisoners. I have absolute authority.'[8] He enforced a regime in which minor infringements of the prison regulations were punished with vindictive sanctions, such as the loss of visits, the withdrawal of newspapers and writing materials; those who dared to protest were further punished with solitary confinement, bread and water and darkened cells. This regime applied only to Niederschönenfeld; right-wing prisoners in the fortress of Landsberg, such as Eisner's murderer Count Arco and later Adolf Hitler, continued to enjoy the traditional privileges of fortress prisoners.

Toller's sense of justice was outraged by the arbitrary and often unpredictable regime, with its daily rota of petty irritations and humiliations. His determination to assert his rights as a fortress prisoner frequently brought him into conflict with the prison authorities. During his four and a half years in Niederschönenfeld, he spent a total of 149 days in solitary confinement, 243 days deprived of writing materials and 24 days without food.

Prison censorship seriously affected Toller's literary work. Several of his manuscripts were confiscated, most notably that of his lyric cycle *The Swallow Book*, in which the censor found passages he considered 'inflammatory' and 'prejudicial to prison discipline'. Toller was finally forced to smuggle the manuscript out of prison, hidden by a comrade who was being released. The manuscript of *Masses and Man*, which had actually passed the prison censor, was seized in a police search at a friend's house, thus delaying publication. He was periodically prevented from writing at all by the withdrawal of writing materials and other disciplinary measures. In a debate on conditions in Niederschönenfeld in the Bavarian Provincial Assembly in March 1922, Ernst Niekisch, then only recently released, described at length 'the systematic attempts to hinder Toller's literary activity'.[9] The government spokesman replied by attacking Toller's veracity and integrity, one of several personal attacks made with the protection of parliamentary privilege which Toller was unable to answer.

Censorship made even letter-writing a burden. 'You become a tightrope walker of the word,' Toller noted. 'Even as you write, you feel the malicious hand of the censor.'[10] Many of the letters he wrote were not forwarded, some of those addressed to him were withheld. An official record of proceedings in the Reichstag was confiscated 'because of political content', a letter from Romain Rolland because it was written in French.[11] He wrote to Netty Katzenstein, the main confidante of his prison letters, that he could never rid himself of the oppressive feeling that even his own thoughts were subject to the will of others.

Imprisonment inevitably brought a halt to Toller's political activity, but these years also saw his political position shift from that of a leading USPD activist to that of an unaligned revolutionary social-ist. During the first years of imprisonment, he had taken a lively, if critical interest in the debate within the USPD. He felt that too many in the party had unrealistic expectations, failing to acknowledge that the revolutionary wave of 1918–19 had now receded: in the present climate, the revolutionary had to concentrate on the day-to-day work of political education and organization.[12]

In June 1921 Toller accepted nomination by the USPD to the Bavarian Provincial Assembly, remaining a deputy for three years without ever attending a sitting. In 1924 he was invited to become the party's leading candidate in the new elections to Landtag and Reichstag, but declined. Instead he announced his decision ('taken long before') to leave the USPD.[13] He thereafter considered himself an independent socialist without party affiliation.

Toller's decision to leave the USPD, and his failure to join another party, owed something to personal temperament. He had always been sceptical of party politics as a vehicle for socialism. While he recognized the role of the party as a focus for working-class aspira-tions, his prison experience increasingly convinced him that party allegiance inhibited the ideal of working-class unity. He deplored the progressive fragmentation of the labour movement: 'the disunity of the working class hampers every major decision.'[14] In his dramatic fragment *Deutsche Revolution*, written in 1920, he compared the ideological wrangling of the left to the doctrinal hair-splitting of the medieval church.[15] He himself continued to advocate Eisner's pre-cept of the 'Einheitsfront', the united front in which workers made common cause across party divisions, a belief which determined his pursuit of broad left unity after 1924 and his support of the Popular Front in exile.

Toller's decision also reflected the conflict he felt between political and creative work. As early as 1921, he wrote to Kurt Wolff: 'I believe that my profession has been decided, the constant tension between the desire to work through action and through literary creation has been resolved.'[16] He felt that the narrower requirements of party politics compromised his artistic independence: he was always careful to differentiate art from propaganda. He believed that membership of the USPD conditioned the response to his work, cutting him off from many of those he wished to address: 'As a writer, I speak to all those who are prepared to listen, no matter which party or group they belong to.'[17]

However, Toller's resignation from the USPD was largely dictated by political events outside prison. By 1924 the USPD had virtually disintegrated. The left-wing majority of the party had joined the KPD in 1920, having accepted the Twenty-One Conditions stipulated by Moscow for acceptance into the Third International. Toller was fiercely critical, considering the Twenty-One Conditions 'fateful for socialism in Europe'. In September 1922 much of the remainder of the party had re-entered the SPD, a decision which Toller denounced as the end of all revolutionary pretensions.[18] The break-up of the USPD left Toller politically isolated between the reformism of the SPD and the sectarianism of the KPD.

Toller's attitude to party politics was undoubtedly greatly influenced by his experience of the bitter internecine strife which broke out between prisoners in Niederschönenfeld. In the beginning, the morale of prisoners had been high, their relations warm and comradely. Men were eager to share both their material possessions and their experiences. 'There was a general desire to confess the most intimate experiences, feelings and thoughts, and to show one another letters from wives and sweethearts'; but, within a few short months, comradeship often turned to hatred under the psychological pressures of close confinement.

> Fifty to sixty prisoners lived penned together in one corridor, year in, year out. Every gesture of one's fellow-prisoners was known, every idiosyncrasy of speech, even a man's smell. Brotherhood changed into enmity. Every

emotional impulse broke on the grating of the cell corridor and recoiled intensified on one's fellow-prisoners,
until in the end a sort of neighbourliness was born out of
sheer resignation.[19]

Differences of political ideology and allegiance produced an atmosphere of mutual distrust and recrimination. Prisoners were divided
over the split in the USPD and the Twenty-One Conditions: such
divisions soon degenerated into a factionalism which mirrored the
political splits in the labour movement outside prison. How far they
poisoned personal relationships is evident in Toller's anecdote of a
young prisoner who came to say goodbye before his release, but
pleaded with Toller that the visit should be kept secret from his
party comrades.[20] Toller attributed these divisions largely to prison
psychosis: 'It is dreadful how it twists and ravages the spirit.' He
himself was clearly not immune from such feelings, as he wrote to
Netty Katzenstein in 1921:

> I am in the grip of a frightening lethargy. And an almost
> pathological dislike of being with other people. It has got
> to the stage where it gives me physical pain to have to
> look at the faces of others. Imprisonment produces
> hostility to all company, smothers sociability, breeds
> misanthropy.[21]

He felt oppressed by the enforced intimacy of prison life, quoting
from Dostoyevsky's *Notes from the House of the Dead*: 'There is one
torture in the prisoner's life which is almost worse than all the others
– it is the enforced living together'; after three years in prison, he felt
that he had lost all inclination for social contact: 'I have acquired all
the virtues and vices of the hermit and I don't believe I shall ever lose
them again.'[22]

There were those, such as the publisher E.P. Tal, who feared that
imprisonment would permanently damage Toller's creative talents, a
fear which he himself was quick to dismiss. Writing undoubtedly
became an emotional necessity, a means of giving some purpose to
the otherwise shapeless pattern of life in prison, in which one day
was almost indistinguishable from the next: 'If I can no longer write,
create, form, observe (each being only a variant of the others), I
should simply dry up inside, or at best become hardened,
encrusted.'[23] His letters frequently mention the difficulty of writing

in an environment which lacked almost any sensual stimulus. The sheer monotony of confinement in a cell measuring fifteen feet by six is succinctly evoked in *The Swallow Book*:

> Sechs Schritte hin
> Sechs Schritte her
> Ohne Sinn
> Ohne Sinn.

> Six paces forward
> Six paces back
> Without sense
> Without sense.[24]

A letter written during his last year in prison summarizes his feelings of social and sensual deprivation:

> I am looking forward to life, I am looking forward to struggles in freedom, to people who do not live in constant fear, to eyes which are not downcast (which every prisoner has after a few days or months), to woods, evenings, nights, to colours and sounds, to innumerable contacts.[25]

The privations of prison life were not least sexual and emotional. It was sex which often dominated the thoughts of prisoners, sometimes finding release in homosexual relationships, though Toller suggested that 'among all the prisoners there were only three real homosexuals'. He later wrote that many prisoners experienced sexual problems after their release. Most found that women 'did not fulfil what prison dreams had promised . . .; not one of the prisoners was unrestrained and natural after his release as he had been before his imprisonment'.[26] How far the shifting pattern of Toller's own relationships was determined by his prison experience can only be a matter for conjecture. Kurt Pinthus later suggested that all Toller's love affairs disappointed him.[27] Certainly, while he attracted frequent admiration and affection from women, none of his friendships matured into a life-long companionship; his only marriage ended in separation.

Life in prison did have some consolations. Toller was able to read more widely than at any other time in his life. He asked Kurt Wolff to send him all the most recent play-texts as they appeared; he was critical of much that was produced, but wrote enthusiastically of Werfel's *Spiegelmensch*.[28] He read novels (Dostoyevsky, Romain Rolland, Knut Hamsun), poetry from Milton and Tasso to Hölderlin and Novalis, literary essays by Landauer and others, philosophical works by Schopenhauer, and the writings of the medieval mystic Meister Eckhardt. He read the Luther bible avidly ('For weeks this book was my only friend') and read widely in politics and economics, including Marx's *Capital* and Engels's *Condition of the Working-Class in England*, as well as Max Beer's *General History of Socialism*. The very breadth and diversity of his reading suggests a search, not only for knowledge, but for ultimate enlightenment.

Despite the deteriorating relations between prisoners, there was also the gift of friendship. Toller was among those who formed a literary group which included Erich Mühsam, Valentin Hartig and Ernst Niekisch. Hartig and Niekisch, who were both party colleagues of Toller's and occupied adjacent cells to his, quickly became his closest friends in prison, the three men spending many hours in literary and political discussion. His relations with Mühsam were less close, but he always retained a high regard for him, commemorating his courageous opposition to the Nazis in his last play *Pastor Hall*.

The letters which Toller wrote from prison were the tenuous link he maintained with the outside world. He corresponded with some of the leading cultural figures of his day – with pacifists like Romain Rolland and Henri Barbusse, whose novel *Le Feu* (*Under Fire*) had deeply moved him in 1917, with the historians of the German labour movement, Gustav Mayer and Max Beer, and with notable literary figures like Stefan Zweig, Else Lasker-Schüler and Fritz von Unruh. Such contacts undoubtedly helped to strengthen Toller's self-esteem, his sense of belonging to a European cultural élite.

He also wrote a large number of personal letters, among them many to his mother. Unable to share her son's political convictions, she had remained unswerving in her devotion to him, a love which Toller had only gradually grown to understand:

> She was estranged from my life and I was hurt that she did not share my ideas . . . Now I see that my way of life – which she does not understand – does not matter to her. She loves me.[29]

For his part, he tried to be a dutiful son; he wrote to her regularly and was greatly concerned when prison discipline prevented him from doing so. Her health was poor and in 1922 he tried to arrange treatment for her in a sanatorium with the help of the writer and satirist Kurt Tucholsky.[30] In April 1923 he suddenly received news that she was seriously, perhaps fatally, ill and applied to the Bavarian authorities for compassionate leave from prison to be at her bedside. The news of her illness had thrown him into such emotional turmoil that he was unable to draft the request himself and had to get a friend to write it for him. He waited for the outcome of his application in a mounting fever of anxiety, but the Ministry of Justice delayed a full four days before transmitting the laconic reply: 'The request of the prisoner Toller is unsuitable for consideration.'[31] His mother did not die, but the experience remained among the most traumatic of his whole imprisonment, helping to focus his feelings for her and to understand hers for him: 'My mother writes me letters of moving tenderness,' he wrote to Netty Katzenstein.[32] Toller also maintained contact with his sister Hertha, with whom he had always had a close relationship. She visited him every year in prison, always arranging her family's summer holiday in Bavaria, so as to be within easy travelling distance of Niederschönenfeld. Toller kept up relations with his mother and sister after his release, visiting them periodically in Landsberg. Such visits were always memorable occasions for the family, when Hertha would lose no chance to make a fuss of her younger brother.[33]

During his last few months in prison, Toller became increasingly apprehensive at the prospect of freedom, being pursued by the idea that he would be unable to adjust to life outside prison, and even more that he could not live up to the political and theatrical reputation he had gained. 'In four months I shall be free. I hardly sleep at night,' he confided to Netty Katzenstein.[34] He found that he could write nothing: 'The urge to write gets weaker and weaker in this place. I am full of plans, but I'd rather bark at the moon than write another scene in here.'[35] He became strangely apathetic, lying on his bed for hours, incapacitated by self-doubt. Such was his apprehension that he even contemplated suicide. Though he was able to resist the impulse, his self-doubt remained:

> Whom shall I meet, whom shall I find again? Who are you and who am I? Many people await me in affection,

> in friendship, in love. Hundreds of letters tell me so. But
> is it me they have affection for, me whose friend they
> are, me they love? Is it not a pipe-dream they are
> pursuing?[36]

The disparity between his reputation and his achievement troubled
him for the rest of his life, one of the threads which led to his
eventual suicide.

Toller served his sentence to the last day. Shortly before he was
due to be released, he was summoned to the prison governor, who
told him that he was to be expelled from Bavaria: since he had not
changed his political convictions, he represented 'a continuing threat
to the security of the Free State of Bavaria'. He was put aboard a
train and escorted by plain-clothes police to the border with Saxony.
Toller's fragmentary autobiography ends at this point: 'I am thirty
years old. My hair is going grey. I am not tired.'[37]

VIII

Plays from a Prison Cell

It has been suggested that Ernst Toller might never have become a dramatist if imprisonment had not afforded him the 'opportunity'. His five years in prison were certainly the most creatively productive period of his life, during which he wrote a play a year for the first four years: *Masses and Man* (1919), *The Machine Wreckers* (1920–21), *Hinkemann* (1921–22) and *Wotan Unchained* (1923). These alone would have been a substantial achievement, but he also wrote a short puppet play, *Die Rache des verhöhnten Liebhabers* (*The Scorned Lover's Revenge*) (1920), two volumes of poetry – *Prisoners' Poems* (1918–21) and *The Swallow Book* (1923) – two 'Sprechchöre' (choral poems for mass declamation), and wrote the scenarios for three 'Massenspiele' (mass spectacles), performed in successive years at the Trade Union Festival in Leipzig (1922–24).

Given the difficult conditions under which he was forced to write, it is little short of astonishing how much he was able to achieve. He rarely felt able to write in the mornings; at other times it was almost impossible to shut out interruptions. He admitted to Kurt Wolff that he often felt oppressed by the enforced community of prison life: 'If I have to be in prison, I often wish I could be allowed to live much more alone.'[1] His most creative time was the evening, but prison regulations did not permit prisoners to use artificial light, so that he was often forced to drape a blanket over his table and creep under it to write by the light of a hidden candle.

Toller later admitted that all the plays he wrote in prison 'suffered from having too much in them'.[2] The reason was that, while prison censorship of letters was severe, literary works were treated more leniently, offering an outlet for thoughts and feelings which were proscribed elsewhere. It is this which gives the plays their particular personal resonance. Literary critics have traditionally grouped them together as 'prison plays', but the term actually conceals a considerable diversity of style and structure – formal and conceptual differences which in fact document Toller's personal and political development during these five years.

Masses and Man

In the forced leisure of imprisonment, Toller had time to reflect at length on his experience of revolution. The plays he wrote are very much the products of that reflection, variations on the theme of socialism and revolution. The most immediate and intense reworking of that experience was *Masses and Man*, written in October 1919 in the fortress prison of Eichstätt.[3] In the months following the defeat of the revolution in Bavaria, he had been troubled by feelings of guilt and remorse which had almost overwhelmed him. The translation of his experience into drama had been a necessary catharsis: 'After experiences the force of which a man can perhaps stand only once without breaking, *Masses and Man* was a liberation from spiritual anguish,' he wrote in retrospect.[4] He completed the play in a single creative burst of three days, without any preliminary drafts: the emotional impulse behind the work could not be more clearly signalled. Toller's experience of revolution had confronted him with the conflict between revolutionary ends and means, between moral principal and political expediency. He now began to see this conflict as inevitable and the situation of the revolutionary himself as inherently tragic:

> The ethical man: living solely according to his own principles. The political man: fighter for social forms which are the prerequisite of a better life for others. Fighter, even if he violates his own principles. If the ethical man becomes a political man, what tragic road is spared him?[5]

This distinction between the ethical and the political, crucial to the dramatic conflict of *Masses and Man*, is derived directly from Kant, whose philosophy Toller had begun to study intensively in prison – a conscious acknowledgement of the continuing influence of Kurt Eisner.

Stylistically, *Masses and Man* is very much an Expressionist play, having strong formal similarities to *The Transformation*. It consists of seven tableaux, which are once more divided into 'real scenes' and 'dream scenes', though the distinction is less clear cut than in the earlier play. The action is universalized, the characters are not recognizable persons but figures representing particular ideas and attitudes. The symbolism of the dream scenes is complex and sometimes obscure, the language elliptical and emotionally heightened. A striking stylistic innovation is the attempt to express collective consciousness in choral passages representing the voice of the masses.

The play's protagonist, the Woman, calls for revolution, but believes it can be achieved through the non-violent means of the mass strike. She is opposed by the Nameless One, who declares that only revolutionary force can free the masses from oppression. The dramatic conflict consists in the clash between their two points of view, the struggle between revolution and reaction providing only the backdrop to the real dramatic argument. What Toller is presenting is essentially the clash between himself and Eugen Leviné (and therefore also between USPD and KPD) in the final days of the Bavarian Soviet Republic. This is not to say that the play is a direct autobiographical account, for Toller has distilled his experience into a dialectic of opposing philosophies of revolutionary action. A brief analytical exposition of the play will help to indicate its significance for his personal and political development.

The first tableau introduces the Woman (also called Sonja Irene L.)[6] who has joined the revolutionary movement from compassion for the suffering of the masses. She is shortly to address them in order to call for a general strike, which she sees as a means, not only of ending the war, but also of precipitating revolution. When her husband appeals to her to abandon her political activities because they will damage his career and his honour, she refuses, feeling that her involvement is a moral imperative.

The second tableau, a 'dream scene', counterposes the system which the revolution must overthrow, symbolized in the workings of the Stock Exchange. Four bankers are discussing a plan to stimulate the war effort by setting up a state brothel, disguised as a sanatorium for 'The Strengthening of the Will to Victory'. The system is not only hypocritical but inhuman, treating men and women as 'war material', components of a mechanism which functions almost independently. It is a recurrent theme of Toller's early work that human beings have been robbed of their humanity by a system in which no one can be fully human. The Woman appears, reminding the bankers that they are dealing with human lives: 'Gentlemen, these are human beings. I say again, human beings.' The bankers respond by organizing a dance for charity, showing the ability of the system to absorb moral idealism. The scene ends with 'the music of clinking gold coins', as the bankers dance a foxtrot round the desk of the Exchange: a grotesque evocation of the dual standards of capitalism.

It is only in the third tableau that the basic conflict of the play emerges explicitly. The scene begins with a succession of mass choruses, in which different groups of workers lament their material suffering. The Woman then addresses them, calling for a mass strike to end the war and usher in a new era of freedom and justice:

> Let strike be our deed! We, the weak, shall become a rock of strength. We shall break our chains without force, and no weapon yet built will be able to defeat us.[7]

Her call is challenged by the Nameless One, an anonymous spokesman of the masses. Even if the strike were to bring the war to an end, he says, it would not change the workers' plight. He ridicules her appeal for non-violent action, declaring there is only one way in which the workers can throw off their subjection:

> The enemy up there won't listen to fine words. Might against might! Force . . . Force! (p. 85).

The Woman protests that she wants no more killing, but the Nameless One dismisses her objection:

> Be silent, comrade. For the sake of the cause. What is the individual worth? Or his feelings, or his conscience? The masses count! (p. 86).

That is, class interest must take precedence over moral principles. The Woman finally throws in her lot with the workers, consciously subordinating moral scruple to revolutionary solidarity. The scene ends with the masses storming out of the hall.

The fourth tableau (a 'dream scene') restates these issues at the level of subconscious apprehension. The scene takes place at night in a 'high-walled yard', a setting which symbolizes the prison of working-class experience. The Nameless One appears and begins to play the harmonica in an invitation to dance. It proves to be a dance of death as prisoners awaiting execution ask to be allowed to join in. The Woman enters as the sentries bring in a prisoner who has the face of her husband. The Woman intervenes to try to save him, but is rebuffed by the Nameless One. The sentry too is deaf to her appeal for mercy: he was condemned to be shot by the other side. Even as she appeals to him, the face of the prisoner changes into that of the

sentry, suggesting that, in killing the prisoner, he is killing himself –
that is, that revolutionary violence only destroys the humanitarian
principles the revolution seeks to establish. At the end of the scene,
the Woman stands beside her husband, inviting them to shoot her in
a gesture which prefigures her later self-sacrifice.

The fifth tableau develops these issues at the level of conscious
experience. The Woman cannot overcome her revulsion to violence.
In the turmoil of defeat, the workers take hostages: the Nameless
One's demand that they should be shot poses the moral dilemma of
the play in its most acute form. The Woman pleads that the murder
of the hostages would be a senseless act of blind rage which would do
nothing to eradicate the system they seek to overthrow:

> I cry: Destroy the system! You, however, want to
> destroy men (p. 96).

The Nameless One accuses her of treachery: whoever is not with
them is against them – repeating verbatim the argument of the KPD
in the final days of the Soviet Republic. As the scene ends, the
building is surrounded by counter-revolutionary forces and the
Woman is taken prisoner, together with the workers.

In the visionary sixth tableau, Toller explores the nature of guilt
and responsibility in a series of visual symbols. The Woman,
chained and shut in a cage, is haunted by headless shadows which
accuse her of having murdered them. At first, she denies her guilt,
but she ends by acknowledging it. In a final vision, she is confronted
by a line of identical figures in prison uniform, representing the
masses. They wear prison clothes both because many revolutionaries
are actually in prison and to symbolize their imprisonment within
the social structure. It is this which determines their actions: 'Masse
ist Muß! Masse ist schuldlos!' ('The masses are necessity. The masses are guiltless!') It is only now that the Woman understands the
true nature of her own guilt:

> O monstrous law of guilt, in which every human being
> *must* become entangled (p. 103).

Guilt is inherent in the human condition, and in any attempt to
change it the determinism of the argument is clearly audible. When
the Woman is finally freed, her freedom is ambiguous, consisting in
recognizing the material limitations on her freedom.

The final tableau takes place in a prison cell, where the Woman is visited by the Nameless One. He has come to help her escape, but she rejects his plan, because it would entail killing one of the guards. Their subsequent exchanges bring the dramatic argument to its climax. The Woman opposes his belief in revolutionary expediency with an assertion of the sanctity of human life. The Nameless One repeats that the interests of the masses must take precedence over humanitarian considerations, even declaring that there is, as yet, no common humanity – only the antithesis between the masses, and the state and its agents. The new mankind will be formed only in the successful revolutionary struggle. The Woman rejects the primacy of the masses, arguing that they are only what social oppression has made of them. She makes a sweeping attack on the use of force, refuting the Nameless One's argument that the masses are fighting for humanity. The methods they use make them no better than the system they wish to overthrow.

> I see no difference. They murder for their country, you for everyone's countries (p. 108).

If the new order is built on such violence, it will be indistinguishable from the old. Their argument ends inevitably in the same deadlock: to use violence is to betray the ideals of the revolution, not to use it is to condemn the revolution to failure. Toller offers no solution – in fact, his intention was precisely to show that the problem was insoluble.[8] Dramatically, he could only resolve the question by resorting to the typical Expressionist motif of redemption through self-sacrifice. The Woman goes voluntarily to her execution, but her death is not in vain, for it forces a change of heart in two prisoners who enter her cell to steal her belongings. The play thus ends on a note of apparent affirmation; however, the ending is unsatisfactory, a personal solution which evades the essentially public issue of the play.

If the Woman insists on the absolute principle of non-violence, finally renouncing force in any circumstances, it must be emphasized that this was not the position which Toller himself espoused publicly – then or later. At his Court Martial, he had insisted that he would not call himself a revolutionary socialist if he believed that force could never be justified. *Masses and Man* is a more private statement, confirming the crucial importance of non-violence for his personality and indicating the emotional difficulty he had in rationalizing his own public position. But he clearly believed that absolute pacifism was tantamount to a renunciation of political action, a belief which is implicit in the 'revolutionary pacifism' he advocated after 1924.

Masses and Man was first produced at the Stadttheater, Nuremberg, though because of police restrictions it could only be given a private performance for trade union members, and even these had to be suspended after only four performances. The repercussion was therefore understandably muted. It was Jürgen Fehling's production at the Berlin Volksbühne in September 1921 which first established the play's international fame.

Masses and Man seems today a strangely archaic work, but the force and freshness of its impact on contemporary audiences is impossible to overlook. The play had an overwhelming success at the Volksbühne, being retained in the repertoire for two consecutive seasons. Many attributed the success solely to Fehling's masterful production, which used an abstract stage set to convey the play's dream-like unreality. Elaborate lighting effects, long flights of steps and carefully orchestrated choral speech and movement combined to create the definitive Expressionist production.[9] Fehling was prepared to concede that part of the success was because Volksbühne audiences were predominantly socialist, but insisted that it was 'in the main due to the inherent dramatic power of the play itself'.[10] The American theatre-writer Kenneth Macgowan stressed that the play 'had been much discussed by American visitors' and was himself impressed by this 'strange and powerful tragedy'.[11]

Among the innovations which had impressed Macgowan and other critics were the mass choruses, which seemed to offer a creative avenue which Toller could pursue. During 1920 he experimented with the literary form of the 'Sprechchor' or choral poem. These were semi-dramatic works containing parts for individual and choral speaking, recited with appropriate dramatic actions, usually to musical accompaniment. They were written for amateur performance by workers' groups at labour meetings and festivals and therefore intended as a public demonstration and celebration of socialist ideals. Toller first experimented with the 'Sprechchor' at the suggestion of Leo Kestenberg, then a cultural functionary of the USPD in the Prussian Ministry of Arts, Sciences and Education, his interest providing one of many examples of the interpenetration of art and politics in the USPD. During 1920 Toller completed two 'Sprechchöre', *Requiem den erschossenen Brüdern* (*Requiem for our Shot Brothers*) and *Der Tag des Proletariats* (*The Day of the Proletariat*), both first performed before the end of that year at the 'proletarische Feierstunde' (workers' evenings) inaugurated by the USPD in Berlin as part of the attempt to encourage the development of art forms which were distinctively proletarian.[12] Toller's choral poems proved extremely popular, being frequently performed and soon inspiring imitation; however, he quickly lost interest in the form, abandoning it after 1920.

The strong vein of determinism in *Masses and Man* was to become increasingly evident in Toller's work. The optimism of *The Transformation*, with its naive belief in the power of spiritual regeneration to effect social change, had proved illusory: 'If only I could believe, as I once did, in rebirth, in purer being,' he wrote in 1920. The disappointment of this ideal is a constant thread running through his correspondence in 1920–21:

> I no longer believe in transformation to a new humanity, to a new 'spirit'. Every transformation is a folding or unfolding. I understand more deeply than ever the tragic and merciful phrase of Pindar's: a man becomes what he is.[13]

Though he had lost faith in the power of socialism to transform mankind ('die erlösende Kraft des Sozialismus'), he continued to consider it 'the new, the necessary form of economic organization, a gigantic work'.[14]

As the emotional impact of revolution receded, Toller attempted to reappraise his political position in search of a more realistic basis for his convictions. He was concerned to integrate his own experience into an historical tradition. In the summer of 1920, he began an intensive study of the theory and history of socialism, 'because I recognize more and more clearly that politics requires more than "conviction", "basic attitude", "ethos", and that thorough and objective knowledge is necessary to master the laws of political action'.[15]

The Machine Wreckers

Toller's efforts to place his experience into an historical framework dictated the choice of historical subject-matter for his next play, written in the winter of 1920– 21.[16] Toller's 'drama from the time of the Luddite movement in England' is based loosely on events in Nottinghamshire in 1811–12, when the local framework-knitters broke up the new machinery which threatened their livelihood.

The realistic subject-matter is matched by a corresponding realism of style and structure. For the first time, Toller abandoned the formal devices of Expressionism – the dream scenes, the symbolic characters, the use of heightened language – in favour of a traditional five-act structure and plot. The setting is historically specific, the characters are identifiable individuals, the dialogue is largely naturalistic. Political reappraisal therefore went hand in hand with creative readjustment, though the process was a long and often difficult one. In contrast to *Masses and Man*, which he had written in one short creative outburst, the new play was the product of lengthy reflection, encompassing several months and at least five successive drafts.[17]

The play opens with a dramatic prologue depicting a debate in the House of Lords concerning a new bill to make machine-breaking punishable by death. Only Lord Byron speaks out against the bill. In the play, Jimmy Cobbett, a politically conscious itinerant workman, returns to his native Nottingham to find the weavers on strike against the introduction of new machinery by the factory-owner Ure. In Jimmy's absence, his brother Henry has worked his way up to become Ure's manager. Hearing that the weavers, led by John Wible, intend to destroy the Machine, Jimmy addresses them and persuades them that their enemy is not the Machine, but the economic system which exploits it. They must work for political change through the nationwide trade union which is now being formed. Jimmy's success antagonizes Wible, whom Henry Cobbett enlists in a plot to get rid of his brother. Wible's plan to destroy the machines is approved by Ure, since it will provide the pretext for more repressive action by the government. Ure employs women and children in the factory to break the strike. While Jimmy counsels negotiations with Ure in the short term, Wible calls for violent action and incites the men to break into the factory and destroy the Machine. Hearing of their intention, Jimmy hurries there to prevent their action. Wible reveals to the weavers that Jimmy is Henry's brother and incites them to kill him as a traitor. After the killing, Ned Lud realizes that Jimmy was right and that they have been misled into attacking the wrong enemy.

Toller had been interested in the Luddite revolt for some time before he actually began work on the play. It represented an extreme example of the conflict between man and machine which so fascinated the Expressionist generation and which is typified by Kaiser's *Gas* trilogy. Toller had himself broached the theme in both his earlier plays, but on this occasion he was interested in its broader historical relevance:

> Last winter I completed a dramatic portrayal, 'The Luddites'. The Luddite movement is one of the first great workers' movements known which plays a role in the history of socialism, also in Marx. A first flaring of the movement which later culminated in the Chartist rebellion.[18]

He was therefore interested in the Luddite revolt as an early example of concerted working-class action – that is, as an historical turning-point. It was a dialectical conception derived from his main historical sources – Marx's *Capital*, the German historian Max Beer's *Geschichte des Sozialismus in England* (*A History of British Socialism*) and Engels's *The Condition of the Working-Class in England*.[19] It was above all Engels's work which suggested the dialectical significance of his material and which also provided many of the details of living and working conditions used in the play.[20]

Toller consciously set out to write 'the drama of a social class'; in correspondence with the historian Gustav Mayer, he stressed that the real protagonist of his play was to be 'the weavers'. In his earlier plays he had portrayed the masses largely in accordance with the theatrical conventions of Expressionism. In *The Machine Wreckers* they emerge from collective anonymity into recognizable individuals. However, their response remains a collective one. They are depicted from a materialist point of view. Their situation is the result of a particular stage in industrial capitalism, in which changes in production have reduced them to the level of a dispensable commodity. Their consciousness is limited by their material environment: they regard the Machine itself as the cause of their misery, attributing almost supernatural powers to it, seeing it as a Moloch to which human beings are sacrificed. The material conditions which cause their desperate revolt therefore also doom it to failure.

Among the mass of weavers, the most important is Ned Lud. Based on the apocryphal figure whose name became synonymous with machine-breaking, he was to embody the dawning of revolutionary consciousness in the working class. Toller intended him to be a typical worker, not a leader: 'In my play too Ned Lud is not a leader. He has the countenance of an upright courageous worker who lacks any qualities of leadership or any knowledge of politics or economics.'[21] Lud's courage is evident in his willingness to keep the union funds, his honesty in his condemnation of the looting of a bakers' shop. He expresses the workers' dawning solidarity, but also their superstitious awe of the Machine. He is Jimmy's first convert among the weavers, but also strikes the first blow against him. He typifies the uncertainty and vacillation which is the product of the weavers' material deprivation. It is only in this material context that John Wible can reassert his influence over the weavers, inciting them to kill Cobbett.

Wible too is a product of his environment, crippled in childhood by a drunken father and trapped by a poverty he is determined to escape from. While he has qualities of leadership, he is also a demagogue, manipulating the weavers' blind fury for his own ends. He can articulate their primitive response to their predicament: 'A Moloch is at large in Nottingham. Destroy it. Or tomorrow it will multiply a thousand times' (p. 140). In fact, he has become their leader precisely because he knows and can express their feelings. He himself is aware of this – and confidently predicts that he understands his fellow-workers better than Cobbett does.

In the character of Jimmy Cobbett, Toller wished to prefigure the emergence of the politically-conscious industrial worker of the twentieth century. Though his political understanding is clearly ahead of his time, he can evoke what the workers dimly aspire to: 'He says what we all feel, what we all want,' Ned Lud declares. He convinces the weavers that it is not the Machine itself which oppresses them, but the system which exploits it, that 'if they control the machines, they can shape their own destiny'. Moreover, he defines the practical steps necessary to achieve that aim: organization and collective action in the (clandestine) union. However, Cobbett himself is clearly less a pragmatic organiser than a utopian idealist. Like Eisner, he seeks to enlighten the workers as to their real political situation in the belief that enlightenment will produce the will to revolution. He evokes a future socialist society in terms of a vision which is innate in every man:

> And yet there is a dream within you! A dream of a
> wondrous world ... a world of justice ... a world of

> communities united in labour ... of people united in
> labour ... Brothers ... join together ... begin, only
> begin ... not I and I and I. No: world and we and thou
> and I. If you *will* the community of all workers, you can
> achieve it (p. 143).

The extent of Toller's continuing ideological debt to Gustav Landauer is evident in this echo of his belief that socialism was always
possible if only enough people willed it. Toller was, however, concerned to re-evaluate the idealist legacy of Landauer and Eisner.
Cobbett's idealism is strongly relativized by the scepticism of the
beggar he befriends. The beggar calls Cobbett a dreamer, telling him
that he sees the workers through rose-coloured spectacles and
accurately predicting his eventual fate at their hands. He does not
dismiss the possibility of future victory, but calls on Cobbett to
recognize the human material he is working with. Cobbett's murder
by the weavers clearly contradicts his own idealism, but his death is
not ineffectual, for it serves to clarify Ned Lud's political understanding. Cobbett's ideas have been defeated, but Lud's last defiant
words make clear that present defeat is tempered by the promise of
future victory:

> Lock us up. We know what we have done and we shall
> atone for having killed him. But others will come after
> us, with greater knowledge, greater faith, greater
> courage than us. Your kingdom is crumbling, O rulers
> of England! (p. 189).

The Machine Wreckers has a number of obvious weaknesses, not
least that Jimmy Cobbett is ultimately unconvincing as an historical
character. Not only is his political consciousness markedly anachronistic (his critique of capitalist production, for example, belongs in
a twentieth-century framework) but his practical proposals are at
odds with his soaring idealism. He lapses too easily into the humanitarian rhetoric of Expressionism, so that the play often typifies Toller's tendency to preach. The critic Stefan Großmann suggested it
was not so much a drama as the collected speeches of Ernst Toller.[22]
   This weakness is compounded by the often uneasy marriage of
realism and symbolism, prose and verse, naturalistic and heightened
diction. The stylistic mixture itself indicates the position of *The
Machine Wreckers* as a work of transition, documenting Toller's

political and artistic development in 1920–21. At a personal level, it was an attempt to come to terms with his experience of revolution by means of historical distancing. At an ideological level, it was an attempt to integrate the idealist inheritance of Landauer and Eisner into a materialist framework of historical development: to follow in Eisner's footsteps in seeking to reconcile Kant and Marx. Despite its weaknesses, *The Machine Wreckers* remains a challenging and interesting play, containing scenes of great dramatic force.

It was these dramatic qualities which Karlheinz Martin was able to exploit in his much-acclaimed production at Max Reinhardt's Grosses Schauspielhaus, which opened on 30 June 1922. The Grosses Schauspielhaus, formerly the home of the Circus Schumann, had been converted and reopened by Reinhardt after the war to stage his experiments in 'mass production'. It had a huge auditorium seating five thousand and a large stage which Martin used to mount tumultuous crowd scenes. The young designer John Heartfield devised a set in which the gigantic machine dominated the stage, dwarfing the weavers and conveying something of the superstitious fear and awe in which they held it. The role of Cobbett was played by Wilhelm Dieterle, who would later make his mark as a film director in Hollywood. Also among the cast was Alexander Granach, who was later known for his close association with the director Erwin Piscator and would play the lead in the latter's production of Toller's *Hoppla*.

The opening night was marked by scenes extraordinary even by the standards of the Weimar theatre. The dramatic impact of the play was heightened by contemporary echoes which transcended its historical theme. Less than a week before the première, the Foreign Minister of the Republic, Walther Rathenau, the architect of the Rapallo Treaty with Russia, was assassinated by nationalist students. When Cobbett was murdered by the weavers during the final scene, many of the audience called out Rathenau's name. The novelist Alfred Döblin noted the politically charged atmosphere in the theatre and the child-like involvement of the audience in the action on stage. Cobbett's speeches were often interrupted by loud applause, while Ure's every appearance was greeted with catcalls. At the final curtain there was prolonged applause, until Karlheinz Martin finally appeared to address the audience, expressing the hope that the new wind blowing in Germany would soon set Toller free.[23] Less than a month later the Reich government, in response to the

Rathenau murder, declared a general amnesty for political prisoners, but the Bavarian government refused to implement it. As for Toller, he had already completed a new play, *Hinkemann*, the reception of which was to be even more explosive.

Hinkemann

Hinkemann, written in 1921–22, was probably Toller's most successful, and certainly his most controversial play.[24] It is also his bleakest, ending on a note of utter pessimism which is almost unbearable.

Hinkemann, cruelly emasculated in the war, has gained a new sensitivity to suffering. His mother-in-law's action in blinding a song-bird appals him, making him doubt if his wife Grete still loves him. His doubt and self-pity cause Grete to seek consolation with Grosshahn, a vulgar womaniser, to whom she confides the secret of Hinkemann's impotence. Desperate for work, Hinkemann finds a job as a fairground strongman, where he has to suck the blood of live rats to amuse a bloodthirsty and degenerate public. In a chance visit to the fair with Grosshahn, Grete sees Hinkemann performing and, shocked into realizing how much he loves her, breaks off her relationship with Grosshahn. Later, in a working-class bar, Hinkemann and other workers discuss their daily lives. Grosshahn arrives, still resentful of Grete's rejection, and betrays Hinkemann's secret to the other workers who burst out laughing. Hinkemann rushes out and collapses. In a nightmare vision, he sees the world for what it is – and sees he has no place in it. Although he ultimately forgives his wife, his belief in her love has been destroyed. His despair drives Grete to suicide and, as the curtain falls, we see Hinkemann preparing to hang himself.

The years 1921–22 were a time of spiritual crisis for Toller, as for many other left-wing intellectuals in Germany.[25] He was increasingly depressed by political developments. The defeat of the revolution was now beyond all doubt; extremism, unemployment and inflation were rife. Toller felt that factionalism had reduced the left to political impotence, being equally critical of the opportunism of the SPD and the ultra-left adventurism of the KPD. Moreover, political disillusionment was exacerbated by a serious decline in his health. He complained of violent headaches which frequently undermined his ability to work.

Toller completed the first draft of *Hinkemann* by October 1921, when he sent it to the Berlin Volksbühne,[26] began to revise the play early in 1922, and completed a final version by June. His prison letters vividly document his state of mind during these months. He was moving towards a tragic view of history, which he increasingly perceived as a recurrent cycle of revolt and repression:

> Read Beer's *General History of Socialism*. The same struggles repeated, the same ideas, the same clash between ideal and reality, the same heroism, the same blind alleys, the same confusion between the needs of the masses and those of the intellectuals . . . from revolution to reaction, from reaction to revolution, the same cycle. What for? Where to? I have a deep, deep homesickness and the home is called: Nothingness.[27]

In a subsequent letter to Beer himself, he confessed that reading the work had thrown him into 'a state of peculiar depression . . . it was weeks before I could shake off this feeling'.[28] It was certainly this 'peculiar depression' which informed *Hinkemann*, despite the strenuous efforts Toller would later make to qualify it.

The play was an attempt to realize the conception of 'proletarian art' which Toller had begun to formulate in 1920 and by 1921 had reduced to the rather generalized definition which accompanied the first published extract from *Hinkemann*:

> Proletarian art *leads* to humanity. It is all-embracing, like life, like death. Proletarian art exists only in so far as the diversity of the inner life of the proletariat offers the artist a way of shaping eternal human problems.[29]

At this stage, he called the play 'a proletarian tragedy', in which, as an explanatory note confirmed, his protagonist was to have representative significance:

> I dedicate this play to you, nameless proletarian, to you, nameless human hero, of whom no page of glory tells, no revolutionary or party history. Your name is to be found only in some police report in one corner of the newspaper, under the heading 'accidents and suicides'. Eugen Hinkemann stands symbolically for you.[30]

The tragedy of the individual was to stand for that of an entire social class. But the tragedy of Hinkemann was to have a further dimension:

> You have always suffered, in every society, in every country and, marked by a dark fate, you will still have to suffer, even when, in some brighter future, a socialist society has been established.

Hinkemann would therefore symbolize not only the suffering of the proletariat within the capitalist system, but the inevitable residue of suffering which no social system could ever alleviate. It was this idea which Toller would emphasize in all his later interpretations of the play; however, it must be said that Toller's original conception was partly vitiated in practice.

Hinkemann has a certain ambivalence of style, fusing elements of realism and Expressionism. For the first time, Toller chose a setting which was local and contemporary: the place is Germany, the time 'about 1921', the milieu proletarian. But the depiction was to be far from naturalistic, the stage directions requiring the working-class milieu to be 'suggested' ('angedeutet'), rather than depicted – using the word coined to describe Expressionist stage technique. Moreover, the central scene of the play is a long visionary interlude in the Expressionist manner.

The ambivalence of style is echoed in the dramatic treatment. Hinkemann is depicted both as the casualty of a socio-economic system – and as the victim of a cruel and incalculable Fate. In the early scenes, his predicament is very much the consequence of an economic system. He is doubly a victim of social oppression, first as a casualty of war – and therefore of the capitalist and militarist interests which unleashed it – but also as a casualty of post-war society, which denies him the right to work and individual dignity:

> I'm just a puppet, whose strings they've pulled and pulled until he's broken. The pension gives us too little to live on – and too much to die on (p. 198).

The difficulties in his relationship with Grete are compounded by the problems of unemployment. He takes his repulsive 'job' at the fairground, because he feels he has no alternative if he is to provide for her – and keep her love. He feels helpless, manipulated by forces beyond his control, as he blurts out to the Showman in accepting his offer: 'Oh, eighty marks . . . oh . . . the likes of me, the likes of me

... we turn about like a ... like a roundabout. Round and round! Round and round! I'll take the job, sir (p. 206).' His impotence is clearly not only physical but social.

If Hinkemann embodies the economic plight of the proletariat, the Showman represents unscrupulous capitalism, exploiting Hinkemann to satisfy the appetites of a degenerate public:

> People want to see blood. Blood! Despite two thousand years of Christian morality. My business takes that into account. So public interest is harmonized with self-interest (p. 205).

The fairground itself, with its lurid and sensational entertainment, is a symbol of post-war society. One aspect of that society is evoked in a visionary interlude which features a chorus of crippled soldiers, playing barrel-organs and singing military songs, conveying a striking image of the destructive legacy of war.

As the drama progresses, the emphasis shifts from the social to the psychological, from the material to the metaphysical. The centrepiece of the play is Hinkemann's discussion with a group of fellow-workers. The characters have names which encapsulate their attitudes: Unbeschwert (Unconcerned) is the dogmatic Marxist for whom the victory of socialism rests on inexorable scientific laws. He dismisses Hinkemann's doubt that socialism can bring everybody happiness: 'We shall create social conditions which are regulated by reason. In three words: a rational humanity – and a rational humanity produces happiness (p. 216).' Knatsch (Trouble) is an anarchist who rejects the Marxist dialectic in favour of the 'revolutionary will of the people'. Singegott (Praisegod) is a pious zealot, whose religion is a substitute for political commitment, while Immergleich (Indifferent) cares about nothing as long as he is left in peace. They argue about the present state of Germany, each stating his own remedy and remaining deaf to all others, their dogmatism and mutual intolerance representing a microcosm of the deep ideological divisions within the labour movement. Significantly, they are all equally insensitive to the implications of Hinkemann's plight. When Grosshahn arrives and callously reveals the secret of Hinkemann's impotence, they all laugh uproariously. Hinkemann rounds on them, bitterly denouncing their cruelty, embourgeoisement and intolerance:

> You fools! What do you know about the suffering of a poor miserable creature? How you'd have to change

before you could build a new world. You fight the
bourgeoisie and yet you are just as puffed up, just as self-
righteous, just as uncaring. Each of you hates the other
because he's in a different party and swears by a different programme. None of you trusts the next man,
none of you even trusts himself (p. 225).

This scene is the dramatic turning-point. Hinkemann's experience
has the force of revelation:

My eyes have been opened. Now I can see. Right to the
bottom. I see men as they are. I see the age we live in.
Sir, the war is back again. Men are murdering each other
and laughing. *Men are murdering each other and laughing*
(p. 228).

Hinkemann's revelation of social reality is enacted in his nightmare
(an Expressionist 'dream scene') in which he encounters a series of
figures evoking the corruption and cruelty of post-war Germany: a
prostitute and her pimp, an old woman who has found the new
Messiah, two Freikorps thugs who revel in their own brutality, a
street salesman peddling quack remedies for the ills of society.

The last act of the play acquires increasingly visionary overtones,
placing Hinkemann's plight in a metaphysical perspective. He
increasingly refers to his injury as an individual misfortune and
himself as the victim of an arbitrary and capricious Fate. He is
completely demoralized. He now sees that life is just a vicious struggle for survival, in which cruel and predatory human beings prey on
their fellows. (Grete pleads with her husband not to leave her alone
in 'a forest full of wild animals'.) Moreover, human cruelty is less a
consequence of social conditions than of human nature itself. Men
are driven by naked instincts which transcend the power of reason:
'Man's living nature is stronger than his reason. Reason is just a
means of self-delusion (p. 244).'

It is the implications of this realization which drive Hinkemann to
despair. He no longer has the strength to fight for his ideals, for he
no longer believes they are attainable. While socialism offers a
rational alternative to the reality he has seen, there is little hope of
achieving it: if men cannot change themselves, what hope have they
of changing society? He finds this conclusion utterly debilitating.

Having lost the strength to fight for his ideals, he no longer has the will to live:

> I don't have the strength to go on. The strength to struggle, the strength to dream. A man who has no strength to dream has lost the strength to live. All seeing becomes knowing, all knowing suffering ... I don't want to go on (p. 245).

The despair of this argument is echoed by Grete, who can see no escape for them: they are trapped in the toils of society like insects in a spider's web, a motif which Hinkemann echoes in his final monologue.

In a world in which human suffering is the inevitable corollary of human cruelty, the victims are chosen quite arbitrarily by an implacable Fate:

> Here I stand, gigantic and ridiculous. In every age there will be men like me. But why does it happen to me? Why me? It strikes at random. It strikes this man and that. It misses the next and the next. What do we know? Where from? Where to? Any day can bring paradise, any night disaster (p. 247).

In this context, there is no pattern or purpose in human history, only deep existential pessimism. The play ends in complete resignation, as Hinkemann prepares the noose with which he will hang himself.

Intellectually and dramatically, *Hinkemann* is totally flawed, but it remains a powerful play with some impressive theatrical moments. Psychologically, it is a record of spiritual crisis, revealing the deep pessimism which Toller had to fight against for the rest of his life and which finally overcame his commitment to a socialist future. Biographically, it is of considerable importance: begun in 1921, completed in 1922, published and first performed in 1923 and revised during the early months of 1924, it preoccupied Toller throughout the last three years of his imprisonment.

The deep pessimism of *Hinkemann* can scarcely have been mitigated by the first reactions to the play. He had submitted the first draft to the Volksbühne in October 1921. The Berlin Volksbühne had originally been founded in the eighteen nineties in order to make theatre accessible to the working class. In the early nineteen twenties, when some four hundred and fifty thousand workers were linked to it through subscription, it represented by far the biggest working-class audience available. Toller had originally hoped that Jürgen Fehling, who had produced *Masses and Man* for the Volksbühne, would also produce *Hinkemann*, but Friedrich Kayssler, the Volksbühne director, finally rejected the play altogether on the grounds that its theme of emasculation made it unsuitable for public performance.[31]

Toller was bitterly disillusioned by such puritanism: the organization he had once revered as 'the proper mediator for proletarian art'[32] seemed to have become a stronghold of artistic conservatism. He deplored the fact that the play would not be performed before the audience for which he had written it – the workers. He must have been all the more gratified when it was accepted by the Altes Theater, Leipzig, for production under the auspices of the Arbeiterbildungsinstitut (Workers' Educational Institute), one of the leading cultural organizations of the labour movement. *Hinkemann* was first produced in Leipzig on 19 September 1923 with great success. *Kulturwille*, the cultural journal of the Institute, described it as 'the outstanding theatre event of the year'.[33]

When the play was first published in 1923 under the title *Der deutsche Hinkemann*, it was widely interpreted as an allegory of Germany, in which the impotence of Hinkemann stood for that of a defeated nation. Rejecting this interpretation, Toller had shortened the original title to *Hinkemann* in order to prevent misunderstanding. The production of the play in Leipzig passed off without incident, but when it was produced in Dresden a few months later, the performance set off a riot.[34]

The production at the Staatstheater, Dresden, came at a time of extreme political tension. In the autumn of 1923, united front governments comprising a coalition of socialists and communists had come to power in Saxony and Thuringia. In Bavaria, the reactionary Kahr dictatorship had moved troops to the border to counter the threat which this development was claimed to represent. Since the central government had failed to assert its authority over these provincial administrations, Germany was once more threatened by separatism and civil war. On 29 October Reichswehr troops intervened to depose the united front government in Saxony. A few days later, in an atmosphere of mounting nationalist expectation, Hitler carried out his beer-hall putsch in Munich. In this context the performance of *Hinkemann* became the occasion of a political scandal out of all proportion to the supposed content of the play.

The production opened on 17 January 1924, the eve of the Anniversary of the Founding of the German Reich, an anniversary offering the pretext for demonstration against the hated Republic. In a well-planned campaign, Nazis and other nationalists bought some eight hundred tickets for the performance. The theatre was resounding to shouts and catcalls long before the curtain went up. Attempts by the director and the cast to calm the audience only succeeded in inciting it still further: to thunderous applause, the audience broke into the National Anthem and the patriotic 'Die Wacht am Rhein', followed by inflammatory speeches full of anti-semitic abuse and anti-Republican slogans. The police showed uncharacteristic restraint, contenting themselves with removing a few ring-leaders and taking their names and addresses before allowing them to return to their seats. The complaisance of the authorities was even more marked in the subsequent trial of seven nationalists for their part in the disturbances. The judge acquitted them, ruling that the play constituted an affront to their patriotic feelings and their personal honour, and that they had therefore acted in self-defence. It was a verdict which became notorious even by the standards of political justice of the Weimar Republic.[35]

The nationalist campaign against *Hinkemann*, in which Toller's name was once more the focal point of political differences within a fiercely divided Republic, was ominously successful, providing an example which the Nazis would follow in the final years of Weimar. *Hinkemann* was taken off in Dresden after the first performance in the face of threats to kill the producer and the actors. Productions planned in Jena and Delitzsch were cancelled after similar intimidation. The production in Vienna was made possible only through the policing of the performance by workers' militia. Such was the notoriety of the play that the planned Berlin production became the subject of discussion in government circles. Toller himself noted that 'high officials of the Ebert Republic are busy over the question of prohibiting the performance'.[36] In fact, Foreign Minister and former Reich Chancellor, Gustav Stresemann, rejected requests to intervene; the Prussian Ministry of the Interior sanctioned the performance which, it ruled, was 'a direct concern of the Republic'.[37] The production – at the Residenztheater – went ahead under heavy police protection. Toller's formal request to the Bavarian authorities to be allowed leave from prison to attend rehearsals was turned down on the grounds that 'the granting of leave for this purpose is incompatible with the due gravity of the execution of sentence'.[38]

The disillusionment and resignation of *Hinkemann* mark the lowest point of Toller's spiritual development in prison: a blind alley from which he could only turn back. In the months following the completion of the play, he made determined efforts to qualify his pessimism and reaffirm his commitment:

> What will Fate bring us in the next few years? Who can prophesy? Germany has lost its way . . . We are moving towards a period of chaos. It will not be 'pleasant and comfortable' to live in Europe in the next fifty years. We must not weary, we must stay watchful, be on guard and be ready.[39]

Wotan Unchained

Toller's change of heart is apparent in his resumption of literary work after several months of silence. His next work was the comedy *Wotan Unchained*, written early in 1923 and published the same year.[40] After the bleak pessimism of *Hinkemann*, it seems almost inconceivable that Toller should write a comedy, as even he conceded:

> At last, after a long, long interval, I can work again. A comedy is developing. I'd never have believed that I could write a comedy. You need to have seen the naive and the sophisticated, the foolish and the painful quixoteries of the human heart and to have acquired a grain of amused wisdom in the process – otherwise, writing a comedy is just a naive attempt at self-deception . . .[41]

The plot follows the career of Wilhelm Dietrich Wotan, a megalomaniac barber who is disillusioned with post-war Germany and dreams up a scheme to save the nation by founding a colony in Brazil. By a shrewd mixture of demagogy and deception, he gains the support of bankers, army officers and aristocrats, and even succeeds in winning the acclaim of the masses. When his scheme is exposed as a fraud, he is arrested, but assured by the authorities that he will be treated leniently.

Toller certainly intended the play as a contemporary satire of resurgent nationalism and anti-semitism. He felt that in *Hinkemann* he had prophesied the fate which had now befallen Germany: '*Wotan*, on the other hand, is intended to help us find a way out of this frenzy of stupidity.'[42] He expressed his disappointment that the play was not to be performed immediately. The new play was therefore an attempt to influence social reality positively: to use satire to undermine the baleful popular attraction of 'völkisch' nationalism by exposing its psychological roots.

Wotan himself personifies this rabid nationalism. He is made in the image of the Teutonic deity, as we see in a prologue which crudely parodies the revival of Teutonic mythology. He is disillusioned with a post-war Germany which has 'deprived the officer of his right to war, the shareholder of his dividends in gold, the official of his titles and medals, the nobility of their ministerial posts' (p. 261). His resentment is explicitly anti-semitic, echoing the 'völkisch' myth of the Jewish conspiracy of world domination: 'The Jews are behind it all! The three hundred elders of Zion! They'll plate their crooked noses with gold. They'll drag blue-eyed womanhood into their filthy bed (p. 260).' He also typifies nationalist resentment of the hated Republic, whose leaders have led Germany into 'chaos and confusion'. He attacks France as the traditional enemy and rails against the 'Dolchstoss' (stab in the back).

Many of these features are the common currency of nationalist ideology in Germany, but other aspects of Wotan show an uncanny similarity to the early career of Adolf Hitler, and it is interesting to note that the play was actually written even before Hitler's beer-hall putsch had made him a national figure. Wotan is a demagogue: it is no chance that he is by trade a barber or 'Schaumschläger' (latherer) – in German slang a 'hot-air merchant'. He chooses Bavaria as his base of operations: in the early twenties, the province had become a haven for various reactionary groups, including the Nazis. Wotan is not only anti-semitic, but specifically denounces Jewish finance capital, using the Nazi watchword of 'Zinsknechtschaft' (interest slavery). Significantly, he reserves his greatest hatred for the 'Red shame'.

Wotan is the little man who suffers from delusions of grandeur. He considers himself an artist, whose genius is unrecognized: he is proud of his ability to draw and complains that his poems have been pirated, his inventions deliberately suppressed. Toller portrays him as a pseudo-Messiah ('dictator and Jesus in one person'). He announces that he will lead his followers into times of greatness. It is not the Marxists, but he who is destined to redeem Europe. When he is arrested, he declares that world history will be his judge and announces that, while in prison, he will write his memoirs. (The play closes on this ominously prophetic note.)

The policeman who arrests Wotan assures him that he has nothing to fear from the law, in two or three days he will be free again. This assurance had a contemporary parallel in the courts' lenient treatment of Hitler, who in September 1921 had led his followers in violently breaking up a meeting of the federalist Bayernbund (Bavarian League) in Munich, had been charged with affray and sentenced to three months in prison – a sentence suspended on appeal.[43] So strong are the analogies with Hitler that it is disconcerting to find that Toller's play was actually inspired by one of his fellow-prisoners who had turned to 'völkisch' nationalism.[44]

It is greatly to Toller's credit that he could acknowledge the appeal of Nazism. In *Wotan* he went beyond the satire of political messianism to suggest the social ground in which Nazism would flourish. Wotan's followers are typical of the social classes which espoused extreme nationalism and ultimately supported Hitler: the retired officer, the reactionary banker, the déclassé aristocrat, the representatives of petty officialdom. Significantly, however, Wotan also succeeds in winning the acclaim of the masses. 'Reaction and petty bourgeoisie are now calling with equal fervour for a dictatorship: they mean a dictator with unlimited powers. These calls reflect a social mood which is frightening, because it has also taken hold of the masses.'[45] He acknowledged that in an economic climate which fostered despair, the discipline instilled in school and barracks left the masses an easy prey to unscrupulous demagogy. *Wotan Unchained* is pessimistic in its portrayal of the ease with which the masses fall under the sway of a political charlatan. The only positive note is struck by a young worker who rejects Wotan's mission to save Europe: 'What does *your* Europe matter? Every burial ground becomes fallow land – and fallow land needs the ploughman.' Toller dedicated the play to 'the ploughmen' who symbolize his faith in the future.

Some contemporary critics found Toller's satire on nationalist megalomania too light-hearted, but the play opens with an explicit warning:

> Oh, public, laugh not too soon. Once you laughed too
> late and paid for your blindness with your living bodies.
> Laugh not too soon, but laugh at the right time (p. 254).

Thematically, therefore, the play anticipates Toller's later warnings against the dangers of fascism, showing that, as early as 1923, he had recognized the social and psychological ground which nurtured it. It is perhaps not surprising that the play failed to find favour in Germany. It was not indeed first performed in Germany at all: its première took place in Moscow in 1924; it was first performed in German in Prague in 1925 and was not finally produced in Germany until 1926, almost three years after it had been written. Toller himself was convinced that the nationalist campaign of intimidation against *Hinkemann* had deterred theatre managements from producing *Wotan*. Nazi groups had threatened demonstrations against the play when it was produced in Prague, though it was only when the play was finally produced in Berlin in 1926 that the reference to National Socialism was made explicit. It was here that Toller's 'Schaumschläger' was first made up to look like Adolf Hitler and here too that Toller changed the ending to comment on the new tactics of the Nazis, who had abandoned putschism in favour of the electoral road to power.[46]

The Swallow Book

Despite the interest of its theme, *Wotan* is a minor play. Toller's major work during 1923 was the lyric cycle *Das Schwalbenbuch* (*The Swallow Book*),[47] which was translated into virtually every major language, carrying his name around the world. The cycle was inspired by the swallows which nested in Toller's cell in the summer of 1922. In a series of free verse poems, he records the feelings prompted by his contemplation of the birds, from misery and despair to wonder and elation, and finally to stoical acceptance and renewed commitment. In the opening poem, Toller is plunged into spiritual crisis by the death of a friend: his fellow-prisoner August Hagemeister had died in Niederschönenfeld in January 1923 through lack of proper medical attention.[48] His death emphasizes the monotony and isolation of imprisonment. Even the intellectual freedom which has kept the poet's integrity is threatened, as imprisonment becomes more and more a state of mind:

> And wherever you look
> Everywhere
> Everywhere you see iron bars.
> Even the child playing in the distant, oh, so distant
>   field, blooming with lupins
> Is forced within the bars that divide your eyes
>   (pp. 325– 6).

Sinking into introspection, the poet is even driven to contemplate suicide. He is summoned back to life by the song of the swallows, a token of the coming spring and hence of the renewal and regeneration which are both the cause and the object of revolution. The swallows symbolize freedom in an environment of repression. The poet feels that imprisonment is not merely a personal misfortune but a symptom of the social condition – he is 'a prisoner incarcerated by prisoners'. The shrill pleasures of a dissolute society cannot hide Man's spiritual poverty:

> All your noise, your shrieks, your croaks
> Your show of pleasure, your How-happy-we-are
> Hahaha
> Cannot drown the faint gnawing
> Of the three secret rats
> Emptiness . . . Fear . . . Loneliness (pp. 337–8).

This desolate view of contemporary society is mitigated by faith in human will to change it; the following poem celebrates the revolutionary vision of youth:

> Already I behold you,
> Youth transformed in revolution.
> Your deed: begetting.
> Your calm: conception.
> Your festival: birth (p. 338).

Hinkemann's debilitating recognition that men could be different, but will not be, is reversed in this evocation of what men could be – and will become. The celebration of youth as the crucial force in social change is a recurring theme in Toller's work. In execution, the poem is a good example of Toller's public manner: idealist in conception, abstract and symbolic in language. Its evocation of social change is rhetorical, failing to suggest how youth can transcend the spiritual poverty evoked in the previous poem. To demonstrate the power of solidarity, Toller is forced to resort to the analogy of the swallows who, in a model of collective action, join forces to harry a sparrow-hawk into dropping its prey.

There follow several poems recording the poet's observation of the swallows, ending with their departure at the onset of winter:

> The swallows gather
> For their winter flight.
> My heart gathers itself
> For winter stillness (p. 349).

But the poet has learnt, through the swallows, a stoic acceptance of what is, and a renewed commitment to the revolution that will be. The keynote of the lyric cycle is therefore pessimism, qualified by faith in the future.

The Swallow Book became the object of a long and bitter dispute between Toller and the prison authorities. Some parts of the cycle, notably the poem inspired by the death of Hagemeister and that celebrating revolutionary youth, were considered by the prison censor to contain

> so many provocative passages that the total effect is agitational . . . In accordance with Section 22 of the prison regulations, *The Swallow Book* has been confiscated, since it contains much which, if published, would be detrimental to prison discipline.[49]

Consequently, the book was not published until 1924 and only reached the publisher at all after being smuggled out of Niederschönenfeld on the person of a prisoner who was being released.

Toller himself was moved from his east-facing cell to one which faced north and which swallows would not frequent. The following April, the birds returned to build their nest in his former cell, but the prison authorities, angered by the publication of *The Swallow Book*, ordered the nest to be destroyed. The swallows built their nest again – and again it was destroyed. The new occupant of Toller's cell pleaded that the swallows should be left in peace, but the prison governor was adamant: 'Swallows should build their nests in the stable. There's room enough there.' The birds then began to build simultaneously in several cells, but their nests were all discovered and destroyed, until finally the swallows gave up. 'The struggle lasted seven weeks, a heroic and famous struggle of Bavarian guardians of the law against the spirit of animal rebellion.'[50]

The Swallow Book is Toller's most celebrated lyric cycle – and also his last. In the years 1924– 33, there is not a single recorded example of Toller's poetry, as though his lyrical impulse had virtually dried up. There are only two isolated examples of his verse during his years of exile.

Mass Spectacles

Among the most interesting – and the least known – of Toller's works in prison were the 'Massenspiele' (mass spectacles) which were devised for performance at the annual Trade Union Festival in Leipzig. The Festival, organized by the Arbeiterbildungsinstitut (Workers' Educational Institute), in collaboration with the trade unions, staged the first mass spectacle in Germany in 1920, when *Spartakus*, a portrayal of the revolt of the Roman slaves, was performed by a cast of nine hundred workers to an audience of fifty thousand.

The mass spectacles were among the most ambitious attempts to create new proletarian art forms. Inspired by the early dramatic experiments in Soviet Russia, they enacted significant episodes in working-class history. They were devised for active collaboration rather than passive consumption, requiring a cast of several hundreds. They were intended to celebrate the socialist heritage, uniting actors and audience in the experience they shared through the common denominator of their class. The Workers' Educational Institute, then dominated by the USPD, three times commissioned Toller to write scenarios for its festivals, which were performed in Leipzig in successive years.[51]

In August 1922 Toller's scenario *Bilder aus der großen französischen Revolution* (*Scenes from the Great French Revolution*) was performed by a cast of three thousand workers under the direction of Alwin Kronacher, who later produced *Hinkemann* in Leipzig. The mass spectacle was, by all accounts, an impressive event; the *Leipziger Volkszeitung* called it 'full of power and life' and concluded that it had been a great success, 'leaving behind a great and uplifting impression'.[52] Toller's scenario covered the years 1789–92, ending with the formal constitution of the Republic. Contrary to historical fact, it portrayed the revolution as a working-class revolt which had culminated in a bourgeois republic: the analogy to the Weimar Republic was unmistakable.

The following year saw the performance of a new scenario by Toller called *Krieg und Frieden* (*War and Peace*). Among the audience of twenty thousand was the English playwright Ashley Dukes, who had brought *The Machine Wreckers* to the London stage earlier that year. The performance was held after dark, illuminated by searchlights:

> The terraced stage was set for the various 'properties' required for the play – such as the outlines of the trenches and barbed wire, national flags and emblems, and huge cardboard figures representing newspapers, through whose mouths megaphones spoke to the crowd. The moving searchlights illuminated scene after scene, showing companies of soldiers in their national uniforms marching to war, rows of priests and statesmen supporting the civilian morale by their nationalist propaganda, the megaphonic press, the speculative bourse, the appearance of young rebels in the armament factories, pacifist risings quelled by the machine-guns of the troops, and finally the fraternization of armies on the field of battle.[53]

Dukes reported that the audience sat enthralled by Toller's dramatic portrayal of their own collective experience. His companion was equally impressed: 'Only a man in a million can dare to be so simple,' he remarked.

The last of Toller's three mass spectacles, *Erwachen* (*Awakening*), an allegorical enactment of the World War, was staged in 1924, being performed by a cast of over a thousand workers. Played on a lake, it portrayed rival great powers fighting for possession of an island – until the crews of the opposing ships revolt, fraternize and erect the Palace of Peace. The spectacle in fact consisted of a dramatic text, written by the director, Adolf Winds, 'based on an outline by Toller'. It seems likely that the subject-matter was prescribed for Toller, since the spectacle was performed as part of a peace rally to mark the tenth anniversary of the outbreak of war. Contemporary reports suggest that it was not a success. There were severe acoustic problems which made much of the dialogue inaudible; there was also criticism of the allegorical treatment of the theme, suggesting that Toller had failed to keep pace with the new realism in the theatre.[54]

Awakening was the last mass spectacle to be performed in Leipzig. They were discontinued after 1924 as the Workers' Educational Institute fell under the political influence of the SPD, which had little interest in such cultural experiments. The mass spectacles have been virtually forgotten, but they remain an important milestone in working-class theatre. For Toller, they were part of the search for an appropriate form of 'collective drama' which he would pursue until the end of the decade.

The Swallow Book was the last work Toller completed in Niederschönenfeld. Early in 1924, he began once more to revise *Hinkemann*, responding to left-wing criticism that the play was defeatist. He was angered by the suggestion that he had abandoned his political commitment: 'as if anyone who senses the tragic limitations of possible happiness through social revolution is therefore any the less determined to fight for the transformation of social disorder.'[55]

He had his own reservations about *Hinkemann* which are symptomatic of the final stage of his political development in prison. In retrospect, he was aware that the play offered no political solutions and confessed that he had even wondered if he should allow it to be performed.[56] He conceded that when he had written the play, he had grasped the theme intuitively, not intellectually.[57] At a rational level, he knew that he could only face up to reality and carry on the struggle 'nonetheless':

> To be able to live without idols, that's one of the decisive things. Idols are the fictions which are supposed to be 'necessary to life'. To be as devout as those who believe in idols and yet not to need any. None at all. Nonetheless to want, nonetheless to act. Whoever can do that is free.[58]

This attitude of commitment without illusions, which runs through the last year of his prison letters, remained typical of him in the years after 1924. It was an attitude which he increasingly wished to illustrate in *Hinkemann* and he now made various revisions for a new edition of the play to be published later that year, inserting new text intended to suggest a positive alternative to Hinkemann's despair and, most important, deleting the stage direction in which Hinke-mann prepares to hang himself.

The revisions to *Hinkemann* close the cycle of Toller's prison plays, a cycle which mirrors his ideological and personal develop-ment, representing a dramatic counterpart to the more prosaic state-ment of his prison letters. Toller's plays not only reflected his development but determined it, their success helping to create the legend which he would never fully escape. By July 1924 his plays had already been translated into the main European languages and been performed around the world.[59] Meyerhold had staged *The Machine Wreckers* and *Masses and Man* in Moscow in 1922–23; the Stage Society had produced the same two plays in London in 1923–24. New York, too, had seen *Masses and Man* in a production by the experimental Theatre Guild, and *Hinkemann* in a version by the Yiddish Art Theatre Group. The latter play had also been staged for textile workers in Leningrad. Before he left prison, Toller had been invited to New York and London and had corresponded with Henri Barbusse about a French translation of his work. He had become a left-wing celebrity whose reputation would now precede him wherever he went.

IX Public Figure and Political Playwright: Toller in the Weimar Republic

1924–1930

When Ernst Toller began his prison sentence in July 1919, he was merely a promising young writer who had strayed into politics. By the time of his release five years later he had become the most famous German dramatist of his generation, whose plays had already been performed in the major theatre capitals of the world. Toller's years of freedom in the Weimar Republic marked the zenith of his fame and fortune in Germany, yet they have received less attention than virtually any other period of his life. There is no comprehensive biographical account of these years, perhaps because the available evidence is scattered and fragmentary, nor is there any cohesive evaluation of his literary work which, despite isolated attempts to salvage individual plays, has been largely neglected. The reasons for this omission lie in the common assumption that, after 1924, Toller's political commitment weakened and his creative powers dried up.[1] There is actually abundant proof to the contrary: his biography in these eight and a half years is the record of a notable contribution to the political and intellectual life of the Republic.

Emerging from prison, Toller had found himself almost embarrassingly famous and not the least of his problems was learning to live with his own fame. He threw himself back into life with a vigour which sought to compensate for the deprivations of imprisonment. He was in almost constant demand for lectures and readings and in the following years made numerous lecture tours in Germany and abroad, which helped to establish the restless pattern of his subsequent life.

Political commitments also claimed much of his time. He campaigned actively for a variety of political causes, his dominant concerns being with questions of political justice and civil liberties, colonial freedom and cultural politics. Though he did not rejoin a political party after leaving the USPD, he did not withdraw completely from organized political activity. He was a leading member of the Liga für Menschenrechte (League for Human Rights), and joined the Gruppe Revolutionärer Pazifisten (Group of Revolutionary Pacifists). He became a familiar figure at international meetings and conferences, addressing the Anti-Imperialist Congress in Brussels in 1927, the Congress of the World League for Sexual Reform in Vienna in 1930, the International PEN Congresses in Warsaw (1930) and Budapest (1932), and the Amsterdam Peace Conference of 1932 at which the 'League against War and Fascism' was formed.

While these activities often distracted him from purely literary work, Toller's creative output during these years was remarkable in both quantity and variety. He wrote no less than five plays: *Hoppla, Such is Life!* (1927), *Bourgeois bleibt Bourgeois* (*Once a Bourgeois always a Bourgeois*) (1928), written in collaboration with Walter Hasenclever, *Feuer aus den Kesseln* (*Draw the Fires*) (1928–30), *Wunder in Amerika* (*Miracle in America*), written with Hermann Kesten in 1930–31, and *Die blinde Göttin* (*The Blind Goddess*) (1931–32). He also completed two radio plays and two volumes of documentary prose, as well as stories, articles, essays, reviews and travel sketches. While some of this work is the small change of literary output, his two best plays of the period represent major contributions to the theatre of the nineteen twenties, effectively disproving the notion of creative decline. Certainly, none of his plays enjoyed either the critical acclaim or the box-office success of his earlier work. When *Hoppla* was produced in Berlin by Erwin Piscator, it was the production rather than the play which was the centre of interest. *Once a Bourgeois always a Bourgeois*, eagerly anticipated as one of the theatre events of 1929, proved to be a complete flop. *Draw the Fires*, though applauded by the critics, found little favour with the public.

Toller's problems derived in part from the inflated expectations created by the sensational success of his prison plays. It was a problem which has been summed up by his friend and publisher Fritz Landshoff: 'As long as he was in prison, he kept the whole of Germany in suspense. Once released, he was robbed of his martyr's crown and subjected to the most rigorous criticism, both as a man and as an artist.'[2] Toller's premonition of the problems awaiting him is evident in the letters her wrote during his last few months in prison. 'I don't want to let myself be acclaimed at festivals and conferences, just because I was in prison,' he wrote to Theodor Lessing.[3] In fact, he found it impossible to escape his own public persona: in the first few months after his release from prison, he was rarely out of the public eye. A brief account of his life during these months serves to indicate both the extent of his fame and the tremendous demands which it made on his time and energy.

Immediately after his release, and expulsion from Bavaria, Toller had travelled on to Leipzig to attend rehearsals for his mass pageant *Erwachen (Awakening)*, where 'he was received enthusiastically by the cast'.[4] He then continued his journey to Berlin, where – still only three days after his release – he appeared before the Legal Committee of the Reichstag to testify on conditions in Niederschönenfeld. In fact, he was able to address only the Social Democrat and Communist deputies of the Committee, the others – in a decision which foreshadowed the later theatre 'boycott' of Toller's work – having refused to hear him. (The only exception was a young Liberal deputy, Theodor Heuss, who was to become the first President of the post-war Federal Republic.)

On the evening of the same day, Toller attended a performance of *Hinkemann* at the Residenztheater, the first time he had actually seen one of his own plays performed. His appearance turned the occasion into a media event, as the normally sober *Vossische Zeitung* reported: 'Photographers, artists, journalists, autograph hunters gave him no peace. After the curtain had fallen, he was forced by the cast into the glare of the spotlight and held shoulder high.'[5] This ecstatic reception was repeated almost everywhere he went in the following weeks. A fortnight later he was guest of honour at the Arbeiterkulturwoche (Workers' Cultural Week) in Leipzig, where the week-long celebrations, attended by over a hundred thousand people, became almost a personal celebration of Ernst Toller. On Sunday 3 August, there was a performance of *The Transformation* in the morning; in the afternoon Toller addressed a mass meeting to commemorate the tenth anniversary of the outbreak of war, while in the evening his mass pageant *Awakening* was performed by a cast of several hundred workers.

Toller's speech to commemorate the war dead had an astonishing impact, moving many of his audience to tears. His rhetorical force and burning sincerity were recorded by the dramatist Günther

Weisenborn, then a young medical student, who witnessed the event from the window of a first-aid station:

> I see him framed in the open window, raised above the masses under lowering clouds of a rainy evening sky: slim, dark and cool. He speaks clearly, still controlled, with quiet outrage, with a nervous elegance which vibrates through all his movements. And then he suddenly bursts forth, hurling a raging denunciation of war and all its works at the cloudy sky over Leipzig, across the massed grey sea of faces of Saxon workers.
>
> This is the will of the masses made word, the grievances of the Leipzig industrial coolie hardened into accusation, this is an event! Ernst Toller transforms the old unspoken yearnings of the workers into words, and in the heat of his tongue the words become a springboard for the rage of the exploited. He stands there in the park, like fire in the trees – young, dark-haired, electric, almost stuttering with emotion, the epitome of the Expressionist . . . He is shaken by flaming hatred, of war and the war-mongers. He is in tears, he is moved and his emotion moves the masses. They know this is no mere Paganini of rhetoric . . . this is Ernst Toller.[6]

Toller's appearance in Leipzig had almost been prevented by one of those bizarre but sinister incidents which were so typical of the justice of the Weimar Republic. On 31 July, at seven o'clock in the morning, he was arrested by the police on the basis of the warrant issued in 1919. The Leipzig Chief of Police was quick to cancel this 'mistake', ordering his release the same day.

After the acclaim of Leipzig, Toller travelled to Switzerland, staying with Emil Ludwig in Ascona. Returning to Germany, he held discussions in Berlin with the Volksbühne, which agreed to produce *The Transformation*. Before the end of the month, he was in Frankfurt for rehearsals of a new production of *Hinkemann*, which opened on 1 September. A few days later, he attended a special matinée given in his honour at the Berlin Volksbühne. Such occasions proliferated. On 5 October there was the first of a series of 'proletarische Feierstunden' (workers' evenings) held at the huge Großes Schauspielhaus in Berlin, which consisted of recitations from Toller's poems and performances of his choral works.

Toller's triumphal progress continued well into 1925. In January he gave readings from his work in the concert hall of the Berlin Philharmonic, reading poems from his collection *Vormorgen* and *The Swallow Book*, and extracts from *The Transformation* and *Masses and Man*. The critic Alfred Kerr reported: 'His clear tenor voice carries all round the packed Philharmonic. Occasionally he drops into the intonation of the preacher. Thousands of young people acclaim him frantically.'[7] Toller's audiences were often predominantly young people, to whose idealism he obviously appealed. Such occasions certainly gave full rein to his strong theatrical talent. As he wrote to an American sponsor in 1929: 'I can say without any false modesty that my dramatic reading of my own work is at least as good as that of any professional actor.'[8] This triumphant celebration of Toller as a revolutionary dramatist evoked a hostile response from his political enemies. A lecture tour arranged for 1925 had to be cancelled in the face of an orchestrated campaign of obstruction. In Stettin it proved impossible to hire a suitable hall, while local papers refused to accept advertisements for the event. In Halle ticket agencies were threatened with a mass boycott by nationalist circles. The critic Alfred Kerr hoped that this unofficial ban would encourage similar action from the left: 'Morally, we have long been in a state of civil war.'[9]

It was not only the political right which felt provoked by these demonstrations of enthusiasm for Toller. His reputation as 'the poet of the working class' had aroused the hostility of the KPD, which sought to undermine his standing by attacking his revolutionary credentials. The communist poet J.R. Becher made a savage attack on him as a 'pseudo-revolutionary' whose work served only to assuage the bourgeois conscience. Such attacks, which were to continue throughout the decade, were an implicit acknowledgement of Toller's reputation. The production of *Hoppla, Such is Life!* in Berlin in 1927 was the subject of no less than nine reviews in successive editions of the KPD's paper *Rote Fahne*.[10]

Toller's release from prison coincided with the beginning of a period of apparent stability in the history of the Weimar Republic. The campaign of passive resistance to the French occupation of the Ruhr had been abandoned; in February 1924, the state of emergency had been lifted. The government of Gustav Stresemann had succeeded in ending the nightmare of inflation by stabilizing the currency. In September 1924 the Reichstag finally accepted the Dawes

Plan, under which an international loan would enable Germany to pay adequate reparations and at the same time make the country attractive to foreign (mainly American) investment. Ahead lay a period of relative stability and prosperity which was to end with the world economic crisis in 1929.

It has often been suggested that Toller was unable to come to terms with the political changes which had taken place during his five-year imprisonment; in fact he was able, despite some initial difficulty, to reintegrate himself into the political life of the Republic. The political position which he adopted during these years, that of an independent socialist advocating a broad left front, was essentially one he had defined before leaving prison. Having decided not to re-enter party politics, he turned to campaigning for particular causes, seeking to promote them through public speaking and political journalism. He campaigned tirelessly on behalf of political prisoners – both his comrades in Niederschönenfeld and others whom he considered to be the victims of political justice. He was also involved in various campaigns against censorship, an issue which increasingly became the touchstone of political repression in the Weimar Republic. He was prominent in the controversy within the Volksbühne in 1926–27 as to the proper role for a People's Theatre, and became a member of the unofficial Committee of Inquiry into the May Day massacres in Berlin in 1929 (see page 148 below). These activities alone would suffice to document Toller's continuing political commitment; they also demonstrate the realism of his judgement and the practical nature of the causes he espoused.

These political commitments were anything but marginal, for they were consistently echoed in Toller's literary work – and often took precedence over it. Interviewed on the day after his release from prison, Toller affirmed that he had no immediate literary plans, being totally preoccupied with the need of the moment – an amnesty for political prisoners.[11] Two days later he testified to the Legal Committee of the Reichstag. His testimony formed the basis for a series of short articles which he published as part of the general campaign for an amnesty, appearing between October 1924 and January 1925 in the political weekly *Die Weltbühne* under the general title 'Dokumente bayerischer Justiz' ('Documents of Bavarian Justice').[12] These pieces formed the backbone of his book *Justiz. Erlebnisse (Experiences of Justice)*, which was published in 1927, helping to prepare the ground for an eventual amnesty the following year.[13]

The book was originally announced for publication early in 1926 under the title *XX. Jahrhundert. Dokumente bayerischer Justiz (20th Century. Documents of Bavarian Justice)*.[14] Toller had certainly completed the manuscript by January 1926, when he sent a copy to Maximilian Harden. By February it was already with the printers, though Toller's correspondence reveals that, even at this late stage, he intended to revise it by inserting a new chapter.[15] Why the book was not published at that time is uncertain, but it did not finally appear until May 1927. The most likely reason for this long delay is that Toller himself felt dissatisfied with the work, apparently feeling that he was still too involved in the events it recorded. Certainly, when he began to revise it early in 1927, the journalist Ernst Feder noted: 'His justice book still not out; only now does he have the necessary distance from the events in prison.[16] The book is in fact admirably detached in tone: an early and striking example of the trend towards documentary literature which emerged in Germany in the last half of the decade.

Toller's original title confirms that he did not intend to give a subjective account of his experience, but an objective documentation of the treatment of (left-wing) political prisoners in Bavaria. 'Every chapter,' he wrote in the introduction, 'illuminates in an exemplary way the spirit of Bavarian justice and, beyond that, the spirit of class justice.' He knew, moreover, that 'legal conditions cannot be seen in isolation, for they too are manifestations of the power of those who rule, symptoms of something more fundamental, something intrinsic to our time'. That is, class justice was the product of a class society.

Toller exemplified his theme of 'class justice' in the crude manipulation of the law to justify the death sentence passed on Eugen Leviné, in the spurious grounds for the charges of high treason brought against himself and others, in the abrupt and arbitrary changes to the regulations for fortress prisoners, in the death by neglect of August Hagemeister (USPD Minister of Welfare in the Bavarian Soviet Republic), in the politically-motivated refusal of the Bavarian government to apply successive Reich amnesties to left-wing prisoners, and not least in his own 'unlawful' expulsion from Bavaria. The specific focus of the book limits its appeal to the modern reader and it has been reprinted only once in post-war

Germany, but there is one section of undoubted interest in which Toller compares the harsh treatment of left-wing prisoners with the leniency shown to their right-wing counterparts. In a chapter ironically entitled 'Gleiches Recht' ('Equality before the Law'), Toller contrasted the indulgence of the court towards Adolf Hitler at the time of the Munich beer-hall putsch with the treatment of a young communist, Lorenz Popp, whom Toller had known in prison. In highlighting the case of Hitler, released on parole after serving only nine months of his sentence, Toller demonstrated the sympathy of police and judiciary with the future Führer: justice was truly a microcosm of the political spirit of the times.

Toller's considerable achievement in *Justice* was acknowledged by perceptive critics. Thomas Mann confessed that it had made 'a terrifying impression' on him, concluding that it would greatly increase the numbers supporting the case for an amnesty. Kurt Tucholsky praised the book's dispassionate tone: 'Toller has almost entirely avoided emotionalism in favour of a conspicuous detachment – he recounts. He gives us facts.'[17] Though written to achieve a short-term political aim, *Justice* has a notable place in Toller's literary development, anticipating the documentary trend apparent in his later work, from the historical drama *Draw the Fires* and the radio play *Berlin – letzte Ausgabe! (Berlin – last edition!)*, to the autobiographical works he published in exile.

Toller's active concern with political justice is also apparent in his campaign on behalf of the imprisoned revolutionary leader Max Hölz, a legendary figure who had won fame as the commander of a Red Army in the Vogtland border area between Saxony and Thuringia. Hölz had later taken part in the communist uprising in the Mansfeld area in March 1921, where he had finally been arrested. He had been sentenced to life imprisonment for the murder of a landowner in the Vogtland, though he had always protested his innocence. A campaign to have Hölz released was launched after a certain Erich Friehe confessed to the murder of which Hölz had been convicted. Toller played a prominent part in the campaign, visiting Friehe in Halle and publishing a polemical article demanding Hölz's release. He spoke on his behalf at mass rallies, published further articles in Germany and abroad and was particularly active in raising money to enable Hölz to have his case reopened.[18]

Toller's involvement in the campaign also took on an intensely personal note. He began a correspondence which reveals a growing warmth and regard between the two men. Hölz's letters pay frequent tribute to Toller's commitment and tenacity: 'I wish my own party comrades had made half the effort you have to get my case reopened.' Their mutual regard turned to friendship as a result of Toller's visits to Hölz in the isolated prison of Sonnenburg, near Küstrin (now Kostrzyn). After the first of these visits, Hölz wrote warmly of his delight that 'Toller the man corresponds to the picture of him that we workers have formed from his plays'.[19] Hölz was finally released under the general amnesty for political prisoners in 1928: he was to die in mysterious circumstances in the Soviet Union in 1933. Toller's campaign illustrates two typical aspects of his political work in the nineteen twenties: the mixture of public speaking and writing in pursuit of a concrete short-term objective, and the strongly personal dimension of his commitment. His evident rapport with Max Hölz naturally owed much to the common experience of imprisonment. He told Jawaharlal Nehru that he felt there was an unspoken bond between them: 'I often think the people who have been in prison form an invisible brotherhood based on suffering and on the greater imagination of heart which prison develops.'[20] He certainly continued to campaign for political prisoners even after the amnesty of 1928. During his visit to the USA in 1929, he took up the case of Tom Mooney and other socialists imprisoned in San Quentin, writing and speaking on their behalf.

Toller campaigned for a variety of political causes in these years, not least the cause of colonial freedom. In July 1926, he joined the Liga gegen koloniale Unterdrückung (League against Colonial Repression), a broad left organization created by the communist publisher Willi Münzenberg. In February 1927, at the instigation of the Communist International, Münzenberg organized an Anti-Imperialist Congress in Brussels, which was attended by representatives of the main colonial liberation movements, among whom were Jawaharlal Pandit Nehru, representing the All-India Congress Party, and Liau of the Chinese Kuomintang, as well as delegates of many European Communist parties. Friedrich Adler, the secretary of the Amsterdam International, had warned member parties against taking part, since the initiative for the Congress had come from the Comintern. The SPD had consequently refused to attend and the only German organizations to send delegates were the KPD, the Liga für Menschenrechte (League for Human Rights) and the League against Colonial Repression. The British Labour Movement was, however, well represented: the ILP had delegated George Lansbury and Fenner Brockway, and the Labour Party Ellen Wilkinson. Brockway already knew Toller from the latter's visit to London in 1925 (see pp. 179–80 below), while Ellen Wilkinson was also an admirer of his work, which she had helped to popularize within the Plebs League.[21]

The Congress voted to establish the League against Imperialism as a platform for anti-imperialist ideas, electing Brockway as its first chairman. Toller attended the Congress in a personal capacity, but took a prominent part in the proceedings, making a speech denouncing the demands by German nationalists for the return of Germany's colonies: 'The age of colonialism is over,' he declared.[22] He was convinced of the historical significance of the Congress and was particularly impressed by the prevailing comradeship, contrasting the 'real League of Nations' forged in Brussels with its counterpart in Geneva, which turned a deaf ear to all demands for colonial freedom. He was disappointed at the failure of the liberal press to report the Congress, which he believed would have far-reaching political effects: in fact, the League against Imperialism slowly atrophied, a casualty of the growing sectarianism between communists and socialists. Toller himself was accused in *Vorwärts* of having participated in a communist propaganda event. The personal echoes of the Congress were more positive: among those he met there was Nehru, a meeting which began a friendship lasting over the next decade. He also renewed acquaintance with Fenner Brockway, an incident from whose life he would dramatize in his radio play *Berlin – last edition!* – amid unprecedented scenes, Brockway was suspended from the House of Commons in 1930, after insisting too vehemently that the House should debate the Indian crisis.[23]

Another cause which Toller espoused was that of pacifism; in 1929, he joined the Gruppe revolutionärer Pazifisten (Group of Revolutionary Pacifists) around the writer Kurt Hiller. At the World Peace Congress of 1925, Hiller's group had seceded from the bourgeois pacifist majority, which had supported the right of the League of Nations to apply sanctions, including armed intervention, a view which Hiller and his circle rejected on the grounds that it would merely serve the interests of the capitalist governments the League comprised. The Group of Revolutionary Pacifists was formed in July 1926, including such prominent left-wing intellectuals as Kurt Tucholsky, satirist and sometime editor of *Die Welt-*

bühne, Alfons Goldschmidt, who combined a career as financial editor of papers like the *Berliner Tageblatt* with work for Münzenberg's International Workers' Aid, Walter Mehring, poet and lyricist, the novelist Klaus Mann and the feminist Helene Stöcker.[24] It represented the view that war was the product of a capitalist society and that pacifism was therefore only possible within a socialist world order. It rejected absolute pacifism, holding that non-violence within a violent society amounted to complicity with that society. Class struggle was a necessary means of bringing about a social and political order which would ensure world peace. The Group was supported by various left-wing tendencies, among them the Theodor Liebknecht faction of the old USPD and the group around the veteran socialist Georg Ledebour. An important point in its programme was the abolition of military service and the recognition of the right to conscientious objection, which it campaigned to legalize, organizing a petition calling for a plebiscite on the question: its political line was therefore opposed to that of the Third International.

The Group was only one of several pacifist groups in the Weimar Republic, exercising little real political influence, but it none the less helps to trace Toller's attitude to the question of non-violence, which remained crucially important for his personality and his political thinking. The inescapable conclusion of his revolutionary experience was that violence was tragically inevitable. His public statements on this theme after 1924 indicate his continuing efforts to come to terms with the problem. He openly acknowledged that unconditional pacifism could not be reconciled with the demands of political action: the revolutionary had to recognize that 'the laws and consequences of his struggle are determined by forces other than his good intentions'. No revolution, he concluded, could dispense with force, but there were 'distinguishing emphases'. The revolutionary socialist rejected force for its own sake and if obliged to use it would regard it as a 'terrible, tragically necessary expedient'.[25] Outlining his position in a statement written for an Esperanto journal in 1928, he wrote: 'All true pacifism is revolutionary. Pacifism which believes it can pacify the world on the foundation of the capitalist system is blind. We must fight this dangerous blindness.'[26] Toller's attitude to pacifism remained remarkably consistent up to 1936, when he began to modify it under the impact of political events.

One of Toller's crucial concerns in these years was the question of

1. Toller as volunteer, 1914

2. Toller in uniform, 1915

3. Toller with Max Weber at the Lauenstein Congress in 1917

4. Toller as prisoner in Niederschönenfeld with Ernst Niekisch, Valentin Hartig and Gustav Klingelhöfer

5. Toller in his prison cell

6. Toller with Netty Katzenstein (Tessa) in Ancona in 1924

7. Toller with (*from left*) Münzenberg, Jawaharlal Nehru, his sister Krishna Nehru, Georg Ledebour, and Henrietta Roland-Holst at the conference of the League against Imperialism in Brussels, February 1927

8. Toller and Lotte Israel in Switzerland, January 1929

9. Christiane Grautoff in about 1932

10. Toller in 1934

11. Obituary photo-
graph in the *Illustrated
London News*, May 1939

censorship, which he had already confronted in Niederschönenfeld and which, in a series of spectacular cases, came to be the yardstick of political freedom in the Weimar Republic. In 1927–28 Toller was actively involved in the campaign to prevent the prosecution of the poet J.R. Becher on a charge of 'literary high treason', a charge which is itself eloquent of the prevailing political climate. Becher had established his reputation as an Expressionist poet during the war, had later joined the KPD and had, as we have seen, become one of Toller's most virulent critics. One of his works had been seized by the police as early as 1925 for allegedly inciting the violent overthrow of the Republic. Becher had been arrested on a charge of high treason, but later released. At this stage, the charges against him were not pressed – nor were they dropped. In February 1926, copies of Becher's novel *Levisite oder der einzig gerechte Krieg* (*Levisite or the only just war*) were seized by the police. During 1927, several communist booksellers were prosecuted for selling books by Becher and the dramatist Berta Lask. In October, the case against Becher himself was reopened and he was charged with high treason. A broad-based campaign was launched to protest against these attacks on artistic freedom of expression, turning Becher's case into a 'cause célèbre'.[27] At a huge protest meeting in the Theater am Nollendorfplatz on 8 January 1928, Toller and Erwin Piscator were among many prominent speakers. Toller called the prosecution of Becher 'high treason against intellectual freedom', declaring that the Weimar state wanted to suppress the revolutionary writer and make it impossible for him to work. Two months later, Toller spoke alongside Becher at a protest meeting of Leipzig workers, attacking the 'class justice' manifested in this case. The campaign for Becher ended in complete success, when the proceedings against him, already twice postponed, were finally dropped under the political amnesty in July 1928. Toller became increasingly involved in such campaigns after 1930, as new emergency decrees making censorship more stringent marked the Republic's decline into dictatorship.

Perhaps Toller's closest links during these years were with the Liga für Menschenrechte (League for Human Rights) which had been formed in 1922 as a counterpart to the French Ligue des Droits de l'Homme. Made sensitive by his own experience to the question of civil liberties, he began a close association with the League in 1926; his correspondence confirms that he played a prominent part as a member of its political sub-committee and found himself in great demand as a speaker, particularly on such topics as political justice or proposed changes in the penal code.[28]

In 1929 Toller became a member of the unofficial committee of inquiry set up by the League to investigate the so-called May Day events. The year had begun with considerable industrial unrest and against a background of strikes, demonstrations and rising unemployment, the SPD, then in government in both Prussia and the Reich, had seen its duty as the defence of law and order. The SPD Chief of Police in Berlin, Karl Zörgiebel, had issued an order banning the traditional May Day marches. The communists and others had organized demonstrations in various parts of Berlin, particularly in the working-class districts of Wedding and Neukölln. Police and soldiers moved in to disperse the marchers and in the ensuing clashes thirty-three workers were killed and hundreds injured. In the aftermath of these events, Carl von Ossietzky, the editor of the political journal *Die Weltbühne*, instituted a committee of inquiry under the auspices of the League for Human Rights.[29] Toller was among its members who also included politicians and journalists. Although the work of the committee was seriously obstructed by the police, which ordered its members to withhold all information from it, it heard numerous eye-witnesses and other independent reports of the events which established that the bloodbath had been caused by indiscriminate action by the police who had opened fire on unarmed demonstrators. Not only the KPD but many independent left-wingers recognized that the SPD had set in motion the machine of state oppression. The May events exemplified the growing mutual hostility of the two working-class parties in the Republic and their tragic failure to make common cause against the emerging threat of Nazism.

In these years, Toller also wrote a body of political journalism which would alone disprove the well-worn argument that he was unable to come to terms with political developments in the Weimar Republic. His articles were written for the leading literary and political reviews of the period – *Das Tagebuch*, *Die literarische Welt* and above all *Die Weltbühne*, the periodical which articulated the voice of the democratic left in the Republic. Some of Toller's articles were marginal comment on the great political issues of the decade, such as disarmament and colonial freedom, but others deal with topical issues of the day, like naval rearmament or the campaign to free Max Hölz. The latter articles, seeking to mobilize public opinion in the short term, and often combined with public speaking, reveal his firm grasp of political reality. The style of his articles matches the subject matter: they are written in a detached and restrained manner, in which material conditions are recorded and used to make a political argument. His article 'Socialist Vienna', for example, records the concrete achievements of socialist municipal government in Vienna as a model for the German labour movement. In 'Homework', he took up the case of domestic workers in the Erzgebirge (in Saxony), describing their appalling conditions in the hope that publicity would result in discussion and eventual improvement. In 'Talk about Battleships', his comments on the immediate issue of German naval rearmament were combined with a critique of the long-term consequences of Social Democratic 'Realpolitik'.[30]

Toller's political insight is most apparent in his speeches and articles on National Socialism. He was more finely attuned than almost any of his contemporaries to the growing threat of European fascism, against which he warned as early as 1927: 'Fascism is such a danger for the European working-class that I believe we should welcome any offensive against it.'[31] In February 1929, speaking on the tenth anniversary of the death of Kurt Eisner, he warned of the consequences of a fascist takeover in Germany:

> A period of reactionary rule lies ahead. Let no one believe that a period of fascism, however moderate, however insidious, will be a short transitional period. The revolutionary, socialist and republican energies which it will destroy will take years to rebuild.[32]

He repeated his warning eighteen months later in an article prophetically entitled 'Reichskanzler Hitler', published immediately after the first substantial electoral gains by the Nazis, in which he accurately predicted both Hitler's seizure of power and the means by which he would consolidate it. He warned explicitly against the 'dangerous illusion', shared by liberals, socialists and communists alike, that Hitler should be allowed to govern, because that would be the quickest way of discrediting him. The Nazis, he argued, were characterized by their 'will to power': Hitler was ready to come to power by democratic means, but once in power, would not relinquish it. He went on to predict with great accuracy the consequences of a Nazi seizure of power: the abolition of social reforms, the purge of SPD supporters from positions of power, the destruction of the trade unions and the use of 'naked brutal terror against socialists, communists and the few remaining (liberal) democrats'.[33] Toller's warning was given at a time when the main left-wing parties still completely failed to recognize the danger which Hitler posed: the SPD still thought in terms of parliamentary alliances, the KPD believed that a period of fascism would merely usher in a proletarian revolution. Toller knew better. Analysing 'The German Situation' in June 1932, he attacked the reduction of sickness and unemployment benefit, stressing the demoralizing effect of poverty and recognizing mass unemployment as a fertile breeding-ground for fascism. He concluded with the accurate prediction that if Hitler came to power he would 'use the constitution to destroy the remnants of that constitution'.[34] The clarity of his insight into the nature and methods of National Socialism is in striking contrast to the almost wilful self-delusion of both SPD and KPD in the years immediately before 1933.

Such was the public figure in the years after 1924, but what of the private man? For the next eight years, Toller was to make his home in Berlin, a city of artistic experiment which had already established itself as the theatre capital of Europe. After staying for some weeks with his friend Ernst Niekisch, Toller moved into an apartment in the leafy suburb of Grunewald, near the forests and lakes on the western edge of the city. In the following years, he frequently changed apartments, moving between a series of addresses in the fashionable districts of Charlottenburg and Steglitz. Literary fame undoubtedly influenced the pattern of his life and it was during these years that he acquired a reputation for good living and epicurean pleasures. During his frequent travels in Germany and abroad, he would usually stay in expensive hotels. He enjoyed good food and was often to be found in small French or Italian restaurants, which he would recommend to close friends. Toller's enemies were quick to criticize such worldly weaknesses, criticism he was equally quick to resent, dismissing 'those unscrupulous bourgeois who accuse a socialist of dishonourable motives if they see him so much as drink a glass of wine'.[35]

Nevertheless, one of the great ironies of Toller's life after 1924 was his gradual isolation from the very class for which he chose to write and in whose cause he had suffered five years imprisonment. In the first years after his release, he received numerous invitations to speak to workers' educational and cultural organizations, but his correspondence confirms that such contacts began to decline after 1927.

His work was, for several years, a focal point for the autonomous Workers' Cultural Movement; workers' theatre groups regularly performed his choral poems – until such works passed out of fashion towards the end of the decade. Toller's relations with the Berlin Volksbühne were also strained, following a contractual dispute in 1926, though it did finally produce *Hinkemann* in November 1927, with Toller himself co-directing and the young Helene Weigel playing Grete Hinkemann.

Toller undoubtedly felt more at home in literary than in political circles. Though he had left the Bohemian life of Schwabing far behind him, he was still sometimes to be seen in the literary cafés of the Kurfürstendamm. Most of his close friendships were with fellow-writers, some of which blossomed into literary collaboration. Among his closest friends were the dramatist Walter Hasenclever, with whom he shared a flat in 1928 while collaborating on the ill-fated musical comedy *Once a Bourgeois always a Bourgeois*, and the novelist Hermann Kesten, for whom he retained a special regard until the end of his life. He also enjoyed a close relationship with his publisher Fritz Landshoff, with whom he shared a flat in the Württembergische Strasse from 1930 to 1933. Landshoff did not meet Toller until 1926 but came to consider him his best friend, enjoying so close a relationship with him that it was said their physical resemblance grew more striking every day. There were other literary friends: the successful biographer Emil Ludwig, whose home in Ascona he visited on several occasions, Kurt Tucholsky, the poet and lyricist Walter Mehring, and the journalist Betty Frankenstein. He particularly enjoyed the company of actors, becoming a close friend of Heinrich George, who played the role of Hinkemann with considerable success in Berlin. He was also friendly with the critic Alfred Kerr, but he did not in general like critics, whose judgements on his work he sometimes resented; he felt that the role of the interpreter was overrated and attacked 'the arrogance of certain critics who think that the writer lives off the critic'.[36]

In the years after 1924 Toller the writer was increasingly difficult to separate from Toller the public figure: he found it impossible to escape his own legend. Emil Ludwig, whom he visited in Switzerland shortly after his release from prison, thought that his spectacular success as a dramatist was premature and advised him to follow the example of Friedrich Schiller: to give up writing plays for a time to allow a period of study and reflection.[37] Toller was too busy pursuing his own public persona to wish to follow such advice. His attitude to his public role was always ambivalent. On the one hand, he courted public acclaim (Fritz Landshoff confirmed that 'he often enjoyed being Ernst Toller'), but he had an equal need for privacy, which periodically led him to avoid public contacts. While his fame fed his vanity, it also induced moods of acute self-doubt. As we have seen, he was constantly troubled by the gulf he perceived between his reputation and his actual achievements, a feeling which probably contributed to his eventual suicide.

Toller's work was frequently interrupted by ill-health. In 1925 illness caused him to cut short a tour of Palestine and the Middle East which had been planned to last several months. In 1927 he was forced to cancel a reading tour, in order to enter a Swiss sanatorium for a period of rest. In June 1928 he was in hospital following a car accident and was ill again later that year. He suffered a long illness just before a tour of the United States in 1929. Despite his precarious health, Toller led a physically active life, sharing the fascination of his contemporaries for physical fitness and sport. He learned to box (a sport which also fascinated Brecht and Grosz) and enjoyed swimming, riding and skiing. He attended popular sporting occasions, like the six-day cycle races at the Berlin Sportpalast, which Georg Kaiser had appropriated for the theatre in his Expressionist masterpiece *From Morn till Midnight*. He also shared the prevailing interest in modern technology, acquiring a taste for motor-cars, though he was apparently a bad driver, and experimenting with the new media of film and radio.

The slackening of Toller's output after 1924 led some to consider him a spent force, and caused him to doubt his own creative ability. He was always an intuitive writer, who wrote in short intensive bursts, often followed by long fallow periods, in which he began to fear that his creative powers had dried up:

> External success has been of little use to me: before each new work, I have thought I am just beginning. And when the creative impulse failed for months on end, I feared it had left me for ever. Only the creative artist knows the acute crisis which then sets in.[38]

After 1924 his silences grew longer, his creative difficulties greater. His work after 1926 was increasingly the product of collaboration. The published text of *Hoppla* clearly reflects the influence of

Piscator. *Once a Bourgeois always a Bourgeois* was written in collaboration with Hasenclever and Kesten and, while the play flopped, his collaboration with both writers flourished. He worked again with Hasenclever on the script of the film *Menschen hinter Gittern* (*Men behind Bars*) in 1931, and in the same year collaborated with Kesten on the drama *Miracle in America*. It was Toller's suggestion that they should write a play together, Kesten describing their method of collaboration as follows: 'Toller and I both wrote a draft of each individual scene, which we subsequently revised together. We then either adopted one or other of these revised versions or we wrote a third version together.'[39] The play itself enjoyed only modest success, but Kesten was to collaborate with Toller again, helping to edit his prison letters in London in 1934–35.

Elsewhere, Toller described his own working methods and habits in some detail:

> I don't write down my ideas. Generally, months pass after the initial idea before I write the work. In these months, when the work is taking shape, I let everything connected with the work flow into me, so to speak. That is, I don't try to outline the details. In general, I can hardly work in the mornings, but on days when I'm writing a major play I work at any time, stopping only when my fingers go numb from writing. If I write in ink, I need a particular pen – and absolute quiet. I smoke a lot, avoid all company. I seldom make a draft. If I do, only an outline sketch. I write very quickly. Even so, too slowly, inspiration comes more quickly than I can write it down. I make a lot of corrections. Before I allow the work to be published, many months may pass during which I continually change whole sections or particular words. I even alter proofs. I see the play, so to speak, afresh when I see it in print for the first time. I never reread the finished book, except when I have to read individual sections at a public reading. Even then, I have to overcome strong reservations before I can do so. Would I ever like to write a work I've completed again? You might as well ask if I'd like to begin a piece of my life again which I've already lived.[40]

Toller's comments give a fascinating insight into the way he wrote, though some of them must be treated with a little scepticism. Certainly, much of his work was written at speed, but revised at leisure. *Masses and Man*, as we have seen, was completed in a single creative outburst of three days; the radio play *Berlin - last edition!* in four. But Toller's claim that he never reread his work after it was published is untrue. He revised *The Machine Wreckers* thoroughly, after its initial publication, in the light of the Berlin production. He was always sensitive to the reception of his work, changing the ending of *Hinkemann* and rejecting the published version of *Hoppla* in favour of an alternative version after the Berlin production. His comments confirm the autobiographical significance of all his plays, in the sense that virtually all are the result of reflection on his own experience. Not for nothing did he term his work 'gelebtes Leben' – a piece of life lived. It is to his work in these years that we must now turn.

X *Political Theatre: Theory and Practice*

Ernst Toller did not develop an elaborate theory of drama, but he did outline a number of prescriptive ideas which, from 1927, were incorporated into his lecltures, and which provide a framework for his own dramatic practice. When he emerged from prison in 1924, not merely the political situation but the cultural landscape had been transformed. The German theatre had abandoned Expressionism. Brecht's early play *Drums in the Night* had presaged a trend towards greater realism which was echoed in other works, such as Kaiser's *Beieinander* (*Next to Each Other*), and finally confirmed by the success of Carl Zuckmayer's comedy *Der fröhliche Weinberg* (*The Merry Vineyard*) in 1925. These were the early examples of what became known as 'Neue Sachlichkeit' (New Objectivity), a literary style appropriate to a period of post-revolutionary stabilization, in which the soaring aspirations of Expressionism were anachronistic. Literary idealism made way for a pragmatic and often bitter realism. The evocation of the 'New Humanity' was replaced by the depiction of the man in the street, hymnic poetry by factual prose, rhetoric by reportage.

It was over three years after his release from prison before Toller's next play *Hoppla, Such is Life!* was published and produced, an interval which contrasts strongly with his output in prison, where he had written a play a year between 1919 and 1923. This long dramatic silence has often been attributed to creative decline, but the real reasons are more complex, relating to his adjustment to life outside prison, not least the creative adjustment to a new cultural climate. While this process is scarcely proof of creative decline, it did entail undoubted creative difficulties: *Hoppla*, written in 1927, was not the first play on which Toller had worked since leaving prison. Early in 1926 he had begun writing a new drama, based on the events leading to the murder of Karl Liebknecht and Rosa Luxemburg, for which he later adopted the title *Berlin 1919*. He was pursuing a new form of 'mass drama' which – by very reason of its experimental nature – he found difficult to realize. Though he worked on the play spasmodically throughout 1926, he never completed it and only fragments of it have survived.

Stories that Toller was writing a new play had begun to appear in the Berlin newspapers in the summer of 1926. The first public confirmation from Toller himself came in an open letter to the journal *Volksbühne*, published in August:

> Stories have been appearing in the press without my knowledge to the effect that I have been writing for the Volksbühne a 'comedy of the slums', 'a dramatic scenario'. The facts are that I am about to complete a play, the title of which is not yet settled and which I shall give to the Volksbühne for production by Piscator.[1]

Toller wrote that he was seeking to realize 'a new form for a collective drama' in the belief that the resources of the conventional theatre were no longer adequate to convey 'the internal face and external atmosphere, the ebb and flow of a great modern mass movement'. The new 'mass drama' had to develop a formal equivalent of the cinema's capacity to show apparently unrelated events so as to make clear their intrinsic connection, to present 'the inner tempo and diversity of the action as a related whole'.

Toller's formal experimentation was inspired partly by the Russian cinema, particularly by Sergei Eisenstein's *Battleship Potemkin* which had begun its triumphal progress through Germany at the beginning of the year and which had so impressed Toller that he had written to Eisenstein, calling it 'the first great collective drama'.[2] Toller's theoretical remarks also betray the influence of the controversial theatre director Erwin Piscator, whose radical experiments in politically committed theatre would dominate the German stage towards the end of the twenties. Piscator, who in 1926 was still under contract to the Berlin Volksbühne, was a forceful advocate of 'political theatre'. He considered the theatre to be a way of advancing revolutionary struggle: drama was 'only a means to an end. A political means. A propagandistic means, a pedagogical means'.[3] In his productions he sought to evoke the social and economic forces which shaped individual destiny, attempting to find the dramatic form appropriate to his revolutionary message. He believed that the traditional devices of theatre production could no longer evoke contemporary social reality and that the theatre had to seek a correlative for social conditions in modern technology. He therefore used projections and loudspeakers, incorporated film into the dramatic action and used documentary details, such as statistics, newspaper reports and official statements, as indirect commentary. The individual character was portrayed, not as an autonomous personality, but as the exponent of a social role.

Toller hoped that Piscator would not only produce the new play but be actively involved in its development, and the two men did in fact spend part of the summer together in the southern French resort of Bandol, between Marseilles and Toulon, 'so that he [Piscator] could get to know the play as it evolved'.[4]

Toller seems initially to have made rapid progress on the play, but as work progressed, he found it increasingly difficult to realize his dramatic conception. The actual course of work on the play, and the creative crisis which ensued, can be partially reconstructed from his letters to Betty Frankenstein, a close friend with whom he would correspond regularly while abroad.[5] Toller had come to Paris in mid-June, awaiting Piscator's arrival with some impatience, and it was not until early July that the two men finally arrived in Bandol. By the end of the month, Toller had completed much of his new play, but was already troubled by creative doubts: 'There are now some fifteen scenes of the play, but whether I have caught what I want – not even the Gods know (29 July 1926).' These doubts quickly grew more serious:

> I sometimes feel that I am shrivelled and dried up. And to laze about with a good conscience, just laze about, is something I can't do. (The play, who knows if that too isn't slipping away from me.) (13 August)

A month later, Toller had virtually completed his first draft but he was so critical of it that he felt he must discard it and begin again. His dissatisfaction heralded a creative crisis which was to last several months:

> I feel very depressed. My travel book on Russia has made no progress. As to my drama, which was already finished up to the final scene, I have torn up half of it – and have no confidence whatever in the other half. I not only turn away in disgust from every sentence I write, even as I write it, but I feel that every thought I think is mediocre and not worth expressing (13 September).[6]

Piscator had returned to Berlin in mid-August and had apparently discussed production of the play with the Volksbühne. A month later he wrote to Toller asking how the play was progressing; Toller replied that it was not finished, nor could he say when it would be. He commented confidentially to Betty Frankenstein:

> The Volksbühne doesn't want to stage *The Transformation*. I had a letter from P. They want the new play, but I won't give them anything I can't stand by. The worst thing is that I notice how indifferent I am to such letters (25 October).

By early October, Toller had left Bandol for Paris, finally moving into Walter Hasenclever's suburban flat at Clamart; but the change of scene did little to resolve his problems and when he left France early in November the play was still unfinished. In the next three months, the Volksbühne continued to press Toller for the play; Toller's reaction is an interesting gloss on his artistic self-perception. He declared he would not be hurried; and would be guided solely by his artistic integrity: 'In the last resort, I am not a baker, who can be expected to have baked his bread by a particular time in the morning.'[7]

He apparently continued to work on the play after his return to Berlin, and several scenes from it appeared in different periodicals during the winter of 1926–27.[8] He also included extracts in his public readings. On 22 February 1927, for example, he gave a reading from his unpublished works, including a total of five scenes from from the 'Massendrama', which were published in the *Volksbühne* journal under the title *Berlin 1919*, the first mention of this title. At this stage, Toller still definitely considered the play as work in progress, describing it as such in his correspondence.[9] He seems to have finally abandoned it only after beginning work on *Hoppla*.

Toller's collaboration with Piscator was able to survive the failure of his 'mass drama'. During 1926 Piscator had staged a number of memorable, if tendentious, productions for the Volksbühne, culminating in March 1927 with the production of Ehm Welk's historical play *Gewitter über Gottland* (*Storm over Gottland*). He had attempted to give the play contemporary relevance by inserting film sequences intended to demonstrate the analogies to modern revolutionary events. The production had become the focus for violent controversy within the Volksbühne movement as to the proper function of a People's Theatre – should it be artistically neutral or politically committed? The Volksbühne management had issued a statement saying that Piscator's production 'violated the fundamental political neutrality' of the Volksbühne.[10] In the ensuing wrangle, which split the Volksbühne into right and left-wing factions, Toller was one of Piscator's most vociferous supporters. At a meeting of the left-wing faction in the Berlin Herrenhaus, he advocated an unequivocally political theatre:

> Drama means conflict, means we must be radical if we are to be anything at all. The proletarian who walks the stage today carries a flag – and that disturbs the petty bourgeoisie. The proletarian of today is not just a man of feeling, he is the bearer of an idea.[11]

It was within the context of this controversy that Toller outlined what he meant by political theatre in an address to the Volksbühne Congress in July 1927:

> If you wish to go back to the original idea of the Volksbühne, you must begin with the living, with our own time. Only the writer who catches the present moment will attain what we call timelessness.[12]

That is, political theatre must be contemporary in subject-matter and realistic in manner; it must seek to influence working-class consciousness by enacting for the worker the reality of his own life:

> The workers are strongly drawn to the portrayal of their own life in the theatre. Ask the Viennese: let them tell you how the workers identified with the performance, how they felt: This is you speaking, this is you taking action. [*Hinkemann* had been put on in Vienna in 1924.]

Political theatre had to mirror political conflict:

> We know that, historically, social struggle takes the form of class struggle. Anyone recognizing that must also endorse the portrayal of that class struggle in the theatre.

While the political dramatist must seek his subject-matter in contemporary reality, he was not merely the 'photographer' of realistic detail, but 'the mouthpiece of the idea at work in the times'. For

Toller, the dominant idea of contemporary society was socialism and the struggle for its realization:

> It is a question of the *path*. We who believe in the social-
> ist path know that it allows of no vagueness, no lack of
> clarity, no liberal utopias of political freedom without
> social freedom. This way must be unequivocal. For us it
> is the path of socialism. And socialism means struggle
> . . . and so our art must be above all an art of struggle,
> not an art of confused good will . . .

Toller's address to the Volksbühne Congress shows the extent - and limits – of Piscator's influence. Contrary to Piscator, Toller was always careful to distinguish between political art and propaganda. He did not discount what he termed 'agitation in artistic form' – indeed he defined his own choral poems in just such terms[13] – but differentiated it sharply from political art. While propaganda sought to arouse its audience to immediate action, political art would articulate the workers' deepest feelings and instincts:

> The question is not whether a work of art should declare
> that the Second or Third International is the only true
> one, leave that to the Proletkult. It is a question of the
> revolutionary atmosphere which pervades a work, which
> fires the worker sitting in the theatre, clarifies what he
> dimly feels and gives his feelings conscious expression.

Toller's collaboration with Piscator also convinced him of the revolutionary potential of documentary drama. Outlining a projected film of the German revolution in 1928, he contended that 'it would be wrong to turn the revolution into a feature film: the film must possess the great historical tension of documentary proof'. Though the film would be partisan, it would be non-party: 'This film cannot be the film of one working-class party, it must have a countenance which the whole working class can recognize as its own.' He hoped that, as in Russia, the working class would actively participate in this enactment of its own history – a clear echo of the idea inspiring his mass pageants. However, it would be a mistake to show only scenes of mass action: the fate of particular individuals must be linked to the collective events.[14]

Toller's insistence that art could not be subordinated to immediate political ends, his move towards individual characterization, and his reliance on the traditional devices of empathy and involvement all serve to locate his theories within the aesthetic debate on the left in Germany in the nineteen twenties. We must distinguish his ideas both from those of the communist-inspired Bund proletarisch-revolutionärer Schriftsteller (Association of Proletarian-Revolutionary Writers), which considered art to be no more than a weapon in the class struggle, and the theories of epic theatre expounded by Bertolt Brecht. It must be emphasized, however, that Brecht did not begin to develop a coherent theory of epic theatre until 1930–31 and that his theories were initially descriptive – retrospective commentary on the plays he had already written. Toller's ideas were always prescriptive: ideas which he attempted to realize in the two major plays he wrote in the last years of the decade – *Hoppla, Such is Life!* and *Draw the Fires*.

Hoppla, Such is Life!

Hoppla, Such is Life! has a crucial place in Toller's development as a dramatist, presenting both an incisive portrait of the Weimar Republic and a critical reappraisal of his own position within it. It was the product of a long period of formal experimentation, an attempt to adopt the technical devices and documentary style of Piscator's 'political theatre'. It was also the result of long political reflection, a dramatic exposition of the social reality into which Toller had emerged after 1924. The play is now generally remembered for Piscator's remarkable Berlin production, which has achieved a permanent place in European theatre history, but it is an accomplished play in its own right, containing, both textually and technically, much of interest for a modern audience.

In its published form *Hoppla* consists of a prologue and five acts. The prologue introduces the key characters of the play – Karl Thomas, Albert Kroll, Eva Berg, Mutter Meller, Wilhelm Kilman – who are awaiting execution in a communal cell after the defeat of a popular revolution. When news is finally received that they are to be reprieved under an amnesty, Thomas loses his reason and is committed to a mental asylum where he spends the next eight years isolated from society. The play proper begins with his release, and traces his experience of social reality through a series of encounters with his former cell-mates. Wilhelm Kilman is now a minister of the new republic; Kroll, Berg and Meller are still socialist activists, continuing the political struggle through their day-to-day work in party and trade union. Thomas accuses Kilman of having betrayed the revolution, but he is almost equally critical of Kroll and Berg who he believes have also abandoned its ideals. Unable to come to terms with a republic bereft of the principles he had fought for, he plans to assassinate Kilman as a dramatic gesture which will stir people from their political indifference, but he is forestalled by a nationalist student, who shoots Kilman and then escapes. Thomas is arrested for the crime and, despairing of 'this madhouse of a world', hangs himself – just as news is received that the real murderer has been arrested.

Toller's original conception of *Hoppla* dated from early 1927, when he had told Ernst Feder that he was working on three different projects, one a 'comedy' of which Feder noted the following outline: 'Political prisoner, sentenced to death, goes mad, ten years in asylum, when he comes out his ex-comrades are ministers etc.'[15] Toller had evidently already begun work on the play, for he included the prologue in the programme of his public readings later that month.[16] At about this time he also showed an outline to Erwin Piscator, whose dispute with the Volksbühne was then coming to a head, and who was already planning to open his own theatre.

In the early months of the year Toller could have worked only intermittently on the play, being distracted by a succession of lectures, readings and speeches. In January he made a lecture tour of Austria, in February he was in Brussels for the Anti-Imperialist Congress, and then in Copenhagen to give the funeral address for the literary critic and historian Georg Brandes. In March he gave a series of readings in Denmark and Norway, and on returning to Berlin on 20 March immediately undertook a further series of speaking engagements. 'In between, I am supposed to finish certain books,' he wrote to Max Hölz in a tone of slight resignation.[17] Toller the public figure had once more upstaged Toller the playwright.

During the spring he must have worked intensively on the play, for by mid-June he reported that he was putting the finishing touches to it. In the same month he reached an agreement with Piscator that he should stage the play as the first production at the new Piscatorbühne, opening on 1 September.[18] Before the end of the month, Piscator had held a first reading at his flat in the Oranienstrasse. Toller had left shortly after for a holiday on the island of Sylt: 'I am so exhausted with people and speaking and writing that all I want to do is warm my belly in the sun,' he wrote.[19] He obviously regarded *Hoppla* as completed, but on his return to Berlin on 20 July, he found that Piscator wanted him to rewrite it.

Piscator had strong preconceptions about the repertoire of his new theatre, in which he intended to present plays portraying contemporary reality from a perspective of Marxist materialism. For his opening production he wanted a play which would present 'a social and political outline of a whole epoch'.[20] While the outline of *Hoppla* had seemed to satisfy this requirement, Piscator was far from happy with the finished script which he found too lyrical and subjective for a documentary exposition of social reality: 'All our efforts in the subsequent course of the work were directed towards providing the play with a realistic substructure,' he wrote (*PT*, p. 207). He proposed a number of changes which were the subject of lengthy and sometimes heated discussion – he recalled that there were arguments lasting days about some passages. With rehearsals due to begin on 1 August, Toller was under tremendous pressure to complete the revisions: Piscator has left a vivid impression of him at work at this time:

> Toller scarcely ever left my apartment. He had made himself at home at my desk and filled page after page at incredible speed with his huge handwriting, consigning the sheets to the wastepaper basket with equal rapidity. And all the while he kept lighting my most expensive cigars and stubbing them out again in the ashtray after a few drags (*PT*, p. 210).

Toller worked quickly, for by 11 August he had completed the final version of the play.[21] His original version had comprised a prologue and four acts, ending with Karl Thomas's recommittal to the mental institution. At Piscator's suggestion he had added a fifth act which ended with Thomas's suicide, and it was in this form that *Hoppla* was finally published. The seeds of all the future arguments about the play are contained in these two endings.

Piscator's criticism of Toller's script had centred above all on the character of Karl Thomas. He complained that Toller had burdened his protagonist with too many of his own emotions, suggesting that Thomas was 'the standard "hero" who recurs in each of Toller's works' (*PT*, p. 209).

Thomas is, however, not the ego-hero of Toller's earlier (Expressionist) dramas: what sets him apart is the critical light in which he is presented. Toller described him as a dreamer, an idealist who wants to achieve the absolute, here and now, and who is unable, or unwilling, to come to terms with political reality. To this extent he is a measure of how far Toller's idealism had been tempered by time and experience. Thomas is, of course, a dramatic device for reviewing political reality, for contrasting the Republic of 1927 with the revolutionary ideals of 1918, but he is equally a means of reappraising those ideals and their relevance to the contemporary political situation. *Hoppla* must indeed be seen as part of Toller's continuing attempt to find a practical basis for his revolutionary convictions: an attempt to convey the political reality of the Weimar Republic and to define his own role within it.

An introductory note states that *Hoppla* is set 'in many countries, eight years after the defeat of a popular revolution;[22] however, despite this claim to universality, the play is set unmistakably in the Germany of 1927, presenting a panorama of the Weimar Republic at the height of its apparent prosperity and stability. Toller paints a bitter and pessimistic picture, taking us behind the façade of gaiety and affluence to reveal a society on the very brink of its own dissolution: a republic without republicans.

With the exception of Karl Thomas, the dramatis personae are not really individuals but social types. Their representative function was acknowledged by Piscator, who rehearsed his actors to play their roles as 'the sharply contoured expression of a social class' (*PT*, p. 214). Toller's exposition of social reality is in fact dialectical, portrayed in a series of conflicting attitudes across the political spectrum. On one side, there is the group of revolutionary activists – Albert Kroll, the class-conscious worker, who had started work by the age of six and who 'knew what kind of society I was living in, and what had to happen to put an end to injustice, before I knew what ten times ten were' (p. 18); Frau Meller, whose political involvement follows the loss of her husband and sons in the war; and Eva Berg, the emancipated young woman of the post-war years, active in party and trade union. Their former comrade Wilhelm Kilman, now a Social Democratic minister, represents the kind of political opportunism which had led the SPD to 'defend' the republic by colluding with its enemies. These enemies are equally clearly presented and differentiated: Baron Friedrich, a functionary in Kilman's ministry, who serves the republic the better to undermine it; Graf Lande, the proto-fascist who advocates a military putsch to overthrow democracy; the War Minister von Wandsring, a militarist conservative, who also favours 'an honest dictatorship', but is convinced that 'the time for firing off is past. What we wish to achieve for the Fatherland, we can bring about legally' (p. 31) (a view also espoused at this time by Adolf Hitler). There is also the banker, a shady operator, motivated solely by greed, who incorporates the cynicism of the new rich.

Toller's play, written for Piscator's stage, paid extended tribute to the technical innovations which were the hallmark of the latter's production style, notably the integration of film into the dramatic action and the use of the 'simultaneous stage'. The film sequence between the prologue and Act I provided the historical perspective on which the play rests, showing the passage of eight years (1919–27) and suggesting their political significance through a series of visual references to key events of the period: the Versailles Treaty, fascism in Italy, the death of Lenin, and the colonial struggle in India and China. Between Acts I and II, Toller outlined a film sequence showing the new role of women in society and providing the social context for the role of Eva Berg – a sequence which Piscator inexplicably cut.

Toller's notes for the producer suggest that 'all scenes can be played on a scaffolding, consisting of different storeys, without change of set'. This structure, comprising different acting areas which could be spotlighted as required, enabled Toller to use a series of short scenes in which he was able to convey the diverse, contradictory nature of social reality. Behind the façade of affluence and gaiety, Toller reveals a society marked by political opportunism, moral corruption, nascent Nazism, cloudy intellectual radicalism, and working-class poverty and resignation. It is a society in which capitalism and militarism once more hold sway, in which, in the words of Walter Mehring's theme song: 'It's just like it was before the war – just like before the next war'.[23]

Toller's portrait of the Weimar Republic combines a considerable advance in dramatic technique with a much firmer grasp of political reality. This reality is revealed not so much through the eyes of Karl Thomas as in the clashes between him and his former comrades – that is, not subjectively but dialectically. Thomas's first visit after his release is to Wilhelm Kilman. He is amazed to find Kilman now a minister of the republic, and even more amazed to see his cynical exercise of power. Kilman's perception of himself suggests the true nature of the republic - and his own objective function as one of its ministers: 'As a minister, I represent no party, but the state. If you have responsibility, my friend, things seem different down there. Power means responsibility (p. 40).' He believes that responsibility is to maintain law and order, considering himself a neutral broker between labour and capital: 'In a democracy, I have to respect the rights of the employer just as much as those of the worker (p. 41).' He is an unashamed apologist for reformism. 'You're like children,' he tells Thomas, 'you can have an apple but you want to have the whole tree (p. 42).' While he prides himself on his pragmatism, claiming that it is he and his like who have 'saved' the revolution, he is curiously short-sighted. He has surrounded himself with his political enemies. Baron Friedrich, formerly his jailer, now significantly holds a post in his ministry; he consorts with the banker who considers democracy no more than a safety valve for popular discontent. Thomas listens to Kilman with mounting incredulity, and finally resignation: 'We speak different languages,' he concludes.

He turns to his former girl-friend Eva Berg, to whom he admits that he cannot cope with the world: 'Since my visit to Kilman, I don't want to go on.' His picture of her is as sentimental as his view of the revolution in which they first met and fell in love. He asks her to come away with him 'to Greece, to India, to Africa – there must be somewhere where simple people live, just live . . . who know nothing of politics, who just live and don't always have to struggle' (p. 50). Berg dismisses his suggestion as romantic escapism: 'So you're disgusted with politics? Do you think you can escape them? . . . The paradise of your dreams doesn't exist (p. 50).' Eva personifies the emancipated woman of the post-war era, matter-of-fact in her attitude to life and love. Thomas is shocked by her unsentimental attitude to their relationship:

> THOMAS: Don't you belong to me?
> BERG: Belong? The word has died. No one belongs to anyone any more . . . Talking to you, I can see that the eight years you were buried alive have changed us more than a century otherwise would (p. 51).

She acknowledges that the revolution was merely an historical episode, a description which upsets and disturbs Thomas. He concludes that the flame of revolution has gone out, but she contradicts him: 'You're wrong. It just burns differently. Less emotionally (p. 52).'

Thomas re-encounters Albert Kroll as a political organizer in the presidential election which occupies the rest of Act II. Kroll personifies the dilemma of the revolutionary in a time of political reaction. Thomas accuses him of 'going along with the electoral swindle', of having lost his ideals and been absorbed into the very system they once fought to overthrow. Kroll retorts that he has not changed his ideals, merely his tactics; he has no illusions about elections, which he calls 'not action, but a springboard for action'. While he counsels patience, 'Because I want to go full steam ahead when the time is right', Thomas demands a demonstrative action which will wake people from their political lethargy: 'Something has to happen. Someone must give an example . . . Someone has to sacrifice himself. Then the lame will walk (p. 66).' Kroll rejects his proposal to murder Kilman as politically damaging. When Thomas accuses him of being a coward, he retorts: 'You seem to think the world should be an eternal firework display for your benefit, with rockets and flares and sounds of battle. It's you who are the coward and not me (p. 67).'

Though his encounters with Berg and Kroll end inconclusively, it is clearly Thomas's attitude which is seen to be unrealistic. Toller himself emphasized that his own sympathies lay with Berg and Kroll: Kroll, in particular, typifies the attitude of 'commitment without illusions' which Toller consistently advocated. 'You must learn to see things straight,' he tells Thomas, 'and still not let them get you down (p. 65).' Toller's dramatic statement emerges much more clearly in his original version, in which Karl Thomas had not hanged himself, but found new courage to continue the struggle, thus endorsing the attitude of his former comrades. In this version, the play ended, as it had begun, with a scene in the asylum between Thomas and the psychiatrist, Professor Lüdin, a structure which Toller adopted not only for reasons of dramatic symmetry, but to reinforce his theme of the madness of the social order. Lüdin represents professional expertise at the service of the state. In the opening scene, he declares that if he were to examine a thousand people, he could certify nine hundred and ninety-nine as mad – that he did not was simply because 'the state has no interest in it'. Madness is defined by 'raison d'état', not clinical diagnosis, a motif which Toller takes up in the final scene of his original version. When

Thomas is returned to the asylum, Lüdin at first accuses him of feigning insanity. Their conversation causes Thomas to recognize the true madness of society:

> What a fool I am. Now I can see things clearly again. You've made the world into a madhouse ... an enclosure in which the sane are trampled underfoot by a herd of galloping lunatics (p. 324).

He recognizes the difference between 'then' (1919) and 'now' (1927), and sees the commitment of his former comrades in a new perspective. But now that Thomas has come to his senses, Lüdin declares him mad; now that he wishes to rejoin his comrades, Lüdin commits him to solitary confinement. Toller's original script therefore ended on a note of bitter cynicism which is more in keeping with the spirit of the play than the suicide ending suggested by Piscator. In the original version of *Hoppla*, Thomas was clearly intended as a self-critique, in which Toller publicly took leave of the revolutionary idealism of his youth.

The suicide ending with which the play was published was the outcome of Piscator's reading of the play. He found Thomas's 'transformation' unconvincing. 'The theme does not plot the course of an erratic adherent of the Revolution ... Thomas is ... an anarchist of the sentimental variety and his breakdown is perfectly logical' (*PT*, p. 209). After much discussion, his conception of the character finally prevailed over Toller's, but the script still did not satisfy Piscator's requirements. To complete the metamorphosis of Karl Thomas, he cast Alexander Granach in the role, instructing him to play the character as a proletarian, not at all the 'sprig of the bourgeoisie' called for in Toller's script. He also made substantial changes to the script during rehearsals, rewriting passages and even inserting new scenes without consulting Toller, who was upset at this autocratic treatment. Relations between the two men became increasingly strained: *Hoppla* was the last play on which they would collaborate.

It was originally intended that *Hoppla* should open simultaneously on 1 September in both Hamburg and Berlin, but while the Hamburg production went ahead as planned, the Berlin première was delayed for two days on account of the elaborate technical preparations. This delay merely heightened the anticipation of what was widely regarded as a major theatrical event.

The technical virtuosity of Piscator's production dazzled audience and critics alike. At the end of the first performance – which lasted four hours – a section of the audience rose to sing the *Internationale*. One critic wrote that Piscator had extended the boundaries of theatre, another that he, just as much as Toller, deserved to be called the author of the evening. The author in fact received little credit for his contribution, the critics being inclined to suggest that only Piscator's production had saved a rather mediocre play. Such criticism is plainly unjust, for *Hoppla* was subsequently produced with great success at many other theatres without the elaborate stage machinery which Piscator employed. It was perhaps Stefan Großmann's comment which went to the heart of the matter: 'A master of the theatre now has his home. He will allow neither supporters nor authors to distract him.'[24]

Toller was dissatisfied with Piscator's production, feeling that the technical effects had often eclipsed the play itself; he was indeed so dissatisfied that he chose to direct it himself when it was produced at the Altes Theater, Leipzig, a few weeks later. He expressed his reservations about Piscator's production in a letter to Alwin Kronacher, the director of the Altes Theater, proposing that the cuts made by Piscator should be restored and his additions deleted.[25] Toller felt that Piscator's film had almost swamped the play and insisted that in Leipzig projections should be used between the acts. He also felt that the figure of Kroll 'which came out far too little in Berlin' should receive greater emphasis. Above all, he regretted the changes which Piscator had persuaded him to make: advance press notices stressed that the Leipzig production would not follow the published text, but a new version based on Toller's first draft. Toller wanted the play to be seen as he had first conceived it: 'Don't forget to write to the Berlin critics,' he urged Kronacher. 'I should like the Leipzig production, in the new version, to be a sort of première all over again.' The Berlin critics did come and some at least felt that the play had been considerably improved by eliminating the changes made by Piscator.[26]

Hoppla excited great interest, helping to re-establish Toller's reputation at home and abroad. Before the end of 1927 – while it was still running in Berlin – it was produced in Leipzig, Frankfurt and Vienna. During 1928–29 it was widely performed abroad, notably in Moscow, Stockholm, Copenhagen, Helsinki and London. The level of interest in Britain can be gauged from the fact that there were no less than three productions in 1929 – at the Gate Theatre, London, the Festival Theatre, Cambridge and the Abbey Theatre, Dublin, so that within two months the play was staged at the three leading experimental theatres in the British Isles.

If *Hoppla* must be accounted a considerable success, it was followed by an even more considerable failure. During 1928 Toller collaborated with Walter Hasenclever on the script of a musical comedy called *Once a Bourgeois always a Bourgeois*, a free adaptation of Molière's *Le Bourgeois Gentilhomme*. Hasenclever, who had written several successful boulevard comedies in the twenties, was not the only distinguished collaborator. The novelist Hermann Kesten, then a young editor at the Kiepenheuer publishing house, wrote the lyrics for the songs, the music was by Friedrich Holländer. The play was to be directed by Alexander Granovsky, Director of the Moscow State Jewish Theatre, which had played a most successful season in Berlin the previous autumn, while the leading role was to be played by Germany's most famous comic actor, Max Pallenberg, still fresh from his triumph in Piscator's production of *The Adventures of the Good Soldier Schweik*.

No text of *Once a Bourgeois* has survived, but Toller's own description confirms that it was a modern version of Molière's comedy, written in the style of a satirical review. The first half of the play comprised a shortened version of Molière's comedy, while the second half was set in 1929, 'in which Molière's characters appear as modern businessmen, swindlers, etc.'.[27] The play was eagerly anticipated as one of the theatrical events of the season and there was even talk of a production by Granovsky for the Theatre Guild in New York the following spring. Toller himself thought 'the play will be very funny and – touch wood – a success'.[28] Its success indeed seemed assured, long before it finally opened at the Lessing Theatre on 21 February 1929, but it turned out to be a disastrous flop. Critics distributed the blame for this failure almost equally. Some felt that the authors' script had served the actors poorly, others that Granovsky's lavish production had overshadowed the play itself; but they were unanimous in pronouncing the result a disaster. In the face of such universal hostility, the production was taken off after only eight performances. Kurt Pinthus called it the biggest flop of the 1928–29 theatre season;[29] Toller himself made no further reference to it. Musical comedy was not his métier and though he would try his hand at it again in *No More Peace!*, he was not much more successful. During 1929 he turned back to the theme which dominated all his majmor work: the November Revolution.

Draw the Fires!

Toller wrote one more play before the end of the decade, the 'historical drama' *Draw the Fires!*, which deals with the unrest in the German Navy in the summer of 1917 – and its revolutionary aftermath.[30] Reichpietsch and Köbis, stokers on the battleship *Friedrich der Grosse* are critical of food and conditions on board and of the navy's ban on socialist newspapers. They contact USPD deputies in the Reichstag, who advise caution, but also encourage them to canvass support for the forthcoming peace conference of socialist parties in Stockholm. Subsequently, Reichpietsch and Köbis, together with Beckers, Sachse and Weber, are elected to an unofficial Food Commission to represent the sailors' grievances. At a meeting of ships' crews on shore, Reichpietsch outlines the USPD peace proposals which receive widespread support. The members of the Food Commission are subsequently arrested and charged with high treason. The examining judge, Schuler, uses brutal and intimidating methods of interrogation to construct a case against the men, confirming that the authorities intend to make an example of them. The five men are found guilty and sentenced to death; Reichpietsch and Köbis are actually executed. The final scene is set in November 1918: when the fleet is ordered to put to sea to engage the British Navy, the crews mutiny and extinguish the fires in the boilers.

Draw the Fires! exemplifies the documentary realism typical of Toller's work after 1925 and which became the dominant trend in Weimar theatre towards the end of the decade. It was one of a growing number of 'Zeitstücke', plays dealing with contemporary themes and written in an objective, documentary style. The main source for the play was the proceedings of the Reichstag Committee of Inquiry into the reasons for the German military collapse of 1918. The Committee of Inquiry into naval affairs, which sat between January 1926 and March 1928, rapidly became a mirror of the growing political polarization of the Republic. While the nationalist right tried to prove that the navy – and hence the nation – had not been defeated by the enemy, but undermined by a left-wing conspiracy at home, the SPD sought to defend itself and to show that the USPD (with which it was now reunited) had not attempted to incite mutiny in the fleet in 1917 but that, on the contrary, the unrest had been the spontaneous result of poor food and harsh discipline.

Draw the Fires!, based on the published record of these proceedings, is among the earliest examples of documentary drama. The published version of the play contained a documentary appendix intended to authenticate all the main dramatic events. In a foreword, Toller stressed that he had taken some liberties with historical facts, altering times and places and even inventing characters, 'because I believe that the dramatist should give the picture of an age, not – like the reporter – photograph every historical detail'.[31] He was nonetheless remarkably faithful to his sources, which are often transposed almost word for word into the dramatic text.

The play has a complex, multi-layered structure, in which the action shifts rapidly in time and place. The opening scene shows the proceedings of the Reichstag Inquiry in 1926; the rest of the play is told in flashback. We return firstly to the Battle of Jutland in 1916, then move on to the events of the 'mutiny' of 1917, while the final scene jumps forward to the revolutionary events at Kiel in November 1918. This 'epic' structure, in which the first and last scenes are linked only dialectically to the main action of the play, is admirably suited to Toller's dramatic theme.

At one level, the play is a 'Justizstück' (judicial drama) portraying a case of corrupt justice within a reactionary society. The opening scene, portraying the Reichstag Inquiry, gives the play itself the character of a judicial investigation. When the committee chairman declares: 'We are not here to decide whether these verdicts were legally correct', he is interrupted by a voice from the wings: 'But we are!' We, the audience, are invited to witness and pass judgement on the events which are then shown in flashback. The central scenes of the play, forming a roughly consecutive narrative of the 'mutiny', make clear that there was no case of high treason, and that the execution of the two men was an act of judicial murder, motivated by political expediency. What we see is not a miscarriage of justice, but a deliberate perversion of it.

The case of Köbis and Reichpietsch has, however, wider implications. In the opening scene, one of the main witnesses to the Inquiry testifies that their execution served to radicalize the fleet, preparing the way for the mutiny of November 1918. The final scene, showing the revolutionary events at Kiel, therefore closes the dramatic circle, placing the judicial murders of 1917 into a revolutionary perspective.

While Toller called his play an 'historical drama', it also had a contemporary resonance. The documentary appendix to the play is divided into three sections, dated 1917, 1918 and 1928. While the first contains a selection of evidence submitted to the Inquiry, and the second documents the events in Kiel, the last section extends the frame of reference into the present. Under the heading 'And what is the Republic doing?', it records the application for maintenance by Reichpietsch's parents on the grounds of the loss of their son – and its rejection by the authorities. The final document pursues this analogy between then and now, quoting the statement by the Naval Prosecutor Dobring (called Schuler in the play) that he would 'shoot these people all over again without any compunction'.[32] Since Dobring was still a senior member of the judiciary, his statement becomes a comment on the reactionary nature of Weimar justice itself. Toller repeated the charge that Dobring had perverted the course of justice in an article in *Die Weltbühne*, challenging him to defend himself:

> Today the tables are turned and you, public prosecutor, now stand in the dock. You must answer for your system . . . You have, like any accused, the right to speak in your own defence . . . Will you speak?[33]

Dobring made no public statement, but he did meet Toller privately, after the latter repeated his charge at a matinee performance of *Draw the Fires!*. Their meeting was reported to have lasted four hours, but what was said can no longer be established.[34]

Draw the Fires! is a significant milestone in Toller's career as a dramatist. It is a well-written play in which his handling of the complex structure demonstrates his increasing technical assurance. It also contains the most coherent political statement of any of his plays. For the first time, he abandoned the subjective ego-hero of his earlier dramas, portraying his five sailors as the *collective* victims of class justice; for the first time, the dramatic conflict is clearly presented in terms of class conflict.

The unrest in the fleet results from the inequality of treatment between officers and men: while the officers mess enjoys good food and fine wines, the lower deck has to be content with 'turnips and porridge', an injustice emphasized by harsh and often senseless discipline. The gulf which divides officers and men is clearly one of class origin, as the men themselves are quick to recognize:

> KÖBIS: The officers can die like us, but they can't live like us.
> SACHSE: That's right, Alvin. For the gentlemen war is the jackpot. For us, it's a losing ticket (p. 140).

The dramatic conflict derives from this social tension.

The officers and the naval authorities clearly belong to the ruling class, their actions emanating from a common ethos which serves to sustain the existing social order. But Toller does not descend to the black-and-white characterization he always deplored. The young officer, Hoffmann, who hides his inexperience behind harsh discipline, is contrasted with the decent and humane Kohler, an officer genuinely concerned for the well-being of his men. Both officers, however, are bound by a code of conduct which transcends their individual differences and which makes Kohler's concern ultimately irrelevant. His attempt to intercede on behalf of the accused men is cursorily dismissed by Admiral von Scheer, who believes that death sentences are necessary in order to maintain discipline – that is, to preserve the military hierarchy and class structure of which Kohler too is part.

Scheer is a representative figure: the nationalist reactionary, convinced of Germany's right to territorial annexations – and the treason of all who oppose them. He does not hesitate to arrange the executions before the court's verdict has even been announced. The main representative of the authorities is the naval prosecutor Schuler, who embodies the perversion of justice in defence of the existing social order. Toller is at pains to lend his character a personal dimension: we first encounter him in an intimate context, dictating a letter to his wife, but he turns immediately from the domestic commonplaces of the letter to make his infamous greeting to the five accused: 'Ah, there are the candidates for death.' From then on, his personal qualities are subsumed in his judicial function. He is aware of the importance of the case entrusted to him, relentless in his pursuit of 'confessions', and prepared to blackmail, intimidate and even invent in order to secure them. Toller was careful to document all the practices he attributed to Schuler, conscious that the authenticity of the character was crucial to his dramatic theme.

If the officers are bound by a common ethos, the sailors are united by their social situation. Sachse articulates their awareness that they are merely 'workers in uniform', unlike the officers, whose trade is war:

> Even if we are coolies and stokers, we are still workers. We were packers and metalworkers and railwaymen and coachbuilders. When the war is over, we shall go back to being packers and metalworkers, railwaymen and coach-builders (p. 147).

The sailors' spokesmen are the five members of the Food Commission. Depicted with unsentimental realism, they are among the most convincing working-class characters Toller created. They first appear during the Battle of Jutland, where they are (deliberately) portrayed as part of the broad mass of enlisted men. Only later do they emerge as spokesmen for popular discontent. The five men are individually characterized, differing widely in political awareness and commitment. Weber largely goes along with the others, failing to see the wider significance of the Food Commission; during the Court Martial, he begins to lie in order to save his skin. Beckers is more committed, but initially considers the men's walkout to be simply a protest against bad food. Sachse is more politically aware, but by no means a dominant figure.

Toller assigns the leading roles to Köbis and Reichpietsch, the dramatic interest resting partly on the psychological and political contrast between them. Reichpietsch is depicted as good-humoured, gregarious, sentimental and somewhat weak. He is a fundamentalist Christian, who believes in the literal force of the commandment 'Thou shalt not kill' – and whose faith determines his political adherence to the USPD. He is politically inexperienced, even naive, accepting the agent provocateur Birgiwski at face value, while Köbis instantly suspects him. Köbis is, from the start, more politically aware than his comrades. He is a natural spokesman for the men's complaints, is the first to suggest the election of the Food Commission and takes the lead in the mass walkout. While others seek to minimize the role of the Food Commission, he sees it clearly as a means of asserting the men's rights. The determination and strength of will which distinguish him from the others emerge during the pre-trial interrogation. Whereas Reichpietsch breaks down under continual questioning, Köbis refuses to make a confession and even Schuler is forced to acknowledge that he is 'the hardest nut'.

The Court Martial confirms Köbis's leadership role. Reichpietsch believes, even at this late stage, in the impartiality of the proceedings, but Köbis has no such illusions. He refuses to defend himself and uses the occasion to declare his revolutionary commitment. He regrets nothing, except that they actually failed to do what the prosecution accused them of – organize a mass strike in the fleet. He ends with a confident prediction that 'Germany will hear our voices, not yours'. The strength of his commitment is confirmed in prison, where he refuses to make a plea for clemency. What finally distinguishes Köbis from the other four members of the Food Commission is that he alone is able to learn from his experience: the legal proceedings against him force him to recognize the true nature of the society which sanctions them. While Reichpietsch still cannot quite grasp what has happened to him, Köbis can put their misfortune into a wider context. When Beckers suggests they should thwart execution by committing suicide, it is Köbis who contradicts him:

> No, lads, drop the ideal. It's galling to be stood against the wall by these people. But every cause demands sacrifices. Our blood will not be spilt in vain (p. 173).

He recognizes that, if they are to die, their death must serve some purpose, and that only their execution will transfigure them into martyrs of revolution. The events of the play's final scene confirm his confidence, lending the men's subjective experience an historical dimension.

Draw the Fires! was first performed on 31 August 1930 at the Schiffbauerdamm theatre in Berlin, where the impresario Ernst-Josef Aufricht had scored a spectacular 'hit' exactly two years earlier with Brecht's *Threepenny Opera*. The production of *Draw the Fires!* marked a peak in the development of the realistic 'Zeittheater'. Brecht's collaborator, Caspar Neher, devised a set simulating a warship in motion; the stage effects included a direct hit by a shell on the engine room. The critical reaction was favourable, most reviewers finding only praise for both the production and the play, but the box-office success of earlier Toller productions was not repeated. Aufricht recalled that thousands of complimentary tickets were sent to trade unions and other workers' organizations in the hope of at least filling the theatre, but even these were not taken up.[35] Despite this failure, *Draw the Fires!* remains one of Toller's best plays: technically accomplished, stylistically consistent and thematically coherent. As an outstanding example of documentary political theatre, it anticipated by over thirty years the work of playwrights like Rolf Hochhuth, Peter Weiss and Heinar Kipphardt in the nineteen sixties.

Draw the Fires! was first conceived as a film and no account of Toller's dramatic work in the Weimar years should overlook his experiments in the new media of film and radio. Film, in particular, was a medium which fascinated many left-wing writers. Lenin, after seeing D.W. Griffith's *Intolerance*, had declared that this, above all, was the medium to communicate the revolutionary message to the masses. There is no doubt that it was the propaganda potential of film which attracted Toller: 'For us socialists, the film could be a weapon of inestimable value,' he commented while still in prison.[36] His belief in the revolutionary potential of film was strengthened by his experience of early Russian cinema and by his collaboration with Piscator. In his original outline for *Draw the Fires!*, he expressed the hope that such a film would be financed jointly by the Volksbühne and the trade unions, but no such support ever materialized. Responding to a newspaper survey in 1929, Toller wrote that the reason he did not write film-scripts was that there were no producers ready to commission them.[37] But he added that he was now writing his first film, referring to a film version of *Hinkemann* on which he had begun work in January and for which the famous Russian director Pudovkin was to be engaged.[38] The project, however, never came to fruition. It was 1931 before Toller finally did write a film, collaborating with Walter Hasenclever on *Men behind Bars*, a German version of the MGM film *The Big House*, an early 'talkie', made in 1930 from the play of the same name by Lennox Robinson.

Radio, like film, symbolized for Toller the inherent ambiguity of technical progress, on which he had reflected while still in prison:

> What you tell me about the radio has made me think. Every technology has a dual potential, one constructive, one destructive. Men have so far used the boldest calculations, the most brilliant inventions in order to kill each other, to gas cities, to lay waste whole countries. This dangerous duality is also intrinsic to the radio.[39]

Radio had the attraction of a mass audience, a fact which Goebbels would later exploit. Toller made several broadcasts between 1927 and 1932 and in 1930 also tried his hand at the medium of radio

drama, to which such well-known writers as Brecht, Friedrich Wolf
and Erich Kästner had already turned. Toller's radio play *Berlin –
last edition!* uses the technique of montage, consisting of a series of
short, loosely-related scenes which enact the headlines from a
newspaper.[40] The play contains a number of references to topical
events, an interesting anticipation of the techniques of the 'living
newspaper', developed in the USA in the thirties. The events themselves range from the momentous to the trivial – from the League of
Nations Disarmament Conference to an interview with a visiting
film-star – but the headlines reduce them all to the common denominator of banality. They become mere items for consumption: an
implicit criticism of the medium in which they are purveyed.

That Toller did not make even greater use of the radio was
because from 1930 the radio authorities began to exercise an internal
censorship which anticipated the eventual 'Gleichschaltung' of the
medium after 1933. The transmission of *Berlin – last edition!* was
actually delayed while the text was referred to the Foreign Ministry
and was finally sanctioned only with 'grave reservations about the
tendency of the play as a whole'.[41] Toller later wrote a second radio
play, *Indizien (Circumstantial Evidence)*, which was broadcast in
Austria in 1932, but was never heard in Germany. It seems to have
been a radio version of Toller's stage play *The Blind Goddess*, which
suffered a similar fate, being premièred in Vienna in 1932 but never
produced in Germany. These examples of censorship were tokens of
wider political developments – and it is to these we must now turn.

XI

Russia and America:
Which World, Which Way?

In the years after his release from prison, Toller became a regular, almost an habitual international traveller. It is sufficient here to record the main destinations in a progressively restless itinerary which, after 1933, was to become almost an end in itself. In March 1925, he travelled to Egypt and Palestine for a lecture tour which was planned to last six months, but which he was forced to cut short through illness. In 1926, he spent ten weeks in the Soviet Union, returning there for the October Revolution celebrations in 1930. He spent the summer and autumn of 1926 in France. He made a number of foreign lecture tours – to England (1925), returning in 1928 and 1929, to Austria (1927), Denmark and Norway (1927) and Sweden and Norway (1928). In 1929 he carried out a three-month lecture tour of the United States. Among other countries he visited were Czechoslovakia (1925), Italy (1925 and 1928), Poland (1930), Switzerland (1924, 1929, 1931 and 1932) and Hungary (1932).

Toller's political reputation preceded him throughout his travels. On his first visit to Switzerland in 1924 he was admitted only after signing a pledge to refrain from political activity and above all from contact with the League of Nations. When he visited Italy in 1928, he was followed wherever he went by two detectives, one of whom quoted passages from *The Swallow Book* to him.[1] He first came to London in 1925 at the invitation of the PEN Club to give lectures and readings from his work, but despite the literary purpose of his visit he had great difficulty in obtaining a visa, finally securing one only through the intervention of Paul Löbe, the President of the Reichstag, with the British passport authorities.[2] Toller's work was already known in London through the productions of the Stage Society. Some idea of his standing can be gained from his engagements in Britain; he not only addressed the PEN Club, but lectured at Cambridge on 'Contemporary Trends in German Theatre' and 'received an enthusiastic reception' when he read parts of *The Swal-*

low Book to a large audience invited by the English Goethe Society at King's College, London.[3]

Toller's closest political contacts in Britain were with the Independent Labour Party (ILP), whose ideology corresponded closely to that of the USPD. He was entertained to lunch at the offices of the party's newspaper *The New Leader*, where he was entertained by the editor H.N. Brailsford, and contributors who included Bertrand and Dora Russell.[4] His plays were read and performed by local dramatic groups affiliated to the ILP Arts Guild, which had been formed to present plays and films for socialist audiences.

Toller did not record his views of Britain, but his occasional journalism includes impressions of many of the other countries he visited, which reveal him as an interested and acute observer.[5] All his travel writing is essentially an account of the political and social conditions he encountered and none more so than the travel sketches which he wrote following his visits to the Soviet Union and the USA. These impressions, published in the miscellany *Quer Durch (Which World: Which Way?)*[6] are not only fascinating commentaries, but indirectly make a cohesive statement of Toller's political convictions, especially his attitude towards the Soviet Union, the touchstone of left-wing commitment in the nineteen twenties.

Toller's Russian and American 'Travel Sketches' are a fragmentary and often anecdotal account of his experiences, in which he reports incidents and encounters, facts and events in the 'objective' style typical of all his documentary prose. Toller's intention, however, was not simply to report but to diagnose, integrating his fragmentary impressions into a coherent social and political critique. The anecdotal approach was no mere accident, but part of a careful and deliberate method: 'You know, of course, that I prefer actual incidents to theoretical descriptions, because they are richer in connotation' (p. 184). In fact, Toller draws few direct conclusions, preferring to make his points through the editorial techniques of selection, juxtaposition and emphasis. In this respect, the book is typical of the social reportage which became an established part of Weimar literature.

Toller's starting-point in considering American and Russian society was to test the fundamental assumption which each made about itself. In the USA he was concerned to examine the extent of political freedom in the 'land of the free'; in Russia, he set out to record the progress towards socialism in the 'first socialist country'.

His impressions, originally written quite separately, became through careful juxtaposition a contrast of opposing political systems. This contrast had a didactic purpose which Toller made explicit in his introduction to the English edition of the work:

> Russia and America – two lands, two ways. Both of them immeasurably rich in their variety of races, landscapes and natural resources. Both young and unimpaired in their belief in their own strength. But the America of today, controlled by a small section of callous financiers, *was* the land of the future. Russia *is* the land of the future.[7]

America

The 'American Travel Sketches' contain Toller's impressions of his visit to the United States from September to December 1929. Toller had come to the USA at the invitation of Ludwig Lore, the editor of the German-language newspaper *Volkszeitung* and President of the International Labor Alliance, to lecture on modern Germany and developments in the German theatre. In an itinerary which covered some twenty American cities and also took him to Mexico, he gave some thirty-five lectures and readings from his work to audiences consisting mainly of workers and students of German origin.[8]

At the time of his arrival, he was hailed by Pierre Loving in the *New York Evening Post* as 'the foremost German playwright of the day', but in fact his work was little known in the USA. The experimental Theatre Guild had produced *Man and the Masses* in New York, but the production had excited no more than polite interest in what was regarded as a theatrical curiosity. Outside New York his work was probably unknown.

Toller's impressions of the United States on the eve of the Depression appear fragmentary, but are in fact arranged into a careful and systematic critique of American capitalism. His theme is outlined in the opening paragraph: ' "You have the freedom, we have the statue" says a line in the revue *Fifty Thousand Frenchman*, now playing in New York. Only the second half of this sentence is true (p. 9).' The lack of real freedom in the 'land of the free' was effectively illustrated by Toller's own immediate experience.

On arrival in New York, he was detained on Ellis Island by the immigration authorities and interrogated about his political opinions. He was finally admitted to the USA only on condition that he took no part in American politics; his visa was limited to three months instead of the usual twelve.

Toller had told the immigration authorities that he remained a radical socialist, a viewpoint which is implicit in his 'Travel Sketches'. He begins by considering the position of the American worker, who he had always thought was much better-off than his German counterpart. The reverse side of this prosperity was the decline of the American labour movement, exemplified by the suppression of the International Workers of the World (IWW), the compliance and corruption of the trade unions and the embourgeoisement of the workers, encouraged by devices such as profit-sharing and equity participation. In fact, the American worker, economically vulnerable through the lack of proper sickness or unemployment insurance, had bought his modest affluence at the price of his virtual enslavement to capital.

The lack of real political freedom is shown to be a consequence of the lack of economic freedom – of productive relations within the capitalist system. Toller exemplifies this in his description of Fords where the division of labour has reached its logical conclusion in the rigid demarcation of assembly-line production. The monotony of the assembly line led to the alienation of the worker from the product of his labour:

> It can therefore happen that a man spends his whole life performing the same hammer blow on a particular car part without ever seeing the finished car which he has helped to build. The capitalist system will however never be able to solve these problems (p. 27).

To underline the inhumanity of capitalism, Toller follows his description of Fords with a visit to a Chicago slaughterhouse, which also used assembly-line production methods: 'If Ford is called the human hell, this is the animal hell.'

From the system of production, Toller turns to its reflection in the country's social institutions, starting with the prison system. He describes a visit to San Quentin, during which he visited 'Death Row'. He saw flower baskets hanging outside each cell and heard a warder recount some of the strange and macabre practices:

> Sometimes the prisoners want to be hanged to music.
> They're well off . . . they get what they want. One wan-
> ted jazz music, so the prison band played jazz dances for
> him. They have better food than we warders do. Even
> chicken for dinner (p. 38).

Toller comments: 'Flower baskets, chicken for dinner, gallows with music. That's civilization.'

The main purpose of his visit to San Quentin had been to meet Tom Mooney, a well-known socialist who had been in prison for many years for a crime he did not commit. Nor was this a miscarriage of justice, but a perversion of it, for he remained in prison long after anyone continued to believe in his guilt, simply because he was a militant socialist. By publicizing Mooney's plight, Toller hoped to contribute to his release, but his case also served to exemplify the misuse of the law in defence of the prevailing economic system, a theme reiterated in a short documentation entitled 'How Socialists are treated'.

Religion served the same objective function of maintaining the capitalist system, since it was a means of sublimating social suffering and discontent. Toller illustrates this in his account of Aimée Sempel McPherson, whom Evelyn Waugh was later to satirize in *Vile Bodies*. Toller stresses the overt connection between business and religion: Aimée had built her Church of the Smiling Light with money from wealthy patrons. Moreover, her sect was only one of many financed by private wealth: 'Everywhere, rich people support these sects, every church has its little "Rockefellers" as patron saints (p. 54).' In 'Aimée', Toller's irony is directed against her obviously fraudulent activity. Her church services were theatrical events, using modern technology and publicity techniques to promote her own position and influence, exploiting the credulity and chauvinism of the American public. Toller would return to the theme of religion as a business in his play *Miracle in America*.

Toller's interest in the 'worldly prophetess' was primarily to show how popular consciousness was permeated by the ethos of capitalism. This is further illustrated in public attitudes to criminality, which ignored the social causes of crime, and even more clearly in the materialist attitudes to sex and love. Prostitution was illegal, but its practice was widespread. Popular attitudes to love were both sentimental and deeply materialistic, virginity being treated as a capital asset to be traded only for marriage. It was the ethos of capitalism which determined the social position of women in America, reducing them often to the role of decorative symbol.

The arts also reflected and reinforced the prevailing economic system. Toller was fascinated by the cinema and particularly by the potential of the 'talkies', which had just been introduced. He admired the primitive vitality of King Vidor's *Hallelujah*, which he thought demonstrated the artistic potential of film, but in general he deplored the limitations placed on the medium by those who owned the means of production. He had hoped to see as many plays as possible in the USA but was disappointed by those he was actually able to see. With few exceptions, the American theatre had degenerated into the business of entertainment for the bourgeoisie. It was dominated by 'whodunnits', drawing-room comedies and musicals, deliberately excluding works of social criticism:

> The theatre in America is an institution for the entertain-ment of the propertied classes. Woe to the authors who portray the reverse side of American prosperity. They are not performed, as in the case of Upton Sinclair. Only small studio theatres will stage them (p. 64).

The objective function of this theatre was to reinforce the social order it portrayed. The arts, which above all should stimulate intel-lectual freedom, contributed to its suppression: 'For in God's own country, which calls itself the land of liberty, there is little evidence of intellectual freedom (p. 63).'

In his last section Toller returns explicitly to his starting-point. In the land of the free, the negro was not only denied elementary political rights, but even deprived of the protection of the law. Toller cites several cases of negroes falling victim to lynch law, but he sees in the subjection of the blacks the seeds of eventual emancipation: 'Today a vanguard of black pioneers are struggling; tomorrow a self-confident army of millions will be fighting for human rights (p. 78).'

Russia

Toller's 'Russian Travel Sketches' are arranged in conscious contrast to his impressions of America. They had originally been written more than three years earlier, recording his impressions of a ten-week visit to the Soviet Union in the spring of 1926. Toller had gone there at the invitation of Anatoli Lunacharsky, the Soviet Commissar for Education – an indication of his considerable standing in the Soviet Union. Though critical of Expressionism, Lunacharsky had personally encouraged the publication and performance of Expressionist plays. At the time of Toller's visit, no less than nine of his works had been published in the Soviet Union; Lunacharsky himself had written a foreword to a Russian edition of his *Prisoner's Poems* in 1925.[9] Toller was not only the best-known modern German playwright in Russia, but the most frequently performed. Meyerhold had produced both *The Machine Wreckers* and *Masses and Man* in his Revolutionary Theatre in Moscow, while *Wotan Unchained* had actually been first produced in Russian translation at the Bolshoi Theatre in November 1924. Meyerhold's pupil, Sergei Varnov, staged several Expressionist plays in Leningrad, including *Hinkemann*.

As the train approached the Soviet border, Toller's feelings were a mixture of anticipation and trepidation:

> All the nerves are taut with expectation. At last! What a feeling! And yet there is something like apprehension. What will I actually find? But the feeling is dispelled by the simple realization: You are in the first socialist country (p. 86).

Toller's journey to the Soviet Union was one made by many European intellectuals in the ninetween twenties. At this historical distance, it is virtually impossible to imagine the widespread enthusiasm which the Soviet Union then inspired among progressive artists, and nowhere more so than in Germany. If the Civil War had isolated Russia until 1921, the Rapallo Treaty, re-establishing diplomatic relations between Russia and Germany the following year, had brought a sudden flowering of cultural relations, producing such organizations as the Society of Friends of the New Russia, whose patrons included Alfred Döblin, Albert Einstein and Thomas Mann.

A steady stream of German intellectuals visited the Soviet Union in the wake of Rapallo, among them journalists like Alfons Paquet and the famous 'roving reporter' Egon Erwin Kisch, critics like Walter Benjamin and Alfred Kerr, the poet J.R. Becher, the academic E.J. Gumbel and other literary men such as Arthur Holitscher, Franz Jung and Ernst Glaeser. They came in search of a brave new world, and most of them found it. Holitscher called the Soviet Union 'our spiritual home', Kerr 'the most grandiose social experiment for 2,000 years', while to Glaeser and F.C. Weiskopf it was simply 'the state with no unemployment'.

Toller was received as a distinguished foreign visitor. He was met on arrival by official delegations from various cultural bodies, interviews and photographs appeared in most newspapers and he was swamped with invitations to speak or appear at meetings. Toller's 'Russian Travel Sketches' were originally written as a series of letters, but though he first began to revise them for publication in 1926–27, he did not publish them until 1930. In fact, he had some reservations about publishing them at all, acknowledging their fragmentary nature and even admitting that they were to some extent already out-of-date:

> Nevertheless, I venture to publish these impressions, because they serve as a document of Russia's development and are an endeavour to investigate spiritual tendencies which after all do not change so quickly.[10]

The 'Russian Travel Sketches' were therefore an attempt to assess the Soviet Union's progress towards socialism, but though he records his impressions of factories and prisons, schools and theatres, he was less interested in social institutions as such than in the 'spiritual tendencies' they manifested – that is, in the development of socialist consciousness.

Toller's impressions have been criticized as bland and uncritical, reflecting to the outside world the régime's own view of itself, but he was a much keener and more critical observer than almost any of the other celebrities who visited the Soviet Union at this time. He was certainly impressed by the achievements which impressed all sympathetic visitors – the progress in education and childcare, the emancipation of women ('Russian women have awoken') and above all the immense will to social reconstruction. But his enthusiasm was tempered by criticism. He recorded the emergence of ideological orthodoxy and conformism and the intolerance of dissent.

Moreover, his impressions are arranged to form a consistent counterpoint to the American sketches, consciously pursuing the same themes and motifs. His comments on Fords have their counterpart in his impressions of a motor factory in Leningrad, through which the position of the worker under socialism is contrasted with that of his counterpart under capitalism. While Ford workers were under surveillance by management spies and company police, Toller was surprised to find that the Russian workers voluntarily submitted to being searched on leaving the factory. In Russia, as in the USA, there were disparities in earnings which seemed incompatible with socialism. If living standards had scarcely improved, the working ethos had been transformed: 'Our everyday life is materially little better than before . . . But in the factory the worker is a human being, not a 'hand', as he used to be (p. 113).'

If Fords represented the alienation of the industrial worker inherent in capitalism, how far could socialism offer the worker a different perspective? Watching early experiments in work study at Moscow's Central Institute of Technology (ZIT), Toller was forced to reflect on the nature of socialist production: 'I feel oppressed. Is this what our goal is? The mechanization of the human being, the deadening of all our creative faculties? (p. 123).' Socialism had not liberated the worker from the tyranny of the machine: this mechanistic reduction of man to a series of predetermined functions had been the basis of the critique of industrial capitalism he had launched in *The Machine Wreckers* and refined in 'Ford'.

Toller's reflections on prison conditions in Russia are once more implicitly contrasted with those in the USA. In Russia he visited Sokolniki, one of the model prisons included in every Soviet guided tour. While the prison régime seemed humane, he was more sceptical than other visitors, such as Harold Laski or the Webbs. He was shocked at the severity of some sentences and bitterly critical of the 'administrative arrest' practised by the GPU. Above all, he knew that 'prison is always something terrible':

> However enlightened the régime, a prison remains a prison. Only those may doubt it who have not experienced prison. This is not the place to discuss whether prisons are among the institutions which socialism has the duty of uprooting, though I am one of those who think so.

He adds: 'Nothing pleases a real human being if he lacks freedom (p. 130).' This reaction of the libertarian socialist to the authoritarian strain in Bolshevism is not an isolated one.

Toller's revolutionary past caught up with him again in Russia. Shortly after his arrival, a defamatory article appeared in *Pravda* accusing him of treachery and defeatism in the Munich Soviet Republic. When he protested, he was initially advised to issue a statement admitting his past errors and acknowledging the revolutionary leadership of the Communist International; he refused, but was finally allowed to publish a reply in *Pravda*. He recounted the incident 'not for its personal side' but because 'the surrounding atmosphere is significant' (p. 96). He felt that it had positive consequence in that many people he met became less reticent in their criticism of conditions in the Soviet Union.

This 'small incident', with its overtones of bureaucracy and conformity, introduces one of the major themes of the 'Russian Travel Sketches': the growth of ideological dogmatism and party orthodoxy. He noted the efforts to instil ideological orthodoxy at the University of the East, where the Party trained its future cadres: 'The most important subject is Leninism. Students' essays are examined to see if their contents are in accordance with the precepts of Lenin (pp. 117–18).' He was uneasy about the burgeoning cult of Lenin, whose image was found in almost every public place. He rejected the explanation that this cult was a concession to popular psychology, a substitute for the religious veneration which was now frowned on. He felt that, on the contrary, its effect was intellectually debilitating:

> For a cult always has a crippling effect on individual responsibility, the development of one's own faculties, its adherents believing that what must be recognized and done has already been recognized and done by their idol (p. 107).

It exploited latent feelings of chauvinism and popular credulity in the same way as the business of religion did in America. Toller is therefore not merely criticizing the cult of personality, but suggesting it will prevent the growth of socialist consciousness. Moreover, 'we should not underestimate the danger that socialist teachings may become articles of faith which are accepted without thinking, as the Catholic accepts his dogma, especially if it also brings a few State benefits' (p. 108).

The dangers of ideological dogmatism were also apparent in the campaign to discredit Trotsky, whose achievement in organizing the Red Army had already disappeared from the official history books. Hearing Trotsky speak, Toller could only admire his rhetorical gifts and his many-sided erudition. By the time Toller's impressions appeared, Trotsky was in exile, but Toller saw no cause to retract and never joined the attacks on Trotsky.

Toller criticized the strict press censorship from the point of view of the libertarian socialist: 'a workers' government must encourage the lively criticism of all workers (p. 161).' He was also aware of the hardening 'party line' in theatre and literature. At the time of his visit, official changes in cultural policy had already begun which would lead to the condemnation of artistic modernism as 'formalist' and the adoption of socialist realism as the approved form of socialist art. While he (mistakenly) detected signs that official censorship was becoming less strict, he also recorded the growing intolerance of non-Party writers, such as Ilya Ehrenburg, Isaac Babel and Boris Pilniak who, while broadly supporting the revolution, had retained their intellectual independence and now suffered the officially-inspired attacks of the 'proletarian' writers organized in RAPP (Russian Association of Proletarian Writers) who condemned their failure to produce what passed for proletarian literature. Official ideology contradicted Trotsky's argument that proletarian art was impossible in a period of social transition. Schools had been set up to teach the principles of proletarian art, in which students were taught 'to see revolutionary events with the eyes of the Marxist, always emphasizing the role of the Communist Party' (p. 167).

Toller's critique of Bolshevism, written essentially in 1926, anticipated some crucial aspects of Stalinism – rigid ideological orthodoxy, the suppression of opposition, the cult of personality, the establishment of socialist realism as the only approved form of art. It is all the more surprising that, on subsequent visits to Russia in 1930 and 1934, he was apparently blind to developments which confirmed his worst fears. He remained, certainly until 1936, a committed if critical supporter of the Soviet Union, as he emphasized in a letter to Lunacharsky:

> Since 1918, since the founding of the Soviet Union, I have been working, both on a political and a literary plane, at countless meetings, in countless essays, manifestoes, resolutions as a friend of the Russian revolution. Not only in Germany but also abroad.[11]

Toller was certainly among the left-wing sympathizers who supported the various pro-Soviet organizations created by the Communist publisher Willi Münzenberg: he joined the League against Imperialism, addressed the founding congress of the Committee of Friends of Soviet Russia in 1928, and was a signatory to the resolution of the International Defence Committee for the Soviet Union in 1930.

Support for the Soviet Union was the common denominator in the twenties amongst left-wing intellectuals. Under the impact of political developments in 1929–30, many of them – among whom were Gustav Regler, Ernst Ottwalt, Ernst Glaeser and Arthur Koestler – joined the KPD, and in view of Toller's long-standing sympathies, it seems pertinent to ask why he did not do the same. Toller's differences with the KPD were firstly historical. His role in the Bavarian Soviet Republic had been the subject of repeated attacks, which had begun during his imprisonment, continued after his release, surfaced during his visit to Russia and culminated in 1929 in a pamphlet by Erich Wollenberg, who had been one of his Red Army aides at Dachau.[12] Toller had defended himself spiritedly, but as he confided to Lunacharsky: 'Such attacks certainly don't damage my enthusiasm for the cause, but I find them incomprehensible and their effect is to embitter me.' Clearly he could only have joined the KPD at the price of disavowing his own past – and equally clearly, he saw no reason to do so.

Toller's differences with the KPD were also ideological. While he had moved decisively away from the anarchism of his political beginnings, he never fully embraced Marxism. He rejected the bourgeois democracy of the Weimar Republic, in which the ruling class manipulated the democratic structure in its own interests; he endorsed the Marxist belief that the very conditions of bourgeois society made class conflict inevitable. While he acknowledged the importance of economic forces, he placed them in a perspective of ethical idealism. He rejected crude economic determinism – the mechanistic interpretation of Marxism which he had caricatured in *Hinkemann*. He viewed the revolutionary process as one of 'dialectical interaction' ('dialektischer Wechselspiel') of economic forces and human will. In a debate on radio with Alfred Mühr, the Nazi editor of the *Deutsche Zeitung* – a debate which exemplifies the political polarization of the Weimar Republic – he emphasized that economic theory must be matched by moral commitment: 'Kant once said that ideas without viewpoint are blind.'[13] He himself consistently evoked socialism in terms of freedom, justice and democracy. His work in the years 1924–33 sought to demonstrate that these ideals had been perverted within bourgeois society and would ultimately be realised only in the economic organization of socialism.

Certainly, Toller did not share the belief of the KPD in the leadership role of the revolutionary party. Revolutions were not instigated by an élite revolutionary vanguard: 'Revolutions are not made' he told Alfred Mühr, 'they are preceded by collapse.'[14] He had experienced the German Revolution as a largely spontaneous response to the breakdown of the prevailing social order, a perception which received an extended exposition in his autobiography. His political thinking in the final years of the Weimar Republic was dominated by the idea of a broad left front, and he could only have been alienated by the growing sectarianism of the KPD, which culminated in the theory of social fascism. Temperamentally, ideologically and politically, he was divided from the KPD.

XII

Dress Rehearsal for Dictatorship
1930–1933

The year 1930 was a watershed in the history of the Weimar Republic. The financial crisis marked the end of economic stability and the effective end of democracy: after March 1930 it was impossible to form a government which commanded a parliamentary majority. In the September elections, the Nazis scored an unexpected triumph, winning 107 seats and becoming the second strongest party in the Reichstag. 1930 also proved to be a turning-point for Toller, the beginning of a decline in his reputation and effectiveness, which can be seen in the reception of his work. *Draw the Fires*, which had opened in Berlin only a fortnight before the Nazis' electoral triumph, was a critical success, but a failure at the box-office; the publication of *Quer Durch* received barely a notice in the press. Neither work was reprinted.

The reasons for this decline lay primarily in the worsening political situation and the abrupt change in public mood which it determined. Fritz Landshoff, director of the Kiepenheuer Verlag, which had published not only Toller, but Brecht, Kaiser, Kesten and other radical authors, recalled that their representatives were suddenly not welcome, their titles no longer in demand.[1] The commercial theatre was dominated by operetta and escapist fantasy. Theatre managers were increasingly unwilling to produce left-wing plays for fear of provoking violent scenes. Toller summed up the situation bitterly in an answer to a newspaper survey: 'The current state of the theatre is that the reactionaries decide which plays can be performed and which can't.'[2] Certainly, none of the plays he wrote after 1930 enjoyed a Berlin première. *Miracle in America*, was first produced in provincial Mannheim; *The Blind Goddess*, was given its première in Vienna and was never performed in Germany.

In an atmosphere of growing political repression, the committed playwright faced the choice of confronting the situation or withdrawing from it. Playwrights such as Brecht and Friedrich Wolf both abandoned the commercial theatre. Wolf, a recent recruit to the

KPD, turned to agitprop and from 1932 ran the Spieltruppe Südwest, a theatre group playing in labour halls and factories, for whom he wrote three short plays. Brecht too abandoned the commercial theatre, devoting himself to the 'Lehrstücke', didactic pieces intended for amateur performance; he also collaborated with Slatan Dudow and Ernst Ottwalt in the agitational film *Kuhle Wampe*, which again had a predominantly amateur cast.

Toller, for his part, seems to have been unable to adapt his work to the political situation after 1930. In the notes on his own plays contained in *Quer Durch* (1930), he had affirmed his faith in the power of political theatre to influence social reality. By the end of the year, he had apparently lost any such hope: 'Books have no effect,' he told Ernst Feder.[3] Toller's disillusion is certainly confirmed in both the plays he wrote in 1931–32, which conspicuously fail to confront the political situation directly. *Miracle in America*, written in collaboration with Hermann Kesten, dramatizes the career of Mary Baker Eddy, the founder of Christian Science. It was Toller who had suggested that they should collaborate, Kesten who suggested the topic of Mary Baker Eddy, his interest having been stimulated by Stefan Zweig's influential essay, which first appeared in 1930.[4] The play is an exposé of Mary's religious pretensions, tracing her rise from obscure faith healer to leader of the richest and most powerful sect in the USA. She is portrayed as a calculating charlatan, who acknowledges the capitalist principle that money is power: 'We shall be rich, millionaires,' she tells her husband Eddy. 'Don't be scared, riches are power. Only power convinces. Nobody believes a poor man.'[5] The play therefore takes up a theme Toller had already broached in his 'American Travel Sketches': the business of religion. Mary Baker Eddy rises to power by ruthlessly exploiting popular credulity: her appeal is knowingly irrational, but her presentation carries complete conviction. Toller obviously felt that she offered parallels with the rise of Adolf Hitler, but such indirect analogies were equally obviously overlooked.

The withdrawal from the political situation is even more striking in *The Blind Goddess*, based on a notorious miscarriage of justice in Switzerland, whose victims Toller had visited in prison in 1931 while they were awaiting the reopening of their case.[6] The play therefore returns to the judicial theme of *Draw the Fires*, but the treatment shows a striking shift of emphasis. *Draw the Fires* was a record of 'class justice' within a revolutionary perspective, but *The Blind God-*

dess contains virtually no implication that the miscarriage of justice it portrays is endemic to capitalism. The play is too specifically tied to the case it portrays, indicting a specific injustice rather than the injustice of society. Toller's protagonist Anna Gerst is transformed by her experience of unjust imprisonment, but her transformation is of personal, not political, significance: she leaves her former lover only to withdraw into private isolation. Both *Miracle in America* and *The Blind Goddess* confirm Toller's talents as a dramatist. The latter, in particular, is a well-crafted play, which was successfully premièred in Vienna, but it remains curiously irrelevant to the political situation of 1932–33, marking Toller's temporary abdication from the role of political playwright.

Toller's disenchantment with political theatre is all the more remarkable in view of the clarity of his analysis of National Socialism. Unlike so many of his contemporaries, he had never dismissed Hitler as a beer-hall demagogue. In September 1930, he was as unprepared as most other observers for the Nazis' sudden electoral success. Kurt Grossmann remembered an occasion on the terrace of the fashionable Café Bauer on Unter den Linden, just before the election, when Toller had confidently predicted that the Nazis would win no more than 25 seats.[7] Even after the election, many on the left were still inclined to disparage the Nazi threat: Toller had no such illusions. In the article 'Reichskanzler Hitler', published three weeks later in *Die Weltbühne*, he warned that 'Reich Chancellor Hitler is at the very gates of Berlin'; the title he chose confirms his awareness that the real danger lay in Hitler's taking power by legal means.

Toller had few illusions about Republican democracy, but he none the less saw the need to defend it. He felt that the only force capable of opposing Nazism was 'the united front of the German trade union movement', doubtless thinking of action along the lines of the general strike which had frustrated the Kapp putsch in 1920, but he was sceptical that it could be achieved. The trade unions were, he wrote, too concerned to protect their funds to mobilize their members.[8] In the deteriorating situation of 1932, he felt that the only means of averting Nazism was the 'creation of a united organization of the working class with clearly defined concrete objectives'.[9] In the autumn of 1932, Toller's signature appeared, together with those of such notables as Albert Einstein, Heinrich Mann and Käthe Kollwitz, under an appeal for cooperation in the forthcoming Reichstag elections between the two main left-wing parties – 'preferably in the form of common candidates, or at least in the form of an associated list'. The mutual hostility of SPD and KPD preempted any such possibility.

Toller's growing certainty of political disaster and his helplessness to avert it did not impair his political commitment. In the course of 1931–32 he was actively involved in various campaigns against the growing censorship and judicial repression. The most notable was the case of Carl von Ossietzky, the editor of *Die Weltbühne*, who in November 1931 was sentenced to eighteen months' imprisonment for 'betraying military secrets', after publishing an article exposing the illegal rearming of the Reichswehr. Despite protests and petitions on Ossietzky's behalf, Hindenburg refused to exercise his presidential prerogative to grant a pardon. On 10 May 1932, when Ossietzky arrived at Tegel prison to begin his sentence, he was met by a group of some eighty friends and supporters who had gathered in defiance of the official ban on public demonstrations. Toller made a short speech, quoting the poet Wieland: 'Writers who address uncomfortable truths to those in power are punished as heretics and criminals.'[10]

At the International PEN Congress in Budapest later that month, Toller succeeded in putting politics on the agenda of such a meeting for the first time in a speech condemning the spread of censorship and the growing suppression of intellectual freedom. Citing specific cases, particularly Ossietzky's, he invoked the writer's political responsibility in the face of fascism:

> What is the point of living if not for justice and freedom? Perhaps my friends and I will no longer be free to speak to you next year, perhaps our voices will be stifled in the cells ... I send greetings to those writers who cannot attend the banquets of the PEN Club, who, because they fought for truth and social justice, languish in prison.[11]

Toller's speech became the focal point of the Congress, leading to bitter exchanges with the Italian delegate Filippo Marinetti. Toller hoped to turn Ossietzky's case into 'an international scandal', but the PEN Congress was too limited a forum to achieve such an aim.[12]

Germany's steady decline into dictatorship was reflected in the increasingly strict censorship. Under an emergency decree of 1931, such novels as Hans Marschwitza's *Sturm auf Essen* (*Attack on Essen*) and Klaus Neukrantz's *Barrikaden am Wedding* (*Barricades in Wed-*

ding) were banned for allegedly 'endangering public order and security . . . and the vital interests of the state'. The same decree was used to prohibit the Brecht-Ottwalt film *Kuhle Wampe*, a ban which provoked a storm of indignation. Toller took the Chair at a protest meeting called by the German League for Human Rights, condemning the censor's decision as 'the most stupid and ridiculous ban the censor has yet produced'.[13]

Toller could speak with some authority, for he himself was no stranger to censorship. As early as November 1930, the transmission of his radio play *Berlin – last edition!* had been delayed at the instigation of Erich Scholz, who was responsible for vetting scripts on behalf of the Ministry of the Interior. It was finally broadcast only over Scholz's 'grave concern about the tendency of the play as a whole and particular scenes contained in it'.[14] In April 1932 Toller was due to give a series of radio broadcasts on his visit to Republican Spain, which were actually programmed and then cancelled, again at Scholz's instigation. *Die Weltbühne* cited the incident as proof of the increasing Nazi influence on the radio, and Scholz had indeed joined the Nazi Party in 1931, shortly after being appointed 'Reichsrundfunkkommissar' (Reich Controller of Radio).

However prophetic Toller's analysis of Nazism, his voice went largely unheard in the last years before Hitler, not least because he lacked an effective political platform – part of the price he paid for his stance as an independent socialist. If he felt helpless to affect the course of political developments, he also felt that he could not leave Germany, where his personal and cultural roots ran too deep.[15] There may have been an additional reason.

Early in 1932 Toller met Christiane Grautoff, the young actress whom he would marry in exile in London three years later. She was the daughter of a distinguished art historian who had also been for many years the chairman of the Franco-German Society. She had begun her stage career as a child actress in 1928 in a play by Carl Zuckmayer, *Kakadu-Kakada*, in which she attracted the attention of the legendary Max Reinhardt, who engaged her for a new play by Ferdinand Bruckner, *Die Kreatur*. Her performance in this play and later in a stage version of Kästner's *Emil and the Detectives* captivated audiences and critics alike: she had become one of the great attractions of the Berlin stage, a genuine 'Theaterwunderkind'.

When Christiane was introduced to Toller by her drama coach Lili Ackermann, she was still not sixteen. She retained a vivid

impression of their first meeting: 'Ernst Toller's eyes were unend-
ingly sad. His flat was small, his study narrow, the window barred.'[16] She would learn that Toller could only write in a small room,
preferably with a single barred window which simulated the physical
conditions of the prison cell in which he had written his greatest
stage successes. The meeting evidently also made an impression on
Toller, who came to see Christiane in her current play, a thriller with
Fritz Kortner. 'From then on, Toller and I saw each other
frequently.' They met mostly at the flat which Toller shared with his
publisher Fritz Landshoff on the Württembergische Strasse. The
pattern of these meetings was quickly established: 'ET and I had a
very strange relationship. It was completely platonic . . . We had
long conversations about his life, about my life, his thoughts and my
thoughts . . . Very soon, he began to read to me from his unfinished
works. "Which do you like best?" he would always ask. He was just
writing the final scene of *The Blind Goddess*.' After a few months,
Christiane told her eldest sister that she had met the man she would
marry. Toller was undoubtedly much less certain, not only because
he was conscious of her age, but also because of the increasingly
threatening political situation.

He had gradually begun to spend more and more time abroad. He
was in Switzerland for much of the summer of 1931 and during the
winter of 1931–32 spent some five months in Spain and North
Africa. In May 1932 he was in Hungary, in the summer he was once
more in Switzerland, spending several weeks in the small town of
Comologno at the summer home of the Zurich lawyer Vladimir
Rosenbaum, who had first drawn his attention to the legal case he
had dramatized in *The Blind Goddess*. Among the other guests at
Comologno were old friends like Kurt Tucholsky and new acquaintances like Secondo Tranquilli, better known under his literary
pseudonym, Ignazio Silone.[17] The latter's fate as a political exile
from fascism was to prefigure Toller's own.

The intellectual and even physical threat to progressive artists in
Germany was now impossible to overlook. In June 1932 von Papen
had become Reich Chancellor, beginning an immediate intensifica-
tion of the campaign against anything seen as 'Kulturbolsch-
ewismus' (cultural Bolshevism). The Nazis, now the largest party in
the Reichstag, openly threatened their opponents. The Nazi paper
Völkischer Beobachter published in August a list of 'those representatives of a decadent and declining era', whose work they would

shortly ban. It included the names of virtually all the leading avant-garde figures in Weimar literature: Fritz von Unruh and Franz Werfel, Friedrich Wolf and Bertolt Brecht, Lion Feuchtwanger and Leonhard Frank, Stefan Zweig and Carl Zuckmayer, Walter Hasen-clever and Ernst Toller. Six months later the Nazis would make good their threat.

Toller himself was all too aware of the prevailing atmosphere. In January 1933 he published a short sketch in a literary journal. It is a dramatic dialogue between a theatre director and his 'Dramaturg' (literary manager), in which the latter enthusiastically recommends a play by a new author, which the director rejects out of hand, contending that this new author must really be a Jew in disguise. The first task of the theatre director, he declares, is to cleanse the theatre of Jews and other subversive elements. It was Toller's last publication in Germany.[18]

XIII

The First Year of Exile
1933

When Hitler became Reich Chancellor on 30 January 1933, it was clear that no left-wing author would be allowed to write or publish freely in Germany and that some would only remain there at the risk of their lives. Ernst Niekisch recalled that Toller telephoned him at this time to ask advice: should he leave Germany or should he stay?[1] Niekisch advised him to leave, but in fact Toller seems to have temporized – towards the end of February, he left Berlin for Switzerland, where he was to make a series of radio broadcasts. It is certain that he intended to return to Germany, but in fact his exile had already begun.

On the night of 27 February, the Reichstag was burnt down. Before the flames had even been extinguished, police and Nazi storm-troopers began a well-planned operation to arrest some 4,000 communist activists and other prominent left-wing figures. They included over 130 Berlin writers and intellectuals – communists like Ludwig Renn and Willi Bredel, the anarchist Erich Mühsam and independent socialists like Ossietzky and Kurt Hiller. Some of them would never retain their liberty. Two hours after the outbreak of the Reichstag Fire, SA storm-troopers broke into Toller's flat to arrest him; not finding him, they ransacked his belongings and left.

Fritz Landshoff, who shared Toller's flat, had also been away from Berlin. When he returned home the following day, neighbours warned him to leave with all possible speed. The SA had already returned in search of Toller and warned they would be back again, a threat which Landshoff found particularly ominous in view of his own striking physical resemblance to Toller.[2]

Toller's absence from Germany, whether prudent or fortuitous, probably saved his life. If he had fallen into the hands of the Nazis, he would almost certainly have shared the fate of Erich Mühsam, who was mistreated, tortured and finally murdered in Oranienburg concentration camp. In the following months, Toller's plays were banned, his books burned, his property confiscated. Most of his personal papers and manuscripts were probably lost or destroyed at this time, certainly few original manuscripts of Toller's work before 1933 have survived. In the introduction to his *Letters from Prison*, Toller recorded that the letters which formed the backbone of the book were rescued by the journalist Dora Fabian, who entered his flat shortly after the SA raid and removed two suitcases full of papers. When the police found out, she was arrested and imprisoned, but resolutely maintained that she had destroyed the papers. After her release, she fled abroad, 'managing in some inexplicable way' to smuggle the papers out of Germany.[3]

On 1 April, in a major speech to introduce the official boycott of Jewish shops and businesses, Josef Goebbels denounced Toller as a public enemy of the Third Reich. Indicting those typical representatives of the Jewish spirit which sought to undermine the New Germany, he named the periodical *Die Weltbühne*, the philosopher Theodor Lessing and – as the leading enemy of the Nazi ideal of heroic militarism – Ernst Toller. 'Two million German soldiers,' Goebbels cried rhetorically, 'rise from the graves of Flanders and Holland and indict the Jew Toller for having written: "the ideal of heroism is the stupidest ideal of all".'[4] On 23 August Toller's name appeared with thirty-two others in the first list of those stripped of their German nationality. The list included those who had most actively denounced Nazism – communists such as Ruth Fischer, Wilhelm Pieck and Willi Münzenberg, socialists like Philipp Scheidemann and Rudolf Breitscheid, the academics F.W. Foerster and E.J. Gumbel and writers like Toller, Feuchtwanger, Tucholsky and Heinrich Mann.

The works of such authors had already been banned. In April the Nazi government had published a black list of authors ranging from Marx to Freud and from Brecht to Thomas Mann. On 10 May their works were publicly burned in one of the archaic ceremonies so typical of Nazism. On the Opernplatz in Berlin, students from the University, led by their new Professor of Political Pedagogy, Alfred Bäumler, and accompanied by the military bands of the SA and SS, burnt twenty thousand books, throwing them into the fire to the accompaniment of ritual incantations: 'Against decadence and moral corruption, for discipline and decency in family and state, I consign to the flames the works of Heinrich Mann, Lion Feuchtwanger, Erich Kästner . . .' Similar scenes were enacted in every other university town in Germany. The book-burnings were not simply a ritual demonstration of the Nazis' wish to suppress all intellectual opposition, but a token of their determination to eradicate the literature of a whole generation. Many of these writers would remain forgotten for more than thirty years in the post-war Federal Republic: a fact which was both a symptom of the Cold War and a retrospective tribute to the success of Nazi cultural policy.

The Reichstag Fire was followed by an exodus of writers and intellectuals on a scale which no country had seen before. Exile was a misfortune which, in the past, had befallen the individual writer, but in Germany in 1933 it became an almost universal experience. The American journalist Dorothy Thompson wrote that 'practically everybody who in world opinion has stood for what is currently called German culture prior to 1933 is now a refugee'. By the time the Law for the Establishment of the Reich Chamber of Culture was proclaimed in 1933, there was hardly a writer of international standing left in Germany who was not in prison or, like Gottfried Benn and Hanns Johst, an enthusiastic supporter of the régime.

Few of those who fled thought they were starting a long exile. There was a widespread belief that the Nazi régime would soon collapse of its own incompetence or, amongst communists, that it would precipitate a workers' revolution. Significantly, most refugees settled at first in the countries bordering on Germany. As Brecht wrote in his poem 'Concerning the Label Emigrant':

> Restlessly we wait thus, as near as we can to the
> frontier
> Awaiting the day of return, every smallest alteration
> Observing beyond the boundary . . .[5]

Toller too had settled 'as close as possible to the borders', spending the first months of exile at the home of Emil Ludwig in Zurich. He too seems to have been awaiting developments in Germany, scanning the newspapers and listening to the stories of refugees who began to arrive in Switzerland in a steady stream. It was during these anxious months that Toller completed his autobiography *Eine Jugend in Deutschland* (*Growing up in Germany*).[6]

Toller's autobiography is often considered to be his finest work: it is certainly an incisive and immensely readable account of his early years, ending with his release from prison at the age of thirty. He had written the book largely in the twilight years of the Weimar

Republic, though some of the final passages were obviously written in exile. He had published some short autobiographical pieces as early as 1926–27, some of which he later incorporated into *Growing up in Germany*, but it was not until 1929 that he actually began work on an autobiography. 'I have a lot of work to do,' he wrote to his American sponsor Ludwig Lore, 'I am beginning to write down my experiences and this will keep me busy for a year or two.'[7] He worked intermittently on the book over the next four years, providing occasional extracts for broadcasts or anthologies.[8] It is clear that in February 1933 he was working on the manuscript, which he took with him to Switzerland: it thus escaped the fate of his other papers which fell into the hands of the Nazis. He continued work on the book during the following months, completing it in August, when he showed it to Kurt Tucholsky.[9] As the Nazis' ruthless consolidation of power forced many refugees to abandon hope of an early return to Germany, the first exile publishing houses were formed, notably the German sections of the Amsterdam publishers De Lange and Querido. Fritz Landshoff, who had taken charge of the German section of the Querido Verlag, met Toller in Zurich in the late summer. The two men quickly agreed terms for the publication of *Growing up in Germany* and Landshoff took the manuscript back with him to Amsterdam, where it was published that autumn, going into a new edition before the end of the year.

Toller did not intend the work to be merely a personal memoir, for he was convinced that his individual experience had representative validity: 'Not only my youth is depicted here, but the youth of a whole generation and a piece of contemporary history as well (p. 7).' His recollections are arranged into a highly stylized narrative, in which events are selected and presented for their wider significance. Toller's foreword, dated 'on the day my books have been burned in Germany', outlines his frankly didactic purpose: 'Anyone who wishes to understand the collapse of 1933 must be acquainted with the events of 1918–19 which I recount here (p. 7). Toller was concerned to show that Nazism was not an inexplicable phenomenon, but one which had its roots in the militarist and nationalist traditions of German history. He was suggesting – and he was among the first to do so – that the reasons for the collapse of the Weimar Republic were implicit in the circumstances of its inception, namely in the failed revolution of 1918.

Toller portrays the November Revolution as a largely spontaneous revolt, in which the masses were driven, not by revolutionary idealism, but by the trauma of defeat and starvation:

> The German Revolution found an ignorant people, a leadership of petty bourgeois bureaucrats. The people called for socialism but hitherto no one had given them any idea of what socialism was. They turned on their oppressors, they knew what they didn't want, but they had little idea of what they did want (p. 111).

A major reason for the failure of the revolution had been the caution and embourgeoisement of the SPD leaders: 'entwined and enmeshed in the old regime', they opposed the revolution in the name of law and order. Toller concludes: 'They hated the revolution. Ebert had the courage to say so (p. 111).'

Toller tells his story from the perspective of 1933. His account of the Soviet Republic is written in the present tense, both to lend the narrative immediacy and to emphasize its contemporary resonance. In Munich, the SPD makes common cause with the enemies of the revolution: Auer 'helps and arms' attempts to set up a Citizens' Defence Force. Toller calls the force a 'forerunner' of the paramilitary groups which disfigured Weimar democracy, commenting pithily: 'One day they will chase off those who helped to bring them into being (p. 114).' The political dilemma of the SPD is illustrated in the plight of the Bamberg government in April 1919 which has to ask for military aid from the Reich: 'Soon the generals are the political masters, the Bamberg government their tool (p. 153).' It is the generals who refuse to negotiate: 'They hate Bavaria because it was the only place where the Republic was strong ... In smashing the Bavarian Soviet, they were aiming at the Republic itself (p. 154).' The point of reference in contemporary reality is here made explicit.

The disunity of the left, which had contributed to the collapse of 1933, was also prefigured in the Bavarian Soviet: 'In Munich, the revolutionaries fight amongst themselves; in Northern Bavaria the opposition is gathering its forces (p. 132).' This factional strife, to which Toller returns again and again, had an added significance in exile, as attempts to form a German Popular Front against the Nazis foundered on the mistrust of the SPD.

The failure of the revolution was above all a failure of socialist consciousness. Wide sections of the working class had been condi-

tioned by the authoritarian ethos instilled in school and barracks.
Toller shows how this spiritual legacy undermined the revolution in
its inception. In the Red Army he commanded it had been necessary
to reintroduce military discipline to maintain any sort of fighting
force: 'Oh, the German worker was accustomed for too long to
obedience, he wants only to obey. He confuses brutality with
strength, authoritarian arrogance with leadership, exoneration from
personal responsibility with discipline . . . (p. 147).' The moral and
political collapse of 1933 is therefore already implicit in the attitudes
and events of 1918–19.

The political climate of the early thirties clearly determined
another major concern of the autobiography, in which Toller
explored, for the first time, his own attitude to his Jewish identity.
As we have seen, he had dramatized his rejection of his Jewish
heritage in his first play, but he later felt that he had sublimated the
problem in his commitment to socialism. There are few references to
Judaism or Jewishness in his work in the twenties, though his
attitude continued to be somewhat ambivalent. He clearly felt drawn
to Palestine, which he visited in 1925 for the opening of the Hebrew
University. He was greatly interested in the pioneering Jewish settle-
ments there, which seemed to practice something close to his own
communitarian ideals, but he considered Zionism an irrelevance: 'I
am not a Zionist . . . Sheer necessity made me a socialist and left no
room for devotion to a cause like Zionism.'[10] He was interested in
some aspects of Jewish culture, but like most Jewish intellectuals in
Weimar Germany, he felt thoroughly assimilated to the German
cultural scene.

The growing visibility of anti-semitism forced him to reappraise
his position after 1929. Born and brought up on the Eastern edge of
the Empire, he was particularly sensitive to the prejudice against
Jewish immigrants from Eastern Europe. *Growing up in Germany*
opens with a section tracing his family's roots in Samotschin back to
the time of Frederick the Great, implicitly distinguishing him from
the anti-semitic stereotype of the 'Ostjude'. Anti-semitism is the
dominant note in his account of childhood. The first memory he
recalls is of a nursemaid telling another child not to play with him
because he is a Jew. His own incomprehension and pain at such
incidents are summarized in the child's question to his mother:
'Why are we Jews?' He recounts his estrangement from Judaism and
his 'terrible joy' when he was not taken for a Jew. The chapter

'Childhood' largely overlaps with the opening scene of *The Trans-formation*, but the perspective differs significantly. The play is a subjective justification of Toller's rejection of his Jewish heritage. The autobiography emphasizes the social pressures of discrimination which cause it: 'I don't want to be a Jew. I don't like children running after me calling me "Jew-boy" (p. 21).'

In retrospect, he suffered deep feelings of guilt: 'I sought to deny my own mother. I am ashamed.' In the final section of his autobi-ography – clearly written after his exile had already begun – Toller reaffirms his Jewish identity. While insisting on the formative role of German language and culture on his personality, he also acknow-ledges his debt to Jewishness:

> But am I not also a Jew, a member of the race which for centuries has been persecuted and hounded, martyred and murdered? . . .

Consciously taking issue with Nazi racial ideology, he asks:

> Am I therefore an alien in Germany? Is blood the only valid test? Doesn't the country I grew up in mean any-thing? Or the air I breathed, the language I spoke, the spirit which formed me? If I were asked, where are your German and where are your Jewish roots I should not know what to say (p. 227).

This passage confirms that the importance of the autobiography for Toller's development lies not in the events themselves but in his retrospective view of them. Under the impact of political develop-ments in 1933, the book was increasingly subsumed into the struggle against Nazism which became his main purpose in exile.

Emil Ludwig later suggested that, in the years immediately before 1933, Toller felt that he had lost his political role: 'As he flitted about vaguely, Hitler came to his aid, giving him a new enemy, a new arena. His flame was rekindled.'[11] The pattern of Toller's life in exile demonstrates his conception of the role of the committed writer, in which the public predominated over the private role. 'If I am work-ing, I am possessed by that work, but I know that we may once again face decisions in which personal commitment is more important than art.'[12] These words, written in 1930, were prophetic of his life in exile, in which all his work was consciously subordinated to the single purpose of exposing the true face of Nazi Germany. It was a campaign which he pursued from every available public platform: in lectures and broadcasts, and in passionate speeches to the various International Writers' Congresses which punctuated the decade. His second public concern was complementary to the first. The extensive relief projects he undertook, first on behalf of his fellow-refugees, and later to feed the civilian population of Spain, were conducted in the context of advancing fascism. These campaigning commitments undoubtedly deflected him from purely literary work, but his literary production during the last six years of his life was nonetheless considerable. As well as a volume of autobiography, he compiled an edition of his prison letters (1935), wrote two plays, *No More Peace!* (1934–35) and *Pastor Hall* (1938), two film scripts, *Der Weg nach Indien* (*The Road to India*) and *Lola Montez* (both 1936–37), as well as poems, essays and articles. All of this work belongs in the context of exile, much of it representing a conscious counterpoint to his speeches and lectures, echoing their themes and often their very words.

Toller began his campaign to convince international opinion of the true nature of the Nazi regime in a speech to the International PEN Congress held in Dubrovnik in May 1933. He had long been critical of the political neutrality espoused by the PEN Club, contending that it was illusory to believe that an international association of writers could ignore political questions. At the PEN Congress in Budapest in 1932, he had spoken on freedom of speech, attacking the growing censorship in many countries, including the host nation. The 1933 Congress was held less than three weeks after the book burnings in Germany, making it inevitable that this question would dominate the proceedings.[13]

Even before the book burnings, the German PEN section had been purged of all Jews and politically unreliable writers, and the official German delegation to Dubrovnik consisted of Hans Martin Elster, Edgar von Schmidt-Pauli and Fritz Otto Busch, three writers who were known for little but their allegiance to the new Germany. Even before the opening of the Congress, they made concerted efforts to counter the prevailing anti-Nazi mood among the delegates on board the special ship taking them from Trieste to Dubrovnik. On the opening day of the Congress, they struck a series of backstairs deals aimed at preventing discussion of the many resolutions critical of Nazi Germany.

In those early days of exile, there was no official organization representing anti-Nazi German authors, and Toller, having been expelled from the German PEN, was invited to attend the Congress as a member of the English delegation. He had not travelled with the other delegates and had not arrived on the first day of the Congress, prompting speculation as to whether he would actually come. He finally arrived on a ship which docked in Dubrovnik early the following morning: one participant recalled that the news 'Toller has come' spread through the town like a forest fire. Toller made his way straight to the conference hall, where his appearance threw the Congress into complete turmoil. Progressive writers clapped and cheered him, while opponents heckled and cat-called.

At this point, the Congress chairman H.G. Wells announced that he had decided to allow an open discussion of the whole question of book-burning and censorship. When he invited Toller to speak, the official German delegation walked out, followed by the Dutch, Austrian and Swiss delegations, while the remaining delegates ostentatiously applauded. It was not in fact until the following day that Toller gave his prepared speech, a furious indictment of the Nazis. He began by referring to his own good fortune in escaping arrest: 'the freedom which I have retained by pure chance obligates me to speak for those who no longer can.'

The main body of his speech was a violent denunciation of the 'Gleichschaltung' of the arts in Germany. He read a long list of authors whose work had been burned, before asking a series of rhetorical questions exposing the complicity of the official German delegation in this suppression of freedom of speech. What, he demanded, had the German PEN section done to protest at the book burnings? Or the persecution of leading scholars and scientists? What had it done to prevent the banning of artists or the blacklisting of authors, or the intimidation of publishers abroad into refusing their work? He called the Nazi regime 'an outbreak of madness and barbarism', rejecting the allegation that his speech was anti-German, since he refused to accept that the Nazis represented Germany. Millions of Germans could no longer speak freely and it was he and the other exiles who must now speak for them. He thus evoked for the first time 'the other Germany' which the exiles claimed to represent and which was to become the unifying theme of exile literature.

Both the applause for Toller's speech, and its echo outside the conference hall, were unparalleled in the history of the PEN. His speech was widely reported in the world press, making him once more an international figure and a symbol of German opposition in exile to the Nazis. A Jugoslav journalist commented that he had rarely seen anyone become so popular so quickly: he had been spontaneously applauded everywhere he went. During the summer, he returned to Jugoslavia for a series of lectures and readings.

Toller's speech in Dubrovnik set the agenda for his political activity in exile. During the following six years, he gave over two hundred recorded speeches, lectures and broadcasts – the actual figure is probably much higher – seeking to expose the brutal reality of the Nazi regime and deny its right to speak for Germany.

In September 1933 Toller arrived in London to testify to the Legal Commission of Inquiry into the Burning of the Reichstag: he was to spend most of the next three years in Britain. The Commission was what we might now call a media event, conceived as a counterpart to the official Reichstag Fire Trial which the Nazis were about to stage in Leipzig. It was the brainchild of the publisher and propagandist Willi Münzenberg, forming part of the campaign to secure the release of Ernst Torgler, Georgi Dimitrov, and the other principal defendants. The *Daily Worker* called it 'the trial of a trial'.[14]

The Commission was comprised of eminent lawyers, drawn from eight different countries and selected for their liberal reputation, under the chairmanship of the Labour lawyer D.N. Pritt. The hearings took place in the court-room of the Law Society, a small room which was packed throughout the proceedings by members of the press and public. Toller was only one of a series of well-known witnesses who included Albert Grzesinski, the former Police President of Berlin, Georg Bernhard, sometime editor of the *Vossische Zeitung*, and Reichstag deputies Rudolf Breitscheid, Paul Hertz and Wilhelm Koenen. One of the principal tasks of the organizing committee was to secure the entry of these witnesses into the country in the face of Home Office obstruction. Toller testified on the final day of the hearings, giving evidence of the attempt to arrest himself and other leading writers. ('I do not know what I was to be charged with. There are thousands of people in concentration camps today who do not know what they are charged with.') He declared his belief that the Fire was part of a pre-arranged plan and closed his address rhetorically: 'I refuse to recognize the right to rule of the present rulers in Germany, for they do not represent the noble sentiments and aspirations of the German people.' Isabel Brown, secretary of the organizing committee, remembered that Toller also addressed public meetings organized around the Commission and spoke of his 'untiring efforts on behalf of Dimitrov and his fellow-prisoners'. He also addressed a meeting at the House of Commons on the conditions in concentration camps, offering to show the MPs a film which a former prisoner had managed to shoot and smuggle out of Dachau – an offer inexplicably refused because of the film's alleged technical shortcomings.

Sceptics like Kurt Tucholsky thought Toller was wasting his time: 'What can Toller testify? It's nonsense. He knows nothing about the matter.'[15] But Toller had recognized that the purpose of the Commission was not to establish the truth, but to discredit the official trial and bring pressure to bear on its verdict. The Commission's findings, which exonerated the principal defendants, were accordingly presented on 20 September, ensuring that the news appeared the following morning to coincide with the opening of the actual trial in Leipzig. There were many on the left who hailed the eventual acquittal of Dimitrov as a significant defeat for the Nazis and a triumph for the international campaign which had been mounted. Toller himself was in no doubt:

> Even dictators bow before public opinion. If world opinion had not made a strong demand, if men who were true to the great traditions of their nations had not lent their aid, would the innocent Dimitrov have been saved from the scaffold?[16]

The Reichstag Fire remained an event charged with emotional and symbolic significance for Toller. He returned to it in 1938 in his last published poem 'Die Feuerkantate' ('The Fire Cantata'), in which he makes the Fire both a symbol of the political repression of the Nazis and a beacon lighting the future generations which will sweep them away.[17]

Following the Inquiry, Toller remained in Britain during October and November to carry out a lecture tour under the auspices of the PEN Club. At this time, he must also have concluded an agreement for the publication of the English version of his autobiography. By the end of the year, he was back in Switzerland. Taking stock of the first year of exile, he could not contain his disappointment. He had hoped to gather his fellow-exiles in a common fight against Nazism, but he found them divided amongst themselves, as he wrote to Emil Ludwig:

> At times I thought of uniting the exiles with the strict discipline of a legion, but it was a futile attempt. The émigrés of 1933 are a confused collection of those exiled by chance – including many Jews who are Nazis manqués, weaklings with vague ideas, paragons of virtue whom only Hitler prevents from being swine, with very few men of conviction among them. German, all too German.[18]

Public disillusionment was compounded by private sorrow. On 28 December 1933 his mother died. For months he had lived with the fear that he would never see her again: his grief at her death echoes in his letters, and in the thinly fictionalized account which he left among his unpublished papers. His sister wrote that his mother had died with his last letter worn in a locket around her neck, like an amulet.[19]

XIV

Exile in London: PEN,
Pacifism and Popular Front
1934–1936

In February 1934 Toller finally settled in Britain, the country which,
he declared a few months later, had become a second home to him.[1]
He lived in London until September 1936, though he continued to
travel widely abroad. In August and September 1934 he was in
Russia; he spent much of the following summer in France, and in
the spring of 1936 he made a six-week tour of Spain and Portugal.
One reason for his decision to settle in London was probably the
relative freedom from the publishing restrictions imposed on the
literary exile in Switzerland, but he nonetheless seems to have felt a
genuine affinity with England. Interviewed by a Finnish newspaper
in 1934, he affirmed that the concept of justice was more alive in
Britain than anywhere else. He had been amazed that even conservative newspapers had called for the release of the German Communist
leader Ernst Thälmann, but in England, he affirmed, there was
nothing unusual about this, which was why a refugeee could feel at
home there.[2]

The greatest problem for most exiles was to turn their back on the
past and adjust to conditions in their adopted country. Many were
unable to find a foothold, but Toller showed a remarkable ability to
integrate himself into British society. He was lionized in London
literary circles. He was elected an honorary member of the English
PEN Club, was invited to lecture to university audiences in London
and Manchester and to address a variety of cultural organizations,
such as the young PEN Club, the British Drama League and the
Society for Cultural Relations with the USSR. His contacts with the
PEN Club were facilitated by the International PEN secretary
Hermon Ould, a long-standing friend who had made the English
translation of *Hoppla* in 1928. Toller was friendly with Kingsley
Martin, the editor of the *New Statesman* and with the writer and
journalist H.N. Brailsford, whom he knew from his previous visits

to London. He was taken up by the well-known *Times* journalist Wickham Steed, who would regularly invite him to Sunday lunch. A particularly good friend was Richard Ellis Roberts, then literary editor of *Time and Tide*, which published much of Toller's literary journalism; Roberts was later the translator of Toller's *Letters from Prison*, and more than once lent him his country home at Stroud (Gloucestershire) so that he could work undisturbed.

During the two and a half years Toller lived in Britain, his work achieved a popularity almost unprecedented for a foreign, let alone a German, writer. His autobiography was published in 1934, his collected plays in 1935 (the only collected edition of his work to appear in his lifetime) and his prison letters in 1936. Several of his plays were also printed or reprinted in separate editions. When his autobiography appeared in English translation, it was reviewed in over a dozen publications, including the *Manchester Guardian*, *Observer*, *The Times Literary Supplement*, *New Statesman* and *Spectator*. His activities were sometimes reported in the press, his essays appeared in *Time and Tide*, *The Bookman* and *The London Mercury*. He engaged in public controversy with H.G. Wells and was translated by Edward Crankshaw and W.H. Auden. In short, he was soon scarcely less of a literary celebrity than he had been in Germany.

Toller's literary reputation in Britain probably reached its peak in February 1935 with the publication of *Seven Plays*. *Draw the Fires* was also published separately to coincide with its production at the Manchester Repertory Theatre – a production which Toller himself praised as the only one which contained all his ideas. Reviewing *Seven Plays*, the Irish playwright Sean O'Casey wrote: 'But Toller's a dramatist and that's the thing that counts. England will be striding nearer to a finer drama when Toller has his London season.'[3] Toller never had his London season, indeed his reputation in Britain rested on a mere handful of professional productions. The parochial and conservative nature of the London stage in the inter-war years meant that the production of foreign or experimental plays was limited to the 'little theatres' or Sunday evening play societies, and Toller's work was no exception. Even at the height of his standing in Britain, his work was produced only by theatre clubs or socialist drama groups. *Miracle in America* and *No More Peace!* were produced by the experimental Gate Theatre in London, besides the Manchester production of *Draw the Fires!*.

Toller's literary standing was, as always, inseparable from his political reputation. His speech in Dubrovnik had established him as a symbol of German opposition in exile. He was able to move freely in progressive political circles, numbering amongst his contacts not only journalists like Kingsley Martin and Wickham Steed, but socialist intellectuals like Harold Laski and D.N. Pritt, Lady Oxford, the doyenne of liberal causes, who entertained him more than once, and Fenner Brockway. The latter, then secretary of the ILP, recalled that Toller had close links with the party, giving advice and contacts for the illegal work it sought to carry out in Germany.[4]

It was of course Germany to which Toller still looked. He contributed to such anti-fascist initiatives as Willi Münzenberg's *Brown Book* and to the campaign for the release of Ernst Thälmann. In 1934 he was elected to the managing committee of the German Freedom Library in Paris, a collection of all works proscribed by the Nazis. Alfred Kantorowicz recorded Toller's enthusiasm for the venture and his crucial role in providing contacts (notably Margot Asquith, Lady Oxford) which led to the establishment of a Society of Friends of the Burned Books in England.[5]

Toller was particularly active in the Free Ossietzky campaign on behalf of the former editor of *Die Weltbühne*, who was a prisoner in the concentration camp of Esterwegen and who had been so badly mistreated that there were fears for his life.[6] Early in 1934 the German League for Human Rights in exile launched an international campaign for his release, in which Toller performed the task of winning the support of the *Manchester Guardian* and other English newspapers. Ossietzky's British wife Maude had sent their daughter Rosalinde to England, but the girl was unhappy there and her mother contacted Toller for help. Toller took a friendly interest in the girl, visiting her more than once and arranging, through Bertrand Russell, for her to attend the progressive private school Dartington Hall.[7]

In June 1934 the League for Human Rights began a new campaign to secure the Nobel Peace Prize for Ossietzky, hoping by this means to force his release. The campaign, loosely coordinated from Paris by Ossietzky's former colleagues Hellmut von Gerlach and Hilde Walter, soon grew to international proportions. In the USA it was led by the physicist Albert Einstein, in Norway by the young émigré Willi Brandt (later to become Federal Chancellor and himself to receive the Peace Prize), in London by the journalist Rudolf Olden, together with Toller and the writer Otto Lehmann-Russbüldt. Toller had already proved himself a shrewd and forceful lobbyist and, together with Olden, succeeded in winning the support of prominent British intellectuals like Aldous Huxley, H.G. Wells, Norman Angell, Bertrand Russell and Virginia Woolf. Toller was careful to remain in the background for fear that his public advocacy might harm Ossietzky, but it was largely at his instigation that articles by Wickham Steed and Elisabeth Bibesco in support of Ossietzky's nomination appeared in *The Times*.[8] Lion Feuchtwanger recalled an occasion in 1935 when Toller, newly married and living in a picturesque but somewhat tumbledown house in Hampstead, entertained an English journalist to win his support for the campaign. Toller was all too successful: 'The man who was to be won for Ossietzky had long been won. He should long since have gone, but he stayed and poor Toller finally had to go out to buy the coffee which was nowhere to be found in the house.'[9]

It was not always so easy. The novelist Ethel Mannin remembered the night when she and Toller, both fresh from a reception at the Soviet Embassy, tried to persuade W.B. Yeats to nominate Ossietzky to the Nobel Committee. This bizarre meeting took place in the lounge at Claridge's, to the accompaniment of loud music from the orchestra. The two poets had made an odd couple as they entered Claridge's: Yeats tall and distinguished, wearing the cloak he would often affect in the evenings, Toller 'short, dark and "foreign-looking"', wearing a picturesquely broad-brimmed hat and looking like something out of the pages of *La Vie de Bohème*'. Toller was at his most passionately persuasive, Yeats listened, but replied that he neither knew Ossietzky nor had any interest in politics. Toller, his eyes beginning to fill with fears, made an emotional appeal, urging that this was not a political matter, but a question of saving a man's life. Yeats was distressed, but insisted that he could not help.[10]

Toller was disappointed, but not discouraged, and was later successful in persuading the Labour academic, Professor Harold Laski, to nominate Ossietzky.[11] The campaign slowly gained wide international support, transcending its initial objective and transforming Ossietzky himself into a powerful symbol of the 'other Germany' the exiles so often sought to evoke. In November 1936 the Nobel Prize Committee finally announced the award of the Peace Prize for 1935 to Ossietzky. Toller, then already in America, greeted the news as a victory for international solidarity, calling for a redoubling of effort to secure Ossietzky's release. In fact, the Third Reich ignored inter-national opinion, refusing to allow Ossietzky to travel to Oslo to receive the prize; he was finally released only to die in hospital in May 1938.

It was in Britain that the typical pattern of Toller's life in exile became established. During 1934–35 he was in great demand as a speaker and lecturer, activities which may initially have been a necessary source of income, but which soon came to take precedence over literary work. He spoke on both literary and political subjects, although the dividing line was increasingly thin. In a lecture at Manchester University on 'The German Theatre Today', he dis-cussed the stylistic innovations of Expressionism and 'Neue Sachlichkeit' – and their suppression by a political ideology which denounced 'all modern experiments as cultural Bolshevism'. He was greeted by prolonged applause which, always conscious of his representative standing, he took as a tribute 'not only to myself, but to all free writers who are not living in the Third Reich'.[12]

The thirties were a decade in which public events forced many writers into political commitment, and this increasing convergence of literature and politics is aptly illustrated by events within the International PEN in 1933–34. Toller's speech in Dubrovnik had begun a rapid politicization of the PEN; in its aftermath he made strenuous efforts to have the German section expelled for violating the organization's basic principles. When the German section finally resigned of its own accord, Toller, Feuchtwanger and Rudolf Olden founded a PEN centre of German writers in exile in December 1933. It was to be 'a centre of free German literature', aiming to counter the propaganda of official Nazi culture, to relieve the isolation of exiled writers and to offer practical help where possible. While its main value was symbolic, its efforts did help, for example, to rescue German-speaking writers from Austria and Czechoslovakia in 1938–39.

When the International PEN Congress reassembled in June 1934 in Edinburgh, politics dominated the agenda. The President, H.G. Wells, set the tone of the proceedings in his opening address:

> When politics reaches up and assaults literature and the liberty of human thought and expression, we have to take notice of politics. If not, what will the PEN Club

be? A tourist agency introducing respectable writers to useful scenery.[13]

The Congress officially recognized the German PEN section in exile, and the exiles were indeed acknowledged as the true representatives of German thought and culture. Toller was given a particularly warm welcome when he rose to address the Congress. Speaking 'as a writer to writers', he made a long plea on behalf of authors still languishing in Nazi prisons and concentrating camps. 'If we believe in the power of the word,' he said, voicing a constant theme of his years in exile, 'then we cannot remain silent.' At the end of the Congress, he proposed a resolution attacking the Nazi government and calling for the release of writers imprisoned without trial, which was passed with only one vote against.[14]

The proceedings in Edinburgh received wide press coverage, being no doubt a source of some embarrassment to the German Embassy, which carefully monitored all Toller's activities. In January 1935 he began a series of lectures which finally provoked the Embassy into direct intervention. A diplomat called zu Putlitz requested a meeting with the Foreign Office on 10 January, at which he raised 'the question of German refugees – he was thinking particularly of Ernst Toller – who travelled the country giving speeches against the German government'. He requested the government to demand an assurance that refugees would refrain from anti-German activities during their stay in Britain – and, on failure to do so, should be deported.[15] The request was politely refused but other efforts to silence Toller were more successful. In the same month, he was invited to address a rally of the Irish Labour League against Fascism on 'National Socialist Germany', but was refused permission to enter Ireland following representations by the German Embassy in Dublin, which gleefully reported to the Wilhelmstrasse: 'Anti-German speech in Dublin by Communist Toller prevented.'[16]

Nazi efforts to silence their opponents abroad did not stop at diplomatic pressure. Publishers and distributors were threatened with economic boycott if they handled books by black-listed authors, refugee groups were infiltrated by Gestapo agents, prominent exiles were kidnapped or killed. The philosopher Theodor Lessing was murdered in Marienbad, the journalist Berthold Jacob was abducted from Switzerland. Toller increasingly feared an attempt on his own life, especially after his friend and collaborator

Dora Fabian was found dead, in mysterious circumstances, with her friend Mathilde Wurm in their Great Ormond Street flat. The inquest concluded that Dora had killed herself after an unhappy love affair: the coroner's verdict was suicide. Toller himself suspected they had been murdered: 'The whole thing seems to me rather dark and doubtful.'[17] He had begun to receive threatening phone calls from anonymous callers; during part of his time in London he certainly enjoyed police protection. In March 1935 he reported attempts by the journalist Hans Wesemann, a former acquaintance now exposed as a Gestapo agent, to lure him to a suspicious rendezvous in France and Switzerland.[18] Ellis Roberts recalled that he was always apprehensive of being followed.[19]

In December 1933 Toller had returned briefly to Switzerland. Early in the New Year he was in Wengen, where he had arranged a secret rendezvous with Christiane Grautoff, their first meeting for almost a year. Christiane recalled that it was bitterly cold, with several inches of snow on the ground. It was during their short stay in Wengen that Toller proposed marriage to her; it was also here that he received news from his sister in Germany of the death of their mother.[20]

Immediately after their meeting, Christiane returned to Germany, where she was playing at the Schauspielhaus in Darmstadt. She had been engaged to play under the direction of Gustav Hartung, whose reputation in the theatre rivalled that of Reinhardt and Jessner, but shortly after the start of the engagement Hartung had fled to Switzerland. Christiane's precocious talent had not escaped the Nazis, who offered her a leading role in a Nazi film eulogizing Horst Wessel, but she had already decided to leave Germany: she later explained that 'she did not care to be a party to a theatre whose theme was race hatred'.[21] She went to Zurich, playing a short season at the Zurich Schauspielhaus, again under the direction of Gustav Hartung, and in spring 1934 rejoined Toller in London. At seventeen, she was less than half his age; her career seemed to be just beginning, his had already passed its zenith.

Like many other German exiles, Toller was living in Hampstead, where he had a small flat at 1 Lambolle Road. He took a room for Christiane in the house next door. Photographs of Christiane at this time show a slim, fair-haired young woman, attractive and apparently self-assured. Contemporaries have described her as charming, self-willed, or even as a 'problem child', but were unanimous about her promise as an actress. Her feelings for Toller were undoubtedly those of romantic love. His for her seem to have been more difficult to define. She was, on her own admission, completely ignorant of both literature and politics, the twin obsessions of his life. They had the theatre in common but he seems to have been drawn principally to her mixture of youth and assurance: 'She is an "old" actress and yet just a "kid", but some people think that she is more mature than I am.'[22]

Christiane was naturally anxious to pursue her acting career, taking lessons in English language and diction from a Miss Borton, who came every day to coach her. It was, however, some two years before Christiane finally made her London stage debut in *No More Peace!* The couple were married in London in May 1935, moving a short distance to take a flat at 27 Belsize Park, which they rented from the actor and writer Miles Malleson. The flat included an attic room which Toller used as a study. It was about this time that he started to go out regularly at nine thirty in the morning, returning some two or three hours later. When Christiane finally plucked up courage to ask him where he went, she learned that he was consulting a psychiatrist, Dr Hilde Maas, in search of a cure for the sometimes suicidal bouts of depression which increasingly shadowed his life. It was Toller's first experience of psychoanalysis, but during the remaining four years of his life, he periodically received psychiatric treatment.

Christiane had already been confronted by Toller's bouts of depression, during which he would often spend days lying apathetically in a darkened room. These attacks were closely associated with feelings of creative inadequacy, which made him fear that his creative talent had finally deserted him. Neither Christiane nor close friends like Fritz Landshoff could decide if these fears were the cause or the effect of his depression. Toller repeatedly implored Christiane not to disclose anything about these periodic breakdowns, which he evidently felt to be a sign of weakness, incompatible with his public persona. His depressions were separated by long periods of 'normality', during which he would play the literary and social role which had been laid upon him. His changes of mood were abrupt and startling. Fritz Landshoff remembered that days of self-imposed isolation would suddenly give way, often in the early hours of the morning, to a compulsive need for company and conversation.[23] Despite these difficulties, the two years which Toller and

Christiane spent in London were their happiest time together. She recalled that she loved England from the first moment she set foot there. Landshoff confirmed that of all the stations of exile, England was the country where Toller felt most at home.

At the time of his marriage Toller seemed to be at the height of his fame and fortune. The publication of virtually his entire work in Britain had given him relative financial independence, which he now used to launch a major campaign to help fellow-refugees in Britain and France. In Germany he had always earmarked a proportion of his income for political causes; in exile, his generosity and willingness to help rapidly became proverbial. René Schickele advised Kurt Wolff in 1935 to seek help from Toller: 'He is kindness itself and knows lots of people.'[24] But Toller himself was well aware of the limits of individual generosity and set out to prompt government action.

Some 8,000 German refugees had settled in France, representing the largest concentration in Europe. While the French government admitted them freely, most were refused work permits and were thus forced to rely on the generosity of friends or the charity of relief committees. Toller spent several weeks in France to study the situation of refugees there, using his findings to make a series of proposals to alleviate their plight. By skilful lobbying, he gained the support of human rights organizations, trades unions and politicians 'ranging from the extreme right to the extreme left'. He then submitted his proposals to the French government and held discussions with the Ministry of Labour. Toller's campaign revealed both his commitment and his flair for publicity, as the communist writer Alfred Kantorowicz noted ironically: 'Toller is here, full of plans, lionized by various cultural and political bodies. He dines often as guest of honour, speaks often and is totally taken up with his own publicity.'[25] Toller doubtless enjoyed the limelight, as this comment suggests, but he was also shrewd enough to realize that publicity was essential to the causes he espoused.

After the apparent success of his campaign in France, he published similar proposals in Britain in July 1935, reporting that his preliminary recommendations had already been accepted by the relief committees, by different churches and by politicians of all parties.[26] His proposals are practical and even pragmatic, concerning the problems of work permits and identity papers and urging countries to help refugees as a matter of enlightened self-interest. He admitted that they could only alleviate the problem, and suggested that a real solution lay in establishing a special office of the League of Nations, citing the example of Fritjof Nansen, the League's first (and only) Commissioner for Refugees. Toller concluded his proposals by stressing that the refugee question could not be viewed in isolation, but only as 'part of the whole struggle for the victory of humanity over barbarism'. He increasingly defined the coming struggle in Europe as one between civilization and barbarism, democracy and dictatorship, peace and war. The problem of peace in the context of the spread of fascism became an obsessive concern: the keynote of his lectures and speeches and the theme of his play *No More Peace!*

The two and a half years which Toller spent in Britain were crucial for the development of his political views, particularly his attitude to pacifism. Peace and disarmament were among the dominant issues in British politics at this time: 1934–35 saw the emergence of the Christian pacifist Peace Pledge Union, the organization of the Peace Ballot, which secured over eleven million signatures for peace through collective security, culminating in November 1935 in a general election fought mainly on the issue of disarmament.

The inescapable conclusion of Toller's revolutionary experience had been that force was tragically inevitable, that absolute pacifism was incompatible with the demands of political action. His own experience anticipated the dilemma of sections of the European left in the thirties, as they attempted to reconcile their traditional pacifism with the need to oppose fascism by force.

Toller's preoccupation with this problem can be read in the titles of such lectures as 'Masses and Man. The Problem of Non-violence and Peace' and 'The Failure of Pacifism in Germany'. In the former lecture, first given at Friends' House, London, in February 1934, Toller was concerned to reconcile private morality and public necessity:

> Whoever today fights on the political plane, in the hand-to-hand conflict of economic and human interests, must recognize that the laws and consequences of his struggle are determined by other forces than his good intentions, that often the means of offence and defence are forced upon him, means which he cannot but feel as tragic, upon which, in the deep sense of the words, he may bleed to death.[27]

He went on to repeat his long-held conviction of the necessity of education for peace. Asking: 'How is peace to be enforced?', he found the answer in 'the banishment of the spirit of violence and war from schools and universities and from the history books'. Toller also referred his argument to international relations, advocating a form of international security in which the great powers would impose economic sanctions on any nation threatening peace. He concluded by praising 'the adventure of peace' and the inspiration of personal example: 'There is no middle way for the man of action. The world needs examples and exemplary lives.'

Toller's attitude changed markedly in 1935–36 under the impact of political events – the reoccupation of the Rhineland, the propaganda triumph of the Berlin Olympics, the outbreak of the Spanish Civil War – changes which are reflected in the later versions of his lecture, which he revised for American audiences in 1936. Though still concerned to reconcile private and public morality, he now translated the problem onto the plane of international politics. He no longer advocated education for peace, for the urgency of the international situation imposed a much shorter perspective. He now answered the question 'How is peace to be enforced?' by insisting, not on economic sanctions, but on the duty of the democracies to resist Hitler collectively.

By the middle of 1936 he had become resigned to the prospect of a new European war. 'The final fight between fascism and the democratic block in Europe will be inevitable', he wrote to Nehru in July, three days after the outbreak of Franco's rebellion in Spain.[28] He deplored the weakness of the League of Nations, 'which is exploited by fascist dictators', and warned that the democratic states must unite against Hitler: 'If not, they will bring about the very thing they want to avoid: war in a near future.' It was not, however, until the end of the year that he gave these private convictions public expression. In a speech to German Americans in New York, he predicted that 'if the world does not succeed in *forcing* Hitler to keep the peace, he will turn Germany and Europe into a pile of rubble and destroy civilization'.[29]

The development of Toller's views must of course be seen in the perspective of the emerging Popular Front. In the final years of the Weimar Republic, he had consistently advocated a broad left front as the only means of preventing the Nazis taking power; in exile he had continued to support united front action. In the meantime, the political climate had gradually become more favourable. Early in 1934 the Comintern had begun to change course, abandoning its former line of denouncing social democrats as 'social fascists' in favour of a policy of active cooperation with other anti-fascist forces. One of the early signposts to the new policy was the Soviet Writers' Congress in Moscow in August 1934. Internally, the Congress marked the culmination of the attempt to impose a more rigid discipline on the arts and to promote socialist realism as the officially-approved form of art; externally, it represented a move to enlist the support of 'left-bourgeois' writers for an anti-fascist front, and Toller was one of a number of foreign delegates invited to attend. His speech to the Congress was hailed as an important contribution to anti-fascist collaboration and was published in the Moscow-based journal *Internationale Literatur*:

> I applaud your resolution. It is important to open the doors wide to all artists fighting fearlessly against fascism, even if their work does not fulfil all the ideological demands you might make.[30]

The cultural dimension of the Popular Front could not be more clearly stated.

Toller had, of course, been a critical supporter of the Soviet Union throughout the twenties. Whatever his reservations, he now recognized the need to defend the world's only socialist state, declaring this defence to be 'the duty of all those who have retained their belief in the historic mission of the working class'. He publicly took issue with H.G. Wells for alleging that the Soviet Union had suppressed intellectual freedom, stating that the two months he had spent there had convinced him that 'the mistakes of the USSR in the early years are being corrected'.[31]

Toller's support for the Soviet Union was an important corollary of his support of the Popular Front. He had expressed his disenchantment with the divisions among German exiles as early as January 1934. Two years later he published a final appeal for unity across political differences: 'The rulers of the Reich have cause for satisfaction. Three years – and what years – have passed in Germany and still here is no united front of its opponents ... Have we learned nothing?'[32] The following month he was among 118 prominent exiles who met in the Hotel Lutétia in Paris to issue an appeal for a German Popular Front. Toller remembered the occasion as one

which had overcome the divisions and the impotence of the opposition to Hitler, an occasion when he had 'sat together with Catholics
and communists, socialists and liberals, trade unionists and
independent writers, all united in the single burning desire to bring
about a Germany of peace, freedom and justice'.[33] However, while
the appeal was endorsed by the entire KPD leadership, as well as by
many left-wing intellectuals, it was rejected by the SPD leadership in
exile.

The problem of peace in the face of advancing fascism is also the
keynote of Toller's literary work in these years, particularly the
poem *Weltliche Passion* (*Requiem*) and the drama *No More Peace!*
Requiem is a 'Sprechchor' or poem for mass declamation, a form
which Toller had pioneered as early as 1920. It is a celebration of
Rosa Luxemburg and Karl Liebknecht, whose fascination for Toller
we have already noted.[34] *Requiem* is narrated by a Chronicler, whose
story is interspersed with choral parts which illustrate and comment
on it. It begins with a celebration of revolution, evoked by the
hammer and sickle, symbolizing productive labour and fruitful
harvest, a vision threatened by the destructive power of war. It is
Liebknecht who personifies opposition to the war. His words inspire
the struggle for 'a Germany of working hands . . . For a Germany of
justice' (p. 176).

When the forces of capitalism and militarism put a price on the
heads of the two revolutionary leaders, they are betrayed and
murdered, but their sacrifice is not in vain, for it will inspire new
commitment. Their example will ensure final victory: the poem ends
with the confident assertion that 'the world will be ours'.

Requiem is a poetic evocation of Toller's belief that 'the world
needs examples and exemplary lives'; it is also a literary document of
the emerging Popular Front, as its subsequent history demonstrates.
It was first published in the periodical *Internationale Literatur*, edited
in Moscow, following Toller's attendance at the Soviet Writers'
Congress, and appeared shortly after in Klaus Mann's liberal journal
Die Sammlung. An English translation was made in 1935, but never
published.[35] It was a poem for performance and it was frequently
performed in Britain, proving popular with workers' theatre groups.
It was seen in street performances in connection with the Peace
Ballot and subsequent general election in 1935 and later became
firmly established in the repertoire of Unity Theatre. In the years to
1939, it became Toller's most frequently performed work, so that

the poet Randall Swingler could write in an obituary that 'there will be many in England who have been moved by his *Requiem*'.[36]

No More Peace!

The comedy *No More Peace!* was the first of two dramas which Toller wrote in exile. The fact that he wrote only two is often cited as evidence of his creative decline; it is much more a consequence of the material conditions of exile. The practical and financial difficulties facing the exiled writer were undoubtedly greatest for the dramatist. As a performing art, drama requires actors, a stage and an audience – and the practical difficulties of bringing them together in the conditions of exile were almost insuperable. The opportunities for German-language production steadily declined. From 1934, censorship made it impossible to produce left-wing plays in Austria, and though there were still limited opportunities in Switzerland and Czechoslovakia, anti-Nazi plays were not felt to be good box-office, a feeling strengthened by Nazi pressure to ban their performance. In practice, the exiled dramatist found that he was writing for a small group of fellow-exiles. If he wished to reach a wider audience, he was obliged to have his work translated and adapted to suit the tastes and conventions of his adopted country. Both the plays Toller wrote in exile illustrate this situation. Both were written in German, but published only in English translation. *No More Peace!* was revised and adapted for the English stage, but was misunderstood by the London critics; *Pastor Hall* was rejected for production in the USA because the translation was considered to be unsuitable. Neither play was published or produced in German in Toller's lifetime.

No More Peace![37] (the title pointedly inverts the name of the 'No More War!' movement) is a satirical musical comedy, a genre Toller had already tried out unsuccessfully in *Once a Bourgeois*. He wrote the play in 1934–35, though he subsequently had to revise it extensively for English production. The original version contained 'several songs, dances and a small ballet',[38] though only the songs which punctuate and comment on the action survive in the final script, and even these are substantially different in the adaptation of W.H. Auden.

In the spring of 1936 Toller and his wife made a six-week car tour of Spain and Portugal where, during their stay in Cintra in mid-

April, they met Auden and Christopher Isherwood. The latter has left a subjective impression of Toller at this meeting:

> ... throughout the supper, it was he who did most of the talking – and I was glad, like the others, merely to sit and listen; to follow with amused, willing admiration, his every gesture and word. He was all that I had hoped for – more brilliant, more convincing than his books, more daring than his most epic deeds.[39]

Toller seems to have made an equally strong impression on Auden, for though it was their first meeting, Auden must have agreed at this time to translate the songs from *No More Peace!* – indeed he must have started work almost immediately, since rehearsals for the production at London's Gate Theatre began barely a month later.

No More Peace! deals with the fragility of peace and the problem of pacifism confronted by an aggressive and irrational ideology. Faced with the problem of writing for a British audience, Toller tried to universalize his theme by using an imaginary setting. The scene alternates between Olympus, among whose inhabitants are Napoleon and St Francis, and the imaginary republic of Dunkelstein. The scenes in Olympus summarize the argument of the play – which is then illustrated by the course of events in Dunkelstein. In the opening scene, Napoleon strikes a wager with St Francis that, despite the appearance of peace on earth, men are still eager to go to war. Dunkelstein is a proverbial haven of peace and stability, but when Napoleon sends a bogus telegram announcing that war has been declared, the country is immediately put onto a war footing.

Despite the fantasy setting, Toller's satire clearly had a factual target: the depiction of war fever in Dunkelstein had obvious analogies with the rise of Nazism. Cain, a barber, is installed as the fascist dictator of Dunkelstein by the country's leading industrialist, Laban, a connection underlining the alliance which had brought Hitler to power. Laban and his fellow-industrialists judge peace and war solely in terms of business opportunity, contriving to profit equally from both, an opportunism summarized in the Financiers' Song: 'You must do the right thing at the right time.' As dictator, Cain appeals to the instincts of blind chauvinism and racial hatred, calling for the purity of blood and soil and proscribing marriage with foreigners. Disturbingly, he does not need to impose his will by force, for the people willingly endorse his dictatorship, echoing his demagogic slogans.

No More Peace! is a dramatic counterpart to Toller's speeches and lectures, particularly the lecture 'The Failure of Pacifism in Germany', written while he was writing the play. There he traced the post-war transition from pacifism to fascism in Germany, a transition suggested in the play by the device of the turn of a placard. In *No More Peace!* Toller portrayed fascism as intrinsically irrational, enacting his view of 'a time in which reason is despised – yes, unreason has risen up and persecutes reason'. In the hysteria following the outbreak of war, no one is sure who the enemy really is: even Cain can only assert that it is the traditional enemy. He orders the corn-fields to be burnt down to ensure that no spies are hiding there and later orders the bombing of Dunkelstein itself: 'This is war, gentlemen. There will be destruction in any case. Better be destroyed by your own bombs than by the enemy's (p. 85).'

The failure of pacifism in Germany, Toller contended, was not so much a failure of reason as a failure of the belief in reason. He gives this failure dramatic substance when Socrates, the personification of reason, returns to earth to proclaim the truth, only to be stoned by the people of Dunkelstein. Napoleon can declare the success of his stratagem, suggesting that the sole purpose of peace is to prepare for renewed war. Men love the adventure and romance of war, he tells St Francis, and even the suffering of war does not deter them: 'Weren't many of them perfectly happy? Happy to die? . . . Well, personally, I call the courage to fight and die, heroism (p. 100).' 'Have so few men the courage to live?' muses St Francis, a question Toller had already addressed in 'The Failure of Pacifism':

> Everywhere, in schools, in books, in films, in the speeches of Republican statesmen, they built monuments to the wrong heroes, raising them into symbols for the youth of Germany. The only merit of these heroes was a more or less heroic death. But youth should have learned to respect and admire heroic life . . . The Republic should have put up monuments to heroic life.[40]

In this and other speeches, Toller was concerned to draw positive conclusions: *No More Peace!* is more equivocal. The supporters of peace do not fare well: Socrates is ridiculed as a madman, Rachel is imprisoned for proclaiming 'no more war'. Nor do the arguments for peace prevail, for peace is finally restored only through divine intervention.

The circumstances of the play's composition and production show how far Toller's work, like that of all refugees, was circumscribed by the material conditions of exile. His correspondence reveals that he had completed the original version of the play by mid-1935, but he made no apparent effort to publish it in German.[41] (Exile publishers published few plays because of the limited sales they could anticipate.) Toller was obliged not only to have the play translated, but, more important, to redraft it extensively for the English stage. According to his translator Edward Crankshaw, he even continued to rewrite parts of it during rehearsal. Most of these changes were intended to make the analogies with Nazism clearer for an English audience. For example, the installation of Cain as dictator by the industrialist Laban is much more explicit, while the poet who puts his talents at the service of the régime becomes, like Goebbels, Minister for Propaganda.

Auden's lyrics demonstrate his own considerable facility with popular light verse, as shown by the following extract from the 'Spy Song':

> Spies in the bedroom, spies on the roof,
> Spies in the bathroom, we've got proof.
> Spies on the lawn where the shadows harden,
> Spies behind the gooseberries in the kitchen garden,
> Spies at the front door, spies at the back,
> And hiding in the coat-stand underneath a mac.
> Spies in the cupboard under the stairs,
> Spies in the cellar, they've been there for years
> (p. 73).[42]

Auden's lyrics are in fact an original composition, for which Toller's text often serves as little more than a basis. Significantly, it was they rather than the play itself which found favour with the critics, who seem to have taken it all purely as entertainment – and found it wanting.

No More Peace! had considerable personal significance for Toller, both as the first play he had written in exile and as a vehicle for the talents of his young wife. He dedicated the play to Christiane, who made her London stage début in the role of Rachel. The relative failure of the play seems to have strengthened his conviction that the theatre was no longer the most suitable medium to convey his message. He had already written the film scenarios which were to take him to Hollywood; shortly afterwards he completed arrangements for an extended lecture tour of the United States.

'Hitler: the Promise and the Reality' – Toller's North American Lecture Tour 1936–1937

In October 1936 Toller left London for a four-month lecture tour of North America. The immediate reason for the tour was Toller's precarious financial situation, but it would nonetheless mark the peak of his anti-Nazi activity in exile. He had obtained a visa only after several weeks of negotiation in London, but on arrival in New York was admitted unconditionally by the immigration authorities. The tour began in New York on 12 October, taking him across the United States via Canada to California, where it ended in Los Angeles in February 1937. There are surviving records of over fifty lectures and radio broadcasts, though the actual total must have been much higher. In the course of the tour he often spoke twice daily, once as many as four times. He spoke on different topics, both cultural and political, but ultimately always addressing the political situation in Germany. He spoke frequently on the theme 'The Theatre in a Changing World', a lecture which ended by considering 'the part of the theatre and of the free writer and actor in Nazi Germany'. He also lectured several times on the theme 'Are We Responsible for Our Times?', but the lecture he delivered most frequently was 'Hitler: the Promise and the Reality'.[1]

Toller defined the purpose of his tour as 'to lecture against Hitler and the Nazi system . . . not only against Hitler's domestic policy, his persecutions and suppression of minorities, liberals and social-ists, but also against his foreign policy which threatens the peace of the world'.[2] The extensive press coverage of the tour records this attempt to enlighten American public opinion about the threat of Nazism: 'Toller sees Hitler as threat to world peace' (*Boston Globe*), 'Appeal to fight Fascism is heard' (*Montreal Daily Star*), 'Spanish war blame put on Hitler' (*Pittsburgh Daily Telegraph*),

'Ernst Toller flays Nazism in stirring speech' (*Anti-Nazi News*, Hollywood).[3]

The manuscript versions of Toller's lectures in the Yale University Library document his intention in greater detail. While there is no surviving manuscript of 'Hitler: the Promise and the Reality', the manuscript of 'Are We Responsible for Our Times' contains a furious indictment of Nazism, in which Toller at one point likens the medicine-man of a primitive tribe in his determination to find a scapegoat: 'The Jews and the Marxists and the French are responsible for all our misfortunes.' Toller began the lecture by tracing the rise of Nazism in the perspective of post-war German history, identifying as a contributory factor the reluctance of the liberal middle class to take social responsibility. Condemning Nazi racial dogma, he called for the League of Nations to intervene to stop the persecution of Jews:

> At a time when the League of Nations has solemnly guaranteed the rights of minorities, the persecution of the Jews is no longer the internal concern of one state, in which other states have no right to interfere. The League of Nations has a purpose only if it watches over the rights of all. Its task and its duty is to compel those states which scorn human rights to abandon their persecution.

Toller clearly hoped to mobilize American public opinion in favour of intervention by the League. He went on to warn that the Nazis' war against 'the enemy within' was merely a prelude to war against 'the enemy abroad' and spoke of 'the dictator who praises peace today . . . the better to prepare for war tomorrow'.[4]

In a clear reference to the Popular Front, he called for 'a common fighting front, uniting across religious and political differences all those who wish to defend civilization'. In a speech in Pittsburgh, he stressed German involvement in the Spanish Civil War: democracy was under attack in Spain. In this and other speeches he advocated 'a peace which will defend itself, not the pacifism of those who refuse to fight under any circumstances'.

Toller addressed a wide variety of audiences, speaking at colleges and universities, to women's clubs, to political, community and cultural groups and at anti-Nazi rallies. The interest aroused was considerable. In Boston, he had an audience of over a thousand at the Ford Hall Forum. In Montreal, where he spoke in a Presbyterian

church, interest was so great that his speech had to be relayed to an
overflow meeting in an adjoining building. In New York he spoke to
3,500 German Americans, in Los Angeles to a mass rally of 6,500 at
the Shrine Auditorium.

The audiences he addressed were largely middle class, comprised
of the liberals and radical intellectuals who supported the New Deal,
and Toller was careful not to alienate them. The lecture 'Are We
Responsible for Our Times?' had originally been written in 1935–36
for a British public. The hand-written corrections to the surviving
manuscripts show that in revising the lecture for American
audiences, Toller edited out Marxist terms, and revised passages
which might have been open to political misunderstanding. Both
here, and in numerous interviews, he stressed that the political
struggle was not one between Bolshevism and fascism, but between
freedom and slavery, democracy and dictatorship. When the *New
York Times* referred to him as 'a Communist leader', he replied
angrily, insisting that he had never been a member of the Communist Party and since 1924 had been a member of no party.[5]

The reports of his lectures stress his fluent command of English
and his charismatic gifts as a speaker. Even a Nazi observer was
forced to concede that his lectures were well structured, effectively
delivered and rapturously received. Toller was also skilful at varying
content and approach according to the composition of his audience.
Addressing New York's German community in a speech entitled
'Our Struggle for Germany', he recalled the progressive social legis-
lation of the Weimar Republic – and its deliberate destruction by the
Nazis. Speaking to a university audience, he stressed the suppression
of academic freedom, to an audience of screen writers and actors, he
highlighted the plight of the creative artist in Nazi Germany.

Toller's denunciations of the Nazis received considerable press
coverage; they were also monitored by Nazi diplomatic representatives. During 1936–37 his police file in Berlin was swollen by regular
reports from German consular and diplomatic officials in North
America. The German Consul in Montreal reported that he had
personally attended Toller's lecture there, describing it as 'a single
outburst of hate against the Germany of today and its leader'. He
regretted that his letter to the *Montreal Star* refuting Toller's attacks
had not been published.[6] It was indeed only later that a concerted
campaign of opposition was mounted, including attempts at disrup-
tion. As Toller rose to address a mass rally in Los Angeles, a group

of Nazi sympathizers staged a noisy demonstration; following the rally he received a number of phone calls threatening to kill him. From then on he was intermittently harassed by Nazi sympathizers and abused in the pro-Nazi German-American press.

It was perhaps in Los Angeles that his words had their strongest resonance. There was virulent opposition to Nazism in Hollywood, articulated through the influential Anti-Nazi League, which counted among its members many leading film directors, writers and actors. The strength of feeling against Nazism, and the sympathetic response he received, undoubtedly helped to influence Toller's decision to return to Hollywood after the completion of his lecture tour. He was also genuinely impressed by the social transformation which he perceived: 'American has undergone a tremendous change since I was last here in 1929', he wrote to Nehru.[7] He felt that, under the impact of economic recession, banal materialism had given way to an awakening social conscience, particularly among the young. The United States seemed to be the only country where the lessons of fascism had been learnt. A large proportion of the population had become 'freedom-conscious' – and he interpreted the re-election of Roosevelt as a resounding endorsement of freedom.

Toller was particularly impressed by developments in the American theatre, which he praised for having 'the courage to face reality and deal with the conflicts and problems of our time'. He admired the work of Clifford Odets and Irwin Shaw, believing that such social plays would lay the basis for 'a real people's theatre in America'.[8] He undoubtedly hoped that his lecture tour would help to promote interest in his plays. He had arrived in New York with three plays – *Draw the Fires*, *The Blind Goddess* and *No More Peace!* which he hoped to have produced on Broadway but, as his friend and agent Barrett H. Clark remarked, his work was far removed in theme and tendency from the traditional Broadway play.[9] Clark attempted to interest college and 'little' theatres in *No More Peace!* – and the play was first produced in the USA by the Vassar Experimental Theatre in February 1937.

Toller also had various contacts with left theatre groups in New York, notably with the New Theatre League, to which most workers' theatre groups were affiliated.[10] A group called the People's Repertory Theatre planned to produce *Draw the Fires* for trade union audiences under the auspices of the Labor Stage, but the project foundered for lack of financial backing.[11] There was, however, a production of *The Machine Wreckers* by an amateur group in New York under the direction of Irwin Swerdlow.[12] However, Toller's most productive relations in the theatre were with the Federal Theatre Project (FTP).

The FTP had been established in 1935 to help alleviate unemployment in the theatre professions: it remains to this day the only theatre organization ever to be subsidized by the US government. At its height the project employed some ten thousand people. The highest price ever charged for a Federal Theatre performance was one dollar, most of the performances being free. Toller's contacts with the FTP were mediated by the Project's Director Hallie Flanagan, who enjoyed a considerable reputation in progressive theatre circles. She had visited Russia in the twenties and had subsequently been among the pioneers of avant-garde theatre in the USA. Her acquaintance with Toller went back to 1929 and the following year she had directed a production of *Masses and Man* at the Vassar Experimental Theatre.

The Federal Theatre repertory consisted of classical and modern plays but was strongly biased towards works with a social theme. Sinclair Lewis's satire on the dangers of fascism, *It Can't Happen Here*, was widely performed under the auspices of the Federal Theatre, opening simultaneously in twenty-one theatres across the USA on 27 October 1936. Toller was the guest of honour at the production in New York and was deeply affected by what he saw: 'I sat on the edge of my seat and cold sweat broke out all over me', he confided to Hallie Flanagan.[13]

Flanagan was full of enthusiasm for *No More Peace!* which she hoped would be widely produced by the Federal Theatre;[14] but there were difficulties, not merely because of the similarity of theme with *It Can't Happen Here*. The Federal Theatre had acquired a controversial reputation because of the radical nature of its repertoire. Its right-wing critics accused it of overt communist sympathies and, in view of Toller's reputation as a 'communist', it was feared that a production of the play would merely provide further ammunition for the project's enemies. It was consequently not until the spring of 1937 that the FTP finally produced *No More Peace!*, giving the play a trial run in repertory in Cincinatti and at a summer theatre on Long Island. It was not staged in New York until January 1938.[15]

The fears of the Federal Theatre were well-founded. The project was finally wound up by Congress in June 1939 after months of investigation by the House Committee for Un-American Activities which branded the social criticism of some productions 'communistic' and 'un-American'. Among the plays most frequently cited by hostile witnesses in these proceedings was *No More Peace!* Toller also planned to write a play for the Federal Theatre in the style of the 'living newspaper', to be called *Forget Europe.* The 'living newspaper', offering the possibility of social and political comment on current events, was a favourite genre of the political theatre of the thirties. It was a form Toller had already adapted in his radio play *Berlin – last edition!* He actually drafted an outline of fifteen scenes for *Forget Europe,* covering events in Nazi Germany, the outbreak of the Spanish Civil War and the early months of Blum's Popular Front government in France. He even made a collection of relevant press clippings, but like so many of Toller's projects in the final years of his life, it was never completed.[16]

Hollywood and After
1937–1938

In February 1937 Toller signed a one-year contract to write film-scripts for MGM, settling in the fashionable Los Angeles suburb of Santa Monica. His reasons were partly financial – he had failed to find a Broadway producer for any of his plays – but his interest in screen-writing went back over a decade. Even before leaving London, he had obviously considered the possibility of working in Hollywood, since he had actually placed two film scenarios in the hands of a Hollywood agent. In a newspaper interview he gave at the time of his arrival in New York, he had named these as *The Road to India*, on the false hopes for peace raised by the building of the Suez Canal, and *Betsy James*, which he somewhat disingenuously described as 'the adventures of an Irish girl' and which seems to have been an early version of a script on the adventuress Lola Montez.[1]

When Toller arrived in Hollywood, the film industry was already dominated by the studio system. MGM was the most powerful and prestigious of all the studios, having prospered under the control of the legendary Louis B. Mayer, the greatest of all the movie moguls. Like all the other studios, MGM was a movie factory, producing over fifty films a year and employing some seventy-five screenwriters. The idea that one writer, alone and unaided, could conceive and execute a complete script was foreign to Hollywood; scripts were customarily turned over to a second writer for rewriting or assigned simultaneously to two or more writers. The low esteem in which writers were held was made clear by Mayer himself, who remarked, when Upton Sinclair ran for governor of California in 1934: 'What does Sinclair know about anything? He's just a writer.' It seemed unpromising ground for a committed left-wing playwright.

Toller, together with Ferdinand Bruckner and Bruno Frank, was in the vanguard of the German writers engaged by the film studios; it is significant that all three had enjoyed considerable success in the theatre, still a major source of talent for the film industry. Hollywood had always been open to foreign talent, particularly from

Central Europe and, even before 1933, directors such as Ernst Lubitsch, Josef von Sternberg, William Dieterle and Erich von Stroheim had established themselves there. Others, like Fritz Lang and Fred Zinnemann, came after 1933 as refugees, but the major German writers who later found a haven in Hollywood – Bertolt Brecht, Lion Feuchtwanger, Alfred Döblin, Heinrich Mann, Franz Werfel and Leonhard Frank – did not leave Europe until after the fall of France.

Few of these later arrivals seem to have had any illusions about Hollywood. Many of them, including Döblin, Frank and Heinrich Mann, were engaged as screen-writers on one-year contracts, largely as an act of practical charity. They did little serious work – and little seems to have been expected of them. Brecht, who arrived in 1941, approached his task with his customary cynicism:

> Every day, to earn my daily bread
> I go to the market where lies are bought,
> Hopefully
> I take up my place among the sellers.[2]

His only screen credit – for the Fritz Lang film *Hangmen Also Die* – was one he subsequently disowned.

Toller, however, seems to have started work with high hopes. While he recognized the commercial nature of the American cinema, he seems to have felt that he could work within the system and even that he could enjoy a certain degree of artistic freedom. He was probably encouraged to think so by the widespread anti-Nazi sympathies he found amongst writers and directors and the fact that such radical playwrights as Lilian Hellmann, John Wexley and Clifford Odets were already working in Hollywood. Moreover MGM had acquired the story for *Lola Montez* – and engaged Toller to write it. He was being paid a salary of a thousand dollars a week, a considerable sum at that time – and one certainly beyond the wildest dreams of most of his fellow-exiles.

Staying at the luxury Miramar Hotel in Santa Monica, Toller was at first beguiled by the earthly paradise of California, in which even the desert bloomed:

> I am settled in a beautiful apartment overlooking the ocean and am trying to spend every free moment, of which there are altogether too few, in the sun at the

beach. My work at MGM gives promise of being very
agreeable and as I hope successful.[3]

Christiane had remained for the moment in New York. Eager to
pursue her acting career, she planned to find work in a stock company. Toller suggested she should follow an intensive language
course to perfect her English diction, recommending a course at the
New School for Social Research.[4]

Some of Toller's friends and acquaintances were amazed to find
him in Hollywood. He wrote to a friend in London:

> The news item is right, I've returned to Hollywood. I am
> writing the Lola Montez film for MGM. Joan Crawford
> will play the title role. Producer is Joe Mankiewicz (Pro-
> ducer of *Fury*).[5]

Toller's mention of *Fury*, the first American film made by Fritz
Lang, is significant. *Fury* was a film with a social message which,
when released by MGM in June 1936, had become an instant hit –
and the first really successful film by an émigré director in Hollywood during the sound era. Its success must have encouraged Toller
to believe that MGM was prepared to produce films of social significance, and that American audiences were ready to watch them.
Given the ethos of MGM, it seems more likely that the studio
regarded *Lola Montez* as a glossy vehicle for Joan Crawford, already
one of its star 'properties'.

Toller, however, was full of optimism about his work on the
script:

> *Lola Montez* grows and has taken on quite a nice size – in
> body and soul. So far I am very happy. There have not
> been any story conferences so far. Up to the present no
> one has interfered with my ideas. What will happen in
> the future, Leo the Lion of MGM will decide.[6]

Lola Montez was in fact growing too fast for his producer:

> In any event, I delivered sixty-four pages of the story to
> him two days ago and he told me again I may take it easy
> and not to work so much.[7]

Toller had easy access to Mankiewicz and saw him often while he
was working on the script, but they do not appear to have developed

a close relationship. As for the proposed star of the film, Toller could only observe.

> Joan Crawford too has great sorrows. Not that she is worried about the events in Spain, but she has decided to invent a new fashion with two different tints in her hair. The Hearst paper writes that she dyed her side hair red and the parting on top of her head black. Perhaps this red color means a secret sympathy with the author of her new film. I am only afraid it will not be red but pink.[8]

By April Toller had moved into an exclusive apartment block, fringed by palm trees, where Christiane finally joined him at the beginning of June. His early optimism about *Lola Montez* had begun to wane. He had completed the script by early June, only to find that the studio was in no hurry to film it. He reported that production had been postponed 'for the time being as the gentlemen in power do not want to make any film with a German locale'.[9] His comment is an interesting gloss on the refusal of the Hollywood studios throughout the thirties to make films which could be construed as anti-German. The script of *Lola Montez* has not survived, but Toller clarified his interest in this exotic figure in a letter to Nehru, in which he describes her as

> that peculiar Irish girl . . . who spent her youth in India, later on appeared as a 'Spanish' dancer in London and then became the friend of King Ludwig I of Bavaria . . . She it was who influenced this monarch's politics for many years most decisively, until the time of that rather comic Munich rebellion of 1848 . . . Strange as history often is, it was this Lola Montez who was the mouthpiece of freedom at the time of European reaction.[10]

Toller's interest was clearly in the contemporary analogies of his material; equally clearly, the studio decided to shelve the script on account of its political context. It was never filmed.

During June Toller was distracted from writing by personal problems. Christiane had fallen seriously ill with tropical dysentery, compounded by pneumonia, and it was several weeks before she recovered. During his time with MGM, Toller was also not immune to the social and physical attractions of Hollywood. He enjoyed the open-air life possible in Hollywood and spent much time on the beach, as well as enjoying horse-riding, which became almost a passion. He particularly sought the company of his fellow-exiles. He spent much time in the company of the writer and director Bertold Viertel (the Friedrich Bergmann of Christopher Isherwood's *Prater Violet*). He also saw a lot of the director Fritz Lang and was often a guest of the novelist Vicki Baum, whose house was practically next door. He and Christiane were also occasional guests of Salka Viertel, who played hostess to the German exile community and had already achieved some prominence as a screen writer for Greta Garbo.

Toller's social contacts were by no means limited to German exiles. He was friendly with the screen writer Hy Kraft, who was also chairman of the Hollywood Anti-Nazi League. Kraft was convinced that Toller would never 'make it' in Hollywood, a topic which they discussed several times: each time Toller was depressed afterwards. Toller was also very friendly with Sidney Kaufman, with whom he collaborated on the script of *Lola Montez*. According to Kaufman, Toller would always write in German and would then work together with Kaufman to produce a final English version.[11]

During 1937 Toller also worked on *The Road to India*, concerning Ferdinand de Lesseps and the building of the Suez Canal. Toller had written the original scenario before leaving London, describing it in an interview given on his arrival in New York as 'the story of a grand illusion'.[12] In February he had asked Kaufman to send him the manuscript from New York as he wished to protect it by registering it at the Authors Screen Guild.[13] A manuscript copy of *The Road to India*, which has survived amongst Toller's papers, contains extensive additions and revisions, confirming that Toller reworked the script in 1937, but it remains only a draft and Toller seems not to have written a final version.[14]

The manuscript of *The Road to India*, in which both text and revisions are largely in German, emphasizes the inability to make the transition from German to English which was perhaps Toller's greatest problem in exile: a problem already indicated by his collaboration with Kaufman on *Lola Montez*. While Toller spoke English fluently, he never learned to think or write creatively in it. He told Hy Kraft that he felt 'imprisoned' in the German language. During the last months of his life he repeatedly told Kurt Pinthus what a catastrophe it was for him never to be able to write in English: 'What is an author who is not heard in his own language and cannot write in another?'[15]

1937 was to prove a fateful year for Toller, beginning a decline in his fortunes from which he never recovered. Yet the year had begun so auspiciously. In January he had been acclaimed at anti-Nazi rallies in Los Angeles and San Francisco. In February *No More Peace!* had been staged by the Vassar Experimental Theatre, followed by no less than three productions by the Federal Theatre. The play was also published later that year, as were his prison letters under the title *Look Through the Bars*. He was still in demand as a speaker and lecturer, frequently breaking off work to carry out speaking engagements. In March he spoke, together with André Malraux, at a mass rally to win support for Republican Spain. In September he gave a broadcast on CBS under the auspices of the Anti-Nazi League. During 1937 he was also involved with Auden and others in a cabaret programme devised by Klaus and Erika Mann, a short-lived attempt to transplant Erika's successful Zurich cabaret 'The Peppermill' to New York.

For all these outward signs of success, the year saw a serious decline in Toller's fortunes, caused by an ominous convergence of public and private misfortune. The Nazis had amply fulfilled his own pessimistic prediction that fascism in Germany would be no short-lived affair. He now privately acknowledged that opposition within Germany, however heroic, was ineffectual: 'Unless an actual crisis arises, one has to reckon with the power of the Nazis who are relentlessly preparing Germany for war,' he wrote in August.[16]

After the end of August there is a sudden and ominous break in Toller's correspondence, lasting several months. He had once again fallen seriously ill, slipping into the acute depression which now increasingly threatened his stability. Letters written to his doctor, Ralph Greenschpoon, complain of sleeplessness and bad nerves which completely undermine his ability to think and act. They indicate a growing dependence on his physician ('You are a doctor, please tell me what to do') and an increasing sense of dissociation. In one letter he refers to himself in the third person, commenting as a detached spectator on his own breakdown:

> It seems more and more to me that the whole case is rather hopeless. The man goes on living from week to week but the ground on which he lived has gone into a thousand pieces. He tries it again and again – but neither

can he make any decision, nor can he see any way which is worth going.[17]

In November, in an attempt to recover from his breakdown, he left Hollywood for Mexico, where he spent some six weeks, much of it riding on horseback through the Sierra: 'I wish you could have come with me,' he wrote to Sidney Kaufman. 'I went on horseback to remote Indian villages, studied the political situation and some of the social reforms and got quite an insight into what is going on. The view that Mexico is turning socialist is romantic . . .'[18]

When Toller returned to Hollywood at the end of the year, he had already decided to escape from this gilded cage. MGM offered to renew his contract, but he declined. Christiane recounts that he sought an interview with Louis B. Mayer himself to ask if his screenplays were finally going to be filmed. Mayer told him they were not, and Toller responded that he did not want to be paid for doing nothing. There is no doubt that he was disillusioned and even embittered by his failure in Hollywood. He was later scathingly critical of the banal optimism which Hollywood sought to purvey: 'It is not the job of the writer to portray a happy ending which is nowhere in evidence in the world today.'[19]

Christiane was no more successful in Hollywood than her husband. Having appeared in films in Germany before 1933, she had hoped to become a Hollywood actress but although she made more than one screen test for MGM, she was never able to begin an American film career. Toller's friends felt that he had been completely unsuited to Hollywood. George Grosz remarked that he was 'too European, too trusting when he was flattered'; Sidney Kaufman felt that 'he never could or would have made a screen writer'.[20] He was unable to adapt to the Hollywood system, could not see the point of story conferences, at which he might be asked to edit a scene for political overtones or redraft it to suit the requirements of a particular star. This failure must be seen in the perspective of literary exile. Bruno Frank and Ferdinand Bruckner, who had also come to Hollywood in 1937, fared little better than Toller. Frank, who had also come with a one-year contract, found the language difficulties insurmountable and left after only seven months. Bruckner too was unhappy and soon went back to New York. Most of those who came later – Döblin, Brecht or Heinrich Mann – had no more success. By the end of January 1938, Toller had decided to return to

New York. He wrote to Sidney Kaufman: 'I am sick of Hollywood – and look forward to seeing no (*sic*) stars, but human beings.'[21]

Toller arrived back in New York on 10 February 1938, moving into the Mayflower Hotel, overlooking Central Park, where he would continue to live until his death. Christiane remained in Hollywood to make a further screen test for MGM. After the unhappy interlude of Hollywood, Toller was anxious to re-establish himself as a dramatist. In January, the Federal Theatre had finally brought *No More Peace!* to New York – but only off-Broadway and to a very muted reception. Toller was eager to secure a Broadway production for one of his plays: 'If only I could get a contract for *Blind Man's Buff* so that I could hope for a certain material security.'[22]

Sidney Kaufman, who saw much of Toller at this time, tried to bring him together with the progressive theatre circles which would best appreciate his work. There were several meetings with the playwright Clifford Odets and with the directors of the Group Theatre, Harold Clurman and Lee Strasberg. The Group Theatre was then at the height of its success in depicting the social problems of Depression America, but there was no place in its repertoire for Toller's new play *Pastor Hall*, which he had completed by June. Clurman was in fact critical of Toller's work, Strasberg even dismissive.[23]

In the early months of 1938 Toller had thrown himself back into work of all kinds. It was at this time that he began working with the American Guild for German Cultural Freedom, an organization founded by an aristocratic refugee from Hitler, Prinz Hubertus zu Löwenstein, who had succeeded in enlisting the support of various prominent American sponsors. The Guild aimed to provide financial assistance for exiled artists and academics, seeking to demonstrate the existence of 'the other Germany' which the exiles were so determined to evoke, and thus to undermine the cultural influence of Nazi Germany abroad. The Guild awarded 'scholarships' to needy cultural refugees and also made grants towards the cost of printing works of exile literature. Brecht's 'Svendborger Gedichte' owed their initial publication in America to a grant from the Guild.

Toller became a member of the Guild's committee, writing numerous 'affidavits' for Guild scholarships on behalf of needy writers and artists, among them Georg Kaiser, Alfred Kantorowicz, Walter Mehring and the artist John Heartfield. He became a regular visitor to Prinz Hubertus's apartment near Washington Square. The

Prince professed to note a change in Toller over the time of their acquaintance, a movement away from a materialist conception towards 'a spiritual and religious view of the world'.[24] During his visit to Europe later that year, Toller made various contacts on behalf of the Guild and continued to play an active part in its work until the end of his life. According to Erika Mann, he attended a committee meeting very shortly before his suicide, at which he pleaded for a small monthly grant for Bodo Uhse and Ludwig Renn, both of whom had just arrived in the United States.

During 1938 Toller also continued to carry out speaking and broadcasting engagements, activities monitored by Nazi diplomats and harassed by their agents and sympathizers. In April he was invited to speak at Queen's College, New York, but the invitation was hastily withdrawn by the college authorities on the grounds that his speech might offend students of German origin, a pretext which obviously reflects pressure by Nazi sympathizers. After a vigorous protest by the Teachers' Union, he was finally allowed to speak, but following the incident he was once more the victim of anonymous phone calls, in which the German caller repeatedly threatened to kill him. These threats continued to the point where Toller was finally forced to ask for police protection.

Toller's physical and mental health were still precarious: from February 1938 he seems to have received regular psychiatric treatment. His letters at this time reveal growing financial worries. Having lost his considerable salary from MGM, he was forced to rely once more on irregular income from royalties and lectures. He suffered continually from homesickness for a Germany which no longer even considered him a German. In one of the concluding passages of his autobiography, he had written of his yearning for the countryside of his native North Germany and his love for the language of Goethe and Hölderlin: 'Is not the German language my language, in which I feel and think, speak and act, a part of my being, the home which nurtured me, in which I grew up?'[25] In his last play *Pastor Hall*, Toller transposed his feelings into dramatic fiction in the character of Erwin Kohn, the Jewish artist who is so homesick for Germany that he returns there, only to suffer the inevitable fate of forced labour in a concentration camp:

> I couldn't bear any longer hearing people speak in a foreign language, I saw the birch-trees on the Wannsee

and I smelt the sand of the Marches and the pine-trees
. . .'26

Toller's own yearning for Germany was sharpened by the growing realization that he might never return there.

These difficulties, largely endemic to life in exile, were compounded by his growing estrangement from Christiane, whose support during his bouts of depression he had come to rely on. Christiane had rejoined him in New York in March, but their relationship now began to deteriorate. In July she finally left him, forming a relationship with Martin Gumpert, a writer and doctor who had managed to establish a practice in New York after fleeing from Germany in 1936. While Toller was deeply affected by this (short-lived) liaison, it was an effect rather than the cause of their estrangement. Neither Toller nor Christiane commented publicly on the reasons for their separation, but it seems clear that Toller's temperamental instability finally made their life together virtually impossible. Fritz Landshoff confirmed that she felt increasingly unable to cope with his bouts of suicidal depression; Toller himself was convinced that she would not have left him 'if our life had not been interfered with by these painful breakdowns'.27 In his last letter to Betty Frankenstein, sent less than three weeks before his death, he wrote: 'Don't try to apportion blame between Christiane and me. It isn't as simple as that. She was very young and wanted to live her own life.'28 Christiane herself suggests that she could no longer tolerate the restlessness and rootlessness of Toller's life. She recalled that the final break came when he announced his intention to go to Spain.29

Pastor Hall

Toller's literary energies during 1938 were devoted exclusively to *Pastor Hall*, written – according to his own note – in New York, Barcelona and Cassis. Both the plays which Toller wrote in exile parallel and complement his role as public speaker and propagandist – and this is particularly true of *Pastor Hall*. In a speech to German-Americans in New York in December 1936, Toller had urged his audience to expose the true reality of Nazi Germany. In *Pastor Hall* that brutal reality is portrayed in the paradigm of the concentration camp, and contrasted to the 'other Germany', evoked in the courageous resistance to Nazism.

Toller's protagonist Friedrich Hall is loosely based on the figure of Martin Niemöller, whose spirited opposition to the Nazis had led to his arrest and trial and who, early in 1938, had been committed to Sachsenhausen concentration camp. Niemöller's trial received wide coverage in the world press. Church notice boards around the world carried the exhortation: 'Pray for Pastor Niemöller.' The wide publicity attending the case undoubtedly influenced Toller's choice of subject, offering a powerful reference to political actuality which few could overlook. Hall is a Protestant pastor, who is opposed to the Nazi régime and who falls into its hands through the spite of Fritz Gerte, an opportunist who has become leader of the local Storm Troop. Gerte wants to marry Hall's daughter and attempts to blackmail Hall, who has corresponded with known critics of the regime, into approving the marriage. When Hall refuses, he is arrested and sent to a concentration camp. The second act is set in the camp, where Gerte has become Commandant. When Hall publicly denounces Gerte, he is sentenced to a public beating, but at this point his courage fails him and he contrives to escape, with the help of a young SS man who is himself shot during the incident. In the final act, Hall overcomes his fear of punishment and death. He decides that it is his duty to speak out against the regime and invites certain re-arrest by returning to his church in order to preach a final sermon against Nazi tyranny (in Toller's first version, Hall dies of a heart-attack just as he is to be rearrested, an ending Toller later found inappropriate).

In theatrical terms, the play is a restatement of the Expressionist theme of transformation, set within the framework of a conventional three-act drama. Its theme is the conquest of fear, an idea which had preoccupied Toller for some time, and which he addressed explicitly in a speech delivered while he was actually still working on the play:

> Fear is the psychological foundation of dictatorship. The dictator knows that only the man who has overcome fear lives beyond his power and is his sole dangerous enemy. For whoever has conquered fear has conquered death.[30]

The fear which buttresses the regime takes concrete form in the concentration camp which is the scene of the second act of the play.

Toller had begun to collect information about the camps as early as 1934, mainly from former prisoners like Willi Bredel, whom he had met in Russia. He was convinced of the importance of documenting these details of organized brutality:

> Herr Hitler says in his speeches, which posterity will count amongst the most inconceivable documents of this age, that refugees are making atrocity propaganda. We don't need to invent atrocities. Ours is the sad duty of the chronicler: to record these atrocities for posterity.[31]

The brutal facts he portrayed had already been recorded in his speeches – a ruthless regime based on hard labour, military discipline and harsh punishment, masquerading as re-education. Gerte tells the camp inmates: 'The Third Reich wishes to educate you to understand what National Socialism means.' There are those who courageously resist this 're-education', like the communist Hofer, who refuses to recant his beliefs and whose file bears the laconic official comment: 'not worth releasing'.

Hall and Hofer are united in their opposition to Nazism, but are themselves divided by ideology. In their discussion, Toller returns once more to the problem of non- violence:

> HALL: . . . There's no question on earth which can't be settled without force, however complicated and entangled it is.
> HOFER: It takes two to arrive at a solution without force, Herr Pastor. It isn't we who invite force, it's the others. Shall I be robbed of my right and say thank you very much? I'd rather die.
> HALL: The courage to die has become cheap, so cheap that I often ask myself whether it isn't a flight from life.[32]

Hoffer then tells the story of Erich Mühsam who, ordered by the Nazi guards to sing the 'Horst Wessel' song, refused and, when they threatened to shoot him, sang the 'Internationale'. Toller cited Mühsam's defiant action more than once in his speeches: 'The poet Mühsam looked death in the eye. And as he looked death in the eye, he outgrew himself, became an image of freedom.'[33] Mühsam's resistance therefore has a symbolic dimension, exemplifying the conquest of fear which transcends physical imprisonment and even death. It is his example which gives Hall the courage to denounce the camp commandant. He refuses Gerte's request to be 'reasonable': 'Yes, I know I should be silent. But silence would be the greatest crime of all.' When he is sentenced to be beaten, however, his courage fails him, and he takes the opportunity to escape.

In the final act, he again confronts Gerte. Having overcome his fear of punishment and death, he refuses to flee the country, announcing instead that he will preach a last sermon – an act of symbolic resistance, intended to inspire emulation:

> HALL (very softly): I will live. It will be like a fire that no might can put out. The meek will tell the meek and they'll become brave again. One man will tell another that the anti-Christ rules, the destroyer, the enemy of mankind – and they will find strength and follow my example (p. 79).

Pastor Hall is not an entirely successful play, moving uneasily between the levels of realism and symbolism. The characters are sometimes unconvincing, their motivation occasionally contrived. It is above all the ending which is unsatisfactory. Hall's last action is a dramatic device which evades the very question it poses: the necessity for an effective opposition to Nazism. Hall's moral example is one which is unlikely to inspire the emulation it seeks to encourage. It is an act of deliberate self-sacrifice, the isolated gesture of an individual, providing a personal rather than a political solution. It is both a measure of Toller's despair at the destruction of effective opposition in Germany and an admission of the political impotence of exile.

The history of *Pastor Hall* is a powerful reminder of the practical problems facing the exile dramatist, emphasizing the necessity of translation and adaptation – and the difficulties inherent in them. Toller had completed the first draft of the play in June 1938 and at that time had several meetings with the publisher Bennett Cerf, who he hoped would publish it. Cerf was quick to point out that it was customary to publish only plays which had already succeeded on Broadway.[34] Toller, on the contrary, needed publication to stimulate production.

Toller brought the first draft of the play with him to London in July: his British publisher John Lane felt that it was 'a perfectly publishable play', but that it would sell few copies unless it were produced on the English stage.[35] The chances of such a production were slim, not only because of the parochial nature of the English theatre. There were firstly the difficulties of translation, a task Toller originally hoped would be undertaken by Thornton Wilder, but later assigned to the poet Stephen Spender.[36] The latter seems to have been a somewhat reluctant collaborator, but he none the less managed to complete the translation by mid-October.[37]

Toller anticipated other obstacles to a London production. In an interview given in October he called the play 'even more topical than *No More Peace!*', adding bitterly that he wished it could be performed in London but doubted if 'it would survive the protests of the German ambassador'.[38] His suspicions were well founded. The Westminster Theatre had 'no doubt of the dramatic value of the play' but felt unable to produce it 'as the theme is too controversial for production in the present state of international affairs – indeed we are very doubtful if the play would get a licence at all for public performance'.[39]

Returning to New York in November, Toller submitted the play for production there, only to have it rejected. His frustration is evident from his letters to John Lane, pleading with them to publish the play before it was produced; he sent a copy of the German manuscript to Fritz Landshoff in the hope that Querido would publish a limited edition.[40] On 12 January 1939 Toller read *Pastor Hall* to an audience of fellow-exiles, whose criticism of the ending persuaded him to change the final scene: Hall would no longer die of a heart attack but would resolve to preach his last sermon.[41]

Meanwhile, Barrett Clark, Toller's American agent, had expressed his reservations about Spender's English version:

> I feel that his translation in many places reads like a translation; that it is stiff and unidiomatic, and finally that, if transferred to the theatre, it would have to be materially revised.[42]

Shortly after, Toller arranged for Hugh Hunt, who had produced *Blind Man's Buff* at the Abbey Theatre, Dublin, to revise and re-edit Spender's version for stage production. These revisions delayed the American publication of the play, which Random House had already type-set by early January. Toller's frustration at the delay is evident in a letter to Barrett Clark: 'How difficult all this is. Every little thing takes five or ten times as long here.'[43]

Though *Pastor Hall* was eventually published in both New York and London, Toller did not live to see it. The play was finally produced in November 1939 by Unity Theatre in Manchester and in 1940 was filmed in a version which the *New Statesman* called 'the first really successful anti-Nazi film'[44] – but by that time it had already been subsumed into British war propaganda. In the USA the film was shown with a prologue spoken by Eleanor Roosevelt, but was none the less banned in some cities after protests by Nazi sympathizers. Toller had dedicated the play 'to the day when this drama can be performed in Germany'. It was produced in Berlin in 1947, when one reviewer called it 'a shattering theatrical experience', but it was probably too soon to confront the Germans with their own recent past. *Pastor Hall* was neither published nor produced in West Germany for another thirty years.

XVII   *Food for Spain*
       1938–1939

In July 1938 Toller returned to Europe, staying briefly in London
before travelling on to Paris for the International Writers' Congress.
He had attended the first of these congresses 'in defence of culture'
in June 1935, but how much had changed in the intervening years!
Then, he had participated in a discussion of 'the role of the writer in
society', a theme which he now took up again in a speech which
amounted to an apologia for his own life and work:

> There have been times when a boundary was drawn
> between the artistic and humanitarian tasks of the
> writer. But our generation has destroyed this boundary.
> [After the war] young writers no longer sought to live in
> the ivory tower which for decades had been the ideal of
> the artist. We knew that it was not so much beauty
> which moved us, as human need. We saw that it was our
> task to portray this need in our work, so as to free
> ourselves from it in reality. We too love the quiet of our
> study and the patient humble labour at our work. But a
> time which betrays the idea of humanity forces us to
> brand this betrayal and to fight, wherever freedom is
> threatened.[1]

It was a conception of the writer's responsibility which he had
outlined at the very start of the decade, aware that 'there are times
when personal commitment is more important than art'.[2]

He was in no doubt now where his own commitment lay. Speaking on the eve of his visit to Republican Spain, he declared
that unconditional pacifism was dead. It was no longer even
plausible to talk of peace, for the world war which would surely
come was already being waged in Spain and China. The slogan
of the day, he cried, was: 'Bring an end to war by organizing the
defence against fascist aggression.' Toller spoke passionately.
Ludwig Marcuse remembered that 'he rapidly warmed to his

theme, until he was finally all ablaze: dark and beautiful, like Savonarola'.[3]

Immediately after the Congress, Toller travelled to Spain, his first visit since the outbreak of civil war. His interest in Spain went back several years – to the winter of 1931–32, when he had made an extended tour of the country. The travel sketches he had later published had been a summary of the political situation of the fledgling Republic, ending with the pessimistic verdict that 'the Spanish Republic is treading in the footprints of Germany'; here as there, a political revolution had left the social structure largely intact.

Toller's fears for Spain had been partly confirmed during his further visit there in the spring of 1936, when the gathering political storm was already evident. Franco's rebellion had taken place only three months later. Toller did not return as a neutral observer; Spain was the great left-wing cause of the decade. For him, as for countless others, it was the front line against fascism, the focus of a campaign of international solidarity surpassing anything yet seen.

Toller spent seven weeks in Republican Spain, much of it in Barcelona, though he also visited the besieged capital Madrid and went to the war front at the time of the Ebro offensive. He went first to Barcelona, travelling by car from Perpignan. After crossing the border, he had expected to drive into a war zone, but the countryside he drove through seemed deceptively peaceful. Even Barcelona itself scarcely seemed to be at war. The beaches on the outskirts of the city were packed with families bathing. As he drove through the suburbs, the streets and squares were thronged with people. Posters shouted from every wall, but while some exhorted the population to resist the enemy, many more advertised cinemas and theatres, concerts and conferences. The whole city seemed on furlough, relaxing outside the theatre of war.

The grim reality of the situation became clear that evening. Despite the pretensions of a menu which recalled better times, the meal in his hotel was frugal. While he was still eating, the sirens suddenly began to wail and the lights went out. He ran out onto the street to find the night sky lit up by searchlight beams which swept across the sky, meeting, intersecting, suddenly illuminating five enemy aircraft. He watched as the fascist planes came in, running a gauntlet of anti-aircraft fire. He heard the whistle of anti-aircraft shells, followed by the burst of shrapnel, then the dull sound of distant explosions as the planes released their bombs. The entire raid was over in ten minutes, but it left forty houses destroyed, twenty-eight people dead and eighty-four injured, all of them civilians.

During the next three weeks Toller witnessed no less than seventeen air-raids. He was deeply impressed by the spirit of the civilian population, whose morale survived not only bombing but chronic food shortages. The population was in fact slowly starving. Fresh fruit and vegetables, meat, milk and eggs had all virtually disappeared from their diet. Not only was the Republic forced to provision its army; Catalonia and Castile were cut off from the agricultural areas which had formerly supplied them, and denied imports through the blockade of Republican ports. The situation was aggravated by the huge influx of refugees into the areas under Republican control. Toller could only admire the fortitude of ordinary people, quoting one young woman who said: 'My stomach is sore with hunger, but it does not matter. One day we shall triumph. There will be time enough to fill the stomach.'⁴

Toller was particularly concerned with Germany's role in the war. During his American lecture tour, he had frequently referred to Spain, particularly to German involvement there. Now he interviewed German and Italian prisoners of war, talking to them at some length, noting the effects of fascist indoctrination. He recognized that Germany's involvement was a dress rehearsal for a wider conflict and was scathingly critical of the sham of 'non-intervention'.

Above all, Toller was anxious to see the war at first hand, and in the early days of September he travelled to the front at the time of the Ebro offensive. A British journalist who accompanied him found him full of energy and optimism. They drove through moonlit countryside, reaching the ruined town of Tortosa near the mouth of the Ebro, where every house had been damaged by bombs and shelling. Toller was horrified at what he saw, writing by torchlight in his notebook: 'Spanish government must immediately send cameramen to Tortosa to show the world the barbarous destruction wrought by fascism.'⁵ It was on the Ebro that Toller addressed men of the International Brigades, telling them that more and more people now recognized the significance of the Spanish Civil War, but that they and their fellow-volunteers had been the pioneers: 'You were the first to bestir the sleep of the world.'⁶

Toller spoke from the heart. His own (unpublished) account of his journey to Spain records the frustration, and indeed guilt, he felt that he had not fought in Spain like so many of his compatriots:

At the end of July 1938, after two years of war, I came to
Spain. I had known the country before the war, lived
there and learned to love its people. When war broke out
and the first volunteers rushed to Spain, I wanted to go
too. However compelling the reasons which prevented
me, they did not satisfy my conscience. Now I was here,
I felt I had to atone for my guilt.[7]

It was this urge to atone, and his first-hand experience of the suffering of the civilian population, which inspired his Spanish Relief
Plan, the project which was to dominate the final months of his life.

Toller had first launched the idea of international relief for the
Spanish people while he was still in Barcelona.[8] Shortly after, he had
been flown into the beleaguered capital Madrid, where he had
witnessed the same scenes he had just left behind: chronic food
shortages, bombed houses, the bodies of women and children in the
mortuary. Despite his anger at the dead, he was more distressed by
the plight of the living. 'I can never forget the faces of those starving
Spanish children,' he later confided to Hermann Kesten.[9] Like so
many of Toller's projects, the Spanish Relief Plan was really an
emotional commitment, rationalized in retrospect. His plan envisa-
ged international aid on the lines of the relief work carried out by the
Hoover Commission in Central Europe after 1918. Governments
would be asked to donate money to buy up food surpluses, by which
method Toller hoped to raise $10 million worth of food supplies to
be distributed to civilians on both sides of the battle lines. Distribution would be carried out by the Quaker Relief Committees.

While in Spain he began to compile a dossier of facts, figures and
photographs, which he hoped would help to convince public opinion
in the liberal democracies to support his plan. He gained the
approval of Spanish church leaders and politicians, of prominent
artists, such as Picasso and José Bergamin, and even discussed his
proposals with members of the Republican government, securing
the support of the Foreign Minister, Alvarez del Vayo. During his
visit to Madrid, he was allowed to broadcast, under the auspices of
the Propaganda Ministry, over the Voice of Spain radio station – a
privilege reserved for favoured foreign visitors. Speaking from an
underground studio close to the front-line trenches, 'hearing as I
speak the roar of bursting shells and grenades', Toller addressed 'my
friends in America'. After sketching his impressions of Republican

Spain, he stressed the government's democratic legitimacy, and the broad support it enjoyed. He thought he had found in Spain the united front he had so long campaigned for: Catholics and Protestants, liberals and socialists, communists and syndicalists had sunk their differences to 'cooperate in a wise narrowness'. The war in Spain was being fought in defence of democracy, but 'to say it frankly, the democracies have let down Spain'. Depicting the heroic sacrifices of the ordinary people, he appealed directly to President Roosevelt to initiate national or international aid for the civilian population, invoking the example of Fritjof Nansen.[10] He had been assured that the short-wave broadcast would be heard in the USA, but he learned later that it had never been received.

After his journey to the battle-front at the Ebro, Toller returned to France, spending some days at Cassis-sur-mer, where he revised the first draft of *Pastor Hall*. On 21 September he arrived back in London to begin canvassing support for his Spanish Relief Plan – only to find that Britain was totally engrossed in the unfolding Munich crisis. He found himself out of sympathy with the dominant mood of appeasement. Ethel Mannin records running into him on a rainy night; they stood in the doorway of a lingerie shop discussing the international situation. Toller was convinced of the need to oppose Germany with force if necessary, rebuking his companion for her stubborn pacifism: 'Hitler cannot be allowed to go on.'[11] He also addressed public meetings, warning of the dangerous consequences of conceding Hitler's claim to the Sudetenland. 'Have no illusions . . . every new concession to Hitler weakens not only the power of the democracies but also the opposition inside Germany.'[12] Ironically, he was speaking on 29 September, the very day Hitler, Chamberlain and Daladier signed the Munich Treaty.

Only in the aftermath of the Munich agreement did Toller begin his campaign on behalf of Spanish civilians. During the following weeks, he conducted – single-handed and largely at his own expense – a campaign of publicity astonishing in its scope and impact. He contacted relief committees and trade unions, Catholic and Protestant clergy; he wrote letters, lobbied public figures, issued press releases and summoned journalists.[13] Christopher Isherwood encountered him among the leather armchairs of a Pall Mall club, waiting to button-hole an archbishop; Isabel Brown found him in the lobby of the House of Commons, waiting impatiently to address a group of MPs. The newspapers were full of his campaign, recording its progress in a succession of headlines: 'Poet's $10 Million Plan for Spain' (*Daily Herald*), 'Playwright's Food for Spain Plan: Duff Cooper's Changed View' (*News Chronicle*), 'Lord Halifax Supports Ernst Toller's Plan' (*Daily Telegraph*).

Though his campaign in Britain was far from concluded, Toller left London on 22 October for Stockholm, where in a whirlwind five days he was received by both the Archbishop of Uppsala and the Swedish Crown Prince, and with their endorsement enlisted the support of the government for his scheme. In Stockholm, his presence provoked vigorous opposition from Nazi diplomats who tried to undermine his credibility with scurrilous attacks on his alleged role in the Munich Soviet Republic. From Stockholm, he went on to Copenhagen and Oslo: in all the Scandinavian capitals he secured promises of support, provided that President Roosevelt would endorse the scheme. By early November he was back in London to conclude his campaign there. He gained the support of the Archbishops of Canterbury and York: the former was 'much impressed' by the weight of his evidence, the latter spoke of 'your great enterprise for the relief of suffering'.[14] Newspapers reported that he was in close touch with Whitehall, and indeed he was, meeting Foreign Office officials who expressed great sympathy with his scheme. Privately, however, the Foreign Office was suspicious of his motives. The official minutes of the meeting contain the marginal note that 'Toller was once a Communist and for all I know still may be'. The Under-Secretary of State, R.A. Butler, added obliquely that the British government could not *associate* itself with such a private initiative.[15]

Ostensibly, Toller seemed to have been astonishingly successful. Christopher Isherwood commented that Toller had caught the ears of the right people: 'He was in the process of becoming a respectable institution.'[16] Isherwood's account suggests something both noble and faintly ridiculous in Toller's efforts. Undoubtedly Toller was happy to be once more at the centre of the stage. Used to public attention, he now found it essential to his self-esteem, an insurance against mounting private despair.

On 10 November, two days before Toller sailed for New York, the first reports of the Nazi-instigated pogrom against Jewish homes and businesses appeared in the British press. Like other refugees, Toller was deeply concerned for the safety of his immediate family. His brother Heinrich had already fled to Prague, but his sister Hertha

and her husband were still living in Landsberg-an-der-Warthe. It
was many weeks before Toller heard that they had been unharmed,
and he remained desperately worried about them.

Before embarking for New York, Toller charged Isherwood with
the task of sending a telegram to President Roosevelt, appealing for
his support for the Spanish Relief Plan; it would duly arrive, signed
by H.G. Wells, E.M. Forster, Storm Jameson, Louis Golding,
Rebecca West, W.H. Auden, Stephen Spender and others.[17] Toller
left London outwardly buoyant and optimistic. Among those from
whom he took his leave was the journalist Hannen Swaffer, whom he
had known since his first visits to London in the twenties. As he left
Swaffer's office, his parting words were: 'Keep on fighting.' Six
months later, Swaffer heard the news of his suicide.[18]

Toller sailed back to the USA on the *Queen Mary*, arriving in New
York on 17 November. To his chagrin, he found that little or
nothing was known of his plan there. In his own terse account, he
notes:

> I always travel tourist class, but this time I got myself a
> cabin in the first class. I wanted to arrive 'in style' in
> New York. We sail up the Hudson. Reporters and pho-
> tographers come on board. They grab hold of a dwarf, a
> giant and a photogenic girl. No one takes the slightest
> notice of me. I had prepared an extensive press release.
> My friends knew that I was coming. What has
> happened?[19]

Once ashore, he learned that opponents of his plan had warned the
American Quakers of his radical reputation. Toller at once tried to
set the record straight. He held an impromptu press conference at
his New York hotel, at which he again outlined his proposals,
appealing grandiosely 'to the moral conscience of the democratic
world'.[20] Shortly after he travelled to Philadelphia to talk to Clarence
E. Pickett, secretary of the American Friends' Service Council,
whom he was able to convince, both of his good intentions and the
support which his proposals already commanded. During the next
few days he campaigned intensively, telephoning, writing letters,
lobbying, speaking. The campaign rapidly gathered momentum:
here too Toller had 'caught the ears of the right people'. He had
turned immediately to the influential columnist Dorothy Thompson,
'always ready to help, if there was a good and useful cause to fight

for'.[21] Thompson, long an admirer of Toller's, threw her weight behind the campaign, publishing an appeal to the government to adopt the plan: 'Intervene – with food!'[22] There were approving editorials in all the New York papers. Dorothy Thompson spoke alongside Toller to representatives of the pharmaceutical industry, appealing for urgent medical supplies.[23]

Toller's success was not gained easily, for political enemies continued to cast doubt on his good faith. His scheme was publicly repudiated by a leading Catholic churchman, Father Ignatius Cox, who claimed that there was no lack of food in Nationalist areas of Spain and that the plan was just a political device to divert food supplies to areas under Republican control. Replying to this attack, Toller insisted that his plan was non-partisan, quoting a League of Nations report to refute Cox's arguments, and stressing the urgency of the situation.[24] He ended with an appeal to 'all men of good will', a phrase he used with some political calculation. In all his public statements Toller sought to emphasize his humanitarian and even unpolitical approach, consciously broadening his message to reach the liberals and moderate conservatives whose support he considered indispensable. It has been suggested that Toller shifted his political position in the final years of his life, becoming a supporter of liberal democracy, but any such shift must be seen in the political context of the period. Toller's political vocabulary remained that of the Popular Front: he supported the Republican government in Spain as the legitimate government and its defence as a defence of democracy. At this time the Communist Party supported, and even founded, organizations with solely liberal and humanitarian aims.

At the end of November Toller wrote directly to President Roosevelt. He was conscious of his own lack of standing, addressing the President 'as a man with no official function, as a writer'.[25] Shortly after, he was invited to Washington to present his proposals. 'The work grows from day to day and I am rather hopeful of good results,' he reported to H.N. Brailsford, who had backed the scheme in Britain and had even lent Toller money to promote it.[26] The financial burden of Toller's work was now becoming acute. 'At the moment, I need badly every sum, even the smallest,' he told Barrett Clark.[27] From 15–23 December Toller was in Washington to present his proposals. He lunched at the White House, at the invitation of Mrs Roosevelt, who promised him that the plan would be submitted to the President. During the following week he had a series of meetings with officials of the State Department to discuss details of the plan. When Toller left Washington just before Christmas the plan had already been approved in principle and even before the New Year Roosevelt had announced the appointment of a special committee under the chairmanship of George Macdonald, a leading Catholic layman, to supervise the detailed execution of the plan. Three million bushels of surplus wheat would be donated to the American Red Cross, the cost of processing it into flour and shipping it to Spain – estimated at half a million dollars – would be raised by the Macdonald Committee, while distribution would be made by the Quaker relief committees in Spain.

Toller at last felt able to relax. For five months he had devoted himself to the project to the exclusion of everything else, now he looked forward to 'resuming my own work'.[28] In January he began to rewrite the final scene of *Pastor Hall*, which he sent to his English publisher before the end of the month.[29] However, work on the play was already overshadowed by the rapidly worsening news from Spain. A few days before Christmas the Nationalists launched a new offensive. On 30 December, the very day that Roosevelt announced the formation of the Macdonald Committee, Franco's troops broke through on the Catalan front. On 23 January they captured Barcelona. Long lines of refugees began to flee over the mountains into France, Madrid was cut off, the defeat of the Republic incontrovertible.

Toller seems to have clung – against all reason – to some shreds of hope. In late February he wrote to Dorothy Thompson that Sweden and Norway had now donated the promised relief funds: 'The Swedish Parliament gave 1,500,000 crowns, the Norwegian 500,000. The money will be used for Spanish children and adults inside Spain and for refugees who were forced to flee from Catalonia . . .'[30] Even such slender hopes were to prove false. On 27 March, Madrid finally surrendered; on 1 April, the American government formally recognized the Franco régime.

The defeat of the Republic, with its wide-reaching political reverberations, was a severe blow to anyone on the left: for Toller, it also meant the collapse of the plan in which he had invested his remaining emotional capital. Shipments of flour were to be diverted to feed refugees from Catalonia, of whom some 400,000 were now in refugee camps in Southern France. Toller himself was always convinced that the supplies already shipped had fallen into the hands of the fascists, an irony which he found almost unbearable. The project had consumed him physically and financially and its failure left him exhausted and disillusioned. He had planned to write a book documenting the Spanish Relief Plan, leaving a manuscript of some thirty pages among his unpublished papers, but abandoned the idea with the collapse of the plan itself. Once more, he was forced to reflect on the fateful discrepancy between dream and reality which, almost twenty years earlier, had been at the heart of his drama *Hinkemann*. 'A man who has no strength to dream has lost the strength to live', he had written then. Now his own strength was failing.

XVIII *Requiem*

By the spring of 1939, Toller had sunk into virtual obscurity. George Grosz, who met him shortly after the fall of the Spanish Republic, found him a sad figure: 'I suddenly saw a man who had once had a succès d'estime: now unsuccessful, bedraggled, bitter, disillusioned, and not even knowing where to find next month's rent.'[1] His health and morale had deteriorated dramatically, his depression had reached chronic proportions. When Ludwig Marcuse arrived in New York on Easter Sunday, Toller was among the small group waiting for him on the quayside – he looked so grey and careworn that Marcuse hardly recognized him.[2] Fritz Landshoff, arriving in New York from Amsterdam later that month, was equally shocked by Toller's appearance: 'His eyes had lost their sparkle, his voice was almost expressionless.'[3]

Toller was increasingly preoccupied with his own health: at the end of his life he was consulting no less than four doctors. Among them was Ralph Greenschpoon, who had treated him in California, to whom he wrote that he was once again in much the same situation as before: 'The worst is the incapacity to work. What that means in times like these and for an emigrant depending entirely upon his daily work, needs no comments.' Later he wrote:

> I am willing to undergo any treatment if there is but the slightest chance to get rid of [these breakdowns] for good. It seems to me that in a good state I am building up life and work and then I am thrown back and have to start all over again.
>
> Human relations are going to pieces, I am unable to help others as I try to do in good times. The uncertainty of my whole existence is growing. All this drives me to sheer despair.[4]

His difficulties were compounded by the mounting anxiety for the safety of his sister. She and her husband remained in Landsberg and Toller was waiting anxiously to hear if they had received permission to emigrate to Palestine. 'Their fate is a nightmare for me' he confided to his old friend Betty Frankenstein, imploring her to do whatever she could.[5] Despite his mounting financial problems, he borrowed five thousand dollars to provide a surety for their entry into Palestine, but they were never to leave Germany. Even more uncertain was the situation of his brother Heinrich, who had been living in Prague, and from whom Toller had heard nothing since the Nazis had occupied the city.

Toller's last appearance in public was in early May at a meeting of the International PEN, organized on the occasion of the New York World's Fair, when he spoke on behalf of the German writers present in memory of the victims of Nazi terror. After the conclusion of the PEN Congress, the delegates had been invited to Washington for an official reception on 11 May in the White House, in the course of which they were briefly presented to President Roosevelt. Klaus Mann, who later recorded his impressions of the occasion, remembered that Toller seemed in better spirits than for many months.[6] His depression seemed to have lifted, and he was lively and talkative. Over lunch, served on a small terrace of the White House, he joined in a particularly animated conversation with Dorothy Thompson, laughing loudly at one of her jokes. After lunch, the writers were given a tour of the White House by Mrs Roosevelt. Toller was impressed by her naturalness and ease of manner, praising it as an example of genuine democracy mixed with aristocratic refinement. Later the PEN delegates had been entertained by Eugen Mayer, the owner of the *Washington Post*. Toller had been delighted by everything, remaining interested and animated throughout the day.

He and Klaus Mann took the train together back to New York. 'It was a rewarding day,' Toller declared, 'we have seen and learned a lot.' In the ensuing conversation he seemed to have regained his self-confidence. While he spoke of his now precarious financial situation, he was more concerned with his plans for the future. He talked at some length about his planned trip to Europe, and about a collection of his political essays and speeches which he hoped to publish in London.[7] It was only when Mann rose to go back to his own sleeping compartment that Toller suddenly burst out, in a voice which trembled on the verge of tears: 'If only I could sleep now . . .' But he could not sleep. The following morning, at Pennsylvania Station, he looked devastated, his face ashen, his eyes dark-ringed. 'I lay awake the whole night,' he said. When they discussed the morning's newspaper headlines, he seemed to have difficulty in concentrating.

Landshoff had suggested to Toller that they should return to Europe together, hoping that a change of scene might bring a change of heart. Toller had agreed to the suggestion, planning to return to London for an extended stay. The two men had actually booked a cabin together on the liner *Champlain* but a week before their planned departure Landshoff fell seriously ill with food poisoning and Toller was quite suddenly left with the prospect of travelling alone. He spent his last weekend packing for the journey. Among the items he sorted out were photos and theatre reviews of Christiane's, which he gave to Sascha Marcuse with the words: 'I'd rather you had them than some stranger.' On Sunday, 21 May, he spent the evening with the Marcuses at their New York apartment, where discussion had turned to the question of suicide. Marcuse had defended the right of the individual to end his own life, Toller had violently disagreed. 'He tended to obscure the reasons for suicide, was very much against my too rational view of it, spoke much about the will to live and so on . . .'[8]

The following day, Monday, 22 May 1939, Toller committed suicide in his room at the Mayflower Hotel. In the morning he had been, as so often, tired and depressed. He spent some time arguing with his agent on the phone, quibbling about a difference of half a per cent. His secretary Ilse Herzfeld had been with him all morning, leaving for lunch at twelve o'clock. Toller had had a lunch engagement, but his guest had failed to turn up. When his secretary returned at one o'clock, she found him dead in the bathroom. He had hanged himself on the hook behind the door with the cord of his dressing-gown.

The precise motive for his act must remain a matter for conjecture, for he left no suicide note. Some fellow-exiles suspected foul play and the police sealed his room to investigate the possibility, but the circumstances in which his body was found precluded any other conclusion than suicide. His manic-depressive temperament had always verged on the suicidal: friends hinted that he had already made one unsuccessful attempt. His action was certainly unplanned. His boat ticket was in his pocket, he had written to friends to expect him; he had even suggested to Hermann Kesten that they should collaborate on a new play.[9]

Erwin Piscator, who had met Toller the day before he died, had found him very depressed by his isolation and lack of success. Such feelings were, of course, common to most German refugee writers.

They had been progressively cut off from their public; many had found that if they were able to write at all, it was only for their desk drawer. Toller felt separated from the very source of his inspiration. While he realized the need to write for an Anglo-Saxon audience, he knew that he was not able to do so directly. The rejection of *Pastor Hall*, partly because of the alleged unsuitability of Spender's English version, was a further unwelcome reminder of Toller's frustrating dependence on his translator. His inability to write in English only reinforced his lack of success: he had faded from public attention in a country which had once fêted him. He was further distressed by a legal dispute in connection with *Pastor Hall*. He had purchased some material for the play from a former concentration camp prisoner, Hermann Borchardt, who had been recommended to him by George Grosz. Borchardt claimed to have written parts of *Pastor Hall*, accused Toller of plagiarism, and threatened legal proceedings if the play was staged or published.

Toller's lack of recent success reinforced his long-held doubts about his own creative ability. He was dismayed by the disparity between his reputation and his actual achievements. He also faced mounting financial problems. The money he had earned while under contract to MGM had been swallowed up by the Spanish Relief Campaign, which he had even borrowed money to pursue. His occasional income had dwindled: his plays were no longer performed, further lecture tours were impossible to arrange. At their last meeting, Toller had asked Kurt Pinthus for help in placing three short stories, saying that he badly needed the money.[10] He admitted that only financial reasons had prevented his divorce from Christiane. Despite his now straitened financial circumstances, he had been unable to adjust his life style, continuing to live in a hotel which was now well beyond his means. His health was a growing preoccupation. He suffered from failing eyesight and insomnia, which made sustained concentration almost impossible. 'Nobody who hasn't been through it can know what it means not to be able to sleep,' he told Klaus Mann.[11] The failure of his marriage had increased his fits of depression.

Toller's personal misfortunes were compounded by political developments which demonstrated the uncertainty of his own future. The annexation of Austria and the march into Czechoslovakia presaged the inexorable advance of Nazism across Europe. He was disillusioned by the mood of appeasement in Britain and France. While fascism was in the ascendant, socialism suffered self-inflicted wounds. The Popular Front was in disarray. The Soviet Union, once a symbol of hope, was now the scene of political terror. Though he never commented publicly on the Moscow show trials, doubtless for reasons of solidarity, close friends later suggested that they were amongst his greatest political disillusionments. He did not live to see the Nazi-Soviet pact, but rumours of such a démarche were already spreading with the resignation of Litvinov as Soviet Foreign Minister. According to Ludwig Marcuse, the prospect of this pact with the devil was an even greater blow to Toller than the appeasement of three democracies.[12] But the greatest blow of all was the fall of the Spanish Republic, and the collapse of the relief project on which he had spent so much time and effort.

The news of Toller's suicide reached Christiane in Hollywood, where she was appearing, with other theatre exiles, in an English-language production of Schiller's *Wilhelm Tell* at the El Capitan theatre. Christiane, who had no understudy, followed the theatrical precept that the show must go on and – in a final irony more terrible than any Toller had contrived for the stage – played her role on an outwardly glittering first night on 25 May.

Toller's death was greeted with shock and sorrow by his fellow-exiles. Thomas Mann spoke for many when he called him a martyr of the time, a victim of the destructive forces they all feared and despised: he was indeed one of a succession of suicides among German refugees. Some of the reactions were tinged with reproach. His fellow-dramatist Ferdinand Bruckner, who had made a radio broadcast with him on behalf of refugees only four days before his death, confessed that 'for the first time, after a friendship of twenty years, I don't understand you', calling his suicide an abdication of his chosen role of public advocate against Nazism, an act which delivered a powerful weapon into the hands of the enemy.[13] Certainly, the Nazi press rejoiced, reporting Toller's death in a gleeful parody of his famous drama title: 'Hoppla, you're dead, but Germany lives!'[14]

At a memorial service on 27 May, attended by five hundred mourners, the funeral orations were given by Oskar Maria Graf for the Association of German American writers, Juan Negrín, the last President of the Spanish Republic, and the novelist Sinclair Lewis. Klaus Mann read a message from his father; Olga Fuchs, formerly of the Dresdner Staaatstheater, recited a poem from *The Swallow*

Book. It was Sinclair Lewis who summed up Toller's significance for a whole generation, calling him 'a symbol of revolution'.[15] The public ceremony was in sharp contrast to the private cremation service the following day, at which only three people were present: Ludwig Marcuse, Toller's cousin Else and an American woman journalist. Two years later, the urn containing his ashes still stood unclaimed in the cellar of the crematorium.

In the weeks following Toller's death, his friends and comrades, scattered in the diaspora of exile, paid individual tribute. J.R. Becher, writing from Moscow, commemorated 'the good comrade'; in France, Lion Feuchtwanger mourned the friend 'who had too much heart for others . . . a candle lighted at both ends which burnt out'.[16] There were very personal words from Alfred Wolfenstein: 'That a fighter should now die younger, more quickly, more suddenly, no longer surprises us and yet Ernst Toller's death moves us as directly as if we had lost a favourite brother.'[17] Perhaps the most apposite tribute came from W.H. Auden in his poem 'In Memory of Ernst Toller':

> Dear Ernst, lie shadowless at last among
> The other war-horses who existed till they'd done
> Something that was an example to the young.[18]

NOTE ON SOURCES

During Toller's lifetime, much of his work was published in English translation, notably his autobiography *I was a German* (1934), *Seven Plays* (1935) and *Letters from Prison* (1936). Unfortunately, these editions are long out of print and not readily accessible to the ordinary reader. Moreover, many of the translations now seem dated and some (e.g. the drama *Draw the Fires* and *Letters from Prison* show substantial variations from the text of the German original). I have consequently chosen not to use them and the translations from Toller's works in the text are my own. Most of Toller's major works are published in *Gesammelte Werke* (Wolfgang Frühwald and John M. Spalek, eds), vols 1–5, Munich, 1978 (cited as *GW* volume number). The accompanying volume of documentary materials *Der Fall Toller. Kommentar und Materialien*, Munich, 1979, is cited as *Der Fall Toller*. Other works of Toller's which are frequently quoted are: *Justiz. Erlebnisse*, Berlin, 1927 (cited as *Justiz*); *Quer Durch. Reisebilder und Reden*, Berlin, 1930 (cited as *Quer Durch*); and *Vormorgen*, Potsdam, 1924 (cited as *Vormorgen*).

I have also made extensive use of documentary sources, among the most important being:

> 1) The papers relating to Toller's trial for high treason, now held in the Bayerisches Staatsarchiv, Munich (cited as 'Trial Papers').
>
> 2) These papers include the transcript of Toller's statement to Staatsanwalt (Public Prosecutor) Lieberich after his arrest in June 1919 (cited as 'Transcript').
>
> 3) The proceedings of the Provisorischer Nationalrat (Provisional National Assembly) and the Bayerischer Rätekongreß (Bavarian Congress of Councils), the stenographic records of which are both held in the Bayerische Staatsbibliothek (cited as 'Provisorischer Nationalrat' and 'Rätekongreß' respectively).

There are several major collections of unpublished letters by Toller:

AK Akademie der Künste, Berlin
BA Bundesarchiv Koblenz
DB Deutsche Bibliothek, Deutsches Exilarchiv 1933–1945, Frankfurt
DLA Deutsches Literaturarchiv, Marbach/Neckar
Texas Harry Ransom Research Institute, University of Texas at Austin
IfZ Institut für Zeitgeschichte, Munich
Yale Sterling Memorial Library, Yale University

Other smaller collections are, where appropriate, cited in full.

Finally, there seems to be some revival of interest in Toller, both in Britain and in Germany. John M. Spalek and Wolfgang Frühwald, editors of Toller's collected works, are compiling an edition of his letters, to be published by Carl Hanser Verlag, Munich. Aufbau Verlag (Berlin and Weimar), is planning a new edition of Toller's work to appear in 1993. In Britain, a new edition of Toller's work in English translation is being prepared by Alan Pearlman, which may help to bring his work the wider audience it deserves.

NOTES

Notes to Introduction

1. The meeting was held on 30 June 1933 under the auspices of the Relief Committee for the Victims of German Fascism. In the end, Toller did not actually appear. See N.A. Furness, 'The reception of Ernst Toller and his works in Britain', *Expressionism in Focus* (Richard Sheppard, ed.), Blairgowrie, 1987.

2. Wilfred Wellock, 'Three Pacifist-Revolutionary Dramas', *Labour Leader*, 15 June 1922, p. 2. Wellock was a life-long pacifist, who became Labour MP for Stourbridge from 1927 to 1931. Toller dedicated his play *Die Maschinenstürmer* (*The Machine Wreckers*) to him.

3. Christopher Isherwood, 'The Head of a Leader', first published in *Encounter*, 1953, reprinted in *Exhumations*, London, 1966, pp. 125–32.

4. *The Saturday Review of Literature*, 31 March 1934.

5. George Grosz, *Ein kleines Ja und ein großes Nein*, Hamburg, 1955, p. 269, first published in English as *A Little Yes and a Big No*, New York, 1946; Ernst Niekisch, *Gewagtes Leben*, Cologne and Berlin, 1958, p. 99.

6. Otto Zarek (with the assistance of James Eastwood), *German Odyssey*, London, 1941, p. 87.

7. Niekisch, op. cit., p. 98. Weber's testimony is reported in *Münchner Neueste Nachrichten MNN*, no. 277, 16 July 1919.

8. *Eine Jugend in Deutschland* (*Growing up in Germany*), GW, IV, p. 235.

9. Niekisch, op. cit., p. 98.

10. J.R. Becher, 'Dem guten Kameraden', *Internationale Literatur*, IX, 7 (1939), pp. 135–6.

11. Emil Ludwig, 'Radionachricht von Ernst Tollers Tod', *Das neue Tagebuch*, 10 June 1939, p. 572.

12. Niekisch, op. cit., p. 98.

13. Grosz, op. cit., pp. 270–1.

14. Author's interview with Fenner Brockway, 14 February 1979.

15. Hermann Kesten, *Meine Freunde die Poeten*, Frankfurt, Berlin, Vienna, 1980, p. 152.

16. Lion Feuchtwanger, 'Dem toten Ernst Toller', *Die neue Weltbühne*, 8 June 1939, pp. 713–15.

17. ibid.

18. Toller, 'Rede auf dem Pariser Kongress der Schriftsteller' (Speech to Paris Writers' Congress), *Das Wort*, III, 10 October 1938, p. 126.

Notes to Chapter I

There is little independent evidence about Toller's childhood and this chapter is therefore based largely on his own accounts, the most important of which are:

i. his autobiography *Eine Jugend in Deutschland* (Growing up in Germany), and references to his childhood in *Briefe aus dem Gefängnis* (Letters from Prison), Amsterdam, 1935. These are reprinted as volumes IV and V of Toller's *Gesammelte Werke*, Munich, 1978 (cited as 'Eine Jugend', *GW*, IV and 'Briefe', *GW*, V)

ii. the transcript of his statement to Staatsanwalt Lieberich after his arrest in June 1919 which is contained in the papers relating to his trial for high treason, now held in the Staatsarchiv, Munich. Reprinted in 'Eine Jugend', *GW*, IV, pp. 239–52 (cited as 'Transcript', *GW*, IV)

iii. the autobiographical notes he sent to Heinar Schilling in 1921, reprinted in H. Daiber (ed.), *Vor Deutschland wird gewarnt* ('Be warned: Germany'), Gütersloh, 1967, pp. 90–105.

I have also drawn on information about the Toller family supplied by Ernst's niece Anne Schönblum.

1. 'Briefe', *GW*, V, pp. 28–9.

2. *Eine Jugend in Deutschland*, Amsterdam 1933; English version: *I was a German*, translated by Edward Crankshaw, London, 1934.

3. Cf. the unpublished autobiographical manuscript 'Death of a Mother' (Yale).

4. Kurt Pinthus, 'Life and Death of Ernst Toller', *Books Abroad*, XIV (1939), p. 4.

5. Cf. Toller's contribution to the anthology *Dichterglaube. Stimmen religiösen Erlebens* (Harald Braun, ed.), Berlin-Steglitz, 1931, particularly pp. 329–30.

6. Else Lasker-Schüler, 'Ernst Toller', *Emuna. Blätter für christlich-jüdische Zusammenarbeit*, Cologne, IV (1969), pp. 259–60. Her poem 'Ernst Toller' first appeared in *Die Weltbühne*, XXI, 1 (1925), p. 17.

7. 'Unser Weg', *Gedichte der Gefangenen*, Munich, 1921, p. 30; translated as 'Our Way', *Letters from Prison*, London, 1936, p. 140 (cited as *LP*). The closing lines of the poem are:

> We will bring the reign of peace on earth,
> We will bring freedom to the oppressed of all countries –
> *We must struggle for the sacrament of earth!*

8. 'Briefe', *GW*, V, p. 31.

9. 'Konflikte der Jugend in Deutschland', *Quer Durch. Reisebilder und Reden*, Berlin, 1930, p. 260 (cited as *Quer Durch*).

10. 'Der Ringende', *Vormorgen*, Berlin, 1924, p. 9. The poem was heavily edited for publication: an earlier MS version, now in DLA, contains eleven lines not included in the version in *Vormorgen*.

11. 'Transcript', *GW*, IV, p. 240.

12. 'Eine Jugend', *GW*, IV, p. 40.

Notes to Chapter II

1. 'Eine Jugend', *GW*, IV, p. 53. Toller's autobiography was written some fifteen years after his war service. In writing this chapter, I have referred to his other autobiographical accounts, to the various references made in his essays, speeches and reviews during the years 1919–30, and to the evidence given at his

trial for high treason. The literal translations of Toller's verse in the text are mine.

2. Thomas Mann, 'Gedanken im Krieg', *Die neue Rundschau*, November 1914, p. 1475; reprinted in Mann, *Politische Schriften und Reden*, II, Frankfurt and Hamburg, 1968.

3. A recent collection of German First World War poetry is contained in *Die Dichter und der Krieg. Deutsche Lyrik 1914–1918* (Thomas Anz, Joseph Vogel, eds), Munich and Vienna, 1982.

4. Richard Dehmel, *Zwischen Volk und Menschheit. Kriegstagebuch*, Berlin, 1919, p. 12.

5. Professor Ludwig Gurlitt (Munich), writing in the periodical *Junge Menschen* II, 24 (1921).

6. Introduction to *Briefe aus dem Gefängnis*, GW, V, p. 9.

7. The poem 'Frühling 1915' is one of a collection in typescript now held in the Bundesarchiv, Koblenz. The poems are among papers formerly held in the NSDAP Hauptarchiv and were presumably among personal papers confiscated after Toller's flat was raided following the Reichstag Fire. 'Frühling 1915' is dedicated to 'RD in admiration' – RD is probably Richard Dehmel, whose work, Toller later wrote, 'meant inexpressibly much to me' – see his unpublished letter to Dehmel, 25 November 1917, Richard Dehmel-Archiv, Staats-und Universitätsbibliothek, Hamburg.

8. 'Gang zur Ruhestellung', *Vormorgen*, Potsdam, 1924, p. 14, translated as 'Going to Rest Billets', *LP*, p. 6.

9. 'Leichen im Priesterwald', *Vormorgen*, p. 17; translated as 'Corpses in the Wood', *LP*, p. 6.

10. 'Briefe', *GW*, V, p. 188.

11. 'Im Westen nichts Neues', *Die literarische Welt*, 22 February 1929, p. 5.

12. 'Eine Jugend', *GW*, IV, pp. 69–70.

13. Letter from Dr Marcuse in 'Trial Papers'.

14. Walter Hasenclever, 'Der politische Dichter', *Tod und Auferstehung*, Munich, 1917.

15. Unpublished letter to Cäsar Flaischlen (DLA).

16. Otto Zarek, with the assistance of James Eastwood, *German Odyssey*, London, 1941, p. 85.

17. 'Den Müttern', *Vormorgen*, p. 21, first published as 'Mütter' in *Kameraden der Menschheit*, Potsdam, 1919, p. 70; translated as 'To the Mothers', *LP*, p. 8.

18. 'An die Dichter', *Vormorgen*, p. 20, not translated.

Notes to Chapter III

1. In evidence given at his trial for high treason, see *Münchner Neueste Nachrichten* (*MNN*), no. 274, 15 July 1919.

2. Letter from Diederichs to Max Weber, 22 July 1917 in Eugen Diederichs, *Selbstzeugnisse und Briefe von Zeitgenossen*, Cologne, 1967. For a contemporary account of the Lauenstein conference, see Marianne Weber, *Max Weber. A Biography*, translated by Harry Zohn, New York and London, 1975. There were in fact two conferences at Burg Lauenstein, the first 29–31 May 1917, the second

29 September–3 October 1917. Toller attended only the second of these, which had the theme 'Das Führerproblem in Staat und in der Kultur' (The Problem of Leadership in State and Culture).

3. H. Daiber, op. cit., p. 92.

4. Unpublished letter to Richard Dehmel, 25 November 1917, Richard Dehmel-Archiv, Staats- und Universitätsbibliothek, Hamburg.

5. See note 3.

6. M. Turnowsky-Pinner, 'A student's friendship with Ernst Toller', *Leo Baeck Institute Year Book*, 1970 , pp. 2121–22. In reconstructing Toller's activities in Heidelberg, I have drawn on this account as well as the various documents contained in Toller's 'Trial Papers'.

7. Toller, 'Bemerkungen zu meinem Drama *Die Wandlung*', *Der Freihafen*, II (1919), pp. 145–46. Reprinted *GW*, II, pp. 360–61.

8. Quoted in Stefan Großmann, 'Der Hochverräter Ernst Toller', reprinted in Toller, *Prosa, Briefe, Dramen, Gedichte*, Reinbek, 1961, p. 474.

9. M. Turnowsky-Pinner, op. cit.

10. *MNN*, no. 274, 15 July 1919.

11. 'Der neue Fall Foerster als Anlaß zum Protest gegen die Einschränkung der politischen Freiheit der Studierenden in Deutschland', Trial Papers, reprinted in *Der Fall Toller*, pp. 29–31.

12. Cf. Toller's unpublished letter to Schickele, 8 November 1917 (DLA).

13. Cf. 'Leitsätze für einen kulturpolitischen Bund der Jugend in Deutschland', *GW*, I, p. 33. Leonhard Frank's story 'Der Kellner' (later published under the title 'Der Vater') appeared in *Die weißen Blätter* in March 1916, extracts from Barbusse's novel from April 1917.

14. Cf. letter from 'Ausschuß der Heidelberger Studentenschaft', *Heidelberger Tageblatt*, 18 December 1917; also Toller's reply, 20 December 1917, (copies of both in 'Trial Papers').

15. 'Aufruf zur Gründung eines Kulturpolitischen Bundes der Jugend in Deutschland' *Der Fall Toller*, pp. 31–33.

16. 'Eine Jugend', *GW*, IV, p. 84.

17. The following outline of Landauer's philosophy is based on his *Aufruf zum Sozialismus*, which was certainly his best-known work and probably the only work of his which Toller had read in 1917. Page references in the text are to the first edition, fourth impression, Cologne 1923 (reprint Verlag Büchse der Pandora, 1978). A valuable exposition of Landauer's life and work is contained in Charles Benes Maurer, *Call to Revolution. The Mystical Anarchism of Gustav Landauer*, Detroit, 1971.

18. Letter to Gustav Landauer, 20 December 1917, *GW*, I, p. 36; 'Leitsätze' – see note 13.

19. 'Die Mobilmachung als Kriegsursache' (Mobilization as a Cause of War), written December 1916, but not published until 1919. Eisner's play *Die Götterprüfung* (Berlin, 1920) was performed in Berlin on May Day 1925.

20. Eisner's essays on Kant were published in the official SPD paper *Vorwärts* in 1904 and reprinted in Eisner, *Gesammelte Schriften* II, Berlin, 1919, pp. 165–86.

21. Felix Fechenbach, *Der Revolutionär Kurt Eisner*, Berlin, 1929, p. 25. Fechenbach's book gives a good account of the January Strike, in which he was a leading participant. See also Eisner's prison diary, *Sozialismus als Aktion* (Freya

Eisner, ed.), Frankfurt, 1975, pp. 58–74. For an historian's account of the strike, see Franz Schade, *Kurt Eisner und die bayerische Sozialdemokratie*, Hanover, 1961. See also Arthur Rosenberg, *Die Entstehung der deutschen Republik*, Berlin, 1928 (*The Birth of the German Republic, 1871–1918*, translated by Ian F.D. Morrow, Oxford, 1931).

22. Trial Papers.

23. Oskar Maria Graf, *Wir sind Gefangene*, Munich, 1965, p. 347. Graf's novel was first published in 1927. There is also an account of the meeting, given by police informers, in Toller's Trial Papers.

24. Cited in *Revolution und Räterepublik in München 1918–1919*, (Gerhard Schmolze, ed.), Düsseldorf, 1969, p. 52.

25. Trial Papers.

26. Cf. 'Ich habe euch umarmt' ('I have embraced you'), *Vormorgen*, Potsdam, 1924, p. 22.

27. *MNN*, no. 274, 15 July 1919. See also Daiber, op. cit., p. 93. For the account in his autobiography, see *GW*, IV, p. 95.

28. Daiber, op. cit., p. 93.

29. ibid.

30. Trial Papers. Some of this testimony is reprinted in *Der Fall Toller*, p. 40.

31. Quoted in Kurt Kreiler, *Die Schriftstellerrepublik*, Berlin, 1978, p. 190.

Notes to Chapter IV

1. *Die Wandlung. Das Ringen eines Menschen*, Potsdam, 1919. Reprinted in *GW*, II, pp. 7–61: page references in the text are to this edition.

2. *Der Sohn*, written 1913–14, was first produced in Prague in September 1916, and first produced in Germany in Dresden in October 1916. *Der Bettler*, written 1912, was produced by Max Reinhardt at the Deutsches Theater, Berlin in December 1917.

3. The most obvious formal and stylistic influences on the play are Strindberg and Sorge, but Toller also knew the work of Hasenclever, admiring his *Antigone*, and Unruh's *Ein Geschlecht*, published in Munich while Toller was a student there in 1917. It is less clear which Expressionist plays, if any, Toller had actually seen on stage.

4. Cf. 'Leitsätze für einen kulturpolitischen Bund der Jugend in Deutschland', *GW*, I, p. 33. See also Chapter III, note 13.

5. 'Bemerkungen zu meinem Drama *Die Wandlung*' dated Eichstätt Fortress Prison, October 1919, *Der Freihafen*, II (1919), pp. 145–46. Reprinted *GW*, II, pp. 360–1.

6. Gustav Mayer, *Erinnerungen. Vom Journalisten zum Historiker der deutschen Arbeiterbewegung*, Munich, 1949, pp. 292–3.

7. Stefan Großmann, 'Der Hochverräter Ernst Toller', in Toller, *Prosa, Briefe, Dramen, Gedichte*, Reinbek, 1961, p. 485.

8. Kurt Wolff to Toller, 2 December 1919, Wolff, *Briefwechsel eines Verlegers 1911–1963* (Bernhard Zeller and Ellen Otten, eds), Frankfurt, 1966, p. 323.

9. Friedrich Wolf, 'Präludium', *Sinn und Form*, XX, 6 (1968), p. 1307. The sketch was written in 1918–19, but not published until 1968.

10. Schickele, 'Der neunte November', *Tribüne der Kunst und Zeit*, VIII, pp. 21, 27–8.
11. Fritz Kortner, *Aller Tage Abend*, Munich, 1969, p. 219.

Notes to Chapter V

1. In writing this chapter I have used the documentary sources listed in the 'Note on Sources' and also the following:

  a) the decrees and proclamations of the two Soviet Republics, many of them signed by Toller, which are held in the Staatsbibliothek, Munich (Monacensia-Abteilung). Many of them are reprinted in Max Gerstl, *Die bayerische Räterepublik*, Munich, 1919.
  b) the proceedings of the 'Betriebsräte' (Works' Councils) during the second (Communist) Soviet Republic, published in the *Münchener Post*.
  c) reports in other Munich papers, such as the USPD paper *Neue Zeitung* and the Communist paper *Münchner Rote Fahne*.
  d) Toller complained that the transcript of his cross-examination often misrepresented his words. His statement to the Court Martial is therefore a better indication of his interpretation of events (cited according to *Münchner Neueste Nachrichten*, 15–17 July 1919 – *MNN*).

I have also drawn on the standard historical works: Allan Mitchell, *Revolution in Bavaria*, Princeton, 1965; Hans Beyer, *Von der Novemberrevolution zur Räterepublik in München*, Berlin, 1957; and Karl Bosl, *Bayern im Umbruch*, Munich and Vienna, 1969.

2. *MNN*, 15 July 1919.
3. 'Ansprache anlässlich der Revolutionsfeier am 17.11.1918', reprinted in Eisner, *Die halbe Macht den Räten. Ausgewählte Aufsätze und Reden* (Renate and Gerhard Schmolze, eds), Cologne, 1969, p. 278.
4. *MNN*, 8 November 1918.
5. 'Provisorischer Nationalrat', Beilage II, pp. 13–23.
6. 'Provisorischer Nationalrat', Beilage III, p. 128. Toller opened this meeting in his capacity as Vice-Chairman of the Workers' Councils.
7. *MNN*, 15 July 1919.
8. 'Provisorischer Nationalrat', 7. Sitzung, 30 December 1918, pp. 186–91.
9. 'Provisorischer Nationalrat', 8. Sitzung, 2 January 1919, pp. 256–8.
10. 'Aktionsausschußsitzung der A-, B- und S-Räte Bayerns', 21 January 1919, Bayerisches Hauptstaatsarchiv, Munich.
11. Letter to Rilke, 29 September 1920, *Rainer Maria Rilke 1875–1975*, catalogue of special exhibition, Schiller-Nationalmuseum, Marbach a.N. (J.W. Storck, ed.), Munich, 1975, p. 239.
12. 'Provisorischer Nationalrat', 5. Sitzung, 17 December 1918, p. 70.
13. 'Rätekongreß', 2. Sitzung, 27 February 1919, pp. 51–2.
14. 'An die Jugend aller Länder', *GW*, I, p. 49, translated as 'To the youth of all nations', *The Crusader*, 7 March 1919, pp. 4,7.

15. 'Rätekongreß', 2. Sitzung, 27 February 1919, p. 52.
16. Unpublished letter from Foerster to Toller, 9 March 1919: copy on file of proceedings against Ernst Niekisch, Bayerisches Staatsarchiv, Munich.
17. 'Transcript', *GW*, IV, p. 242.
18. 'Eine Jugend', *GW*, IV, p. 123.
19. The account of this meeting follows Ernst Niekisch, *Gewagtes Leben*, Cologne and Berlin, 1958, pp. 66–71.
20. Cf. Daiber, op. cit., p. 94.
21. Georg Escherisch, *Der Kommunismus in München*, VI, p. 8. This series comprises eight pamphlets, of which number VI deals with 'Die Scheinräterepublik', Munich, 1921.
22. The proclamation is reprinted in *Revolution und Räterepublik in München 1918–19* (Gerhard Schmolze, ed.), Düsseldorf, 1969, p. 271.
23. Cf. KPD leaflet, Bayerische Staatsbibliothek, Monacensia-Abteilung.
24. Lenin's telegram is reprinted in *Die Münchner Räterepublik. Zeugnisse und Kommentar* (Tankred Dorst, ed.), Frankfurt, 1969, p. 109.
25. Landauer to Mauthner, 7 April 1919, *Gustav Landauer. Sein Lebensgang in Briefen* (Martin Buber, ed.), vol. II, Frankfurt, 1929, p. 413.
26. 'An das Proletariat', proclamation dated 10 April 1919, signed by Toller, Bayerische Staatsbibliothek, Monacensia-Abteilung.
27. A. Rosenberg, *Die Geschichte der Weimarer Republik*, Frankfurt, 1961, p. 70.
28. Tilla Durieux, *Eine Tür steht offen. Erinnerungen*, Berlin, 1954, p. 133.
29. *Münchener Post*, 23 April 1919.
30. Cf. *Revolution und Räterepublik in München*, pp. 332–3.
31. *Münchner Rote Fahne*, 25 April 1919.
32. Toller's statement, dated 26 April 1919, is quoted in Gerstl, op. cit., pp. 108–9.
33. *MNN*, 15 July 1919.
34. *Münchner Rote Fahne*, 29 April 1919.
35. *Münchner Rote Fahne*, 30 April 1919.
36. Robert G.L. Waite, *Vanguard of Nazism: The Free Corps Movement in Postwar Germany, 1918–1923*, Cambridge, Mass., 1952.
37. The following paragraphs are based on Prinz Löwenstein's own recollections in Thomas Bütow, *Der Konflikt zwischen Revolution und Pazifismus im Werk Ernst Tollers*, Hamburg, 1975, Anhang, pp. 72–5.
38. See Trautner's statement on file of proceedings against him, Bayerisches Staatsarchiv, Munich.
39. 'Eine Jugend', *GW*, IV, p. 169.

Notes on Chapter VI

1. *Münchner Neueste Nachrichten*, 5 June 1919.
2. *Der Fall Toller*, p. 72.
3. Stefan Großmann, 'Der Hochverräter Ernst Toller' in Toller, *Prosa, Briefe, Dramen, Gedichte* (Kurt Hiller, ed.), Reinbek, 1961, p. 482.
4. See *Justiz*, pp. 84–7.
5. Toller's trial was reported in the leading national newspapers, such as the *Vossische Zeitung, Frankfurter Zeitung, Berliner Tageblatt, Vorwärts*, etc., as well

as in the Munich papers. My account is based on those in the *Münchener Post* and *Münchner Neueste Nachrichten*, 15, 16 and 17 July 1919.

6. *Der Fall Toller*, p. 79.

7. Großmann, op. cit., p. 484.

8. *Münchner Neueste Nachrichten*, 17 July 1919.

9. 'Schlußwort vor dem Standgericht', *GW*, I, pp. 49–51, which reprints the text published in the *Münchener Post*, 17 July 1919. Toller's final address also appeared, in a slightly different version, in *Münchner Neueste Nachrichten*, 17 July 1919.

10. See note 8.

Notes to Chapter VII

1. Letter to Tessa (i.e. Netty Katzenstein), undated (1920), *Briefe*, *GW*, V, p. 22 (hereafter cited as *GW*, V). Netty Katzenstein's husband Erich, a doctor, had fled to Switzerland in the aftermath of the Soviet Republic. Netty had remained in Munich, visiting Toller in prison more than once, rejoining her husband in Ascona in 1921.

2. Letter to Kurt Wolff, 13 July 1920, Wolff, *Briefwechsel eines Verlegers* (Bernhard Zeller and Ellen Otten, eds), Frankfurt 1966, p. 324.

3. O.M. Graf, 'Gedenkrede auf Ernst Toller', *Sinn und Form*, XXI (July 1969), pp. 897–900. Toller's years in prison are probably the best-documented period of his life, the events and experiences of these years being recorded in successive autobiographical works - *Justiz. Erlebnisse* (*Experiences of Justice*) (cited as *Justiz*), *Eine Jugend in Deutschland* (*Growing up in Germany*) and above all in *Briefe aus dem Gefängnis* (*Letters from Prison*). Further letters of Toller's from this period are published in Wolff, op. cit. and Kasimir Edschmid, *Briefe der Expressionisten*, Frankfurt, 1964; some unpublished letters are held in the Akademie der Künste, West Berlin and the Theaterarchiv of the Märkisches Museum, Berlin, GDR.

4. Unpublished letter, Kaufmann to Toller, December 1919 (AK).

5. 'In erster Linie Beamter', *Justiz*, p. 95.

6. Letter to Tessa, 30 January 1922, *GW*, V, p. 90.

7. *Gedichte der Gefangenen. Ein Sonettenkreis*, Munich, 1921, reprinted *GW*, II, quotation p. 330.

8. *Justiz*, pp. 93–4.

9. See the stenographic record of the proceedings of the Bavarian Landtag, session of 21 December 1921: Bayerische Staatsbibliothek, Munich. Extracts from the record are published in *Der Fall Toller*, pp. 128–33.

10. *Justiz*, p. 90.

11. Letter to Romain Rolland, undated (1921), *GW*, V, p. 76.

12. Letter to the editor of the newspaper *Kampf*, and letter to K., both undated (1920), *GW*, V, pp. 48–50.

13. Letter to Tessa, 25 February 1924, *GW*, V, p. 177, and to Paul Z. (i.e. Paul Zech, Expressionist dramatist), 4 May 1924, *GW*, V, p. 192.

14. Letter to K., 7 February 1922, *GW*, V, p. 94.

15. 'Deutsche Revolution', *Das Tagebuch*, 26 March 1921, pp. 358–65.

16. Letter to Kurt Wolff, 12 November 1921, Wolff, op. cit., pp. 328–9.

17. Letter to Paul Zech, 4 May 1924, *GW*, V, p. 192.

18. Letters to Tessa, 9 October 1920, *GW*, V, p. 55 and 30 September 1922, *GW*, V, p. 130.

19. 'The sexual life of prisoners', introductory essay by Toller to Joseph Fishman, *Sex in Prison*, London, 1935, p. vii.

20. Letter to Tessa, 30 January 1922, *GW*, V, pp. 90–1.

21. Letter to Tessa, 3 March 1921, *GW*, V, p. 63.

22. Letter to Tessa, 27 April 1922, *GW*, V, pp. 101–2.

23. Letter to Tessa, 4 October 1921, *GW*, V, p. 79.

24. *Das Schwalbenbuch*, *GW*, II, p. 331.

25. Letter to Walter Fabian, 6 December 1923, *GW*, V, p. 170.

26. Fishman, op. cit., p. xii.

27. Kurt Pinthus, 'Life and Death of Ernst Toller', *Books Abroad*, XIV (1939), pp. 3–8.

28. Letter to Kurt Wolff, 19 January 1921, Wolff, op. cit., p. 325; letter to Tessa, 2 February 1922, *GW*, V, pp. 92–93.

29. Letter to Tessa, 27 April 1922, *GW*, V, pp. 101–02.

30. See Kurt Tucholsky, *Ausgewählte Briefe 1913–35*, (Mary Gerold-Tucholsky and Fritz J. Raddatz, eds), Reinbek, 1962, pp. 124–5.

31. *Justiz*, p. 113.

32. Letter to Tessa, 23 October 1923, *GW*, V, p. 168.

33. Communication from Toller's niece Anne Schönblum, 1988.

34. Letter to Tessa, 16 March 1924, *GW*, V, p. 184.

35. Letter to Dr N., 25 February 1924, *GW*, V, p. 183.

36. Letter to Tessa, 11 July 1924, *GW*, V, p. 194.

37. 'Eine Jugend', *GW*, IV, p. 235.

Notes to Chapter VIII

1. Letter to Kurt Wolff, 13 July 1920, op. cit., p. 325.

2. *Quer Durch*, p. 288.

3. *Masse-Mensch. Ein Stück aus der sozialen Revolution des 20. Jahrhunderts*, Potsdam, 1921. Reprinted in *GW*, II, pp. 63–112: page references in the text are to this edition. Toller wrote the first draft of the play in October 1919 and had completed revisions to it by June 1920. It passed the prison censorship in July – see letter to Kurt Wolff cited in note 1.

4. Letter to Theodor Lessing, undated (1920), *GW*, V, p. 36.

5. Letter to Tessa (i.e. Netty Katzenstein), 12 November 1920, *GW*, V, p. 50.

6. Toller's protagonist was inspired by Sarah Sonja Lerch, the Russian-born wife of a Munich university professor, who had joined the anti-war group around Eisner and played a leading role in the strike committee. Arrested at the same time as other strike leaders, she committed suicide in Stadelheim Prison two months later.

7. Toller inserted the line 'Gewaltlos werden wir die Ketten sprengen' only in the second edition of the play (Potsdam, 1922), in order to emphasize her belief in the *revolutionary* effect of non-violent action.

8. *Quer Durch*, p. 282.

9. Extensive details of the production are given in K. Macgowan and R.E. Jones, *Continental Stagecraft*, London, 1923, pp. 144–56. These are also dis-

cussed in Renate Benson, *German Expressionist Drama. Ernst Toller and Georg Kaiser*, London, 1984.

10. Jürgen Fehling, 'Notes on the production of *Masse-Mensch*' in *Masses and Man*, translated by Vera Mendel, London, 1923.

11. Macgowan, op. cit., pp. vii, 144.

12. *Der Tag des Proletariats. Ein Chorwerk*, Berlin, 1920, also including *Requiem den erschossenen Brüdern*, which had been first published in the USPD yearbook *Die Revolution*, Berlin, 1920. The text of both 'Sprechchöre' is reprinted in *Arbeiterkulturbewegung in der Weimarer Republik. Texte. Dokumente. Bilder* (Wilfred van der Will and Rob Burns, eds), Frankfurt, Berlin, Vienna, 1982.

13. Letter to Anne-Marie von Puttkamer (editor at Kurt Wolff Verlag), 22 May 1921, Wolff, op. cit., p. 328. Cf. also letter to Tessa, 18 May 1921, *GW*, V, p. 66.

14. Letter to Tessa, 1 September 1920, *GW*, V, pp. 34–35.

15. Letter to Tessa, undated (1920), *GW*, V, p. 31.

16. *Die Maschinenstürmer*, Leipzig, Vienna, Zurich, 1922. Reprinted in *GW*, II, pp. 113–90: subsequent page references in the text are to this edition.

17. Letter to Tessa, 27 January 1921, *GW*, V, p. 59.

18. Letter to Anne-Marie von Puttkamer, see note 13.

19. Letter to Gustav Mayer, 7 February 1921, *GW*, V, p. 60, also Toller's notes in *Die Glocke*, VII, 43, 16 January 1922, reprinted in *GW*, II, p. 361.

20. For an extended analysis of the historical sources and their treatment, see my *Revolutionary Socialism in the Work of Ernst Toller*, Bern, Frankfurt, New York, 1986, pp. 156–62, and N.A. Furness, 'Fact and Symbol in *Die Maschinenstürmer*', *Modern Language Review*, 1978, pp. 847–58.

21. Unpublished letter to Gustav Mayer, 2 January 1921 (Istituto Giangiacomo Feltrinelli, Milan). Toller's letters to Mayer, to whom he had originally written for help in supplying historical source material, shed interesting light on his dramatic conception and particularly his characterization.

22. Stefan Großmann, 'Toll, Toller, am Tollsten', *Das Tagebuch*, 15 July 1922, reprinted in *Der Fall Toller*, pp. 135–37.

23. Döblin's review, which first appeared in the *Prager Tageblatt*, is cited in *Der Fall Toller*, pp. 137–8.

24. First published under the title *Der deutsche Hinkemann. Eine Tragödie in drei Akten*, Potsdam, 1923. Reprinted in *GW*, II, pp. 191–247: page references in the text are to this edition. The play was reprinted in 1924 under the title *Hinkemann*. A second (revised) edition, also entitled *Hinkemann*, appeared in the course of that year.

25. Two well-known examples are the poet J.R. Becher and the dramatist Friedrich Wolf. Becher, a member of the USPD in 1917 and of the KPD in 1919, was disillusioned by the defeat of the revolution and in 1920–21 suffered from moods of despair and nihilism. He resumed political commitment in 1923 with a public declaration for the KPD. Wolf, as a member of the USPD, had taken part in the fighting in the Ruhr in March 1920. In the spring of 1921, he had joined the anarcho-community in Worpswede, only to leave it shortly afterwards in disillusionment. Becher was later to become Minister of Culture in the GDR, Wolf its first ambassador to Poland.

26. See Toller's unpublished correspondence with the Volksbühne (Märkisches Museum, Berlin, GDR), particularly his letter to Dr Oskar Anwand (Deputy Artistic Director of the Volksbühne), 21 October 1921. This correspondence confirms that, in the course of negotiations regarding the production of the play, Toller was persuaded to make considerable revisions to his original manuscript, before the play was finally rejected in July 1922.

27. Letter to Tessa, 20 March 1922, *GW*, V, pp. 98–9.

28. Letter to Max Beer, 7 July 1923, *GW*, V, p. 158.

29. 'Anmerkung zur proletarischen Kunst', *Volksbühne* II, 3 (January/February 1922). Toller repeated this formulation on several other occasions in 1921–22, e.g. 'Brief an einen schöpferischen Mittler' which serves as a foreword to the second edition of *Masse Mensch*; 'Ernst Toller über proletarische Kunst', *Vorwärts*, 28 April 1922; letter 'to a worker', undated (1922), *GW*, V, pp. 116–17.

30. Toller, *Die Hinkemanns. Eine proletarische Tragödie in drei Aufzügen* (extract corresponding to Act II, Scene I of the published play), *Volksbühne*, II, 3, p. 93.

31. Cf. letter to Kurt Wolf, 12 November 1921, Wolf, op. cit., pp. 328–9; cf. also postcard from Toller to Dr Anwand, 17 July 1922, requesting the return of the manuscript (Märkisches Museum) and letter to Tessa, 14 August 1922, *GW*, V, pp. 112–13, in which Toller quotes at length from a letter from the Volksbühne.

32. Unpublished letter to Dr Anwand, 30 October 1921 (Märkisches Museum).

33. *Kulturwille*, III (1924), p. 50.

34. Details of the theatre scandal in Dresden appeared in the contemporary press and are summarized in Carel ter Haar, *Ernst Toller. Appell oder Resignation?* Munich, 1977. For Toller's own account, see letter to Tessa, *GW*, V, pp. 177–80.

35. See Heinrich Hannover and Elisabeth Hannover-Drück, *Politische Justiz 1918–1933*, Frankfurt, 1966, p. 255.

36. Letter to the editor of the *Tagebuch* (i.e. Stefan Großmann), 14 April 1924, *GW*, V, p. 191.

37. See Wolfgang Frühwald, 'Nachwort' in the edition of *Hinkemann* in the Reclam Universal-Bibliothek, Stuttgart, 1974, p. 92). Cf. also Gustav Stresemann, *Vermächtnis. Der Nachlaß in drei Bänden* (Henry Bernhard, ed.), Berlin, 1932–33, vol. 1, p. 548.

38. This judgement by the Bavarian Minister of Justice, Franz Gürtner, was used by Joseph Roth to preface his review of the Berlin production of *Hinkemann* in *Vorwärts*, 15 April 1924. As Minister of Justice, Gürtner showed great complaisance towards Adolf Hitler, lifting a threat of deportation against him in 1924.

39. Letter to B., 19 July 1923, *GW*, V, p. 160.

40. *Der entfesselte Wotan*, Potsdam, 1923. Reprinted *GW*, II, pp. 249–302: page references in the text are to this edition. An author's note states that the play was 'written in the serene power of growing early spring'.

41. Letter to Kurt Wolff, 5 February 1923, Wolff, op. cit., p. 330.

42. Letter to the actor Max Pallenberg, 20 June 1923, *GW*, V, p. 154.

43. Toller evidently knew of this incident, referring to it in *Justiz*, pp. 53–6.

44. 'Dichter über ihre neuen Werke. Ernst Toller: *Der entfesselte Wotan*', *Die Szene*, January 1926, reprinted in *Der Fall Toller*, pp. 363–5.
45. Letter to B., 28 June 1923, *GW*, V, p. 155.
46. Unpublished letter to Dr Lutz Veltmann, 15 January 1926 (DLA).
47. *Das Schwalbenbuch*, Potsdam, 1924. Reprinted *GW*, II, pp. 323–50: page references in the text are to this edition.
48. Toller describes Hagemeister's death and the subsequent dispute between prisoners and judicial authorities in *Justiz*, pp. 129–44.
49. Letter to the President of the German Reichstag, Paul Löbe, 19 September 1923, *GW*, V, pp. 162–5. First published as one of the 'Dokumente bayerische Justiz, *Die Weltbühne*, 20 January 1925.
50. 'Nestersturm', *Justiz*, pp. 122–4. This account was included as an epilogue in later editions of *Das Schwalbenbuch*.
51. For an account of the mass spectacles in Leipzig, see Klaus Pfützner, *Die Massenfestspiele der Arbeiter in Leipzig*, Leipzig, 1960; see also Ludwig Hoffmann and Daniel Hoffmann-Ostwald, *Deutsches Arbeitertheater 1918–1933. Eine Dokumentation*, Berlin, 1961, pp. 33–4.
52. *Leipziger Volkszeitung*, 8 August 1922, reprinted in *Der Fall Toller*, pp. 140–2. See also Pfützner, op. cit., pp. 20–4.
53. Ashley Dukes, 'A poet of the German Revolution', *The New Leader*, 11 December 1925, p. 11. See also Pfützner, op. cit., pp. 25–6.
54. *Leipziger Volkszeitung*, 15 July 1924. See also Pfützner, op. cit., pp. 26–8, Hoffmann, op. cit., p. 34.
55. Letter to Alfred Kerr, 6 April 1923 in K. Edschmid, *Briefe der Expressionisten*, Frankfurt, 1964, pp. 133–4. He repeats this idea in a letter to Stefan Zweig, 13 June 1923, *GW*, V, p. 112.
56. Letter to Ernst Niekisch, 28 February 1924, *GW*, V, p. 180.
57. Letter to the Director of the Dresdner Staatstheater, 1 February 1924, *GW*, V, pp. 176–7.
58. Letter to Tessa, 16 March 1924, *GW*, V, pp. 184–5.
59. Cf. letter to Tessa, 24 November 1922, *GW*, V, p. 13. Full details of translations and productions of Toller's plays are contained in Spalek, *Bibliography*. Information about the production in Leningrad is contained in Toller's letter to the actor Alfred Beierle, 7 April 1924 (Märkisches Museum).

Notes to Chapter IX

1. For examples of this view, see William A. Willibrand, *Ernst Toller and his Ideology*, Iowa City, 1945, and Walter H. Sokel, 'Ernst Toller' in *Deutsche Literatur im 20. Jahrhundert* (Otto Mann and Wolfgang Rothe, eds), Bern and Munich, 1967. More recent critics have taken a more favourable view of Toller's work after 1924 – see, for example, Thomas Bütow, *Der Konflikt zwischen Revolution und Pazifismus im Werk Ernst Tollers*, Hamburg, 1975, and Rosemarie Altenhofer, *Ernst Tollers politische Dramatik*, unpublished dissertation, Washington University, 1976.
2. Fritz Landshoff, 'Ernst Toller. Eine Radiosendung', *Germanic Notes*, XV (1984), pp. 41–2.
3. 'Briefe', *GW*, V, p. 193.

4. *Leipziger Volkszeitung*, 17 July 1924, quoted in Spalek, *Bibliography*, no. 1366.

5. Quoted in *Der Fall Toller*, p. 162.

6. Quoted in Rothe, *Ernst Toller*, Reinbek, 1983, pp. 17–18.

7. Alfred Kerr, *Die Welt im Drama* (Gerhard F. Hering, ed.), Berlin and Cologne, 1954, pp. 162–3.

8. Unpublished letter to Ludwig Lore, 29 November 1928 (AK).

9. *Der Fall Toller*, pp. 164–5.

10. Cf. Becher, 'Bürgerlicher Sumpf. Revolutionärer Kampf', *Das Wort* (Halle), February 1925. The successive critiques of *Hoppla* appeared in *Die Rote Fahne* on 6, 7, 8 and 9 September 1927; reprinted in *Die Rote Fahne* (Manfred Brauneck, ed.), Munich, 1973, pp. 273–87.

11. *Der Fall Toller*, p. 161.

12. *Dokumente bayrischer Justiz* appeared in *Die Weltbühne* between 16 October 1924 and 20 January 1925.

13. *Justiz. Erlebnisse*, Berlin, 1927, reprinted Berlin, 1979.

14. See advertisement in *Deutsche Revolution*, Berlin, 1925, p. 15.

15. Unpublished letter from Toller's secretary to Ferdinand Luttner, 2 February 1926 (AK).

16. Ernst Feder, *Heute sprach ich mit . . . Tagebücher eines Berliner Publizisten* (C. Lowenthal-Hensel and Arnold Paucker, eds), Stuttgart, 1971, pp. 105–6, entry for 18 February 1927.

17. Thomas Mann in *Berliner Tageblatt*, 31 July 1927; Ignaz Wrobel (i.e. Kurt Tucholsky), 'Der Rechtsstaat', *Die Weltbühne*, 12 July 1927.

18. Cf. Toller, 'Max Hölz', *Die Weltbühne*, 1 February 1927 and 'Die Erschießung des Gutsbesitzers Heß', *Die Weltbühne*, 3 May 1927. See also the unpublished correspondence between Toller and Hölz, in Bundesarchiv, Koblenz (BA).

19. Hölz to Toller, 20 May 1927; see also Hölz's letter of 23 September 1927 (BA).

20. Toller to Nehru, 21 July 1936, in Nehru, *A Bunch of Old Letters*, London, 1958, p. 198.

21. See Richard Dove, 'The Place of Ernst Toller in English Socialist Theatre 1924–1939', *German Life and Letters*, January 1985, pp. 125–37. For an account of the Brussels Congress, see Fenner Brockway, *Inside the Left*, London, 1942.

22. Toller's speech to the Congress was reprinted as 'Gegen Kolonialimperialismus' in *Quer Durch*. For his report on the congress, see 'Der Brüsseler Kolonialcongreß', *Die Weltbühne*, 1 March 1927. Toller's enthusiasm is noted by Ernst Feder, op. cit., pp. 103, 105.

23. See Brockway, op. cit. For a discussion of the incident and Toller's dramatization of it, see Richard Dove, 'Fenner Brockway and Ernst Toller. Document and Drama in *Berlin – letzte Ausgabe!*', *German Life and Letters*, October 1984, pp. 45–56.

24. See Kurt Hiller, *Leben gegen die Zeit*, vol 1, 'Logos', Reinbek, 1969, p. 163, also Alf Enseling, *Die Weltbühne. Organ der intellektuellen Linken*, Münster, 1962.

25. Toller's main statements on pacifism are contained in 'Antworten', *Die Weltbühne*, 6 January 1921; 'Eine Ansprache', *Die sozialistische Erziehung*

(Vienna), February 1925; *Deutsche Revolution*, Berlin, 1925; *Quer Durch*, pp. 98–9.

26. See his statement on revolutionary pacifism to the Esperanto journal *Laborista Esperanto Asocio*, 'Sammlung Ernst Toller' (AK).

27. The proceedings against Becher are described in Alfred Klein, 'Der Hochverratsprozeß gegen J.R. Becher', *Aktionen, Bekenntnisse, Perspektiven* (Deutsche Akademie der Künste, eds), Berlin and Weimar, 1966.

28. See his unpublished correspondence with the League (AK).

29. An account of the work of the committee is contained in C.v.Ossietzky, *Rechenschaft*, Frankfurt, 1972.

30. 'Das sozialistische Wien', *Die Weltbühne*, 15 March 1927, 'Heimarbeit', *Die Weltbühne*, 21 June 1927, 'Sprechen wir vom Panzerkreuzer', *Welt am Montag*, 26 November 1928.

31. *Vorwärts*, 16 February 1927. It was at Toller's instigation that Angelika Balabanov was invited to speak in Berlin in March on 'The Spiritual Face of Fascism' – cf. his unpublished letter to the League for Human Rights, dated 22 January 1927.

32. 'In Memoriam Kurt Eisner', *GW*, I, pp. 165–8.

33. 'Reichskanzler Hitler', *Die Weltbühne*, 7 October 1930 (reprinted in *GW*, I, pp. 69–73).

34. 'Zur deutschen Situation', *GW*, I, pp. 73–6.

35. *Quer Durch*, p. 289.

36. ibid.

37. Emil Ludwig, 'Radionachricht von Tollers Tod', *Das neue Tagebuch*, 10 June 1939, p. 572.

38. *Quer Durch*, p. 296.

39. Personal communication from Hermann Kesten.

40. 'Zur Physiologie des dichterischen Schaffens', *Die literarische Welt*, 28 September 1928, p. 204.

Notes on Chapter X

1. 'Das neue Drama Tollers', *Die Volksbühne*, 15 August 1926.

2. Babette Gross, *Willi Münzenberg. Eine politische Biographie*, Stuttgart, 1967, p. 184.

3. Erwin Piscator, *The Political Theatre*, London, 1980, p. 23. This is the English translation (by Hugh Rorrison) of *Das politische Theater*, Berlin, 1929 (reprint Reinbek, 1979). For an account of Piscator's life and work, see John Willett, *The Theatre of Erwin Piscator*, London, 1978.

4. See 'Korrespondenz mit Bühnenschiedsgericht' (AK). This (unpublished) account, concerning Toller's dispute with the Volksbühne over its failure to honour an agreement to produce *Die Wandlung*, is undated, but must have been written in March 1927. It was written in response to a letter from the Volksbühne, dated 26 February 1927, and sent by Toller to his publisher. He also sent a copy to Alfred Kerr – see letter of 29 March 1927 (AK).

5. Betty Frankenstein was editor of the *Jüdische Rundschau* from 1925 to 1938. Toller's surviving letters to her in the Deutsches Literaturarchiv, Marbach, none of which has been published, include some fifteen letters he wrote

from France between 18 June and 6 November 1926. The dates of individual letters quoted are given in the text.

6. The 'travel book on Russia' is a reference to the 'Russische Reisebilder' (Russian Travel Sketches) which Toller eventually published in *Quer Durch* in 1930. See Chapter XI.

7. 'Korrespondenz mit Bühnenschiedsgericht' (AK).

8. See *Kulturwille* III, 12, 1 December 1926, p. 246; *Kunst und Volk. Mitteilungen des Vereines 'Sozialdemokratische Kunststelle'*, II, January 1927; *Die Volksbühne*, 1 March 1927.

9. Unpublished letter to Alfred Kerr, 20 February 1927 (AK).

10. Quoted in *The Political Theatre*, p. 147. Piscator's account of the Volksbühne controversy is given on pp. 95–110. A less committed account is given in Cecil W. Davies, *Theatre for the People. The Story of the Volksbühne*, Manchester, 1977, pp. 103–11; see also Willett, op. cit., pp. 63–5.

11. Piscator, op. cit., p. 158.

12. Toller, 'Rede auf der Volksbühnentagung in Magdeburg' (Speech to the Volksbühne Conference in Magdeburg), *Das Tagebuch*, 2 July 1927, pp. 1074–8. Subsequent page references in the text are to this publication. Toller's Magdeburg speech was a contribution to the debate on the artistic policy of the Volksbühne, containing in embryo the conception of theatre he would develop in two later essays: 'Bemerkungen zum deutschen Nachkriegsdrama', in *Die literarische Welt*, 19 April 1929 and 'Arbeiten', in *Quer Durch*.

13. *Quer Durch*, p. 167.

14. 'Wer schafft den deutschen Revolutionsfilm?' (1928), *GW*, I, pp. 117–19. This article contains the first published outline of *Draw the Fires*.

15. Ernst Feder, *Heute sprach ich mit . . . Tagebücher eines Berliner Publizisten* (C. Lowenthal-Hensel, A. Paucker, eds), Stuttgart, 1971, pp. 105–06 (entry for 18 February 1927).

16. A handbill advertising this reading is among the papers in the Bundesarchiv, Koblenz.

17. Unpublished letter to Max Hölz, 22 March 1927 (BA).

18. Unpublished letter to Dr Alfred Landsberg, 16 June 1927 (AK); See also *Berliner Tageblatt*, 15 June 1927.

19. Unpublished letter to Landsberg, 1 July 1927 (AK).

20. Piscator, *The Political Theatre*, London, 1980, p. 207. Subsequently cited in the text as *PT*.

21. Unpublished letter to Alfred Kerr, 11 August 1927 (AK).

22. *Hoppla, wir leben! GW*, III, p. 10. Subsequent page references in the text are to this edition.

23. Walter Mehring, *Die Gedichte, Lieder und Chansons des Walter Mehring*, Berlin, 1929, p. 39.

24. *Der Fall Toller*, p. 186. A selection of reviews in the Berlin press is cited by Piscator in *The Political Theatre*, pp. 218–20, which contains a full account of Piscator's production (pp. 206–17) (see also John Willett, op. cit., pp. 84–7).

25. Unpublished letter to Alwin Kronacher, 19 September 1927 (AK).

26. For reviews of the Leipzig production, see Spalek nos. 2781, 2795, 2797, 2825 and 2846.

27. Unpublished letter to Ludwig Lore, 10 January 1929 (AK).

28. Unpublished letter to Alwin Kronacher, 19 December 1928 (AK).

29. Walter Hasenclever, *Gedichte, Dramen, Prosa* (Kurt Pinthus ed.), pp. 44–5.

30. *Feuer aus den Kesseln. Historisches Schauspiel von Ernst Toller*, Berlin, 1930. An acting version of the play, showing a number of revisions, also appeared in 1930. This version has been reprinted in *GW*, III, pp. 119–84; subsequent page references in the text are to this edition.

31. *Feuer aus den Kesseln*, Berlin, 1930, foreword, p. 7. Among Toller's departures from historical truth are that while eleven sailors were actually indicted, Toller reduced this to the five who were originally sentenced to death. He also brought the men together on one ship, presumably for reasons of dramatic economy. While the figure of Schuler largely corresponds to the naval prosecutor Dobring, some of the practices attributed to him were in fact used by his fellow-prosecutors Breil and Loesch.

32. *Feuer aus den Kesseln*, documentary appendix, p. 167.

33. 'Einladung an Dobring', *Die Weltbühne*, 1 October 1930, reprinted *GW*, III, pp. 335–6.

34. Ernst Feder, op. cit., p. 271 (entry for 11 November 1930).

35. Ernst-Josef Aufricht, *Erzähle, damit du dein Recht erweist*, Berlin, 1966, pp. 101–3.

36. 'Film und Staat' (1924), *GW*, I, p. 115.

37. 'Die Auftraggeber fehlen', *Vossische Zeitung*, 31 March 1929, reprinted *GW*, I, p. 125.

38. Unpublished letter to Ludwig Lore, 10 January 1929 (AK).

39. 'Briefe', *GW*, V, p. 187.

40. *Berlin – letzte Ausgabe!* in *Frühe sozialistische Hörspiele* (Stefan Bodo Würffel, ed.), Frankfurt, 1982. A detailed analysis of the play is contained in my article 'Fenner Brockway and Ernst Toller: document and drama in *Berlin – letzte Ausgabe!*', *German Life and Letters*, October 1984, pp. 45–56.

41. Quoted in Christian Hörburger, *Das Hörspiel der Weimarer Republik*, Stuttgart, 1975, pp. 21–2.

Notes to Chapter XI

1. The incident in Italy is recounted by Hermann Kesten in *Meine Freunde die Poeten*, Frankfurt, Berlin, Vienna, 1980, p. 150.

2. Cf. Löbe's letter to the British Passport Control Office, Berlin, 14 November 1925 and Toller's letter of thanks to Löbe, 20 November 1925 (AK).

3. 'Ernst Toller in England', *Die Volksbühne*, 1 January 1926. For details of Toller's reading at King's College, see *Publications of the English Goethe Society*, New Series 3 (1926), p. 144.

4. 'Communism in Munich and Palestine. What Ernst Toller saw', *New Leader*, 11 December 1925, p. 3. This issue of the *New Leader* also included an article on Toller by Ashley Dukes, a woodcut portrait of him by Clare Leighton (see frontispiece above) and a translation of one of his poems.

5. Cf. 'Reise nach Kopenhagen' ('Journey to Copenhagen'), *Die literarische Welt*, 18 April 1927, 'Das sozialistische Wien' ('Socialist Vienna'), *Die Weltbühne*, 15 March 1927, and the series of articles on 'Das neue Spanien' ('The New Spain'), published in *Die Weltbühne* between 12 April and 21 June 1932.

6. *Quer Durch. Reisebilder und Reden*, Berlin, 1930 (reprint Heidelberg, 1981). Page references in the text are to the reprinted edition.

7. Author's preface, *Which World, Which Way?*, translated by Hermon Ould, London, 1931.

8. Cf. Toller's unpublished letters to Emil Ludwig, 4 January 1929 and Ludwig Lore, 10 January 1929 (AK).

9. Cf. John M. Spalek, 'Ernst Toller: the need for a new estimate', *German Quarterly*, XXXIX (1966), No. 4, pp. 581–98.

10. *Which World, Which Way?*, London, 1931, pp. ix–x.

11. Unpublished letter to Anatoli Lunacharsky, 16 October 1928 (AK).

12. See Paul Fröhlich, *Die bayerische Räterepublik. Tatsachen und Kritik*, Leipzig, 1920 and Toller's reply in *Die Weltbühne*, 6 January 1921. It was Fröhlich who wrote the attack on Toller published in *Pravda* in 1926. See also Rosa Leviné, *Aus der Münchener Rätezeit*, Berlin, 1925 and Erich Wollenberg, *Als Rotarmist vor München*, Berlin, 1929, as well as Toller's response in *Neue Bücherschau*, VII, 10 (1929).

13. *Nationalsozialismus. Eine Diskussion über den Kulturbankrott des Bürgertums*, Berlin, 1930, p. 33.

14. ibid., p. 11.

Notes to Chapter XII

1. Interview with Fritz Landshoff, 16 July 1982.

2. Quoted in Hans-Albert Walter, *Deutsche Exilliteratur 1933–1950*, vol I, Darmstadt and Neuwied, 1972, p. 268.

3. Ernst Feder, op. cit., p. 271 (entry for 5 October 1930).

4. Personal communication from Hermann Kesten. Zweig's essay 'Das Leben und die Lehre der Mary Baker Eddy' first appeared in *Die neue Rundschau* and was reprinted in *Die Heilung durch den Geist*, Leipzig, 1931.

5. Toller, Kesten, *Wunder in Amerika* (mimeographed acting version), Berlin, 1931, p. 34. The play was published in English as *Mary Baker Eddy*, translated by Edward Crankshaw, in *Seven Plays*, London, 1935.

6. *Die blinde Göttin. Schauspiel in fünf Akten von Ernst Toller*, Berlin, 1933; published in English as *The Blind Goddess*, translated by Edward Crankshaw, London, 1934. For Toller's visit to the two defendants in prison, see his article 'Giftmordprozeß Riedel-Guala', *Die Weltbühne*, 13 October 1931.

7. Kurt R. Grossman, *Ossietzky. Ein deutscher Patriot*, Munich, 1963, p. 248.

8. 'Reichskanzler Hitler', *Die Weltbühne*, 7 October 1930, reprinted *GW*, I, pp. 69–73.

9. 'Zur deutschen Situation' (1932), *GW*, I, pp. 73–6.

10. Grossmann, op. cit., p. 11.

11. 'Rede in Budapest', *Die Weltbühne*, 7 June 1932.

12. Kurt Tucholsky, *Unser ungelebtes Leben. Briefe an Mary* (Fritz J. Raddatz, ed.), Reinbek, 1982, p. 537.

13. Brecht, *Kuhle Wampe*, Frankfurt, 1969, p. 184.

14. Quoted in Christian Hörburger, *Das Hörspiel der Weimarer Republik*, Stuttgart, 1975, pp. 21–2.

15. See note 3.

16. The following is based on an unpublished autobiographical manuscript by Christiane Grautoff, written during the early nineteen seventies which is now in the possession of John M. Spalek (Albany, N.Y.), whom I thank for drawing it to my attention.

17. Kurt Tucholsky, *Briefe aus dem Schweigen 1932–35* (Mary Gerold-Tucholsky and Gustav Huonker, eds), Reinbek, 1977, p. 10.

18. 'Der Autor Alois Kronberg', *Die literarische Welt*, 20 January 1933, pp. 3–4.

Notes to Chapter XIII

1. Ernst Niekisch, *Gewagtes Leben*, Cologne and Berlin, 1958, p. 103.
2. Interview with Fritz Landshoff, 16 July 1982.
3. Author's introduction to 'Briefe', *GW*, V, p. 11.
4. Quoted in the introduction to *GW*, I, p. 9.
5. Translated by Stephen Spender in Bertolt Brecht, *Poems* (John Willett and Ralph Manheim, eds), London, 1976, p. 301.
6. *Eine Jugend in Deutschland*, Amsterdam, 1933. Reprinted as volume IV of the *Gesammelte Werke*: page references in the text are to this edition.
7. Unpublished letter to Ludwig Lore, 10 January 1929 (AK).
8. Cf. 'Kampf mit dem lieben Gott' in *24 Neue Deutsche Erzähler* (Hermann Kesten, ed.), Berlin, 1929, and Toller's contribution to *Dichterglaube. Stimmen religiösen Erlebens* (Harald Braun, ed.), Berlin-Steglitz, 1931. Toller also gave at least one radio broadcast dealing with his recollections of childhood – cf. 'Radio. Ernst Toller erzählt sein Leben' in *Vossische Zeitung*, 1 June 1930.
9. Cf. Toller's letter to Hermann Kesten, 18 July 1933, *Deutsche Literatur im Exil. Briefe europäischer Autoren 1933–1949* (Hermann Kesten, ed.), Frankfurt, 1973, p. 41.
10. Toller's comments were made in an interview he gave to the periodical *The American Hebrew*, 3 June 1927, p. 178.
11. Emil Ludwig, 'Radionachricht von Ernst Tollers Tod', *Das neue Tagebuch*, 10 June 1939, p. 572.
12. *Quer Durch*, p. 296.
13. The following account is based on contemporary press reports, on materials contained in *Der deutsche PEN-Club im Exil 1933–1948*, Frankfurt, 1980, and on eye-witness reports, such as that of Mitar Papic, 'Ernst Toller auf dem PEN-Kongreß in Jugoslawien 1933', *Weimarer Beiträge*, XIV (1968), Sonderheft 2, pp. 73–7. The text of Toller's speech to the Congress is reprinted in *GW*, I, pp. 169–73.
14. *Daily Worker*, 14 September 1933. This section is based on contemporary press reports and on correspondence with Isabel Brown, who was secretary of the organizing committee for the Inquiry.
15. Tucholsky to Walter Hasenclever, 15 September 1933, *Ausgewählte Briefe 1913–35*, Mary Gerold-Tucholsky and Fritz J. Raddatz, eds), Reinbek, 1962, p. 274.
16. *The Scotsman*, 19 June 1934, p. 12.
17. 'Die Feuerkantate', *Das Wort* (Moscow), June 1938, pp. 35–36. Toller also submitted the poem to the *London Mercury* in an English translation by the

American poet Muriel Rukyser – cf. his letter 20 July 1938 to R.A. Scott-James (Texas).

18. Unpublished letter to Emil Ludwig, 11 January 1934 (DLA).

19. Cf. his unpublished letter to Mr Boswell (John Lane Publishers), 7 January 1934 (Bodley Head Archive), and his correspondence with Betty Frankenstein (DLA). The story 'Death of a Mother' is among the Toller papers in the Sterling Library, Yale. Cf. also Dorothy Thompson, 'Death of a Poet', *New York Herald Tribune*, 24 May 1939, p. 23.

Notes to Chapter XIV

1. Author's introduction to *Seven Plays*, London, 1935. The introduction is dated 17 October 1934.

2. See *Der Fall Toller*, pp. 204–5.

3. *New Statesman and Nation*, 13 February 1935.

4. Author's interview with Fenner Brockway, 19 January 1983.

5. Alfred Kantorowicz, *Politik und Literatur im Exil*, Hamburg, 1978, pp. 277–8.

6. Comprehensive accounts of the campaign to free Ossietzky are contained in Kurt R. Grossmann, *Ossietzky. Ein deutscher Patriot*, Munich, 1963; Elke Suhr, *Carl von Ossietzky. Eine Biographie*, Cologne, 1988; Ludwig Hoffmann et al., *Exil in der Tschechoslowakei, in Großbritannien, Skandinavien und Palästina*, Leipzig, 1980 (Vol V in the series *Kunst und Literatur im antifaschistischen Exil 1933–1945*). Toller's own role emerges partly from his correspondence with Hilde Walter in the Hilde-Walter-Nachlaß, Institut für Zeitgeschichte, Munich.

7. Elke Suhr, op. cit., p. 222.

8. Unpublished letter to Hilde Walter, 2 January 1935 (IfZ).

9. Lion Feuchtwanger, 'Dem toten Ernst Toller', *Die neue Weltbühne*, 8 June 1939, pp. 713–14.

10. Ethel Mannin, *Privileged Spectator*, London, 1939, pp. 82–4.

11. Cf. Toller's correspondence with Hilde Walter in January 1935.

12. *Manchester Guardian*, 17 February 1934.

13. *The Scotsman*, 19 June 1934, p. 11.

14. *The Scotsman*, 19 June 1934, p. 12 and 21 June 1934, p. 12.

15. See *Exile in Great Britain* (G. Hirschfeld, ed.), London, 1984, p. 36.

16. See *Der Fall Toller*, p. 209.

17. Unpublished letter to Mary Meloney, 27 April 1935, Columbia University Library, New York.

18. Unpublished letters to Mary Meloney, 28 March and 27 April 1935 (Columbia).

19. *Daily Herald*, 23 May 1939, pp. 1–2.

20. See Christiane's unpublished manuscript. The following is based partly on her account, partly on Toller's correspondence and the comments of contemporaries.

21. 'Mr Toller on the Cinema', *New York Times*, 1 November 1936, Section X, p. 5.

22. See note 17.

23. Author's interview with Fritz Landshoff, 16 July 1982.

24. Schickele to Wolff, 12 October 1935, Wolff, op. cit., p. 219.

25. Unpublished letter from Alfred Kantorowicz to Rudolf Olden, 5 March 1935 (DB).

26. 'The Refugee Problem', *Political Quarterly*, VI, 3 (July–September 1935), pp. 386–9.

27. 'Masses and Man. The Problem of Non-Violence and Peace', London, 1934. This publication is a pamphlet published by the Friends' Book Centre, a copy of which is now held in the Deutsche Bibliothek. Toller had used precisely this form of words in his speech *Deutsche Revolution* (Berlin, 1926) and had already repeated them in his autobiography – see *GW*, IV, pp. 138–9. A revised version of the pamphlet entitled 'Man and the Masses. The Problem of Peace', probably written in 1936 in the USA, is reprinted in *GW*, I, pp. 78–85.

28. Letter to Jawaharlal Nehru, 21 July 1936: Nehru, *A Bunch of Old Letters*, London, 1958, p. 199.

29. 'Unser Kampf um Deutschland', a speech delivered in December 1936, *GW*, I, p. 207.

30. *Internationale Literatur*, IV, 5 (1934), pp. 42–4.

31. 'Stalin and Wells. A Comment by Ernst Toller', *New Statesman and Nation*, 3 November 1934, pp. 614–15.

32. 'Mahnung', *Die neue Weltbühne*, 30 January 1936, p. 153.

33. 'Unser Kampf um Deutschland', *GW*, I, p. 206.

34. *Weltliche Passion. Ein Chorwerk*, *Internationale Literatur*, IV, 4 (1934), pp. 3–8, also in *Die Sammlung*, II, 4, December 1934, pp. 174–82. Page references in the text are to the latter publication. The poem refers to Liebknecht's exemplary gesture in publicly denouncing the war in 1916, which led to his arrest and imprisonment, and to the murders of Luxemburg and himself in January 1919.

35. Two typescript versions of the translation by Alexander Henderson, both undated, are held in the Yale University Library. The date can be approximately inferred from two unpublished letters from Toller to the British composer Christian Darnton, held in the British Library, the first dated 25 May 1935, the second undated but evidently written in June 1935, which mention the work and its translation.

36. *Daily Worker*, 24 May 1939. For further information about the various performances of *Requiem*, see my article 'The place of Ernst Toller in English Socialist Theatre', *German Life and Letters*, January 1985, pp. 125–37.

37. *No More Peace! A Thoughtful Comedy*, translated by Edward Crankshaw, lyrics adapted by W.H. Auden, London, 1937. Subsequent page references in the text are to this edition. The German version, written in 1934–5, was not published in Toller's lifetime; the manuscript, held in the Yale University Library, is now published in *GW*, III.

38. Unpublished letter to Christian Darnton, 13 July 1935, British Library.

39. Christopher Isherwood, 'Head of a Leader', *Exhumations*, London, 1966, pp. 125–126.

40. 'Das Versagen des Pazifismus in Deutschland', *GW*, I, p. 188.

41. See Toller's unpublished letters to Betty Frankenstein, 27 December 1934 (DLA) and to Christian Darnton, 13 July 1935 (BL). Fritz Landshoff confirmed to me that Toller did not even offer the play to the Querido Verlag.

42. Cf. Toller's original text, *GW*, III, p. 226.

Notes to Chapter XV

1. See John M. Spalek and Wolfgang Frühwald, 'Ernst Tollers amerikanische Vortragsreise 1936–37', *Literaturwissenschaftliches Jahrbuch*, VI (1965), pp. 267–311.
2. Letter to Jawaharlal Nehru, 30 March 1937 in Nehru, *A Bunch of Old Letters*, London 1958, p. 221.
3. See Spalek, *Ernst Toller and his Critics. A Bibliography*, Charlottesville, 1968.
4. 'Sind wir verantwortlich für unsere Zeit?', first published in 'Ernst Tollers amerikanische Vortragsreise' (see note 1).
5. See *New York Times*, 1 and 4 February 1937.
6. See *Der Fall Toller*, pp. 213–17.
7. Letter to Nehru, 30 March 1937, Nehru, op. cit., p. 222.
8. Speech at National Book Fair, New York, *New York Times*, 10 November 1936, p. 23.
9. Letter from Barrett H. Clark to Toller, 23 December 1936 (Beinecke Library, Yale). Clark, editor and theatre critic, was at this time Executive Director of the Dramatists' Play Service, set up by the Dramatists Guild to handle members' rights for non- professional productions. Through the Dramatists Play Service, Clark acted as Toller's agent.
10. Cf. Toller's correspondence with Ben Irwin of the New Theatre League in 1936–37, copies of which are in the Clark collection, Beinecke Library.
11. Toller to Barrett Clark, 1 December 1936, Beinecke Library.
12. Toller to Irwin Swerdlow, 20 April 1937, Sterling Library, Yale.
13. Hallie Flanagan, *Dynamo*, New York, 1943, p. 105.
14. Flanagan to Toller, 22 December 1936, copy in Clark collection, Beinecke Library.
15. See Hallie Flanagan, *Arena*, New York, 1940, pp. 155, 319. For reviews of these productions, see *New York Times*, 4 June 1937, p. 26, and 29 January 1938, p. 13.
16. Toller's outline for *Forget Europe* is among his papers in the Sterling Library, Yale, as are some of the relevant press clippings.

Notes to Chapter XVI

1. 'Mr Toller on the Cinema', *New York Times*, 1 November 1936, X, p. 5.
2. 'Hollywood', translated by Michael Hamburger, in Bertolt Brecht, *Poems* (John Willett and Ralph Manheim, eds), London, 1976, p. 381.
3. Unpublished letter to Barrett H. Clark, 9 February 1937, Beinecke Library, Yale.
4. Unpublished letter to Sidney Kaufman, 20 February 1937, Sterling Library, Yale.
5. Unpublished letter to Fritz Joss, 24 February 1937, Leo Baeck Institute, New York.
6. Unpublished letter to Barrett H. Clark, 11 March 1937, Beinecke Library.
7. Unpublished letter to Sidney Kaufman, 24 February 1937, Sterling Library.

8. Ibid.

9. Unpublished letter to Denis Johnston, 23 June 1937, John M. Spalek archive (Albany).

10. Letter to Nehru, 30 March 1937 in Nehru, op. cit., p. 222.

11. Interview with Sidney Kaufman, conducted by John M. Spalek, 27 June 1982. I am grateful to Professor Spalek for allowing me to hear this interview.

12. See note 1.

13. Unpublished letter to Sidney Kaufman, 20 February 1937, Sterling Library.

14. The manuscript is held in the Sterling Library, Yale. It comprises 139 typed pages, with numerous handwritten corrections and additions. Toller's renumbering of the original pages makes clear that, in revising the original manuscript of some ninety pages, he also lengthened it. The script is in German with occasional passages in English.

15. Pinthus, 'Life and Death of Ernst Toller', *Books Abroad* XIV (1939), p. 7.

16. Letter to Nehru, 23 August 1937, Nehru, op. cit., p. 243.

17. Unpublished letter to Dr Ralph R. Greenschpoon, undated, but written in November from Mexico City (Spalek archive). Toller wrote two letters to Greenschpoon from Mexico: the handwriting in both is irregular, the syntax often disjointed.

18. Unpublished letter to Sidney Kaufman, 11 January 1938, Sterling Library.

19. Speech to Paris Writers' Congress, *Das Wort*, October 1938, p. 124.

20. Grosz, *A Little Yes and a Big No*, New York, 1946, p. 337; Spalek interview with Sidney Kaufman, see note 11.

21. Unpublished letter to Sidney Kaufman, 3 February 1938, Sterling Library.

22. Unpublished letter to Dr Ralph Greenschpoon, 29 April 1938 (Spalek archive).

23. Spalek interview with Sidney Kaufman, see note 11.

24. Hubertus zu Löwenstein, *Abenteuer der Freiheit*, Frankfurt, 1982, p. 198.

25. 'Eine Jugend', *GW*, IV, p. 227.

26. *Pastor Hall*. A play in three acts, translated by Stephen Spender, London, 1939. This is the first published version of the play. The German version, published in *GW*, III is based on the German typescript held in the Sterling Library, Yale.

27. Author's interview with Fritz Landshoff, 16 July 1982; unpublished letter to Dr Ralph Greenschpoon, 19 April 1939 (Spalek archive).

28. Unpublished letter to Betty Frankenstein, dated 1 May 1939 (Marbach). The letter was actually sent some days after the date.

29. See Grautoff manuscript.

30. Speech to the Paris Writers' Congress, p. 125.

31. 'Unser Kampf um Deutschland' (1936), *GW*, I, p. 203.

32. *Pastor Hall*, London, 1939, p. 52.

33. Speech to the Paris Writers' Congress, p. 125.

34. Unpublished letter, Bennett Cerf to Toller, 7 November 1938, Sterling Library.

35. Unpublished letter from John Lane (Mr Howe) to Curtis Brown (Mr Halliday), 19 July 1938, Sterling Library.

36. Unpublished letter to Isabel Colborn, 23 July 1938, Sterling Library.

37. Cf. unpublished letter, Toller to Denis Johnston, 16 October 1938, Sterling Library. Spender himself could say little about the circumstances of the translation, except that he 'did it because asked to do so by Toller' (communication from Stephen Spender, 20 January 1986).

38. *The Star* (London), 19 October 1938, p. 7.

39. Cf. letter from Ronald Jeans to J.B. Pinker, Toller's theatre agent in London, 25 November 1938, Sterling Library.

40. Unpublished letter from Toller's secretary to Fritz H. Landshoff, 10 January 1939, Sterling Library.

41. The typescript copies of Spender's translation of *Pastor Hall* in the Sterling Library all have the first ending, the German typescript the second. The German text of the first version, in which Hall dies on stage, was published in *Das Wort* (Moscow), January 1939, pp. 42–51. Toller had completed the new version of the final scene by 20 January, when he sent it to John Lane.

42. Unpublished letter, Barrett Clark to Toller, 28 December 1938, Sterling Library.

43. Unpublished letter to Barrett Clark, 27 January 1938, Beinecke Library.

44. *New Statesman*, 1 June 1940, p. 700.

Notes to Chapter XVII

1. 'Rede auf dem Pariser Kongreß der Schriftsteller' (Speech to Paris Writers Congress), *Das Wort*, October 1938, pp. 122–6.

2. *Quer Durch*, p. 296.

3. Ludwig Marcuse, *Mein zwanzigstes Jahrhundert*, Zurich, 1975, p. 205.

4. 'Madrid-Washington', *New Statesman and Nation*, 8 October 1938, pp. 521–2.

5. *Time and Tide*, 27 May 1939, p. 686. The article is unsigned, but was probably written by R. Ellis Roberts, the periodical's literary editor and the translator of Toller's *Letters from Prison*.

6. Frederick R. Benson, *Writers in Arms*, London 1968, p. 40.

7. From the unpublished typescript of a projected book on the Spanish Relief Plan, Sterling Library, Yale.

8. Cf. *New York Times*, 15 August 1938, p. 8.

9. Hermann Kesten, *Meine Freunde die Poeten*, Frankfurt and Berlin, 1980, p. 151.

10. See note 4.

11. Ethel Mannin, *Privileged Spectator*, London, 1939, pp. 307–8.

12. 'A Minority Hitler never mentions', *Tribune*, 14 October 1938, p. 13. Toller's speech was delivered at a meeting in Conway Hall, also addressed by Wickham Steed.

13. Toller's correspondence regarding the Spanish Relief Plan has survived virtually in its entirety and is held in the Sterling Library, Yale.

14. Letter from Cosmo Lang, Archbishop of Canterbury, 11 November 1938 and William Temple, Archbishop of York, 10 November 1938, both in Yale.

15. Cf. Foreign Office records in Public Record Office, Kew (ref. FO 371/22614).

16. Isherwood, op. cit., p. 127.

17. A copy of the telegram is among the Toller papers in Yale.

18. *Daily Herald*, 23 May 1939, pp. 1–2.

19. From the unpublished MS of the Spanish Relief Plan, see note 7.

20. *New York Times*, 18 November 1939, p. 7.

21. See note 7.

22. *New York Herald Tribune*, 30 November 1938, p. 21. See also leading article, ibid., 2 December 1938, p. 24.

23. *New York Herald Tribune*, 9 December 1938, p. 11.

24. *New York Herald Tribune*, 5 December 1938, p. 7 and 8 December 1938, p. 24.

25. Toller's letter to Roosevelt, 23 November 1938 and his accompanying memorandum are in the Sterling Library, Yale.

26. Unpublished letter to H.N. Brailsford, 7 December 1938, Sterling Library, Yale.

27. Unpublished letter to Barrett Clark, 13 December 1938, Beinecke Library, Yale.

28. Unpublished letter to Volkmar von Zuelsdorf, 24 December 1938 (DB).

29. Unpublished letter to John Lane, publishers, 20 January 1939, Sterling Library, Yale.

30. Unpublished letter to Dorothy Thompson, 20 February 1939 (IfZ).

Notes to Chapter XVIII.

1. Letter from George Grosz to Hermann Borchardt, in *George Grosz. Briefe 1913–59* (Herbert Knust, ed.), Reinbek, 1979, p. 276. The letter is wrongly dated 1938; the content indicates that it was written after Franco's victory and before Toller's death, i.e. April or early May 1939.

2. Ludwig Marcuse, *Mein zwanzigstes Jahrhundert*, Zürich, 1975, p. 253.

3. Author's interview with Fritz Landshoff, 16 July 1982.

4. Unpublished letters to Ralph Greenschpoon, 8 April and 19 April 1939 (Spalek archive).

5. Unpublished letter to Betty Frankenstein, 1 May 1939 (Marbach); see also an earlier letter, dated 27 February 1939 to the same correspondent. Toller's fears were all too well-founded. Hertha and her husband were unable to leave Germany. In 1941 they moved from Landsberg to Berlin; on 9 December 1942 they were deported to Auschwitz and are assumed to have been murdered there a week later. Heinrich Toller was deported from Prague to Theresienstadt and is assumed to have died in 1945. (Information supplied by Anne Schönblum [Haifa], 1988.)

6. Klaus Mann, 'Letzter Tag mit Toller', *Die neue Weltbühne*, 22 June 1939, pp. 784–8.

7. Cf. Toller's unpublished letter to John Lane (Mr Howe), 24 December 1939, in which he refers to the collection under the working title *Time My Companion* and mentions the possibility of publication in spring 1939.

8. Letter from Ludwig Marcuse to Hermann Kesten, 15 June 1939 in *Deutsche Literatur im Exil* (Hermann Kesten ed.), pp. 82–3.

9. Kesten, *Meine Freunde die Poeten*, Frankfurt/Berlin 1980, p. 153.

10. Kurt Pinthus, 'Life and Death of Ernst Toller', *Books Abroad* XIV (1939), pp. 3–8.

11. See note 6.

12. Marcuse, op. cit., p. 255.

13. Bruckner, 'Abschied von Ernst Toller', *Die neue Weltbühne*, 8 June 1939, pp. 715–16.

14. *Berliner Lokalanzeiger*, 23 May 1939.

15. *New York Times*, 28 May 1939, III, p. 6.

16. Becher, 'Dem guten Kameraden', *Internationale Literatur*, IX (1939), 7, pp. 135–6; Feuchtwanger, 'Dem toten Ernst Toller', *Die neue Weltbühne*, 8 June 1939, pp. 713–14.

17. Wolfenstein, 'Ernst Toller', *Die neue Weltbühne*, 1 June 1939, pp. 677–80.

18. W.H. Auden, 'In Memory of Ernst Toller' (May 1939), in *Collected Poems* (Edward Mendelson, ed.), London, 1976, p. 198.

BIBLIOGRAPHY

Primary Sources

i) Anthologies

Seven Plays, London, 1935.
Prosa, Briefe, Dramen, Gedichte, with a foreword by Kurt Hiller, Reinbek, 1961.
Gesammelte Werke (Wolfgang Frühwald and John M. Spalek, eds), five volumes, Munich, 1978.

ii) Plays

Die Wandlung. Das Ringen eines Menschen, Potsdam, 1919; translated by Edward Crankshaw as *Transfiguration* (in *Seven Plays*).
Masse-Mensch. Ein Stück aus der sozialen Revolution des 20. Jahrhunderts, Potsdam, 1921. The second edition, Potsdam, 1922, includes Toller's foreword (addressed to Jürgen Fehling), 'Brief an einen schöpferischen Mittler'; translated by Vera Mendel as *Masses and Man*, London, 1923 (in *Seven Plays*).
Die Maschinenstürmer. Ein Drama aus der Zeit der Ludditenbewegung in England, Leipzig, Vienna, Zurich, 1922 (second edition, also 1922); translated by Ashley Dukes as *The Machine Wreckers*, London and New York, 1923 (in *Seven Plays*).
Hinkemann. Eine Tragödie in drei Akten, Potsdam, 1923. Originally published as *Der deutsche Hinkemann*; translated by Vera Mendel as *Brokenbrow*, London, 1926 (in *Seven Plays* under the title *Hinkemann*).
Der entfesselte Wotan. Eine Komödie, Potsdam, 1923.
Hoppla, wir leben! Ein Vorspiel und fünf Akten, Potsdam, 1927; translated by Hermon Ould as *Hoppla!*, London, 1928 (in *Seven Plays* under the title *Hoppla, Such is life!*).
Feuer aus den Kesseln. Historisches Schauspiel. Anhang historische Dokumente, Berlin, 1930; translated by Edward Crankshaw as *Draw the Fires!*, London, 1934 (in *Seven Plays*).
Wunder in Amerika. Schauspiel in fünf Akten, with Hermann Kesten, Berlin, 1931 (mimeographed acting version); translated by Edward Crankshaw as *Mary Baker Eddy* (in *Seven Plays*).
Die blinde Göttin. Schauspiel in fünf Akten, Berlin, 1933; translated by Edward Crankshaw as *The Blind Goddess*, London, 1934 (in *Seven Plays*).
No More Peace! A Thoughtful Comedy; translated by Edward Crankshaw, lyrics adapted by W.H. Auden, music by Herbert Merrill, London, 1937 (the original German version not published in Toller's lifetime, now in *Gesammelte Werke*).
Pastor Hall. A play in three acts, translated by Stephen Spender with assistance from Hugh Hunt, London, 1939 (original German version not published in Toller's lifetime, now in *Gesammelte Werke*).

Berlin – letzte Ausgabe! – radio play, unpublished in Toller's lifetime, now in *Frühe sozialistische Hörspiele* (Stefan Bodo Würffel, ed.), Frankfurt, 1982.

iii) Poetry and Prose

Der Tag des Proletariats. Ein Chorwerk, Berlin, 1920.
Gedichte der Gefangenen. Ein Sonettenkreis, Munich, 1921.
Das Schwalbenbuch, Potsdam, 1924; translated by Ashley Dukes as *The Swallow Book*, London, 1924; also translated by Ellis Roberts and included in *Letters from Prison* (see below).
Vormorgen, Potsdam, 1924; translation of some poems from *Vormorgen* by Ellis Roberts included in *Letters from Prison* (see below).
Justiz. Erlebnisse, Berlin, 1927.
Quer Durch. Reisebilder und Reden, Berlin, 1930. First two parts (*Reisebilder*) translated by Hermon Ould as *Which World, Which Way?*, London, 1931.
Nationalsozialismus. Eine Diskussion über den Kulturbankrott des Bürgertums zwischen Ernst Toller und Alfred Mühr (published transcript of radio broadcast), Berlin, 1930.
Eine Jugend in Deutschland, Amsterdam, 1933; translated by Edward Crankshaw as *I was a German*, London, 1934.
Briefe aus dem Gefängnis, Amsterdam, 1935; translated by R. Ellis Roberts as *Letters from Prison*, including poems and a new version of *The Swallow Book*, London, 1936. Published in USA as *Look through the Bars*, New York, 1937 (includes a new foreword by the author).

For the location of unpublished letters by Toller and other collections of documentary material, see 'Note on Sources' (p. 267).

Secondary Sources

i) General Historical and Cultural Background

Thomas Anz and Michael Stark (eds), *Expressionismus. Manifeste und Dokumente zur deutschen Literatur 1910–1920*, Stuttgart, 1982.
Thomas Anz and Joseph Vogel (eds), *Die Dichter und der Krieg*, Munich and Vienna, 1982.
Karl Bosl (ed.), *Bayern in Umbruch*, Munich, 1969.
Keith Bullivant (ed.), *Culture and Society in the Weimar Republic*, Manchester, 1977.
Cecil W. Davies, *Theatre for the People. The Story of the Volksbühne*, Manchester, 1977.
Walter Fähnders and Martin Rector, *Linksradikalismus und Literatur*, Reinbek, 1974.
Peter Gay, *Weimar Culture. The Outsider as Insider*, London, 1969.
Heinrich Hannover and Elisabeth Hannover-Druck, *Politische Justiz 1918–1933*, Frankfurt, 1966.

C.D. Innes, *Erwin Piscator's Political Theatre. The development of Modern German Drama*, Cambridge, 1972.

Thomas Koebner (ed.), *Weimars Ende. Prognosen und Diagnosen in der deutschen Literatur und politischen Publizistik 1930–1933*, Frankfurt, 1982.

Kurt Kreiler, *Die Schriftstellerrepublik*, Berlin, 1978.

Egbert Krispyn, *Anti-Nazi Writers in Exile*, Athens, Georgia, 1978.

Kenneth Macgowan and R.E. Jones, *Continental Stagecraft*, New York, 1923.

F.N. Mennemeier and F. Trapp, *Deutsche Exildramatik 1933–1950*, Munich, 1980.

Alan Mitchell, *Revolution in Bavaria 1918–19*, Princeton, 1965.

Michael Patterson, *The Revolution in the German Theatre 1900–1933*, London, 1981.

Anthony Phelan (ed.), *The Weimar Dilemma. Intellectuals in the Weimar Republic*, Manchester, 1985.

J.M. Ritchie, *German Expressionist Drama*, Boston, 1976.

J.M. Ritchie, *German Literature under National Socialism*, London, 1983.

Arthur Rosenberg, *Die Entstehung der Deutschen Republik*, Berlin, 1928; translated by Ian F.D. Morrow, *The Birth of the German Republic, 1871–1918*, Oxford, 1931.

Arthur Rosenberg, *Entstehung und Geschichte der Weimarer Republik*, Frankfurt, 1955.

A.J. Ryder, *The German Revolution of 1918*, Cambridge, 1967.

Richard Samuel and R. Hinton Thomas, *Expressionism in German Life, Literature and Theatre*, Cambridge, 1939.

Walter H. Sokel, *The Writer in Extremis. Expressionism in Twentieth-Century German Literature*, Stanford, 1968.

Frank Trommler, *Sozialistische Literatur in Deutschland*, Stuttgart, 1976.

Hans-Albert Walter, *Deutsche Exilliteratur 1933–1950*, Darmstadt and Neuwied, 1972.

Matthias Wegner, *Exil und Literatur. Deutsche Schriftsteller im Ausland 1933–1945*, Frankfurt and Bonn, 1968.

John Willett, *Expressionism*, London, 1970.

John Willett, *The New Sobriety. Art and Politics in the Weimar Period 1917–33*, London, 1978.

C.E. Williams, *Writers and Politics in Modern Germany (1918–1945)*, London, 1977.

ii) Autobiographical and Documentary Sources

Ernst-Josef Aufricht, *Erzähle, damit du dein Recht erweist*, Frankfurt and Berlin, 1966.

Martin Buber (ed.), *Gustav Landauer. Sein Lebensgang in Briefen*, two volumes, Frankfurt, 1929.

Ashley Dukes, *The Scene is Changed*, London, 1942.

Tilla Durieux, *Eine Tür steht offen*, Berlin, 1954.

Kasimir Edschmid, *Briefe der Expressionisten*, Frankfurt, 1964.

Kurt Eisner, *Sozialismus als Aktion. Ausgewählte Aufsätze und Reden* (Freya Eisner, ed.), Frankfurt, 1975.

Freya Eisner (ed.), *Kurt Eisner. Die Politik des libertären Sozialismus*, Frankfurt, 1979.

Felix Fechenbach, *Der Revolutionär Kurt Eisner*, Berlin, 1929.

F.W. Foerster, *Erlebte Weltgeschichte 1869–1953*, Nuremberg, 1953.

Max Gerstl, *Die Münchner Räterepublik*, Munich, 1919.

Oskar Maria Graf, *Wir sind Gefangene*, Munich, 1965.

Stefan Großmann, *Der Hochverräter Ernst Toller. Die Geschichte eines Prozesses*, Berlin, 1919, reprinted in Toller, *Prosa, Briefe, Dramen, Gedichte*, Reinbek, 1961, pp. 473–98.

Alfred Kerr, *Die Welt im Drama* (Gerhard F. Hering, ed.), Cologne, 1954.

Hermann Kesten, *Meine Freunde die Poeten*, Munich, 1959.

Hermann Kesten (ed.), *Deutsche Literatur im Exil. Briefe europäischer Autoren 1933–1949*, Frankfurt, 1973.

Gustav Landauer, *Aufruf zum Sozialismus*, Berlin, 1919.

Rosa Leviné, *Aus der Münchner Rätezeit*, Berlin, 1925.

Rosa Leviné-Meyer, *Leviné. The Life of a Revolutionary*, Farnborough, 1973.

Ludwig Marcuse, *Briefe von und an Ludwig Marcuse* (Harold von Hofe, ed.), Zurich, 1975.

Charles Benes Maurer, *Call to Revolution. The Mystical Anarchism of Gustav Landauer*, Detroit, 1971.

Ludwig Morenz, *Revolution und Räteherrschaft in München. Aus der Stadtchronik 1918–1919*, Munich and Vienna, 1968.

Jawaharlal Nehru, *A Bunch of Old Letters*, London, 1958.

Ernst Niekisch, *Gewagtes Leben*, Cologne and Berlin, 1958.

Erwin Piscator, *Das politische Theater*, Berlin, 1929; reprinted Berlin, 1963; translated by Hugh Rorrison as *The Political Theatre*, London, 1978.

Paul Raabe, *Die Autoren und Bücher des literarischen Expressionismus*, Stuttgart, 1985.

Ludwig Rubiner (ed.), *Kameraden der Menschheit. Dichtungen zur Weltrevolution*, Potsdam, 1919.

Günther Rühle (ed.), *Theater für die Republik 1917–1933 im Spiegel der Kritik*, Frankfurt, 1967.

Gerhard Schmolze (ed.), *Revolution und Räterepublik in München 1918–19 in Augenzeugenberichten*, Düsseldorf, 1969.

Jürgen Serke, *Die verbrannten Dichter*, Weinheim and Basel, 1977.

Kurt Tucholsky, *Ausgewählte Briefe 1913–1935* (Mary Gerold-Tucholsky and Fritz J. Raddatz, eds), Reinbek, 1962.

Wilfried van der Will and Rob Burns, *Arbeiterkulturbewegung in der Weimarer Republik*, 2 vols, Frankfurt, 1982.

Hansjörg Viesel, *Literaten an der Wand. Die Münchner Räterepublik und die Schriftsteller*, Frankfurt, 1980.

Kurt Wolff, *Briefwechsel eines Verlegers 1911–1963* (Bernhard Zeller and Ellen Otten, eds), Frankfurt, 1966.

Erich Wollenberg, *Als Rotarmist vor München*, Berlin, 1929; reprinted Hamburg, 1972.

The best source of information on the cultural trends of the period are the literary and cultural periodicals, the most useful being:

Die Aktion, Berlin, 1914–32.
Die weißen Blätter, Leipzig, 1913–16, Zurich, 1916–18, Berlin, 1919–20.
Internationale Literatur, Moscow, 1933– 39.
Die literarische Welt, 1925–33.
Die neue Rundschau, Berlin, 1914–33.
Die Sammlung, Amsterdam, 1933–35.
Das Tagebuch, Berlin, 1920–33 (continued in exile as *Das neue Tagebuch*, Paris, 1933– 40).
Die Weltbühne (formerly *Die Schaubühne*), Berlin 1918–33 (continued in exile as *Die neue Weltbühne*, Vienna, Prague, Paris, 1933–39).
Das Wort, Moscow, 1936–39.

iii) Critical Works on Toller

Rosemarie Altenhofer, *Ernst Tollers politische Dramatik*, unpublished dissertation, St Louis, Mo., 1977.
Renate Benson, *German Expressionist Drama: Ernst Toller and Georg Kaiser*, London, 1984.
Thomas Bütow, *Der Konflikt zwischen Revolution und Pazifismus im Werk Ernst Tollers*, Hamburg, 1975.
Richard Dove, *Revolutionary Socialism in the Work of Ernst Toller*, Bern, Frankfurt, New York, 1986.
Manfred Durzak, *Das expressionistische Drama. Ernst Barlach – Ernst Toller – Fritz von Unruh*, Munich, 1979.
Rene Eichenlaub, *Ernst Toller et l'expressionisme politique*, Paris, 1980.
Jost Hermand (ed.), *Zu Ernst Toller. Drama und Engagement*, Stuttgart, 1981.
Carel ter Haar, *Ernst Toller. Appell oder Resignation?*, Munich, 1977.
Klaus Kändler, *Drama und Klassenkampf*, Berlin and Weimar, 1970.
Dorothea Klein, *Der Wandel der dramaturgischen Darstellungsform im Werk Ernst Tollers 1919–1930*, unpublished dissertation, Bochum, 1968.
Michael Ossar, *Anarchism in the Dramas of Ernst Toller*, Albany, N.Y., 1980.
Malcolm Pittock, *Ernst Toller*, Boston, 1979.
Martin Reso, *Der gesellschaftlich-ethische Protest im dichterischen Werk Ernst Tollers*, unpublished dissertation, Jena, 1957.
Wolfgang Rothe, *Ernst Toller*, Reinbek, 1983.
John M. Spalek, *Ernst Toller and his Critics. A Bibliography*, Charlottesville, 1968.
William A. Willibrand, *Ernst Toller and his Ideology*, Iowa City, 1945.

NAME INDEX

Ackermann, Lili, actress and drama coach, 196
Adler, Friedrich (1879–1960), Austrian politician, Secretary of Socialist International, 144
Alvarez del Vayo see Vayo, Julio Alvarez del
Angell, Norman (1872–1967), English writer and pacifist, winner of Nobel Peace Prize 1933, 214
Arco-Valley, Graf Anton von (1897–1945), army lieutenant, murderer of Kurt Eisner, 66, 82, 97
Arp, Hans (1887–1966), Dadaist poet, 35
Asquith, Emma Alice (1864–1945), countess of Oxford and Asquith, 213
Auden, W. H. (1907–73), English poet, 212, 225, 227, 256, 265
Auer, Erhard (1874–1945), Bavarian SPD politician, 63, 67, 82, 203
Aufricht, Ernst-Josef (1898–1971), theatre manager and producer, 176

Babel, Isaak (1894–1941), Russian-Jewish writer, 189
Bachmair, Heinrich Franz (1889–1960), Munich bookseller and publisher, 21
Ball, Hugo (1886–1927), Dadaist poet, 35
Barbusse, Henri (1873–1935), French novelist and pacifist, 36, 56, 102, 135
Baum, Vicki (1880–1960), popular novelist and screen-writer, 239
Bäumler, Alfred (1887–1968) Nazi educationalist, Professor of Political Education, University of Berlin, 200
Becher, Johannes R. (1891–1958), writer and poet, later GDR Minister of Culture, 5, 21, 28, 140, 147, 185, 265, 278n
Beer, Max, German Labour historian, 102, 119
Benjamin, Walter (1892–1940), literary critic and essayist, 185

Benn, Gottfried (1886–1956), medical doctor and poet, 201
Bergamin, José (b. 1897), Spanish writer and critic, 253
Bernhard, Georg (1875–1944), newspaper editor and politician, 208
Bernstein, Eduard (1850–1932), SPD politician and political writer, 41
Björnsen, Björn (1859–1942), Norwegian actor and writer, 92
Blum, Leon (1872–1950), French socialist politician, 234
Borchardt, Hermann (1888–1951), writer and Professor of German, 263
Brailsford, H. N. (1873–1958), English writer and journalist, 180, 211, 257
Brandes, Georg (1842–1927), Danish literary historian and critic, 162
Brandt, Willi (b. 1913), SPD politician, Federal Chancellor 1969–74, 213
Brecht, Bertolt (1898–1956), poet and dramatist, 1, 3, 8, 152, 155, 161, 178, 192–3, 196, 198, 200–201, 236, 241, 242
Bredel, Willi (1901–64), writer and novelist, 199, 246
Breitscheid, Rudolf (1874–1944), SPD politician and Reichstag deputy, 200, 208
Brockway, Lord Fenner (1889–1988), British ILP, later Labour, politician, 6, 145, 213
Bröger, Karl (1886–1944), worker-poet, 31
Brown, Isabel (1894–1984), British communist organiser, 209, 254
Bruckner, Ferdinand (1891–1958), Austrian poet and dramatist, 196, 235, 241, 264
Busch, Fritz Otto, Nazi writer, 206
Butler, R. A. (1902–82), British conservative politician, 255
Buxton, Charles Roden (1875–1942), British writer and politician, 66